AN INTRODUCTION TO THE OLD TESTAMENT AND ITS STUDY

An Introduction to the Old Testament
and Its Study

Robert L. Cate

BROADMAN PRESS
Nashville, Tennessee

© Copyright 1987 • Broadman Press
All rights reserved
4212-33
ISBN: 0-8054-1233-6
Dewey Decimal Classification: 221
Subject Heading: BIBLE. OLD TESTAMENT
Library of Congress Catalog Card Number: 86-24412
Printed in the United States of America

Library of Congress Cataloging-in-Publication Data

Cate, Robert L.
   An introduction to the Old Testament and its study.

   Includes bibliographies.
   1. Bible.   O.T.—Introductions.   I. Title.
BS1140.2.C37   1987   221.6′1   86-24412
ISBN 0-8054-1233-6

To Bob, Jr., who feels deeply,
loves freely, and has the courage
to step to the beat
of a different drummer

Preface

"Of making many books there is no end," said the author of Ecclesiastes (12:12). In no sphere of knowledge is this truer than in the field of Old Testament introduction. Each year a new crop of books ventures into the field, and the library shelves are already full to overflowing. The very surfeit of such works makes any new attempt questionable.

The Old Testament, the book about which all these other volumes are written, is an ancient book. Parts of it are more than three thousand years old and all of it is more than two thousand years old. This raises two additional questions. First, hasn't everything been said in these intervening years which can be said about the Old Testament? Second, of what possible value can the study of such an ancient collection of materials be to anyone facing the crises of the modern world? Can it have any significance today?

These are serious issues. I will, therefore, answer them seriously in order to justify my venture into the field.

The Present Need

Considering the questions raised in reverse, the Old Testament is a part of the Christian Bible (as well as being the Bible of Judaism and a foundation for Islam). As such, it has had a significant effect on world history. It is also the record of the religious interpretation of the rise of Israel as the nation of the Jews. This makes its study important for all those interested in or concerned with world history. Of far more significance is its statement of faith. As a part of the Christian Scriptures, it is believed by millions to be a part of God's word to all humanity. This is a claim which needs to be taken seriously. If it is true (as I believe it is), then we need to hear God's voice as He speaks to us through it. Even were it not true, we would need to study the Old Testament in order to understand its impact upon those who by faith accept it as God's Word and try to apply it to their lives. Thus, in spite of the fact that the Old Testament is an ancient book, it is still a book of significance in our world.

Admitting that there is a need to study the Old Testament does not justify a new introductory book. Here we face a different issue. Human knowledge is steadily expanding. Through the work of historians, archaeologists, linguists, scientists, and scholars of many other disciplines, new facts are constantly brought to light, new information is discovered which relates to old facts, and new methods are developed for relating and interpreting old materials. All of this means that older introductions, for all of their value, are inadequate today.

Consider an illustration from the scientific world. When all we had to consider were the earth and falling objects, Newton's law of gravity was quite sufficient. But as our horizons of knowledge expanded into outer space and the inner atom, we needed new approaches. At that point, Einstein proposed his theory of general relativity. It was adequate for its day. But as we have probed more deeply into the atom and farther into space, Einstein's theory has also become insufficient. Something new in physical theory is needed. In time it will come. In the world of Old Testament studies, similar things have happened. With the knowledge explosion of the last four decades, new knowledge has demanded new methods and fresh interpretations.

Now we are face to face with the first issue: With all of the Old Testament introductions published, why should I write another? Several related answers moved me to write this book. First, significant work has been done in the field of Old Testament scholarship which needs to be analyzed, evaluated, and then synthesized for the new student in the field. Second, Baptists have made major contributions to the study of the Old Testament over the years. This may be because we take seriously the fact that the Old Testament is a part of our Scriptures and believe that its message must be understood and applied to life. However, the last major Old Testament introduction by a Baptist which has attained wide use is Clyde T. Francisco's *Introducing the Old Testament* (Broadman Press, first published in 1950 and revised in 1977). For its day, it was reasonably good, but the revision was inadequate in some places and incomplete in others. Thus, there is a present need.

The third reason for a new introduction to the study of the Old Testament is that there is an abysmal ignorance of both the content of the Old Testament and the approaches to its study. Some of what is popularly said about its content or its study is either incomplete or simply wrong. What you do not know about the Old Testament and its study is not nearly as dangerous as what you do "know" which is just not so.

My fourth reason for approaching this study is quite personal. In my years of ministry through pastoring and teaching and in my own personal study, the Old Testament has become a living book about real people to me. God has spoken to me through it. I want to help others have a similar experience. My desire to help others hear God speak clearly from the pages of the Old Testament is the primary justification for this labor of love.

The Proposed Study

Scholars are not in complete agreement about what belongs in an introduction to the Old Testament. Some introductions simply recount the history of the ancient Hebrews, fitting each book into what the author considers the appropriate historical slot. This is a somewhat questionable approach, since it is quite unclear as to where some books actually fit. Many of the shorter books are very difficult to date. This approach is also questionable because some books relate to two time periods. Thus 1 and 2 Chronicles recount the history of the Southern Kingdom up to the Exile (early sixth century) but appear to have been written during the postexilic era. They speak *about* one period but *to* a second one. It is quite difficult to decide how to deal with these books in such an approach. An even stronger objection to this approach is that, while focusing upon the content of the Old Testament, the major methods of Old Testament study are wholly ignored.

A second major type of Old Testament introduction directs attention to one or more of the methods of serious Old Testament study, but generally ignores the content. Granted that to become competent students of the Old Testament, we need to be familiar with these methodologies, know how to use them, and know their strengths, weaknesses and limitations. Such an approach can become quite sterile, leading simply to a study of the Old Testament as literature while ignoring the fact that it was, and is, a book of faith. To ignore this is to miss the major reason for studying the Old Testament. A person can become an "expert" in how to study the Old Testament and know almost nothing about its content. For these reasons, I find this approach alone unacceptable.

The third major type of Old Testament introduction seeks to incorporate both of the preceding approaches. This is the approach I have used in this book. We shall first begin with an introduction to the various methods used in Old Testament studies, pointing out the contributions which each approach has made and can make while carefully noting the limitations of each as I see them. Then we shall turn to the content of the Old Testament itself, seeking to provide an overview of each book, a survey of its content, and a summary of its faith proclamation. Here I shall generally follow the organization of the Hebrew canon for reasons which we shall consider later.

My Personal Pilgrimage

To help you understand my approach to the Old Testament and its study, I want to share some of my personal pilgrimage of faith. I grew up in a home where both of my parents were Christians. I don't remember a time when I did not love Jesus. Every Saturday I saw my father working on his Sunday School lesson at the kitchen table. He taught the same class for about fifty years. Bible stories as read or told by my mother were a part of my heritage.

As a freshman in college, however, I became aware that there was something missing from my life and that the "something" was spiritual. During that year I read my New Testament through three times. I immersed myself in spiritual works, teaching a Sunday School class of nine-year old boys. It was all to no avail. In the summer following, the young lady I was dating asked me if I were a Christian. I gave all the standard answers. "Of course I am. I am a church member. I teach Sunday School. I read my Bible. I am American!" But she ignored all this, saying, "But have you made a personal commitment to the Lordship of Jesus?" She said nothing more at that point, and neither did I. Before the week was over, however, I made such a commitment. That has made all the difference. (By the way, I later married the girl, and we have shared love, life, and ministry ever since.)

During my last year of college, I felt God calling me "to preach." I didn't know all that call entailed, but I knew I was supposed to do something special vocationally. During the latter part of my senior year, I served as pastor of a small country church whose people lovingly put up with a struggling young preacher. In the fall, after graduating from college as an electrical engineer, I enrolled in The Southern Baptist Theological Seminary and began my ministerial training. Dr. Clyde Francisco introduced me to the Old Testament. Suddenly, a book which had contained only a few unrelated stories of interest and some isolated texts became a living book. Its people came alive and the voice of God spoke from its pages.

At that point, I became sure of what God wanted me to do. I was to devote my life to making the Bible live for people. From that time to this, I have not doubted my task. From my student pastorates in Tennessee and Kentucky, through the five years at the First Baptist Church of McRae, Georgia, and the ten-and-a-half years at the First Baptist Church of Aiken, South Carolina, and on to the more than ten years on the faculty of Golden Gate Baptist Theological

Seminary, my task has been to make the Bible (and in particular, the Old Testament) live. My every sermon, article, book, and ministry has been devoted to this task. That is why I have written this book. I want to make the Old Testament live for you. There is no other reason.

My Presuppositions

Finally, you as a reader and student need to be aware of my presuppositions. They govern my approach to the Old Testament, control the ways in which I handle evidence, and ultimately will make this work unique in spite of all of its similarities to other works in the field. You need to evaluate my presuppositions in the light of your own; for in the interaction between our basic beliefs, your understanding of my words will be correct or incorrect.

The first four of my presuppositions have to do with my faith, my commitment to the lordship of Christ. These, for me, are not debatable. Upon these my life and ministry are built; they determine who I am and what I do. The fifth presupposition is not fundamental to my person but is fundamental to this book, for it relates to my purpose in writing.

The Nature of God

For me, the beginning point of all things is God. I believe that God is, that He exists. More than this, I am fully committed to the concept that *God is love*. However, for all its profundity, this statement is too abstract. More to the point is that God loves all people. This means to me that God's plan and purpose is to do His very best for everyone, including you and me. I am totally and completely convinced that God intends for us to experience His best. This does not always mean that His best for us is what we want. Like a child, I may prefer chocolate ice cream when spinach is best or play when study is best. God's wisdom knows the best and plans it.

The Predicament of People

Even though God's will for me is good, in my freedom I can and do thwart that will by sin. I am a sinner, a rebel against God's will. You, too, are a sinner and a rebel. All people are sinners. As sinners, you and I are not only morally wrong but can be intellectually wrong as well. Anyone who believes that all people are sinners should acknowledge that his or her ideas may be flawed. Indeed, the reality of sin makes such flaws inevitable.

Further, my sin has alienated me from God. He has not rejected me; I have rejected Him. In my helpless and hopeless predicament, I need salvation, redemption, forgiveness, and transformation. You need these, also, and so does everyone else. (Perhaps we need some fresh language since these terms do not communicate well to ordinary people in the modern world. At least for the moment, however, we shall stick with "the language of Zion," for I am writing primarily to Christians and not to the lost.)

The Divine-Human Encounter

God loves (desires good for) me, even while I am a rebel against that love. He has acted to redeem people, including you and me. In Christ Jesus, He demonstrated once for all His love by taking my sin upon Himself and giving me new life in Christ. I am born again through my faith in Christ by God's grace. This is salvation.

Having saved you and me, God calls us to Himself and then sends us forth into His world as servants. We are all called to serve God in His world. This is His best will for us.

Furthermore, God has not left us to our own devices at this point. He speaks to us, revealing His will to us. This is done in at least three ways. First He speaks to us in the world, both in nature and history. The Christian who ignores either risks missing God's will. God also speaks to us in His Word, the Bible. This should drive us back to the written Word again and again. Further, God speaks to us by His indwelling Spirit Who guides us into truth. You and I must listen to the voice of God and seek to obey Him.

The Search for Truth

If my task as a Christian is to do God's will, then I must know that will. Thus, I spend my life on a search for His truth. The Christian has nothing to fear from truth, for any truth is God's truth. The Christian has an obligation to search for truth.

In this book and in your study, you will find many things new to you. Consider and evaluate them analytically and seriously. Do not cast away any of your old ideas until you have found something better. My task and purpose is to strengthen your faith, not to destroy it, to challenge it so that in the end it will really be *your* faith, not just something you have inherited. Never settle for anything less than truth.

The Format of This Book

This book is a first introduction to the Old Testament and its study. Those who are already familiar with the field will recognize my indebtedness to all those who have gone before me. The new student who pursues the subject further will soon discover the same. But the beginning student can sometimes be distracted by a multiplicity of footnotes and citations. Thus, one of my basic presuppositions is that footnotes must be kept to a bare minimum so as not to intrude upon the learning process. For those who want to pursue a subject further, I will periodically offer suggestions for further study. There is also a detailed list of such suggestions at the end of the book.

I have found my years of studying the Old Testament to be both exciting and rewarding. The task has frequently been difficult, but it has never been boring. Through the pages of the Old Testament, I have met people who were faced with the issues of life which confront me. I have learned from their successes and failures. Most important of all, God has confronted me, transforming my life and thought. I welcome you to this study. May God bless you in it.

Contents

AN
INTRODUCTION
TO THE
OLD TESTAMENT
AND ITS STUDY

Part I
General Considerations

1

The Old Testament as Word of God

The first priority in any approach to the Old Testament is to establish as precisely as possible the basic nature of the book. Countless millions of people claim the Old Testament to be the inspired Word of God. Is this claim true? If so, what is meant by the claim?

A very obvious fact is often overlooked by scholars, ministers, and laypeople: The Christian churches possess the Old Testament precisely because they preserved it. Admittedly, the Old Testament is the Bible of Judaism. As such, it should be taken seriously. On the other hand, it has been read, studied, and preached by Christians over the centuries, not as the Jewish Scriptures but as part of the Christian Scriptures. Christians have preserved it because they have heard God speak through its pages. The Christian affirmation has been that God's Word confronts human life from the pages of this ancient book. This brings us back to our basic questions: Is the Old Testament the inspired Word of God, and if so, what is meant by this claim?

I am going to try to separate what the Bible claims for itself at this point from what people have said about it. Further, we need to differentiate in our thinking between facts and theories. Facts are true. They are observable, demonstrable. Theories, on the other hand, are human attempts to explain known facts. Theories are interpretations and explanations based upon present knowledge. Theories change; facts do not.

Once I had a recurring soreness in my heel. The doctor treated it as neuritis, giving periodic injections and countless pills. We eventually noticed that the pain always came after the days I had preached. Only then did we discover a lump in the heel of my best shoes, the ones I wore when I preached. The basic fact was a pain in the heel. The theory to explain the pain had to change as new facts were discovered.

This is true in every area of life and in every field of knowledge. Much trouble and heartbreak can occur in the area of religion when people make no distinction between facts and theories. We must seek to avoid confusing facts and theories.

Inspiration

I believe the Bible is inspired. So what? Does my believing it make it so? Does the fact that someone else does not believe it make it not so? For me, this is a faith commitment. Why have I made this commitment?

During the days of Jesus' life and the days of the early Christians as reflected in the New Testament, there was no New Testament. The only Scriptures which they had were those of the Old Testament. Examine with me the claims these early Christians made about the Old Testament.

Two things seem to stand out in the claims made in the biblical passages relating to inspiration.

1.   Inspiration is a fact.
2.   Inspiration is a process.

Before attempting to justify these conclusions, we need to define *inspiration*. One person says, "I believe the Bible is inspired." Another suggests, "The painting of Michelangelo is inspired." A third announces, "The sight of the sun setting behind the snow-covered mountains was so inspiring." The term is clearly used of different things in different ways. What does it mean for us?

The word *inspiration* comes from two words which mean "to breathe into." When applied to the Old Testament or to the Bible, it means that God has breathed into the words. The idea probably derives from the account of God breathing the breath of life into the first man (Gen. 2:7). I use the term *inspiration* in this way. To say the Scriptures are inspired is to say that they are "God-breathed."

Inspiration is both a fact and a process. Several significant passages must be considered at this point. We are clearly taught that inspiration begins with God's Spirit moving upon the hearts and minds of His people. "No prophecy ever came by the impulse of man, but men moved by the Holy Spirit spoke from God" (2 Pet. 1:21). A real revelation from God has its starting point with God. This is so simple and obvious that it is often overlooked. Furthermore, inspiration begins as God's Holy Spirit starts to stir someone from among His people.

Another admonition defines the process further. A foundational proclamation advises: "All scripture is inspired by God and is profitable for teaching, for reproof, for correction, and for training in righteousness, that the man of God may be complete, equipped for every good work" (2 Tim. 3:16-17). Here we are told that not only were the writers and speakers inspired, their words also were inspired, they were God-breathed. We must again remind ourselves that when this quotation was first written it was most likely being applied to the Old Testament, since the New Testament had not yet been written. The Bible itself proclaims that in some way the very words of the Old Testament have been breathed into by God.

A final concept was added to these teachings both by the apostles and by Jesus Himself. "First of all you must understand this, that no prophecy of scripture is a matter of one's own interpretation" (2 Pet. 1:20). Perhaps in explanation of this kind of idea, Jesus told His disciples: "I have yet many things to say to you, but you cannot bear them now. When the Spirit of truth comes, he will guide you into all the truth" (John 16:12-13). Here is proclaimed the idea that God's Holy Spirit inspires (breathes into) the interpreter of the Scriptures.

A fully developed concept of inspiration must include all of these ideas: The process begins with God, moves through the original speakers and writers, fills the very words themselves, and carries on to the contemporary interpreter. Any concept of inspiration which is less than this is less than what the Bible claims for itself.

After stating what the Bible claims for itself, the going gets tougher, for a number of theories have been proposed to explain these facts. Some theories explain inspiration as if God dictated His word to His writers and speakers as if they were nothing more than stenographers. This fails to consider that the Bible books reflect various human styles, vocabularies, and degrees of mastery of language arts and skills. Other theories explain inspiration as if it only applied to the original manuscripts. To me, this creates problems with my understanding of God. It seems to me to reflect a very weak God if He could inspire the original writers and not control the ongoing process. Further, if only the original words are inspired, what authority does my modern translation have? Still other theories claim that only the ideas are inspired. This claim, however, ignores the fact that the Bible clearly claims more than this for itself.

The better part of wisdom causes me to pause at this point in an affirmation of both faith and mystery. The faith statement is that the Bible is fully inspired, both in its origin and as it comes to us. Yet the ultimate nature of its inspiration belongs to God. We may attempt to explain it, but such explanations are still only human theories—no more. In humility, I will trust that God did it and still does it. It is ultimately a matter of faith.

Revelation

A part of the teachings of the Bible regarding inspiration bring us face to face with the concept of revelation. God inspired His Scriptures for the purpose of revealing something. This is variously stated as "truth" (John 16:13), a basis for "teaching, for reproof, for correction, and for training in righteousness" (2 Tim. 3:16), to "glorify [Jesus]" (John 16:14), and to proclaim Him (Luke 24:27). Jesus is God's ultimate Word to the world (John 1:1-5), but God spoke and still speaks through the Bible, revealing Himself and His will and purpose for all humanity.

The Old Testament is a record of God's unveiling of Himself and His will. This is important to remember while studying the Old Testament, for it will help in understanding its content and intent.

If we fail to see and hear God through the pages of the Old Testament, the failure is not because we lack some secret key. The failure lies much closer than that. If we fail to see God's revelation, it is because we fail to study His revelation seriously, with diligence. If a visitor to Switzerland fails to see the Alps, it is simply because he did not look, not because they were hidden. The same is true of God's truth in the Old Testament. God reveals Himself in it. If we do not see Him, the fault is ours, not His. He is not trying to hide from us. To the contrary, He is drawing near to us. The Old Testament is revealing God, uncovering His hiddenness, making Him visible. We must open our eyes to see Him.

However, we must always remember that the Bible is God's Word in human language. God did not invent a new, divine language to speak to people. He spoke in the common language of the day, to common people. This means that the revelation in the Bible is always conditioned by human limitations of space and time. Words are limited. No finite human words can contain all the truth about an infinite God. The more profound an idea, the more difficult it becomes to express. I can describe a blade of grass with precision. To define love is far more difficult. Furthermore, a person can be in only one place at a time. Ezekiel or Jeremiah or Isaiah could only be in one place at any particular time. Their messages were limited, initially, to that place. If the people of Jerusalem heard Isaiah preach a certain message, the people of Samaria didn't. Although this appears to be quite obvious, much biblical study falters at this point. There is a human limitation.

Further, God is revealing sense, not nonsense. God's message made sense to the speaker and hearers when it was first given. It must have made sense originally, even if there may have been a far more profound meaning which they missed. The leaders of Jerusalem did not seek to execute Jeremiah because they did not understand him but precisely because they did. There was a revelation which they heard and saw. There is a revelation which we can and should see and hear.

Authority

The Old Testament has an authority inherent in its pages. The Bible is the Christian's authority in religious matters. It has a clearly stated purpose: "These are written that you may believe that Jesus is the Christ, the Son of God, and that believing you may have life in his name" (John 20:31). Beyond this, the Bible becomes the textbook of faith and life (2 Tim. 3:16-17).

The Bible is not a book of mathematics, science, history, home economics, or medicine, though it has all of these subjects in it. It is not even *a* book of faith. It is *the* book of faith which makes demands, challenges allegiances, calls to service, and forces decisions.

We must face the issue of the authority of the Old Testament for Christians. It has been much abused. The Old Testament provides the roots from which the New Testament faith grew, *but it is not the New Testament.* Thus it must be understood in the ultimate light of the New Testament revelation of God in Jesus Christ. Its teachings on slavery, war, diet, and other issues must be viewed from the standpoint of Christ. The Old Testament does have authority, but its authority is shaped and guided by the Lordship of Jesus.

Jesus accepted the Old Testament as authoritative upon Himself and proclaimed its authority to others (Matt. 23:23; Luke 10:25-28). But to accept it as fully authoritative at every point, the ultimate word on every issue, is to ignore the fact that Jesus modified its teachings at some points, enlarged upon them in others, and ignored them in still others (Matt. 5:17-48; 12:1-8).

The authority of the Old Testament is real. It has a binding relationship upon the life of the Christian. But it does not stand on its own; it stands only in relationship to the ultimate authority of its Author and as a part of the whole revelation of God.

The Old Testament is, thus, the Word of God to humanity. It is not God's ultimate Word, Jesus is. But it is a part, a major and significant part, of His written Word to sinful people. We must hear Him speak through it.

2
The World of the Old Testament

The Old Testament is not just a book; it is a collection of books, an entire library. It was written over a period of more than a thousand years and reflects, contains, and proclaims God's revelation to and through Israel during that time. It is a religious book, a book of faith and worship. The contemporary reader, unfortunately, finds that much of this collection of ancient scrolls is not easily understandable.

At first, "You shall not kill" (Ex. 20:13; Deut. 5:17) seems easy to understand. But even that becomes difficult when we try to define "kill." Is it limited to murder? Does it apply to soldiers in battle or to governments? Just what is meant?

The task of understanding and interpreting becomes more difficult with, "You shall not boil a kid in its mother's milk" (Ex. 23:19). The laws regarding slavery are more difficult still (Ex. 21:1-11,20-21,26-27). Furthermore, none of us has ever seen a Jebusite or a Perizzite. We do not normally even begin to know who or what they were.

The Old Testament was not written in a vacuum but in a real world, by real people who lived in specific places at specific times, facing real problems. If we are going to have any understanding of the Old Testament and its message, we have to learn as much as possible about the world of the Old Testament, including its history, its cultures, its languages, its geography, and its climate. The task is formidable but well worth the effort.

Archaeology

The science of archaeology has probably been the most useful and most abused of all disciplines which have been brought to bear on the task of understanding the Old Testament. It has been useful for it has brought to light most of what we know (outside of the Old Testament) of the culture and history of Israel and her neighbors during the biblical period. It has been abused primarily by those who fail to grasp what biblical (or Syro-Palestinian) archaeology is all about.

Biblical archaeology is not intended *to prove* the Bible. This kind of approach is bad archaeology and questionable theology. The truth of the Bible does not depend upon archaeology but faith. If belief in God's revelation depends upon archaeology, it is based upon a shaky foundation, indeed. The truth of God's dealing with Noah in the Flood is unaffected by whether the ark is ever found. God's message is not affected by anyone's scientific achievement.

Neither is archaeology a treasure hunt. It is not merely looking for great monuments or items of gold, silver, and precious stones which can be displayed in museums. These are of interest and of value, but they are really insignificant when compared with archaeology's major task. Further, the finding of such treasures frequently distracts persons from grasping the most significant contribution which archaeology has made to biblical studies.

Biblical archaeology is intended to shed light upon and give insight into the world of the Bible. It is here that its major contribution has been and will continue to be made. Occasionally, archaeologists discover ancient manuscripts or libraries which give us major information about the world of the ancient Near East at a particular place and time. Among these have been the Nuzi documents, which shed light upon the patriarchal times, the Ras Shamra (or Ugaritic) documents which give an understanding of Canaanite religion and culture, and the Dead Sea Scrolls which open up a part of the world of Judaism during the end of the Old Testament era and the beginning of that of the New Testament. To these may be added the Ebla materials, which reflect prepatriarchal culture and customs, and the libraries of Assyria and Babylon, giving us a history of those nations. In addition to these kinds of manuscripts, monumental inscriptions from all over the ancient Near East and fragments of military correspondence, business records, and the like occasionally come to light. Such things paint very graphically the luxurious life of the last days of Samaria and the tragic pathos of soldiers seeing the nation of Judah come to an end before the onslaught of Babylon.

Yet, for all the value of these things, archaeology has made a far more valuable contribution to the student of the Old Testament. Archaeologists working in the Near East have uncovered cultural remains from the daily lives of these people who lived in Bible times. We have discovered how they worked and lived. Such discoveries make those ancient people become living persons whom we can, to some extent, begin to understand. Their inventions and changes in life-style make many of the differences found in their cultures from one era to another understandable.

Details of archaeology's contributions to our understanding of biblical people can be found in any good book on archaeology. I will point out such contributions from time to time as we deal with specific issues in individual books. For our purposes at this point, the issue of most importance is that you clearly understand what archaeology is and is not seeking to accomplish.

Geography

Many beginning students know little about Old Testament geography. The geographical features of the ancient Near East played a very significant role in the region's history. A good set of maps is invaluable in the study of the Old Testament. Following historical developments on maps will help the student understand the major forces behind these developments.

In considering the entire Old Testament world, several major features grasp the attention. Beginning with the southwest, the land of Egypt was essentially the long narrow band of the Nile River Valley, sandwiched between great, high, arid desert regions. With the exception of the broader delta region where the Nile emptied into the Mediterranean Sea, the fertile and habitable region of Egypt was seldom more than ten miles wide, though the land was hundreds of miles long. The Nile Valley was highly fertile due to the annual flood caused by the melting snows in the highlands of Ethiopia. This flood deposited highly fertile silt, making crops fairly easy to grow when the land was irrigated with water from the Nile.

To the immediate east of Egypt is the Red Sea, with the Sinai Peninsula jutting into its northern reaches. The peninsula is primarily desert, with high mountains in its southern part. A narrow fertile coastal plain extends along the border of the Sinai and the Mediterranean Sea. This coastal plain connects Egypt with Palestine.

Palestine itself served as a broader, but still narrow, region of fertility to the north of Sinai. It was bordered on the west by the Mediterranean and on the east by the great Arabian Desert. Due south of Palestine was another desert wilderness. To the north were massive mountain ranges. Further north and east were the headwaters of the Tigris and Euphrates Rivers. Between Palestine and this region were the cities of Damascus and Hamath and the territory of the Syrians, a relatively fertile region watered by the rivers Abana and Orontes.

In the upper reaches of the Tigris and Euphrates river valleys was the nation of Assyria. To the southeast, in the lower part of the valleys was Babylon. Further to the north and east were very mountainous highlands.

In viewing the Old Testament world as a whole, two facts stand out. Most of the region was hardly habitable, due either to deserts, mountains, or seas. The part of the land which was habitable centered around rivers or coasts. The habitable region, as a whole, is approximately crescent shaped, beginning with the Nile Valley, moving up the coastal plain and Palestine, through the region of Syria, and then down through the Tigris-Euphrates Valley. This region has come to be known as the Fertile Crescent. It is primarily in this region and among its peoples that the events of the Old Testament occurred.

Of more detailed interest to the Old Testament student are the geographical features of Palestine itself. The name comes from the Philistines who once played a significant role in its history. This little strip of land is about 165 miles long, about 40 miles wide at the top and about 75 miles wide at the base. On this small stage was played out all the drama of the history of the Hebrew kingdoms.

Palestine is divided into four north-south divisions. Beginning on the western edge bordering on the Mediterranean Sea is the Coastal Plain. This is sometimes called the Philistine Plain in the south and the Plain of Sharon in the north. It ends abruptly in the north, where Mount Carmel juts out into the sea. It was a highly fertile, well-watered region which was easy to settle and cultivate. It has no natural harbors but was quite desirable for its agricultural qualities throughout all biblical history.

Moving eastward, the second major north-south division is the Central Highlands. This is rough, rocky, and highly defensible. It was difficult to cultivate but made excellent territory for shepherds and nomadic or guerrilla-type warriors. Major settlements in this region in the earliest days were only possible where there was an abundant water supply, such as at Jerusalem. However, with the invention of slaked lime, about 1250-1200 BC, it became possible to make cisterns watertight. Rainwater could be collected during the rainy seasons and stored for the long dry months. Such water supplies made settlements throughout the region possible. Eventually, these settlements became quite numerous.

The third major north-south division is the great Jordan rift. The land drops quickly from the Central Highlands to the Jordan Valley, a major geological fault. In the north, the land drops from Mount Tabor at an elevation of about 1,850 feet to the surface of the Sea of Galilee, which is almost 700 feet below sea level. In the south, it drops from Jerusalem, about 2,500 feet above sea level to the surface of the Dead Sea, with an elevation of almost 1,300 feet below sea level. This is the lowest surface on earth. The Jordan River makes its torturous way from the Sea of Galilee down to the Dead Sea. The Jordan rift, while rising slightly to the south of the Dead Sea, continues on to the Gulf of Aqaba.

The land east of the Jordan Valley rises sharply to the Transjordan Plateau, the fourth north-south division. This quickly fades away into the arid wastes of the great Arabian Desert.

Three other major geographic regions must also be identified. In the south of the land, a small pie-slice shaped region of foothills intrudes between the Philistine Plain and the Central Highlands. This is known as the Shephelah. Further south, on a line approximately equal to the southern tip of the Dead Sea, the entire region fades away into a rough, arid, hostile region known as the Negev. The final major geographical feature of the land is a long, narrow valley which runs eastward from the Mediterranean just north of Mount Carmel. It cuts through the Central Highlands almost all the way to the Jordan Valley. This is variously known as the Plain of Sharon, the Valley of Esdraelon, and the Valley of Megiddo.

In addition to knowing the location and nature of the major geographic features of the land, it is also important for the student to know the major highways and their general location. Four major north-south highways and one minor east-west highway were of significance. The most important highway is known as the Way of the Sea. It came southwest from Damascus, cut north of the Sea of Galilee, across the Valley of Megiddo, through the mountain pass at Megiddo, and then followed the Coastal Plain all the way into Egypt. Probably second in importance was the King's Highway, which followed the Transjordan Plateau south from Damascus beyond the southern end of the Dead Sea where it split. One part went west toward Egypt, and the other went south toward the Gulf of Aqaba. The highway got its name from the fact that the kings who attacked the region of Siddim in the story of Lot followed this route (Gen. 14).

The third important highway is known variously as the Water Parting Route or the Central Highlands Route. It followed the spiny backbone of the land from north to south and was quite difficult to travel. It was seldom used for moving major armies or caravans. The fourth route followed the Jordan Valley from the north to the ford at Jericho, where it connected with the only east-west route of significance. This east-west route connected Jerusalem with Jericho and went on eastward across the ford there.

The importance of these routes cannot be stressed too much. Palestine itself was a land bridge between Egypt and Mesopotamia. Every army which moved between these regions had to travel along one of these highways and thus they were of both strategic and economic significance. For example, during the period when the Northern Kingdom of Israel and the Southern Kingdom of Judah existed side by side, Israel straddled all four routes while Judah was only on the Water Parting Route. That brought greater prosperity in trade to the Northern Kingdom but made it much more of a military target. The history of the two kingdoms reflects that situation quite clearly. Thus geography can be seen significantly to affect a nation's history.

Climate

The land of Palestine is approximately at the same latitude as the state of Georgia. The location determines its basic climate, subject to the modifications caused by its geography. The amounts of rain which fall decrease in proportion to the distance from the Mediterranean. It also decreases from north to south. However, no part of the land receives regular, abundant rainfall.

The summers are generally hot and dry. They begin in May or June and last until September. Then comes a brief period of "the former rains" which is followed by the cold winter season and the annual "winter rains." The success of the crops depended upon the winter rains. When the winter rains failed, the harvest was sure to be scant. The cold of Palestine's winter is not excessive, but it is felt because of its contrast with the summer heat. The rains also made the cold more cutting. The winter rains do not fall daily but are common throughout a general rainy season.

The winter season is followed by another brief season known as "the latter rains." Adequate rains in that period could make the crops quite abundant.

Normally the winds blow from the Mediterranean into Palestine. That brings the rain in its season and the heavy dews during the summer. However, occasional climatic aberrations occur when the strong sirocco blows from the desert. This wind brings the high heat and dry dust of the Arabian Desert. It has a devastating effect upon vegetation, as well as upon man and beast. Because of its utter destructiveness, it came to be symbolic to the prophets of the judgment of God (Jer. 4:11-13; Jonah 4:8).

As can be easily imagined and quickly documented, the weather and climate were important to Hebrew history. In addition to affecting directly the prosperity of the people, they also affected military action. Armies generally marched in the drier seasons. David's sin with Bathsheba is dated by the expression: "In the spring of the year, the time when kings go forth to battle" (2 Sam. 11:1). Deborah's defeat of the Canaanites seems to have been aided by a thunderstorm which caused the river Kishon to overflow, thus bogging down the chariots of the Canaanites (Judg. 5:4, 19-21). Thus a knowledge of Palestine's climate also aids our understanding of Hebrew history and the message of the Old Testament.

History

Perhaps the most important area of knowledge for the study of the Old Testament is that of ancient Near Eastern history. Our particular interest lies in those nations and peoples who interacted with the Hebrews during the Old Testament era. Yet, for all of its importance, the knowledge of Old Testament history is something in which too many interpreters are sadly lacking. There is no way to comprehend the message of the Old Testament with any degree of mastery apart from a knowledge of the history of the era.

Numerous sources are available to the student who wants to reconstruct this period of history. First of all, the biblical records themselves include historical books (Joshua, Judges, 1 and 2 Samuel, 1 and 2 Kings, 1 and 2 Chronicles, Ezra and Nehemiah). Other Old Testament books which are not as much concerned with history and events reflect a great deal of more or less incidental historical information.

To the biblical sources must be added the official records of the ancient kingdoms with whom Israel came in contact. Generally thorough records from Egypt throughout the biblical era are available. The Assyrian king lists and their eponym list are also sources for study. The eponym list identifies each year of Assyria's history by some important event or person. Further, the Babylonian king list is now also completed. Finally, among the official records, some information from the Persian empire exists. These all clearly overlap and interact with one another and with the Hebrews, allowing comparison, evaluation, and correlation.

Further sources of historical information related to this era come from ancient historians, such as Herodotus and Josephus. Admittedly, their work is occasionally questionable and must be assessed in the light of other information. Also, ancient monuments which were frequently erected to commemorate some great victory or event add their details to the data on the Old Testament period. Finally, astronomical and geographical data are useful, particularly as such items may be identified from modern observations. Of course, new discoveries in archaeological investigations regularly add to the store of knowledge.

Yet, possessing all of this historical data and being able to use it are two quite different things. Ancient data were normally given in the terms of the reigns of kings. "In the third year of Asa king of Judah, Baasha the son of Ahijah began to reign over all Israel at Tirzah, and reigned twenty-four years" (1 Kings 15:33), or "In the eighteenth year of King Josiah, the king sent Shaphan . . . the secretary, to the house of the Lord" (2 Kings 22:3) are examples. The problem for the historian is to convert all dates into an absolute chronology. It is both a complex and a difficult task.

No one can grasp ancient history without mastering ancient chronology. Further, there is no such thing as an approximately correct chronology. Either something happened at a particular date or it did not. Yet there is nothing wrong with admitting both modern limitations and ignorance. Scholars seek to arrive at a chronology which is as accurate as possible, given the present state of knowledge. On the other hand, due to the confusing state of some knowledge and the gaps in other parts of it, the fact is that much of scholars' ancient chronological reconstructions is only approximately correct. Thus, different historians frequently give slightly different dates for identical events. On the other hand, given the distance of modern research from such events, it is amazing that historians can come as close as they do to agreement.

In trying to establish an ancient chronology, some dates are quite certain. These are the stackpoles around which to reconstruct the history. Reconstruction begins with recorded astronomical events whose dates can be calculated. At the present time, two are of major significance. In ancient Egypt, the civil calendar was correlated with the appearance of a star called Sothis. This star appeared at the same place on the horizon at the same time of the first day of the year every 1,460 years. This knowledge allows us to give absolute dates to some of the Egyptian records. In Assyria an eclipse of the sun was recorded which we know occurred on June 15, 763 BC. On this stackpole, other dates in Assyrian history may be established. Where Assyrian and Egyptian history touch Hebrew history we can begin to establish an absolute chronology for the Old Testament era. Six major dates can be calculated in this way at the present.

1. In 853 BC, Ahab, king of Israel, fought at the Battle of Qarqar against Assyria.

2. The Black Obelisk of Shalmaneser III portrays Jehu, king of Israel, paying tribute to the Assyrians in 842 BC.

3. Samaria, capital of the Northern Kingdom, fell to the Assyrians after a three-year seige in 722/21 BC.

4. Although not directly involving the Hebrews, Babylon finally defeated the Assyrians at the Battle of Carchemish in 605 BC, and Nebuchadnezzar became king of Babylon.

5. Jerusalem fell to the Babylonian army in 587/86 BC.

6. In 539 BC, Cyrus, king of Persia, allowed the Jews to return to their homeland from their exile in Babylon.

Given these fixed dates, the diligent historian can begin

to calculate both backward and forward to try to establish other dates. This process, of course, must be constantly checked with correlations within the Bible and with foreign synchronisms.

However, it is not as simple as it at first seems. Some problems are quite complex. Consider, for example, the problems of the reigns of the kings of Israel and Judah. In the Southern Kingdom of Judah, Rehoboam reigned seventeen years (1 Kings 14:21), Abijam reigned three years (15:2), and Asa reigned forty-one years (v.10), for a combined total of sixty-one years. In the Northern Kingdom of Israel, Jeroboam reigned twenty-two years (v.25), Nadab reigned two years (v.25), Baasha reigned twenty-four years (v.33), Elah reigned two years (16:8), Zimri reigned seven days (v.15), and Omri reigned twelve years (v.23), for a combined total of sixty-two years. It was at this point that Ahab began to reign (v.29), but this is said to be Asa's thirty-eighth year. This would mean that while sixty-two years had passed in the north, only fifty-eight years had passed in the south (17 + 3 + 38 = 58). This is a significant problem. Following the chronology onward, the problem gets worse.

Numerous solutions have been proposed, but the one commonly used is to ignore the problem, pretending it isn't there. That just won't do. The problem will not evaporate. A solution to this problem is proposed in this book in the study of the Books of 1 and 2 Kings.

The historian and biblical interpreter must also deal with other problems of Old Testament chronology. The major problems appear to be:

1. the date of the Exodus event,
2. the dates of the patriarchs,
3. the dates of the judges,
4. the life spans of ancient peoples, and
5. the chronology of the postexilic period.

Before we can find solutions to these problems, we must first admit our ignorance. Until we arrive at that point, we shall never find solutions. This is precisely the way God deals with us. We have no hope of spiritual salvation until we admit our sinful limitations. We have no hope of deliverance from ignorance until we admit our own limitations of knowledge.

For our purposes at this point, we need to consider the results of a study of ancient Near Eastern history as it relates to the Old Testament. The following historical outline of the Old Testament era will serve as a framework for the rest of our studies.

The Prepatriarchal Period

The prepatriarchal period extended from the beginning to the time of Abraham, sometime around 2000 BC. In this period the historian finds interest in the rise of Egyptian and Mesopotamian civilizations. As far as the Old Testament is concerned, in this period we are not dealing with history as we know it today but with scattered accounts describing the sin predicament of mankind. The biblical background for this period is found mainly in the early chapters of Genesis (1:1 to 11:32).

The Patriarchal Period

With the call of Abraham (Gen. 12:1-4), we move onto the real stage of Hebrew history. Hebrew or Old Testament history is quite different from what we normally find in history books. The history of the Bible is not a record of events simply as events. It is a record of what God was doing with, to, and through His people Israel. As such, it is perhaps best described as "salvation history," "redemption history," or even "holy history." This is more commonly described by biblical historians or theologians by the German term, *Heilsgeschichte*. The prime concern in the Old Testament narratives was not so much what people were doing as what God was doing. It is imperative that we remember this.

The patriarchal period included the time of Abraham, Isaac, Jacob, and Joseph. This appears to fit into the era around 2000 to 1700 BC. The Nuzi tablets give a great deal of cultural background to our understanding of the biblical material related to this era (Gen. 12:1 to 50:26). Surface exploration of Palestine reveals that the central hill country was basically unsettled at that time, thus allowing the patriarchs the freedom to move easily through the region.

The Sojourn

We know very little of the period of the sojourn, and the chronological difficulties are quite complex. However, for reasons which I shall discuss in connection with our study of the Book of Exodus, it appears most likely that this period extended from about 1700 to about 1300 BC. The biblical narrative is almost nonexistent (Ex. 1:1-6). Israel and his family went into Egypt as refugees from famine. They stayed because the living was easy. But by the end of the era, they were slaves of the Egyptians.

The Exodus, Conquest, and Settlement

The narrative relating to these events is largely found in the books of Exodus through Judges (Ex. 1:7 to 24:18; 32:1 to 34:35; Num. 9:15 to 36:13; Deut. 1:1 to 34:12; Josh. 1:1 to 24:33; Judg. 1:1 to 21:25; 1 Sam. 1:1 to 9:27). This era also has major chronological difficulties which are not certainly solved, but this era appears to have extended from around 1290 to 1020 BC.

This period began with the time of God's deliverance of Israel through Moses. It included the giving of the covenant at Sinai and the period of wilderness wanderings. Following Moses' death, Joshua led the people in the conquest of Canaan. He was followed by a succession of judges, leaders who helped the people consolidate both their hold on the land and their faith. The last of the great judges was Samuel.

The United Monarchy

With the anointing of Saul as king of Israel, the little nation took its place on the stage of history among the kingdoms of the ancient Near East. The people of Israel always seem to have been more aware of their tribal identity than of their national identity. The personalities of Saul, David, and Solomon held the tribes together briefly, for a period extending from around 1020 BC to 931 BC. This is described in 1 Samuel 10:1 to 31:13; 2 Samuel 1:1 to 24:25;

1 Kings 1:1 to 11:43; 1 Chronicles 10:1 to 29:30; and 2 Chronicles 1:1 to 9:31.

During the united monarchy, the religious and political institutions of Israel took shape. A sense of national identity and purpose came to the fore. Under the leadership of David, the nation reached its point of greatest territorial expansion. Furthermore, the nature of the nation and its kings' relation to God and His law was clearly established. However, the union of the tribes under Saul, David, and Solomon was at best only tenuous. It did not long endure.

The Separated Kingdoms

The division of the united monarchy into two kingdoms is frequently described as if it were something new. The separation of the kingdoms was actually more of a return to the earlier sense of tribalism than a new development. Following Solomon's death in 931 BC, the northern tribes established a kingdom separate from the southern tribes. From that time onward, the Northern Kingdom was called Israel and the Southern Kingdom was Judah.

During the period when both kingdoms existed, Israel was normally stronger economically and militarily than Judah. In addition to the normal material from the historical books (1 Kings 12:1 to 22:53; 2 Kings 1:1 to 17:41; 2 Chron. 10:1 to 28:27), some of the books of the prophets Amos, Hosea, and Isaiah also furnish historical detail for this era. The Northern Kingdom came to an end under the assault of Assyria with the fall of Samaria in 722/721 BC. Many of its citizens were carried away into exile at this time.

Judah continued to exist as a separate nation for more than a century (2 Kings 18:1 to 25:30; 2 Chronicles 29:1 to 36:23). For this period as well, parts of the books of the prophets Isaiah, Jeremiah, Ezekiel, Micah, Habakkuk, and Nahum also add historical detail. Throughout this period of Judah's separate existence, it was essentially weak, normally at the mercy of the mightier empires.

With the fall of Jerusalem to the armies of Babylon in 587/86 BC, the Hebrew experiment at kingship came to an end. It had been a story of apostasy, idolatry, and rebellion. The leaders of the land were carried by King Nebuchadnezzar to Babylon.

The Period of the Exile

Following the end of the kingdom, it appeared as if Israel would cease to exist. The land of Judah was devastated and only the poorest people had been left behind. Those in exile in Babylon fared far better. They were essentially free to do anything they wished except to return home. In fact, many of the Hebrews in exile seem to have prospered.

A great deal of Israel's theology took shape during this period. Much of the idea of redemptive suffering and substitutionary atonement upon which the New Testament writers later drew to describe Jesus' ministry was formulated in Babylon under God's leadership. No other nation in the ancient world had a faith which survived such a catastrophe. Israel alone found the light of God in the darkness of suffering.

Babylon did not exist long after conquering Judah. The once-mighty empire fell to the Medo-Persians in 539 BC. Cyrus allowed all the Babylonian exiles to return home. Among them were the Hebrews. Many Hebrews had been so successful in Babylon that they did not wish to go home. However, a large group did return to Judah to begin the task of reconstruction.

The Postexilic Period

In the years following the return from exile in 539 BC, the Persian Empire generally maintained peace throughout the ancient Near East. For a period of almost two centuries, the Persians reigned supreme. The Hebrew people obviously benefitted from that time of peace, but we know very little of the events which involved them. Only brief glimpses of their situation are afforded to us.

Immediately after the return, the Hebrews apparently experienced great difficulties and allowed the task of rebuilding the Temple of Jerusalem to languish. In 520 BC,

Haggai and Zechariah called them back to this task and the second Temple was completed and dedicated in 516 BC.

The curtain is raised only partially on Hebrew experiences in the next century by the Books of Ezra, Nehemiah, and Esther. This period appears to have basically been a time of consolidation and stabilization. In this era, the synagogue was established as a religious center and Judaism emerged as a religion.

With the rise and expansion of Greece, primarily under the military influence of Philip of Macedon and his greater son, Alexander, the days of the Persian empire were numbered. Alexander's defeat of the Persians at the battle of Thermopylae in 333 BC brought the Persian suzerainty to an end. Palestine passed under Greek domination, and the Old Testament era essentially came to an end. The major emphasis of God's redemptive action with His people drew to a close. The stage was set for the main act in God's great drama of redemption, the gift of His Son.

Against this historical background, we must study the Old Testament and seek to understand its message. Any attempt to try to understand the Old Testament without a knowledge of history is doomed to failure. The Old Testament was produced in its own world, with geography and history as its setting. When placed within that setting, its people are better seen as living people and its content as a living book.

3

The Content of the Old Testament

Three basic issues must be confronted at the outset in any approach to the study of the Old Testament. The first of these is the issue of exactly which books are a part of the Old Testament. Related to this are the questions of how, why, and when these books began to be regarded as authoritative. Here the issue of the Old Testament canon is raised and must be considered.

Having arrived at an understanding of which books belong to the Old Testament, the second issue is what content actually belongs in these books. The study of the text of the Old Testament is usually known as "text criticism." *Criticism* is not a negative word. In much modern usage, a critic is against or opposed to something. However, to criticize something is to study it seriously, to analyze it. Thus the discipline of Old Testament text criticism is the serious study of the text of the Old Testament with the intent of trying to discover what was originally written.

Related to the two issues of canon and text is the third issue, linguistic studies. It is not enough to know what books belong in the Old Testament. It is not even enough to know what was the original content of these books. We must also come to grips with the ancient language, including its grammar, syntax, and lexicography, to determine what the text really meant. Only as we have dealt with all three of these issues can we, with any degree of confidence, begin to approach the study of the Old Testament itself.

45

The Canon of the Old Testament

The word *canon* comes from a Greek word which means a standard or a rule. As applied to the Bible, the term has come to refer to those books which are the standard, which are regarded as authoritative. Most people have never thought about how or when the books of the Old Testament came to be collected and accepted as authoritative.

In considering the subject, two basic questions must be answered. First, what can be discovered about the process by which the thirty-nine books which make up the Old Testament came to be collected and accepted as authoritative for life? The Old Testament itself refers to numerous other books which were available, but which were not accepted as authoritative. In addition, copies of ancient books and of parts of books which were not so accepted have been discovered (some of the Dead Sea Scrolls, for example). It is simple to say that some books were inspired and others were not. The issue, however, is what human processes were used of God in order to determine this.

The second basic question regarding the process of canonization which must be addressed relates to the different Old Testament canons which are around. Protestants accuse Catholics of having added books to the Old Testament. The Roman Catholics respond with the accusation that Protestants have left some books out of the Old Testament. In addition to these differences, the Eastern Orthodox churches have yet a different canon from either of these, both in the number of books and in their order. Can any data in the process of canonization help explain this confusing situation?

The Hebrew Bible is divided into three major sections. The first section is called by the Hebrew word *Torah,* which means "law." It is also sometimes called by the Latin name, *Pentateuch,* which is based on the Latin word for "five." This section is made up of the first five books of the Bible: Genesis, Exodus, Leviticus, Numbers, and Deuteronomy.

The second major section of the Hebrew Bible is called the *Nebhi'im,* which means "prophets." This is further subdivided into the Former Prophets, which include Joshua, Judges, 1 and 2 Samuel, and 1 and 2 Kings, and the Latter Prophets, which include Isaiah, Jeremiah, Ezekiel, and the Twelve (what Christians call the Minor Prophets). Many people normally identify the Former Prophets as history books. Perhaps the fact that the ancient Hebrews regarded these as prophets should be significant to us. (I shall return to this issue when we study these books.)

The third section of the Hebrew canon is called the *Kethubhim*, also known as the Writings, or by its Latin title, the *Hagiographa* (The Wise Writings). This includes all the rest of the books of the Old Testament: Psalms, Proverbs, Job, the Megilloth (or Scrolls, made up of the Song of Songs, Ruth, Lamentations, Ecclesiastes, and Esther), Daniel, Ezra, Nehemiah, and 1 and 2 Chronicles.

The Jews do not call these books the Old Testament, for they of course do not accept the *New* Testament. Their most common title for what we call the Old Testament comes from taking the first letter of each of the three sections: T(orah), N(ebhi'im), K(ethubim). To these they add vowels to make it pronounceable, calling the entire collection the *TANAK*.

Within the biblical history, we can possibly determine the latest date at which a particular book or section of the Old Testament was regarded as authoritative, that is, when it was demonstrably canonical. Obviously, there is no way we can demonstrate when it was *first* accepted, if that date is different.

Biblical Evidence

The "book of the law" was found in the Temple in 621 BC during the reign of Josiah (2 Kings 22:8 to 23:25). Josiah accepted it as the authoritative basis for a major religious reform in Judah. This is the first documentary evidence of any book being accepted as an authoritative sacred Scripture, governing faith and life. Although most scholars agree that this book was related to our present Book of Deuteronomy, unfortunately there is no way in which an actual identity can be proven. However, it was clearly a step in the canonization process.

The next identifiable step is found with Ezra's return from Babylonia in 458 BC with the "law of . . . God" in his hand (Ezra 7:14). Fourteen years later, he read what is called "the book of the law of Moses" in the hearing of all the people (Neh. 8:1-3). The reading took all morning. This may have been the whole Pentateuch. The length of time required to read it would fit in well with its present length. What he read was both presented by Ezra and accepted by the people as an authoritative Scripture.

The beginning of a canon of the prophets may have been when the prophet Isaiah placed an obligation upon his disciples to preserve his words (Isa. 8:16). Jeremiah was clearly preserving an authoritative word from God when he employed Baruch to write his messages in 605 BC (Jer. 36:1-32). Although King Jehoiakim did not accept Jeremiah's scroll as authoritative, the royal court seems to have done so.

Unfortunately, no clear Old Testament evidence concerning when any of the Writings were accepted as authoritative can be found.

In the New Testament, writers used the expression "the law and the prophets" or "Moses and the prophets" (Matt. 5:17; 7:12; Luke 16:31; 24:27; John 1:45; Acts 24:14; Rom. 3:21). Many Christians have interpreted those expressions as referring to the entire Old Testament. Given the three-fold division of the Old Testament canon, the expressions more likely refer specifically to the first two parts. That is all that can be claimed with certainty. Thus by the New Testament era, the first two sections of the Old Testament canon appear to have been collected and accepted.

After the resurrection, Jesus spoke of "the law of Moses and the prophets and the psalms" as bearing witness to Him (Luke 24:44). Jesus could have been referring only to the Book of Psalms, or He could have been using a figure of speech for the entire collection of the Writings. Paul's reference to "all scripture" as being authoritative is too indefinite to be of any help with this issue.

Jesus made a reference to a string of murders extending

all the way from Abel to Zechariah (Luke 11:51). This sounds like a reference to the two extremities of a book, like "from beginning to end," or "from Genesis to Revelation." Abel, of course, was the first person murdered in the Old Testament (Gen. 4:8). Zechariah's murder, on the other hand, is less well known, but the reference is apparently to the prophet killed in the time of Joash (2 Chron. 24:20-21). However, when we remember that the Books of Chronicles close the section of the Writings, which in turn conclude the Hebrew Old Testament, Zechariah's stoning becomes the last murder in the Old Testament. Thus it would appear that Jesus' reference would indicate that both He and His hearers knew the Old Testament collection in its present form, although not everyone had as yet accepted it as authoritative.

Extrabiblical Evidence

When the Samaritans and the Hebrews split from one another, the Samaritans kept the Pentateuch as it is found in the Hebrew Bible. They also kept a version of the Book of Joshua, but it is widely divergent, recording history from Joshua to the time of the Romans. Thus it would appear that only the canon of the Torah was firmly established by that time. The date of the split is strongly disputed, but it certainly could not have been earlier than Ezra and Nehemiah, for they had troubles with the Samaritans which ultimately led to the split. The date can thus be no earlier than 450 BC and can be hardly later than 350 BC. It appears most likely to have been near 400 BC. Furthermore, extrabiblical sources from the fourth century BC onward seem to treat the Law as authoritative.

A writer known as Ben Sirach identified the Latter Prophets as Scripture and listed them in the same order in which we now have them (Ecclesiasticus 48—49). He also listed books known as the Writings, but omitted Daniel and Ezra. Ben Sirach's work is dated about 200 BC.

The Jewish general, Josephus, and the Jewish Talmud (in *Baba Bathra*) point to the canonical Jewish Scriptures as coming into existence between Moses and Ezra. Josephus listed it as containing the five books of Moses, thirteen books of the prophets, and four books of hymns and regulations for life. These two sources are probably to be dated in the early Christian era.

With the rise of Christianity, the Jews became defensive about what actually belonged to their Scriptures. Two rabbinic councils appear to have been held in Jamnia (Jabneh) in AD 90 and in AD 110, for the purpose of determining their authoritative canon. After extensive debate, particularly centering around Ezekiel, Proverbs, Song of Songs, Ecclesiastes, and Esther, and raising some questions about the Books of Chronicles, the Hebrew canon, as we now have it, was established.

During the last two centuries before the time of Jesus, the Jewish people were scattered throughout the Mediterranean world. As a consequence, many Jews away from Palestine no longer spoke Hebrew. In order to meet their needs, the Scriptures were translated into Greek. An ancient legend states that seventy rabbis locked in seventy separate rooms came out with identical translations. While there is no truth to the legend (the whole process apparently lasted more than a century), it did give the title to this Greek version of the Old Testament. It is known as the Septuagint (abbreviated LXX) from the Greek word for *seventy*.

The LXX had fourteen more books than the Hebrew canon, and the books were in a different order. It came to be known as the Alexandrian canon, since its writing and distribution centered in Alexandria in Egypt. The Hebrew canon, on the other hand, is known as the Palestinian canon.

Essentially, the Roman Catholics adopted the Alexandrian canon as their version of the Old Testament. Protestants, on the other hand, prefered the Palestinian canon. This explains the basic difference between the two major canons. (The Orthodox churches of the East added a few more books to the LXX.)

The Bible which most Protestants use today has the books in the Old Testament found in the Palestinian canon but in the order of the LXX.

Conclusion

While there is much we do not know about the process of canonization of the Old Testament, there are several things which stand out with clarity. First, there is no way by which we can establish any date as a time when a part or the whole canon *first* began to be accepted as authoritative in matters of faith and practice. Second, the Torah was clearly completed and accepted as authoritative at the latest by about 400 BC. Third, the Nebhi'im was completed and recognized as authoritative by about 200 BC. Fourth, the Kethubim was apparently in the form in which we now have it by the time of Jesus' ministry, around 30 AD. However, we cannot certainly regard it as having been generally recognized as authoritative Scripture until somewhat later, perhaps as late as the time of councils of Jamnia (ca. AD 90-110).

The Text of the Old Testament

The Old Testament was written primarily in Hebrew, with one major section (Dan. 2:4*b* to 7:28) and several minor passages (Ezra 4:8 to 6:18; 7:12-26; Jer. 10:11) in Aramaic, a language related to biblical Hebrew. (Hebrew and Aramaic are both a part of the Semitic family of languages.)

Originally, the text of the Old Testament was written without vowels. This always opened the door to a possibility of confusion, but the context usually helped. To illustrate, consider the English word *DG*. This could either be *dig, dog,* or *dug.* If the passage was telling of something barking, the word is obviously *dog.* If the context spoke of excavating a well, *DG* would be *dig* or *dug,* depending upon the tense needed.

However, the situation with Hebrew was more complex than just the omission of vowels. In the interest of conserving space, many ancient writings left no space between words and sometimes broke a word between lines. Yet, this is also not overly difficult to a person familiar with the language. Consider the following illustrations.

TWNKLTWNKLLTTLSTRHWWNDRWH
TYRPBVTHWRLDSHGHLKDMNDNTHSK

With only a little thought, this old nursery rhyme can be read quite easily: "Twinkle, twinkle, little star, How I wonder what you are. Up above the world so high, Like a diamond in the sky!"

Much of the Old Testament was oral before it was written. Now we would consider that this would in itself give rise to multitudinuous errors. Further thought denies this, however. If you have ever had read or told a favorite story to a child, you will know what I mean. On occasions when I was tired and tried to shorten the story by leaving something out, a little voice would cry out, calling my attention to the omission. Many ancient narratives were told over and over again around campfires. When there was an omission or error, there were many voices to correct it.

The original writing of a document was the next step in the process. After the documents were written, the scribes or *sopherim* made copies as needed. About the fifth or sixth century AD, groups of special scribes known as Masoretes arose. They developed a set of accents and vowels to keep the ancient records accurate. They transmitted the tradition (Hebrew: *masora*) of the text. Among the New Testament churches copies of the New Testament were made for evangelistic and missionary purposes as well as for worship and study. Many copies of these books were made and preserved. The Old Testament was not so handled. New copies were generally not made until an old one was wearing out. When a new one was made, the old was then generally burned or buried. Very few copies were left. As a matter of fact, the oldest complete copy of the Hebrew Old Testament (usually abbreviated as MT for Masoretic Text) which we possess is the Codex Leningradensis. It is dated about AD 1008, more than a thousand years after the completion of the last Old Testament book. This codex is in the public library in Leningrad. It is usually abreviated as "L," or "B19a" (from a cataloging system).

Until the early part of the twentieth century, we possessed almost no other Hebrew witnesses to the text of the Old Testament. At that point, workmen rebuilding an old synagogue in Cairo, Egypt, uncovered an ancient storeroom or Genizah which had a large number (more than 200,000) of fragments of ancient Hebrew manuscripts, many of which were biblical. But the discovery of the Dead Sea Scrolls after World War II was the greatest boon to Old Testament textual studies. Parts of many Old Testament books from the period just before and just after the life of Jesus were recovered. We now have full copies of several Old Testament books and large portions of almost all of the Old Testament canon. Only the Book of Esther is not represented. At one fell swoop, Hebrew textual studies were moved more than a thousand years backward toward the original manuscripts.

In addition to these witnesses to the text, we also have the Samaritan Pentateuch which is of value at least for the study of the text of the Pentateuch. We also have the texts of ancient translations from the Hebrew into other languages. Obviously these have to be used with care by students of the text. When divergences appear, it may be due more to the nature of translation than to a divergent text. Among the more important of these ancient witnesses are the Septuagint (LXX) and the Aramaic Targums, which are basically pre-Christian in date. To these must be added the Old Latin (ca. AD 150), the Vulgate (ca. AD 390-405), the Coptic version (ca. 3rd-4th century AD), and the Syriac Peshitta (ca. 4th century AD).

With the study of these witnesses, Old Testament text criticism has moved steadily forward. The purpose of Old Testament text criticism is to try to establish what the first written manuscript of any book said. The study of ancient texts and versions has allowed text critics to determine that mistakes have occurred in text transmission for three basic reasons.

Alteration

The alteration of a text in copying sometimes occurred by the simple transposition of consonants. That would usually happen when the copyist was inattentive to his task. Such errors also occurred through auditory or visual confusion.

If one person were reading a text to another, the scribe might confuse two words with identical sounds. In Isaiah 9:3 the King James Version renders a phrase: "Thou hast multiplied the nation, and *not increased the joy"* (author's italics). That negation is strange in the very heart of a passage on joy. The Hebrew word for "not" is pronounced *lo*. But another word with identical pronunciation but different spelling means "to him." The second word was found in the Dead Sea Scrolls, making the passage read: "Thou has multiplied the nation, thou has increased joy to him" (author's translation). Visual confusion shows up where two letters looked quite similar and the copying scribe chose the wrong one.

The final way by which texts were altered was by deliberate, dogmatic substitution. For example, Saul had a son by the name of Eshbaal ("man of Baal," 1 Chron. 8:33). However, the prophets were incensed at a king naming his son after the pagan god Baal, so they called Saul's son by the name of Ishbosheth ("man of shame," 2 Sam. 2:8).

Additions

The Old Testament text was also changed over the years through the process of addition. Remember that the writing took place over many centuries; language changed. Scribes, therefore, occasionally changed an uncommon word for a common one. More often, their attention slipped and they copied the same letter, word, or phrase twice. This process is called dittography. Also, occasional marginal notes were copied by a later scribe, apparently thinking the note was something which had been left out.

Omission

Scribes also omitted items in the same ways they added them. When the identical word or phrase occurred twice in a passage, they might let their eye slip from the first to the second, omitting the material between. Also, as marginal notes were sometimes incorporated into a text as an addition, they were also omitted sometimes when they shouldn't have been. A scribe might have put in the margin something he had left out but which should have been there. A later copyist assumed, wrongly, that the marginal note was merely a comment and not part of the text and left it out completely.

The discovery of the Dead Sea Scrolls demonstrated two things to Old Testament text critics. In moving almost a thousand years backward, we found numerous mistakes in the text as it had been transmitted, just as had been expected. However, not a single change has been discovered which has made any difference in any significant teaching of the Old Testament. It would appear that, while God left His scribes free to be human and make human errors in the transmission of the Old Testament, His Spirit has so controlled the process that His message has been preserved.

The study of the text of the Old Testament is now on firm enough ground that the contemporary student can handle the text with confidence. While Old Testament students do not have the massive evidence in such studies that the New Testament textual critics do, they have enough to be able to face the text in its present form with assurance.

The scribes of the Old Testament handled their text with care, respect, and reverence. To demonstrate this, consider the summary of Saul's kingship. "Saul was . . . years old when he began to reign; and he reigned, . . . and two years over Israel" (1 Sam. 13:1). Somewhere along the way a mouse or an insect ate a hole in an ancient manuscript. Anyone can see that numbers ought to be supplied in these blanks. Yet scribes never yielded to that temptation. They passed on the text as they received it, holes and all, so great was their reverence for the sacred Scriptures.

Language and Linguistics

Having confidence in the canon and the text, however, is not enough. We must know what the text meant if we are going to interpret it. Here we come to grips with the whole area of linguistic science. We must determine the meaning of words and idioms and understand the grammar and syntax.

Words cannot be assumed to be understood just because

we know generally what they mean. For example, God said through Malachi: "I have loved Jacob but I have hated Esau" (Mal. 1:2-3). Our normal usage would describe both of these terms as emotions. It is hard to comprehend a loving God hating Esau. A more thorough study of the use of these two words for love and hate in the Old Testament reveals that they are primarily actions, not emotions. This word for love means "to choose" and the word for hate means "to reject." Thus the statement becomes one of grace. In choosing Jacob, God did not choose Esau. Esau was rejected as God's chosen instrument.

The full process of linguistic science is really beyond the scope of this book. On the other hand, we shall have to use the results of such studies from time to time. It is here that we get into the basic task of interpretation. That, however, must follow introduction.

4

The Message of the Old Testament

A major element of the foundation to any study of the Old Testament is an attempt to answer the question: Why do we have the Old Testament at all? Admittedly, giving an answer to the question at this stage of our study is quite preliminary. Any answer which we give now may have to be modified later. At the same time, unless we begin our study with some idea as to why we possess the Old Testament, we are quite likely to spend a great deal of time floundering around in the pursuit of issues which are actually irrelevant to our basic study.

The Old Testament was originally preserved by the Jewish people as their Holy Scripture. They still preserve it for the same reason. Furthermore, parts of the Old Testament are included in the Koran, the sacred scriptures of Islam. These religions are both quite important in our world. Thus the Old Testament is of major importance because of its influence over people whose faith is either Islam or Judaism. Beyond this, a study of the Old Testament becomes important for any student of ancient Near Eastern history or of comparative religion, and for those who seek to understand the roots of modern Judaism or modern Mohammedanism.

While all these may be important reasons for the study of the Old Testament, they are hardly sufficient to justify the massive amount of attention given the book by Christians of all ages and times over the past nineteen centuries. Christians have studied this book for far different reasons.

57

The Purpose of the Old Testament

For contemporary Christians, one of the prime reasons for studying the Old Testament is that it has been preserved by earlier Christians as a part of our sacred Scripture, the Holy Bible. With simple faith we state that we have the Old Testament because God wanted us to have it. That is obviously correct. But that faith statement causes us to ask, Why does God want us to have the Old Testament? Is it possible for us to find an answer to this question?

Perhaps we can narrow the field of our answer by identifying some negative answers. We do not have the Old Testament simply as a book of ancient history. There are many sources for ancient history. I find it a bit difficult to believe that God went to all the effort of inspiring and preserving such a massive amount of material simply for us to have one more source for ancient Near Eastern history. Furthermore, the same sort of thing can be said of science or mathematics. These things can be learned in other and far easier ways. This does not mean that the Old Testament does not contain history or science or mathematics. What it does mean is that these are not the primary or even very important reasons for studying the Old Testament.

Now we must direct our attention to formulating a more positive statement of the Old Testament's purpose. The place to begin is to ask why the early Christians preserved it as a part of their Bible.

Recognizing that most of the earliest Christians were Jews who became followers of Jesus Christ (who was Himself a Jew), some people have suggested that the Old Testament was preserved by the early followers of Jesus simply because they were conservative Jews. They were seeking to preserve the core of their old faith as it was expanded and enlarged by Jesus. This is a possibility, at least insofar as some of the early disciples were concerned, but it does not address the fact that the gospel was quickly preached to Gentiles who became converts. They had no Jewish roots. In fact, one of the earliest church councils was held to decide whether Gentile Christians had to become Jews (Acts 15:1-

29). At that time, no such requirement was placed upon Gentile Christians. With that decision, there was no reason for Christians to keep the Old Testament simply as a Jewish book. They were freed from any commitment to it merely for its Jewish background.

The Old Testament was preserved by the early Christians for one major reason: They believed that Jesus Himself was the fulfillment of the Old Testament. In addition, they believed that the Christian community itself was the new Israel of God and that they were the new recipients of the ancient promises to Israel.

Jesus Himself took that approach to the Old Testament. Following the resurrection, He confronted two disciples on the road to Emmaus. They were struggling with doubt as to the reality of the resurrection reports and whom Jesus had really been. "Beginning with Moses and all the prophets, he interpreted to them in all the scriptures the things concerning himself" (Luke 24:27). To those who in His lifetime opposed Him, Jesus very pointedly asserted: "You search the scriptures, because you think that in them you have eternal life; and it is they that bear witness to me" (John 5:39).

The author of Hebrews directed attention to the same point. In dealing with the new covenant, he pointed out that those who enter this new covenant become the recipients of the "promised eternal inheritance" (Heb. 9:15). But the promised inheritance of which he spoke was that which was originally promised to Israel in the Old Testament.

The only Bible which the early Christians had was the Old Testament. The first books of the New Testament were apparently not written until almost twenty years after Jesus' death and resurrection. Yet the early Christians had been clearly preaching the gospel throughout that period of time. The texts which are identified in the Book of Acts as the bases for those early sermons are all Old Testament texts. In the Old Testament, the Christians found the foundation for the proclamation that "in Christ God was reconciling the world to himself" (2 Cor. 5:19).

We can say with reasonable certainty that the Old Testament has been passed down to us because the early Christians and believers after them saw in it the promises which were fulfilled in Jesus and through Him in themselves. The New Testament often quotes the Old as the basis of the Christians' faith. Not only is the New Testament the fulfillment of the Old, the faith of the New Testament appears to have its roots firmly implanted in the Old.

The Old Testament is at its very base a book of faith. That was the proclamation of ancient Israel. From that proclamation, the New Testament faith sprouted and grew. A brief overview of Israel's faith proclamation, consideration of God's revelation to them and through them to us, will aid our understanding of individual books and sections of the Old Testament. Obviously an introduction to the Old Testament cannot give a major amount of attention to the full message of the Old Testament. That is the task of biblical theology in general and Old Testament theology in particular. However, this collection of books was drawn together because they had something in common. They are not just unrelated books on a library shelf. Instead, they are part of a single collection with a common commitment.

The Major Themes of the Old Testament

The Old Testament is not a theology book. However, it is solidly from beginning to end a theological book. It does not set forth a systematic statement of Israel's faith in God. Yet it clearly introduces us to the God whom the Hebrews knew and with whom they related throughout their history. Since there is no systematic presentation of Israel's faith within the Old Testament, any attempt to systematize its faith is obviously going to be forced upon the Scripture by the one who does it. But any attempt to try to understand Israel's faith without systematizing it leads to frustration and confusion. The faith of the Old Testament grew through living experience. I am going to break into that experience and attempt to describe what appears to be the heart of the Old Testament faith. This can best be done through presenting a series of dual ideas which the Old Testament writers kept in tension.

The Focus: God and Man

The Old Testament can be described as a drama with two main characters, God and man. Some have suggested that Israel (rather than mankind) was actually the second major character in this divine drama, but it appears that Israel can be understood from a Christian viewpoint as essentially the sum of all humanity focused into one people. Thus mankind is the better designation of the second character of the divine drama.

Both of these central figures are introduced within the first chapter of the first book. God is clearly the central focus of Genesis 1, His name occurring twenty-nine times. Man is also introduced in that same chapter, identified as having been created in the image of God (v.26). However, the biblical narrative directs much more attention to mankind in the next chapter, as we see both man's finitude and grandeur. Man is introduced as being dust, but God-breathed dust (Gen. 2:7).

God is introduced in the Genesis material as the sovereign Lord of creation, the One who spoke the universe and all which is in it into being. Nothing exists which did not come into being as the result of the express will and purpose of the divine Creator. Man is introduced plainly as the creature of the Creator. Man is not sovereign, yet exercises a limited authority over the world which was given to him by his Creator (Gen. 1:28).

To the person who begins reading the Bible with Genesis 1, it appears that the most important picture of God in the Old Testament must be the fact that He is Creator. This is obviously important. However, as one reads all the rest of the Old Testament, one discovers that the primary emphasis is upon God as Redeemer, Savior. The Old Testament portrait focuses far more upon God's redemptive activity in the Exodus than it does upon His identity as Creator. Furthermore, in spite of the exaltation given to man in Genesis 1 and 2, the major image of mankind in the Old Testament is one of his sinfulness, his rebellion against the One who created him.

The entire library of the Old Testament continually tells the story of the interactions and the interrelations of God and mankind. The rest of the first eleven chapters of Genesis show the sinful rebellion of God's human creatures and the consequences of those acts. Beginning with Genesis 12, the story focuses upon one man, Abraham, and his family. God began working out His redemptive purposes for mankind, calling that particular man to start a pilgrimage which would result in his being a blessing to all humanity (Gen. 12:1-4).

All the rest of the Old Testament is the ongoing story of how God went about the business of redeeming people from the consequences of their own actions. From the patriarchal wanderings through the deliverance from the slavery of Egypt and continuing through the monarchy to the Exile and beyond, the whole narrative tells of mankind's rebellion and sin and God's love and concern, resulting in both judgment and deliverance.

When the Old Testament narrative directs attention upon the acts of people, its concern is always upon those acts as they relate to the will and purpose of God. When the prophets and the psalmists turn our attention to the mighty acts of God or to His holiness and glory, these are continually portrayed against the background of human experience.

The Old Testament never seeks to prove the existence of God. On the contrary, it assumes God's existence because He is met in the normal affairs of life. What the Old Testament did for its own day and does for us is to point out that life is always lived in relation to God. We either live in obedience, submission, and service or we live in rebellion and alienation. Either way, in the Old Testament human life is always understood in relation to God. Furthermore, God is never presented as the sum of a series of theological propositions. Rather, He is always described in terms of a Person who is met, as One who is known by what He does.

The Choice: Election and Covenant

The second pair of ideas which the Old Testament keeps in tension is that of election and covenant. These concepts are of major importance to any full understanding of the faith of Israel.

From the earliest strata of Old Testament traditions and continuing throughout, we find a major emphasis upon God's free choice of Israel as an act of grace. God chose Abraham as His instrument to begin the process of deliverance (Gen. 12:1-4). Through Abraham and the patriarchs, He ultimately chose the nation of Israel as the ongoing instrument of His blessings to humanity. He chose Moses as the human agent of deliverance from Egypt, Joshua as the instrument through whom the land was to be given, David as the representative king, and Amos, Hosea, Isaiah, Jeremiah, and others as His messengers. Over and over again, the prophets and the singers of Israel directed attention back to the supreme choice of Israel in the Exodus experience. A major point of the entire Old Testament canon is God's free choice of people to accomplish His purposes. This record of God's choices in the Old Testament directs our attention to the fact that His choices were primarily for service. God chose His instruments to accomplish His purposes.

Yet God's choices or His election are not properly understood apart from the Old Testament's understanding of covenant. This, too, is a theological idea which binds the Old Testament together. God made a covenant with Noah to spare the world another such judgment as had been experienced in the Flood (Gen. 9:8-17). He made a covenant with Abraham and with his offspring to give to them the land of Canaan (Gen. 15:18-21). He made a covenant with Israel which was mediated by Moses at Sinai (Ex. 24:3-8). That covenant was renewed periodically throughout Israel's history. God made a covenant with David that his house would always have a representative upon the throne of Israel (2 Sam. 23:5).

To Israel, the concept of covenant seems generally to have

included two major factors. First, there was always the awareness of divine obligation. God took upon Himself the obligations of the covenant. In a very real sense, this was a divine promise. Sometimes the covenantal obligations of God had already been demonstrated in His free choice. The second obligation which the covenant implied was Israel's obligation to be faithful and obedient. The covenant par excellence was the one given at Sinai, where the Ten Commandments set forth the basic obligations laid upon Israel (Ex. 20:1-17).

Throughout the Old Testament, the tension between the ideas of election and covenant informs every description of God's relation with Israel and Israel's relation to God. It clearly carries over into the New Testament where Jesus described His ministry and mission in terms of a new covenant as well as in terms of His choice (Luke 22:20; John 6:70).

The Problem: Sin and Deliverance

The third pair of ideas which are central to the thought of the Old Testament focus upon the plight of humanity. From the third chapter of Genesis, mankind's problem with sin comes to the fore and never leaves our attention. Theologically, the problem of sin is presented in the Old Testament as the frightful pride of humanity. Sin is portrayed as being based first upon mankind's desire to replace God as Sovereign. At the very least, man is motivated to "be like God" (Gen. 3:5). Sin is also depicted as deliberate disobedience. Knowing what God desired and had commanded, the first man and the first woman and all subsequent people consciously and willfully disobeyed. Sin is clearly presented as a deliberate choice of humanity, not something slipped into by accident.

The story of humanity's descent into sin went on, ultimately arriving at the place where the evil imagination took absolute control of thought and action (Gen. 6:5). Clearly, external demonic forces of evil are described, but the ultimate problem was and is mankind's. In the final analysis, the Old Testament is quite clear that we cannot blame our sinful condition on external forces.

The Old Testament also declares that sin separates or alienates humanity from God. In the story of Eden, Adam and Eve, in their guilt and shame, hid from God; God did not hide from them (Gen. 3:8). With the entrance of sin, the relationship which God had intended to exist between Himself and His human creatures was spoiled. The sin story of the Old Testament continues without relief throughout each page. It includes the rebellion of nations and peoples, but it also includes each individual. Extending from the greatest to the least, all have sinned. Thus the psalmist sang in sorrow of the fool who said

> "There is no God."
> They are corrupt, they do abominable deeds,
> > there is none that does good.
> The Lord looks down from heaven upon the children of
> > men, to see if there are any that act wisely,
> > that seek after God.
> They have all gone astray, they are all alike corrupt;
> > there is none that does good,
> > no, not one (Ps. 14:1-3).

Moses was a murderer (Ex. 2:12). David was both an adulterer and a murderer (2 Sam. 11:1-21). Jeremiah couldn't find a single righteous person in Jerusalem (Jer. 5:1-5). From beginning to end, sin is a problem. From man's standpoint, there was no solution; mankind could do nothing to restore the broken relationship. If that were the whole story, it would have been bleak indeed.

However, the Old Testament also presents a companion idea to the sin of humanity: God acts to deliver His people. What man could not do for himself, God sought to do for him. The first hints of God's acts of deliverance are presented in the story of Eden where sin began. God covered the nakedness of man, but He also announced that ultimately the forces of evil would be crushed by the seed of woman (Gen. 3:15, 21). Beyond that, God called Abraham

(Abram in the narrative at this point) to become the agent and instrument of His blessing to "all the families of the earth" (Gen. 12:1-4). All the rest of the Old Testament is a record of how God proceeded in His plan of delivering humanity from the curse of sin. While quite aware of God's continual acts of redemption, the Old Testament is also aware that the whole story was not there. The presentation of the message of deliverance ends with a forward look, a look of hope.

The Dilemma: Justice and Mercy

To the people of the Old Testament, as well as to modern people, the idea that mankind's sin problem could be met by the redemptive acts of God posed a dilemma. Justice demanded that sinful rebellion be punished. But the divine acts of deliverance seemed either to preclude or to ignore the demands of justice. At this point the Old Testament revelation confronts the next pair of ideas through which their faith developed: justice and mercy.

The Old Testament proclamation from beginning to end is that sin must be punished. Justice is both a part of God's nature and part of the world which He created. From the earliest narrative, the announcement was made that sin had consequences. "Of the tree of the knowledge of good and evil you shall not eat, for in the day that you eat of it you shall die" (Gen. 2:17). The law added bluntly that "every man shall be put to death for his own sin" (Deut. 24:16). The prophets continually called Israel to an awareness that justice demanded that sin be punished. There was no other alternative.

At the same time, the Old Testament was quite aware that God Himself tempered His justice with mercy. Man could not make scarlet sin white, but God could (Isa. 1:18). That which made this possible was the love of God. Thus God agonized:

> How can I give you up, O Ephraim!
> How can I hand you over, O Israel!
> How can I make you like Admah!

> How can I treat you like Zeboim!
> My heart recoils within me,
>> my compassion grows warm and tender.
> I will not execute my fierce anger,
>> I will not again destroy Ephraim;
> for I am God and not man,
>> the Holy One in your midst,
>> and I will not come to destroy (Hos. 11:8-9).

In response, the sweet singers of Israel acknowledged that God did act in mercy as well as in justice. Both are a part of the Divine nature and purpose.

> When I declared not my sin, my body wasted away
>> through my groaning all day long.
> I acknowledged my sin to thee,
>> and I did not hide my iniquity;
> I said, "I will confess my transgressions to the Lord";
>> then thou didst forgive the guilt of my sin (Ps. 32:3,5).

The divine righteousness demands that sin be punished. The divine mercy at the same time seeks for a way of deliverance for the sinner. This combination also points to the ultimate working out of God's purposes in the proclamation of the gospel.

The Revelation: Word and Wisdom

The Old Testament also states that the faith which Israel proclaimed was not at all dependent upon Israel's own discovery. To use a more modern expression, Israel's faith was based upon God's revelation. The next pair of ideas are basic to the faith of the Old Testament: word and wisdom.

The Old Testament writers were totally convinced that the message they proclaimed came to them through the revelation of God, although that was not the common term which they used. Of major importance in Israel's proclamation of God's revelatory process was the concept of the word which God revealed to His spokesmen. Over and over again the prophets said, "The word of the Lord came unto me," or some phrase of similar wording. The creation account is punctuated by the phrase, "And God said." The concept is found throughout the Old Testament, placing a concrete emphasis upon the fact that Israel and her spokesmen were quite aware that their ultimate faith and message came to them from God.

This, however, is not the only concept of revelation which Israel had. The Old Testament spokesmen for God were also quite aware that God spoke through human wisdom. They were firmly convinced that God spoke through the natural world. That message is available to all people everywhere.

> The heavens are telling the glory of God;
> 　　and the firmament proclaims his handiwork.
> Day to day pours forth speech,
> 　　and night to night declares knowledge.
> There is no speech, nor are there words;
> 　　their voice is not heard;
> yet their voice goes out through all the earth,
> 　　and their words to the end of the world (Ps. 19:1-4).

The Old Testament writers were also quite aware that God spoke through human wisdom. An entire wisdom movement grew up in Israel, as in other lands, and the people directed their attention to what made the good life. In Israel, the wisdom movement produced major works such as Job, Proverbs, Ecclesiastes, and the Song of Solomon. Solomon was remembered as the great wise man and was acknowledged as the founder of the Hebrew wisdom movement. This movement not only produced its own literature but also significantly affected the work of some of the prophets (e.g., Amos and Jeremiah) as well as numbers of the psalms (e.g., Pss. 1, 15). Followers of this movement clearly believed that God revealed Himself in both nature and the human intellect. Israel's understanding of this kind of revelation was that it came through a mind devoted to God, one which was openly a part of the covenant people.

Thus, to Israel, God's revelation came both through His word and through human wisdom. Both avenues were subsidiary to the origin. In both instances the revelation was God's. The wisdom movement did not discover truths about God, it met God in human experience when He allowed

Himself to be found. It was always God's revelation, not mankind's discovery.

The Life: Law and Love

Another pair of concepts which were central to Israel's faith proclamation had to do with God's revelation of His expectations for Israel. Even a superficial reading of the Old Testament reveals that Israel's life and worship were wholly governed by law. In fact, they even called the first and major portion of their Scripture, the Torah, Law. The life they were called upon to live was a life controlled by law.

To the Hebrews the law of God was something good, something to rejoice over, and something to sing about. After three verses describing the laws of God, the psalmist cried,

> More to be desired are they than gold,
> even much fine gold;
> sweeter also than honey
> and drippings of the honeycomb.
> Moreover by them is thy servant warned;
> in keeping of them there is great reward (Ps. 19:10-11).

Further, he proclaimed,

> Great peace have those who love thy law;
> nothing can make them stumble (Ps. 119:165).

This praise and acclaim of the law sounds strange to most people today. To us, law is normally regarded as an infringement of our liberties. To the ancient Hebrews, however, it was not so. In the world in which Israel lived, most nations believed that their gods were capricious. No one could ever be sure exactly what the gods demanded. The law let the people of Israel know precisely what God expected of them. Even more, the law made life livable. A game is not playable without rules. Life becomes livable only when it is governed by law. To Israel, the law made it clear how the people were to serve God and treat one another.

Unfortunately, too many people think of the faith of Israel only as a religion of the law. That is a false picture. The

Old Testament clearly shows that love played a major part in life as well. The Hebrews were told to expect love from God and to show love to God (Ex. 20:6). Furthermore, they were called upon to "love your neighbor as yourself" (Lev. 19:18). The fact that Israel very narrowly defined who its neighbor was does not get rid of the fact that such love was commanded. Admittedly, the full love of God and the full demands of love from God's people did not become clear until the New Testament, but the Old Testament has a major emphasis upon the fact that the godly life was to be controlled both by law and love.

The Relationship: Fidelity and Infidelity

The seventh pair of ideas that were a major part of Israel's faith relate to the response to God. The Hebrews had been chosen by God and had covenanted with Him to be His people. Yet their history showed that committing themselves to be God's covenant people and being His covenant people were two radically different things. Israel's response to God was supposed to be one of fidelity.

From the beginning, Abraham was called to a life of trusting obedience (Gen. 12:1-3a). The other patriarchs and their families were expected to follow their ancestor's lead. As often as not, they failed. After Israel had been delivered from the Egyptian slavery and had settled in the land of Canaan, its history was one of habitual infidelity.

> Whenever the Lord raised up judges for them, the Lord was with the judge, and he saved them from the hand of their enemies all the days of the judge; for the Lord was moved to pity by their groaning because of those who afflicted and oppressed them. But whenever the judge died, they turned back and behaved worse than their fathers, going after other gods, serving them and bowing down to them; they did not drop any of their practices or their stubborn ways (Judg. 2:18-19).

Such practices followed Israel's history throughout. Most of the kings were described as doing "what was evil in the sight of the Lord." Further, the prophets regularly pointed out the awesome and awful infidelity of their people.

> Ah, sinful nation,
>> a people laden with iniquity
> offspring of evildoers,
>> sons who deal corruptly!
> They have forsaken the Lord,
>> they have despised the Holy One of Israel,
>> they are utterly estranged (Isa. 1:4).

Jeremiah underscored this problem, proclaiming,

> Be appalled, O heavens, at this,
>> be shocked, be utterly desolate,
> says the Lord,
> for my people have committed two evils:
>> they have forsaken me,
> the fountain of living waters,
>> and hewed out cisterns for themselves,
> broken cisterns,
>> that can hold no water (Jer. 2:12-13).

From beginning to end, Israel's relationship to God was punctuated by rebellion and turning away. At times, the people considered themselves to be forsaken by God. They were wrong. *They* had forsaken God.

While Israel regularly and habitually forsook God, God remained loyal to His commitment. Judgment came upon the people, surely. But it was a judgment with an evangelistic aim. God punished them for the purpose of bringing them back to Himself. Amos announced this most vividly by describing a series of judgments and ending each description with the refrain: "yet you did not return to me" (Amos 4:6, 8-11). Hosea further identified the amazing loyalty of God's love, holding on to His people when they let go of Him.

> When Israel was a child, I loved him,
>> and out of Egypt I called my son.
> The more I called them,
>> the more they went from me;
> they kept sacrificing to the Baals,
>> and burning incense to the idols.

> I will not execute my fierce anger,
>
> ....
>
> and I will not come to destroy (Hos. 11:1-2, 9).

To the end of its history, Israel was informed and reminded that God was loyal. The amazing loyalty of God stands out even more emphatically when contrasted with the ongoing story of Israel's infidelity.

The Process: Defeat and Victory

Perhaps the strangest and possibly the most significant pair of theological concepts which were revealed to Israel about God relate to defeat and victory. The significance of these ideas are frequently missed by many interpreters of the Old Testament because they are unfamiliar with the Old Testament world and very familiar with the Christian proclamation made from this side of the cross. In the world of the ancient Near East, the defeat of a nation was considered to be a defeat of the god or gods of that nation. Gods of defeated nations were considered to be weaker than the gods of the victors. In light of this, considering all of the defeats which Israel suffered, it is amazing that the Hebrews considered their God to have any power at all.

The history of the Hebrew people could almost be described as one long story of defeats. Under Joshua, the invaders were defeated at Ai (Josh. 7:2-5). The entire period of the judges was one defeat after another. During the time of Samuel and for much of Saul's reign the Philistines gained supremacy over Israel. In the time of the kingdoms, there was a major period of Syrian supremacy. The Assyrians totally destroyed the Northern Kingdom and brought Judah under submission for almost a century, and the Babylonians brought ultimate defeat and exile to Judah. Even after the deliverance from exile, the Hebrew people were under Persian and Greek domination.

This whole story raises the question of how a people who experienced so much defeat could ever come to believe that their God was the sovereign Lord of the universe? The answer is particularly striking: Through defeats Israel came to an awareness that her God was sovereign. The people discovered the amazing truth from God of representative suffering. Israel developed what theologians have come to call a theology of exile or a theology of suffering. This is especially visible in the message of Isaiah 40—66 and of Ezekiel. It is also seen in a different way in the message of Hosea, where he learned through a heart broken by an unfaithful wife that love becomes victorious through suffering. God revealed two truths to Israel through suffering. The people's suffering and defeat was frequently (not always) the punishment for their sin. When suffering and defeat were for sin, they were designed to be both penal and evangelistic. Sin was being punished, but Israel was being brought back to God. The second truth is the more profound: Suffering and defeat could be atoning, redemptive for others. This is most profoundly proclaimed in the songs of the Suffering Servant.

> Surely he has borne our griefs
> and carried our sorrows;
> yet we esteemed him stricken,
> smitten by God, and afflicted.
> But he was wounded for our transgressions,
> he was bruised for our iniquities;
> upon him was the chastisement that made us whole,
> and with his stripes we are healed (Isa. 53:5-6).

This idea of representative suffering is clearly enlarged and proclaimed to all of the exiles in Isaiah 40:1-11. There they were acknowledging suffering for their own sin, but the double suffering was intended to proclaim to the world that Judah suffered not because God was weak but because He was strong. All the other nations could proclaim that victories showed the strength of their gods. Only the people of the Old Testament proclaimed that defeats showed the power of their God. Any god can use a victory. Only the sovereign Lord of the universe can use a defeat to accomplish His will.

The Future: Promise and Hope

The final pair of ideas Israel used to proclaim her faith are promise and hope. The Old Testament is filled with God's promises to Israel. The people of Israel clung to God's promise to Abraham to "make of you a great nation, . . . and make your name great," but they forgot that as a part of that promise they were to "be a blessing" (Gen. 12:2). They also clung to the promise of the gift of the land of Canaan, which was rooted in Abraham's experience where God promised, "To your descendants I give this land" (Gen. 15:18).

Israel's understanding of the promises of God was enlarged by the covenant experience at Sinai. There the people were told: "Now therefore, if you will obey my voice and keep my covenant, you shall be my own possession among all peoples; for all the earth is mine, and you shall be to me a kingdom of priests and a holy nation" (Ex. 19:5-6). Those covenant promises were repeated again and again at covenant renewal ceremonies throughout Israel's history, becoming the essential part of faith. While Israel regularly forgot that God's promises also placed responsibility upon it and laid obligations on it, the promises were there and Israel clung to them with tenacity.

In addition to national promises, Israel also retained the promises that there would always be an offspring of David upon the throne of Israel (2 Sam. 7:1-17). In the ongoing processes of time, the Hebrew people saw the kingdom divide and many of David's descendants fail to be what God intended them to be, even as David himself had failed on more than one occasion. Finally, this promise was transferred from the anointed king to the ultimate King, the Messiah. (The Hebrew word for anoint is *mashiach,* from which we get the word *messiah*. The New Testament word *Christ,* comes from the Greek word for anoint, *christos*.)

The promises of God gave rise to the hope of Israel. Its hope involved the coming of the Messiah, the ultimate establishment of the kingdom of God (as seen in Israel) upon the earth, and the final vindication of God and His purposes

in the Day of the Lord. All of that was expected to finally
to produce an ideal age upon the earth. This hope is beauti-
fully described:

> It shall come to pass in the latter days
>   that the mountain of the house of the Lord
> shall be established as the highest of the mountains,
>   and shall be raised above the hills;
> and all nations shall flow to it,
>   and many peoples shall come, and say:
> "Come, let us go up to the mountain of the Lord,
>   to the house of the God of Jacob;
> that he may teach us his ways
>   and that we may walk in his paths."
> For out of Zion shall go forth the law,
>   and the word of the Lord from Jerusalem.
> He shall judge between the nations,
>   and shall decide for many peoples;
> and they shall beat their swords into plowshares,
>   and their spears into pruning hooks;
> nation shall not lift up sword against nation,
>   neither shall they learn war any more
> (Isa. 2:2-4; cf. Mic. 4:1-3).

Thus the Old Testament comes to an end with a strong
faith and a distinctively forward look. The faith which Israel had developed through the inspiration and revelation of
God had laid a solid foundation upon which the ministry
and message of Jesus could be built. It provided the forms
by which the New Testament evangelists proclaimed their
faith. It even provided the language of that faith proclamation. Above all else, the Old Testament was Israel's proclamation of faith. It is not the Hebrews' story, it is God's story.
It is not what they had done for God, but what God had done
for and through them. Yet, they were quite aware that it
was not the full story. The story ends looking forward.

Interpreting the Old Testament

Since the Old Testament is the proclamation of Israel's
faith, since it is a part of the revelation of God, and since we
study it for its religious message, we need to carefully inter-

pret that message and proclaim it. The science of interpreting and applying the religious message of the Bible is called hermeneutics. The name comes from the name of the Greek god Hermes, who was the messenger of the gods to human beings. Thus hermeneutics is the science of bringing God's message to people. It does little good to have a message from God if it is not interpreted so that it can be understood. It does even less good to have such a message if it is interpreted poorly or carelessly. It does no good at all and usually does much harm if God's message is interpreted wrongly. Thus it is important that every student of the Old Testament develop a proper technique for interpreting and applying it. While the process of interpreting the Old Testament cannot be covered in detail in an introduction such as this, some basic principles can be set forth. In addition to guiding the student to develop interpretive skills, they will also help one to avoid some of the more obvious pitfalls which beset the way.

In developing an adequate technique for interpreting the Old Testament, several basic truths must be acknowledged. First, the Old Testament is both a divine and a human book. It is inspired by God and, therefore, has authority over human life. While we acknowledge the divine side of the Old Testament, we must also remind ourselves that God used human authors and speakers who were limited by space, time, and language. The second basic truth we must face is that the task of interpreting such a book must be undergirded by prayer and submitted to the leadership of God's Spirit. Finally, God has granted us intellect, and He holds us responsible for using the mind He has given. God will hold us accountable for the interpretations which we give. This is not just a matter of giving information which may be in error, it can be a matter of life and death. Thus the task must be taken seriously and should be undertaken with fear and trembling.

Certain steps should be followed in the process of interpreting any Old Testament text. If followed with diligence and consistency, these will help us to come to a proper interpretation and application of any passage.

Determine What the Text Says

This involves two specific steps. First of all, we must find out as nearly as possible what the original speaker said or the original writer wrote. This involves the discipline of Old Testament textual study. Most of us are not and will never be competent in this area. This is where we seek the best results of competent scholars. The present state of Old Testament textual studies gives us a high degree of confidence in the text which we now have.

But determining what the actual words of a specific text were is only a part of the process. The second part is determining what those words really communicated. This involves a study of language, grammar, syntax, word meanings, and geographical and historical references. Again, for most of us, we rely for this upon our translators. However, do not accept any particular translation simply because you like what it says. Compare translations constantly. Seek to determine why they differ in places. By such a process you will build up both the experience and the expertise to begin to determine which are the better and which are the less valuable translations. No interpretation of any Old Testament passage can be any better than the text from which you begin. If your text is in error or you do not understand it, your interpretation is quite likely to be in error. Once you have achieved confidence that you know what a text says and that you understand its words and linguistic characteristics, then you are ready to move on to the second step.

Determine What the Text Meant

The basic presupposition of all biblical interpretation is that *God is the God of sense, not of nonsense.* This forces us to the conclusion that whatever an ancient text said made sense to the original spokesmen and their audience. The spokesmen would not have proclaimed something meaningless. The hearers would not have preserved the messages if they had not made sense. Therefore, before we can move further in the process of interpretation, we must seek to determine (insofar as is possible) what a text originally meant. This may not, and frequently does not, exhaust its full meaning. But it is the point at which we must begin.

In order to do this, we must identify the literary category of the text. Prose is interpreted one way, poetry another. Prose speaks to the mind, poetry to the emotions. We must also be sure that we understand the context of any passage. What was the book trying to accomplish? How did our particular passage help in this? Since we believe that the Old Testament is a part of God's revelation, there must be a purpose behind the organization of any block of material. We must seek to come to grips with that purpose.

Moving on, we must also seek to determine the historical setting of our passage. It may have been reporting something that happened at one time but communicating it to a far later age. Consider the fact that 1 and 2 Kings and 1 and 2 Chronicles essentially cover the same era. Why do we have two accounts of the same events? If, as most interpreters agree, the Chronicles material was written much later than that of Kings, the material that has been left out and the additional material that was included should give us clues to the purposes of the later writers. Further, unless we can identify the historical setting, we may (and probably will) miss the significance of some historical references.

We must also seek to identify the theological context of a passage. For example, we will miss a major part of our understanding of the Book of Job unless we realize that it was written in a time and to a people who assumed that all suffering came as the result of sin and all prosperity came as the consequence of godly living. The Book of Job plainly refutes such a basic position. It is important for interpreting any passage that we come to grips with what was going on in the theological world of Israel at that time.

Next we must seek to evaluate the levels of understanding revealed in any passage. In the Old Testament, there are frequently at least three levels of understanding to a passage. There is the popular level, which is where the ordinary people were. In addition, there was the priestly understanding, or the "official" faith of Israel. These two were sometimes identical and sometimes quite different. Beyond this, the prophetic level of understanding was frequently different from both of the others. In fact, most of the preaching of the prophets was an attempt to contradict one or the other levels. For example, it is easy to treat all of the Book of Job as if it were on the same level of understanding. Yet the final words of God in that book point out that Job's friends had not "spoken of me what is right, as my servant Job has" (Job 42:7).

At this point, having followed all of these avenues of investigation, we should be ready to draw conclusions about what a particular passage meant. All of the study in the world does no good until we can finally put down succinctly what a passage meant.

Determine What the Text Means

The next step in our process of interpretation is to move from the ancient setting to our modern one. Since we are dealing with Scripture, the modern or contemporary meaning of a passage may, and frequently does, go far beyond its ancient meaning. But its modern meaning grows out of its ancient meaning. We dare not divorce the modern meaning of a passage from its ancient roots. World history does not stand still. Ancient meanings were limited by ancient culture. In a new situation, we must find new meanings for ancient words. Jesus Himself set the example. In the Sermon on the Mount, He took numerous Old Testament commands and pointed out new interpretations for them (Matt. 5:21-48). He identified the thrust or movement of a passage and carried it further *in the same direction*. This is precisely what He told His disciples to do. "I have yet many things to say to you, but you cannot bear them now. When the Spirit of truth comes, he will guide you into all the truth; . . . for he will take what is mine and declare it to you" (John 16:12-14).

This is our task. We must take the study we have done and determine the thrust, moving into our world and culture. Until we can apply a message clearly and succinctly to our day with a meaning rooted and grounded in its past, we will not have completed the task. God gave us the Old Testament as a part of His revelation. Until we have determined what it means to us today in our world, we may as well not have had it at all.

5

The Study of the Old Testament

In beginning a thorough study of the Old Testament, we need to be aware of how the Old Testament has been studied in the past. This is helpful for several reasons. First, if we are aware of the major methodologies which have been used in studying the Old Testament, how they have been applied and the results they have accomplished, we are better able to evaluate the present state of Old Testament studies in any particular instance. Simply put, it is sometimes easier to see where we are going if we know where we have been.

Second, if we are aware of the failures of particular avenues of inquiry, we can avoid the same pitfalls. Conversely, if we know of significant successes in certain kinds of study, we do not have to replow the same furrows again. That allows us to build on the assured results of earlier Old Testament study while avoiding the weaker foundations.

Third, as we investigate and critique the various approaches which have been made to the study of the Old Testament, we will be in a better position to evaluate commentaries and other treatments of the Old Testament or any of its parts. In other words, if a book were written before the development of a particular approach to the study of the Old Testament, we should not expect it to be aware of that approach. In the same manner, if a book were written or a study made before a particular archaeological or literary discovery, then it did not have the benefit of that information as evidence for its conclusions. For example, books written before the late 1940s did not have the advantage of the Dead Sea Scrolls for textual studies as these have only been available for use since that time.

Before we proceed further with our survey of the major approaches to the study of the Old Testament and with the history of their development and their use, we need to consider some definitions. In general, most serious study of the Old Testament is called critical study. This does not mean that it is study which is opposed to the Old Testament or which is seeking to undermine faith in its revelation or in the God behind that revelation. Unfortunately, the noun *critic* and the adjective *critical* have very negative connotations in our time. However, that is not the way the words have been used in Old Testament studies and is not a part of their actual definition. A critical study is simply a systematic, serious study. I shall use the term in that fashion.

We need also to come to grips with the meaning of a theory (or a hypothesis) and the difference between a fact and a theory. A fact is something which is true, regardless of time and circumstances. A theory, on the other hand, is an attempt to explain known facts. Facts do not change. Theories change as new facts are discovered which do not fit into old theories. We should be careful not to get theories and facts confused. We must accept theories for what they are, simply working attempts to explain the facts as we know them at present. But we must always be ready and willing to cast aside existing theories in favor of better ones. Furthermore, we need to be aware that serious biblical students can and do debate about theories. We can have different theories to explain known facts. In fact, in this way, the study of the Old Testament (or anything else, for that matter) advances.

Old Testament studies have been going on from the time of the Old Testament itself. Certain words and phrases have become a part of the literature on the subject. Not everyone likes all of them and some people would wish other terms were used. However, students being introduced to the subject must become familiar with the basic language of the discipline in order to proceed with studies in other books. Where it is necessary, as I give further definitions, I will explain why I think certain terms are too limited or are inadequate.

The critical study of the Old Testament has been divided into two basic categories: "lower criticism" and "higher criticism." The terms are not descriptive of anything except the intellectual pride which believes that certain kinds of study are more important and/or difficult than others. However, each approach to the study of the Old Testament is usually classified under one or the other of these headings.

Lower criticism includes two subdisciplines: "textual criticism" and "linguistic criticism." We have already considered the discipline of text criticism in Chapter 3. Linguistic criticism relates to the meaning of words and the use of language. Words have histories. We need to study words to see, for example, if Isaiah used a word differently from the way Jeremiah did or if it were used differently in the Northern Kingdom than in the Southern Kingdom or differently in the tenth century than in the fourth century. We need also to study grammar and syntax to see how various ideas were expressed. All of this falls into the category of linguistic criticism.

Higher criticism, on the other hand, is much broader and includes numerous subdisciplines. Among these are "literary/historical criticism" (which is sometimes broken into two separate areas), "form criticism," "tradition criticism," "rhetorical criticism," "structural criticism," and "canonical criticism."

Literary/historical criticism seeks to analyze each book of the Old Testament in terms of its literary components. Each book is divided into its prose and poetical segments. Literary style is studied for evidence on how the book was put together in its final form. In addition, the historical information given in a book is studied in an attempt to evaluate how the history was recorded, when it was recorded, and for what purposes.

Form criticism is an analysis of passages which appear to have a common form or outline. The assumption is that passages with common outlines may have had common purposes and places in Israel's life and worship. Anyone who has ever outlined a passage of the Old Testament and compared that outline with another similar passage has already practiced some kind of form criticism. Common forms which seem to have a common place in Israel's worship are assumed to have a common *Sitz-im-Leben* (life situation).

Form criticism also insists that common forms were used in aiding the oral transmission of texts. The form was used to transmit material in order to ensure that all essential and significant details were included.

Tradition criticism seeks to explain how certain types or kinds of oral traditions were collected and passed on. For example, such materials were usually collected by groups around specific worship centers. Jerusalem in the south was obviously such a center. Bethel, the major shrine of the Northern Kingdom, was another. It would have been expected that Davidic material would have been collected and passed on in the south. The absence of such material would have been expected at the northern shrine. Other cycles of traditions were probably gathered at Shechem, Beersheba, and similar places. The study of the collection and transmission of such traditions is tradition criticism.

Two very new areas of Old Testament critical studies are rhetorical criticism and structural criticism (or structuralism). Rhetorical criticism is usually defined as looking for the unusual in forms while seeking to confine form criticism to looking only at the common items in forms. The differences usually point out what a speaker or writer was trying to emphasize. Structuralism on the other hand has not even attained a common definition among its adherents. Its avowed purpose is to look for "deep" or "hidden" structures within biblical material. It sometimes seeks new structures where common statements may take on new or additional meaning. At other times it appears to look for common or systematic structures which developed within a narrative or poem or shaped that piece of literature.

The newest area of Old Testament critical studies has come to be called canonical criticism. The emphasis here, rather than seeking to focus upon how biblical material can be analyzed into its component parts, is to focus upon the whole. The canon of the Old Testament is the one given fact. We have it in the form that it has come down to us. Canonical criticism calls our attention to the book as a whole. The attempt is made to see the message as a whole rather than the individual messages of the individual parts.

The History of Old Testament Studies

The Old Testament has been used from its earliest days as a source of devotional material. It has also been read fairly regularly for its great literature. Although both of these uses are quite important, they fall outside the limits of its study as a document of faith.

The serious study of the Old Testament falls into four historical periods. Of course, history, like life, does not really fall into neat compartments. Some overlapping occurs between periods as well as some moving backward and forward in the ongoing process.

The Early Period

The earliest scholars of the Old Testament were the Jewish scribes. They studied and analyzed the text, seeking to pass it on in its proper form. The authorship of parts of the Old Testament was considered by the authors of the Talmud. In *Baba Bathra,* a statement of the authorship of Old Testament books was set forth.

> Moses wrote his own book and the section concerning Balaam, and Job. Joshua wrote his own book and eight verses of the Law (Deu. 34:5-12). Samuel wrote his own book, and Judges, and Ruth. David wrote the book of Psalms together with ten elders, namely Adam, Melchizedek, Abraham, Moses, Heman, Jeduthaun, Asaph, and the three sons of Korah. Jeremiah wrote his own book, and the book of Kings, and Lamentations. Hezekiah and his college wrote Isaiah, Proverbs, the Song of Songs, and Ecclesiastes. The men of the great synagogue wrote Ezekiel, the Twelve (Minor Prophets), Daniel, and Esther. Ezra wrote his own book and the genealogies of the book of Chronicles as far as himself.

Such statements were grounded in curiosity regarding authorship. However, they were based on theological belief rather than upon actual research.

Early Christian writers and their opponents also set forth opinions on authorship. A few of them began to be guided by the beginnings of actual research into the biblical text. Porphyry, a heathen philosopher of the third century AD, dated the Book of Daniel to the reign of Antiochus Epiphanes (2nd century BC) based upon an historical analysis of the text. Jerome (early 5th century), known for his translation of the Bible into Latin in the Vulgate, identified the Book of Deuteronomy with the lawbook found in the Temple during the reform of Josiah. This discovery later proved to be a major key to Pentateuchal studies, but its real significance was not recognized for centuries. Theodore of Mopsuestia at about the same time rejected the titles of the psalms, concluding that they had been added long after the writing of the psalms themselves. From the same era, Augustine deduced that the Scriptures were generally written long after the events they recorded. About a century later, Junilius questioned the Mosaic authorship of the Pentateuch, due to the recurring phrase: "the Lord spoke unto Moses," suggesting that this was not the way anyone would write about something he had personally experienced.

At about this time in the history of such studies, the Roman Empire collapsed and Europe was plunged into what has come to be called the Dark Ages. The mere struggle for survival was so great that little opportunity was afforded for serious Bible study.

The Middle Ages and the Reformation

In the fifteenth and sixteenth centuries, a fresh impetus to biblical studies was given by three major developments: (1) the invention of the printing press, (2) the Renaissance, with its emphasis upon the serious study of everything, and (3) the Reformation. Andreas Bodenstein, also known as Carlstadt, suggested that since the Book of Joshua was of the same style as the Pentateuch, those books were all written by the same person. He coined the term *Hexateuch* for the first six books of the Old Testament. He also pointed out that Moses could not have written the account of his own death and burial (Deut. 34:5-12). Martin Luther and John

Calvin both questioned the Mosaic authorship of the Pentateuch. Calvin also questioned the authorship of Joshua and Samuel. However, both insisted that the issue of the identity of the human author of a book was relatively unimportant. In 1574 the first Catholic to join the list of critical scholars, Andreas Masius, suggested that Ezra compiled all of the history from Joshua through Kings, using many different sources. In 1589 Benedict Pereira, a Jesuit, wrote a commentary on Genesis, holding that while Moses wrote parts of it the book had been significantly enlarged long after his death.

An English philosopher, Thomas Hobbes, in 1651 outlined the aims and methods of a critical study of the Old Testament. In applying these methods, he then rejected the overall Mosaic authorship of the Pentateuch, suggesting that Moses wrote those portions which he is said to have written and nothing more. He further concluded that Joshua and Samuel had nothing to do with the books which bear their names. He ultimately concluded that much, if not most, of the Old Testament was written in the postexilic period of Israel's history.

An additional development of this era was the first serious approach to the study of the transmission of the biblical texts. Cappellus, a French Protestant, and Marinus, a French Catholic, began the discipline of text criticism in 1658 and 1659 respectively. They applied this to both the Greek and the Hebrew texts of the Old Testament.

The Beginnings of Modern Old Testament Criticism

The work of three men stand out as establishing the real foundations of most modern Old Testament criticism. The first of these was a Jewish philosopher, Baruch Spinoza. In 1670 he published the first serious analytical criticism of the Old Testament. He based his work on the earlier studies of a twelfth-century rabbi (Ibn Ezra). Three common expressions indicated to him that much of the Old Testament was written long after the events reported. "Beyond Jordan," referring to the land on the east side of the Jordan, had to have been written by someone on the west side, not by a person standing in the east. Further, "and Moses wrote" had to have been used by someone other than Moses. Finally, "the Canaanite was then in the land" was clearly written in a time when the Canaanites were no longer in the land. Starting from these points, he concluded that Genesis through Kings was a single work compiled from a series of different documents. He also discussed the authorship and date of other books, concluding that Psalms was basically postexilic and that Chronicles was from the Maccabean era. He further concluded that the final compilation of the canon could have been no earlier than the time of the Maccabees. For these views, he was excommunicated from the synagogue.

The second founder of modern Old Testament studies was Richard Simon, a French priest whose book was published in 1678. He was the first to note that numerous duplicate accounts of similar events appear to be present in the Old Testament. In his study of these, he pointed out that most such accounts had decidely different writing styles reflected in them. This forced him to the conclusion that such evidence indicated different authors. He proposed a school of inspired scribes who compiled, edited, and abridged the Old Testament continually from Moses to Ezra. Furthermore, he studied the Latin Vulgate (the Bible of the Catholic Church) and compared it with both the Greek and the Hebrew, pointing out numerous errors in the Vulgate. For this his book was confiscated even before it was circulated. He did manage to get one edition published later in Holland.

A Protestant by the name of Clericus took up the task of textual criticism in 1697 and for the first time began to apply the same scientific approach which had been made to secular texts of antiquity. Clericus assumed and insisted that any ancient book should have its text studied by the same methods. That was a major departure from the belief that sacred writings had to be studied differently.

The work of these three men was seminal for Old Testament studies. Their importance is not so much in the theories which they proposed as in the methods which they used. They insisted that conclusions drawn about the text, authorship, and date of the Old Testament and each of its books must be based upon facts and not upon theology. They insisted that biblical criticism be scientific. Theories explaining the origin and authorship of any part of the Old Testament had to be the consequence of such investigation and not the preconceived basis of it. All subsequent critical study of the Old Testament proceeds from this foundation.

The First Documentary Theory. A major development took place in 1753 with the work of a French physician, Jean Astruc. He noted that in Genesis two different names for God occurred, Yahweh (or Jahveh) and Elohim. He further noted that frequently, when there appeared to be duplicate accounts of the same event, one name would occur in one and the other in the other. Based upon this analysis, he identified two major documents and nine or ten minor ones. Ultimately, he upheld the Mosaic authorship of the Pentateuch but insisted that Moses compiled Genesis from earlier sources and then wrote Exodus, Leviticus, Numbers, and Deuteronomy.

J. G. Eichorn followed with the first great modern introduction to the Old Testament (ca. 1780 to 1783). He is known as the founder of the science of Old Testament introductory studies, dealing with the text, the canon, and the questions of authorship. Using the criteria of the divine names, he also seriously examined the literary, linguistic, and stylistic characters of the sources. He fairly well abandoned the theory of Mosaic authorship of the Pentateuch. Shortly thereafter, K. D. Ilgen (1798) distinguished a second Elohim source in Genesis. The two Elohim sources, according to Ilgen, had decidedly different internal characteristics.

In the following decade (ca. 1805 to 1807), W. M. L. De-Wette rediscovered the work of Jerome which had identified Deuteronomy with the lawbook of Josiah's reform. He pointed out that it differed quite radically from the style of the material in Genesis through Numbers and concluded that it was written in the age of Josiah. He also began to question the historicity of some of the narratives. Acknowledging the work of DeWette, Franz Bleek (1822) resurrected the work of Carlstadt, pointing again to the close literary connection between the Pentateuch and Joshua.

At this time, the scholars following these approaches had suggested that at least four major documents lay behind the Pentateuch. These were a Yahwistic source (J), two Elohistic sources (E1 and E2), and a Deuteronomistic source (D). In addition, there was some attempt to trace these sources beyond the Pentateuch into Joshua.

The Fragmentary Theory. Parallel to the latter part of the development of the first documentary theory, some scholars moved in a different direction. In 1792 Alexander Geddes, a British Catholic priest, suggested that the Hexateuch contained many fragments which dated from the time of Solomon. He claimed that these had been created and preserved by two groups of scribes using Elohim and Yahweh respectively. This idea was picked up and carried further by J. S. Vater in 1802. Beginning with the use of the divine names and adding literary and linguistic analysis, Vater projected a total of thirty-nine different fragments which had been essentially put together by a scissors-and-paste method. These fragments were dated from early times to the Exile, when they were finally compiled in their present form.

This approach was the result of carrying literary criticism to extremes. It was obviously self-destructive, being doomed because it overlooked the very important fact of the obvious unity of the Pentateuch.

The Supplementary Theory. A modification of the first documentary theory came about with the work of young Heinrich Ewald. In 1823, at the age of nineteen, Ewald set forth to prove the unity of Genesis. Ewald's investigations, however, convinced him that there was a diversity of authorship. In 1830 he suggested that the second Elohistic source was the only one which exhibited coherence and structure in and of itself. In other words, he claimed that E2 was the only source which could have stood alone as an independent document. He proposed, therefore, that this was the basic document of Genesis and that it had subsequently been supplemented by other, later additions. His arguments were accepted by Bleek (1836) and DeWette

(1840). For a time, this position was also held by Franz Delitzsch (1852).

At this point, a major reaction set in. The reaction insisted that the studies which had been made had moved too far away from the concept of the inspiration of the Scriptures. This reaction was led in England by Pusey and in Germany by Hengstenberg. They were joined by numerous others, Franz Delitzsch among them.

The Documentary Theory. At this point, the world of Old Testament scholarship began to move even more rapidly. DeWette had proposed that there was an obvious development in religious ideas in the Old Testament and that this could be used in establishing the relative dates of both books and sources. By dating Deuteronomy (D) to the seventh-century reform of Josiah, he had given a fixed point from which others could be established.

In an unpublished thesis in 1833, Edward Reuss claimed that much of the narratives of Judges-Kings is in conflict with the idea that the laws of the Pentateuch were in force during these times. He claimed that Jeremiah was the first prophet acquainted with a written law and that he only knew Deuteronomy. Vatke put forth the same ideas shortly thereafter, but Vatke's research was characterized by a strong commitment to the philosophy of Hegel. Hegelian philosophy characterized most Old Testament study for the next fifty years.

In 1853, Hupfeld dealt with the methodology of Old Testament introductory science, defining the task as that of finding out what the writings were originally and seeking to explain how they had come to be what they are. He rediscovered Ilgen's second Elohistic source, concluding that it was characterized by an extreme interest in the Levitical priesthood and in things relating to that. He called this source Priestly (P). He ultimately identified four sources in the Pentateuch which had all originally had an independent existence: J, E, D, and P. These, he suggested, embodied even earlier materials from other sources.

K. H. Graf, a pupil of Reuss, published views similar to Hupfeld's in 1866. He dated the laws of P later than those of D. Graf's work was picked up and developed by A. Kuenen, a Dutch scholar, in 1869. It remained for Julius Wellhausen in 1878 to amass large amounts of evidence for this theory and almost convince the world. Wellhausen concluded that the first document was J, written around 850 BC. E was then written around 750 BC and these two were compiled about 650 BC. He claimed that D was written in 621 and was added to the JE material about 550 BC, during the Exile. He believed that P was written in the postexilic era, about 450 and that the entire compilation of the Pentateuch was completed around 400 BC. Wellhausen assumed that the material in each source reflected the history of the time of compilation rather than the history which each purported to tell.

S. R. Driver in England (1891) picked up Wellhausen's approach and propogated those views with vigor in the English-speaking world. Robertson Smith in Scotland also had great influence on their adoption. But Wellhausen's methodical and systematic representation was the overwhelming factor in their popularity.

Followers of this approach began to try to apply Wellhausen's methods to the further analysis of the documents. They began to identify subsources in each document (J1, J2, E1, E2, etc.). At this point, it appeared that the theory was headed toward the same self-destruction which the fragmentary theory had experienced.

Twentieth-Century Developments

With the turn of the century, a radical new development came which is tied into the work of Hermann Gunkel. In 1906 he established what has come to be called form criticism of the Old Testament. Gunkel's study was based on the material of the Old Testament and also upon the culture of Israel's neighbors. He identified common forms in Israel's literature which appear to have been used in common life situations (*Sitz-im Leben*) in Israel. Many of these forms, he said, were similar to those of other nations. Denying that anyone could write a history of Israel's literature, he insisted that a history of the development and use of literary forms could be written. He further insisted that a long use of oral traditions preceded any written materials in the ancient Near East. Contrary to what might be thought from modern experience, such oral traditions would have attained a fixed form quite early and would have been passed on with considerable accuracy.

Eissfeldt picked up Gunkel's work, insisting upon the importance of the history of traditions. He sought to identify geographical and cultural centers in Israel where particular traditions would have been maintained. He also sought to find historical reasons as a basis for the reasons leading to their ultimate compilation. Based upon this work, he proposed that the task of Old Testament introduction was to present the history of Old Testament material from its earliest formulations until its final compilation. The most significant contribution of Gunkel and Eissfeldt may rest in their insistence that the date when something may have been committed to writing has no bearing upon either its historical accuracy or its antiquity.

Two different approaches to the study of Deuteronomy were made at this time. Holscher proposed that Josiah was attempting to purify the worship of Jerusalem in 621 BC and that Deuteronomy was the product of this reform, to be dated about 500 BC. On the other hand, Adam Welch dated the compilation of the Book of Deuteronomy to the time of Solomon. He proposed that it had later been preserved by the people of northern Israel and carried south to Judah following the fall of Samaria in 722 BC.

Edward Robertson combined the work of Welch with that of Gunkel and Eissfeldt, suggesting that when the Hebrews entered the land under Joshua, they had a nucleus of law. The people split up after the conquest, setting up shrines around the land. With the reunion under Samuel, a new code was given: Deuteronomy, the law of the centralized administration. Shortly thereafter the traditions of the other shrines were compiled as a form of introduction to Deuteronomy.

Numerous other contributions followed. H. S. Nyberg in 1935 stressed the reliability of the Masoretic Text (Hebrew) of the Old Testament. He further underscored the reliability of the oral traditions which lay behind it. H. Birkeland (1938) reaffirmed the secondary nature of writing in the ancient Near East, claiming that it was normally used only to preserve oral material from destruction in times of crisis.

A different approach to the science of introduction was made by Martin Noth who, in a series of publications from 1942 to 1948, pointed out that Deuteronomic material is essentially not present in Genesis through Numbers. He further demonstrated that the entire corpus from Joshua through 2 Kings is predicated upon the Deuteronomic faith. He, therefore, identified the Books of Joshua, Judges, 1 and 2 Samuel, and 1 and 2 Kings as the Deuteronomic History (DH).

Picking up the contribution of Noth, Ivan Engnell (1945) further underscored the Deuteronomic nature of the Joshua-Kings material. He also insisted that, based upon an analysis of the forms and oral nature of Israel's traditions, the material in Genesis through Numbers is on the whole quite ancient, although it was put into its final form rather late. He insisted that there never were any coherent documents but that there were various cycles or strata of traditions. These could be appropriately named J, E, D, and P, but not in the sense which Wellhausen had used the titles. With this work, the death knell of the old Wellhausen approach was sounded.

Numerous other introductions have followed since World War II, but there have only been four major developments. The first of these is connected most closely with the names of George Mendenhall and Norman Gottwald. They sought to bring the study of the Old Testament into the realm of sociological studies. The basic assumption was that the religion and faith of Israel was primarily to be understood in terms of the sociology of ancient Israel. Such an approach totally eliminates any concept of the religion of Israel as revelatory. With this approach, the Old Testament ceases to be a part of the revelation from God, for there was no revelation. At the very most, such an approach assumes that if Israel had any unique understanding of God it was the result of natural historical forces and rested upon their own religious insights. While still creating some stir among Old Testament scholars, the approach leads up a blind alley insofar as any ultimate significance for the understanding of faith. On the other hand, the approach has forced the world of Old Testament scholarship to come to grips with the fact that Israel had a sociology, the study of which can give us some fruitful new insights into Israel's historical development and faith pilgrimage.

The second recent development in Old Testament criticism was initiated by James Muilenburg who in 1968 sought to supplement the use of form criticism with rhetorical criticism. Form criticism seeks to discover the common forms of Old Testament materials and the common *Sitz-im-Leben* of those materials. Rhetorical criticism begins with those results and seeks to analyze the differences between common forms, trying to trace the development and unique dimensions of each individual writer's or editor's thought. It has been suggested (perhaps rightly so) that this is not a new development built upon form criticism but the recovery of one of the original intents of the method. The debate about terminology is not settled. The value of rhetorical criticism seems to be of major significance, regardless of what we call it.

Structuralism or structural criticism in Old Testament studies is a relatively recent application to biblical studies of a philosophical approach to knowledge which has been applied in almost every arena of intellectual investigation. It has been acclaimed by some as the most significant tool in biblical and theological studies which has ever been developed. Others, on the other hand (and I am numbered among them), consider it to be little more than a tempest in a teapot. The structural critics themselves have not been able to arrive at an acceptable definition of what they are doing. It appears that what is being said is that language has a structure which exists outside of time, that is, the structure is not affected by the historical processes. If this is true, then history becomes meaningless as an aid to understanding the development of the Old Testament. The structure of each passage is supposed to carry some significant meaning. The whole approach is quite nebulous, has made no visible contribution to Old Testament studies, and appears to lead absolutely nowhere.

The fourth and most recent development in Old Testament critical studies was proposed by B. S. Childs in 1979 in his *Introduction to the Old Testament as Scripture*. He used the term *introduction* in its classical sense, for he did not seek to write for the novice but for the expert in the field. Childs's major thrust has come to be called canonical criticism. The term *canonical* appears in almost every chapter. While acknowledging all the studies which have gone before and making frequent references to them, he did not concern himself with an attempt to analyze how each book came to be in its present form. Rather, he assumed that this has been done. Furthermore, he directed his concerns to the fact that the Old Testament as a whole and each book individually has been presented to us as it now is. What we actually possess is the canon, preserved and passed on by a community of faith.

Childs's concern was to try to discover precisely what is being proclaimed by the canonical forms of the books, and he asked that of the books both individually and collectively. He emphasized both the unity and the final form of each book rather than the many sources which might rest behind it. Childs demanded that serious scholars come to grips with the Old Testament text as it has come down to us. This emphasis is quite refreshing in the field of biblical scholarship and is obviously needed. That it has been ignored by so many for so long is almost unbelievable. The approach of Childs at least takes quite seriously a faith in divine revelation and inspiration, while at the same time acknowledging the fact that God revealed Himself to historical people within the limits of their own history.

Having traced with admitted brevity the history of Old Testament critical studies, we are now ready to examine where contemporary scholarship presently stands in those studies. The following materials must be understood in the light of the process which has brought us to this present position. They must also be understood as certainly not being the final word in the process. The studies still go on.

Major Methodologies in Old Testament Studies

While seeking to understand where contemporary Old Testament scholarship stands on major issues, the student needs to remember the differences which exist between facts and theories. Facts remain the same. We may learn new facts, but old facts do not change because of this. On the other hand, theories are human attempts to explain known facts. Theories do change. They change with the discovery of new facts or with a new understanding of old facts. Biblical students get into trouble confusing facts with theories. This section deals strictly with theories. Theories in Old Testament studies are attempts to try to understand how we got the books which make up the Old Testament. They are of value only so long as they deal honestly with the facts. But the theories of how we got the Old Testament cannot and do not alter the fact of divine inspiration. These theories merely help us to try to understand how God worked in preparing and preserving the Scriptures which we now have.

Some scholars of Old Testament studies will certainly disagree with how I categorize the following materials. Some would like to have seven or eight categories. However, for the sake of simplicity, I have identified five major approaches to the study of the Old Testament. They are clearly not mutually exclusive. Most contemporary Old Testament scholars use all of these methodologies to some extent. The serious student of the Old Testament must be familiar with these and should examine them to see if they enhance the understanding of the Hebrew Scriptures.

Literary or Source Criticism

Literary or source criticism is concerned with seeking to understand the literary processes by which particular books or segments of Old Testament books were put together in their present form. It also attempts to identify the historical background of each passage and the nature of the material contained within it. Finally, it attempts to deal with the questions of the authorship of each individual book.

A major example of such an approach can be found in the study of the Pentateuch. The first literary issue which has to be considered is that of Mosaic authorship. The King James Version of the Bible clearly identifies these books as having been written by Moses, calling Genesis "The First Book of Moses," Exodus "The Second Book of Moses," and so forth. The tradition that Moses wrote the Pentateuch is quite ancient, although it does not appear to go nearly as far back as the Hebrew kingdom. However, most scholars today believe that the Pentateuch was compiled from a series of sources and traditions, all of which were brought into their final form after the time of Moses.

Almost no scholar today would hold to the old Wellhausian view that there were four documents which were each written at a particular time and later collated. The Wellhausian approach made the assumption that the separate documents were the creations of their own time and had little or no historical value or validity except as they reflected the particular beliefs of the time of their writing.

On the other hand, many scholars do believe that these four basic sources probably did have separate existences. The general consensus today, however, is that each of these collections of material are based upon ancient oral traditions. Thus, even though the final shaping of a particular stand or stratum may have taken place late in Israel's development, the traditions which are recorded in it have a long prehistory and can be handled with confidence.

The Hebrew people had traditions which went back to their earliest patriarch, Abraham. Almost certainly some written materials were part of these strata, but most were probably oral. However, we must not assume that simply because something was oral it was inaccurate. Neither can we assume that something which was written down never had any existence prior to its writing.

The general assumption of literary critics today is that the earliest strand of the Pentateuch used the name Yahweh for God. This strand has come to be known as the

Jahwist (or Yahwist) and is usually identified as J. It is considered to have assumed its final form about 950 BC in the southern part of the Hebrew kingdom and to have been preserved around the Jerusalem Temple. The material in this stratum of tradition is bold and vivid, making extremely interesting reading. Possessing a high degree of patriotism, these narratives recorded the kinds of human interest detail that make such stories both memorable and entertaining. The heroes and heroines were living people, and no attempt was made to cover the human weaknesses which they possessed. God is described with bold anthropomorphisms. The great movements of history are of minor significance in the J stratum when compared with the affairs of daily life.

The second Pentateuchal strand has been identified as E, since the most common name for God in it is Elohim. The material contained within this stratum is called Elohistic. It is usually assumed that this material took its final form around 850 BC, probably in the Northern Kingdom after the monarchy had divided following Solomon's death. After the call of Moses in Exodus 3 and 4, this source also uses the name Yahweh for God. This material is more disturbed by moral issues than was J and describes God in more majestic and transcendent terms. In this stratum God communicated with mankind through more dreams and visions, and angels played a more significant part in the narrative. Scholars find it quite difficult in some places, particularly after the call of Moses, to separate the J and E material. It is generally assumed that the E material was gathered by the religious leaders of the Northern Kingdom after the division of the kingdoms so that they would have their own independent traditions, without having to be dependent upon those of the Southern Kingdom.

This theory further describes these two strata as having been woven together with care and skill about the time that the Northern Kingdom was destroyed by Assyria (722 BC). According to this approach, as the Northern Kingdom died, there was great danger that their religious heritage would die with them, so their traditions were carried southward by refugees. It is quite probable that the material was still primarily oral and was then woven together with the J material.

The third strand of Pentateuchal material is primarily found in Deuteronomy and has come to be known as D. Almost certainly, Deuteronomy, or at least the major part of it, was the book found in the Temple during the reform of Josiah (2 Kings 22:8-11; 622 BC). It served as the basis for Josiah's further reform. This material is found almost nowhere else in the Pentateuch, although it appears to have served as the theological foundation for Joshua, Judges, 1 and 2 Samuel, and 1 and 2 Kings. The compilation of this material is usually assumed to have taken place shortly before its discovery in the Temple. However, some scholars believe that the Deuteronomic material was originally collected in the time of Solomon, probably about the time of the dedication of the Temple. These believe that when the kingdom divided, this material was carried to the north and was preserved there until the final overthrow in 722 BC. Scholars believe that, at that time, the priests from the north either wrote the material down and sent it southward to preserve it or carried it themselves as refugees. The material was then hidden somewhere in the Jerusalem Temple. Since the Temple was so abused and disused during the reign of Manasseh, the hidden scroll was not found until the refurbishing of the Temple during Josiah's reform. Either way, we know for certain that it was in writing by the time of Josiah's reform of Judah's religion.

Scholars generally assume that the D material was added to the JE material at the time of the fall of Judah before the forces of Babylon in 586 BC. At such a time, the nation was in danger of losing all of its religious heritage and the compilation would have served to preserve those traditions, letting the JE material serve as an introduction to Deuteronomy.

At the time of the fall of Judah, the leaders of the land, including the priests, were carried captive to Babylon. The literary critics believe that the fourth strand of Pentateuchal material was gathered together at that time, again for the reason that it was in danger of being lost. This material is called Priestly (identified by P) because of its intense interest in things related to the priests and the Levites. The law codes are contained in this material along with the history which relates to them. P material is quite interested in details, recording the genealogies and the tables of statistical details. The narratives of this strand are pedantic and are very difficult reading. When a person who is reading the Bible through comes to Pentateuchal material which he or she desires to skip, it is almost always P. The dating of P's final compilation is usually assigned now to about 550 to 500 BC. Shortly before or after the time of the return from Exile (539 BC) all of this material was joined together.

The foregoing theory is not necessarily the correct one. Whatever approach is taken to the literary composition of the Pentateuch, several features must be considered. First of all, the analysis must deal with the variations of the divine names, the varieties of styles which accompany such variations, and some apparently duplicate accounts. Secondly, the analysis must deal with the fact that numerous references to geography give the impression of having been written from within Canaan rather than from without. Third, numerous historical references appear to have been written after the date of the events recorded, for explanations are given which would not have been necessary for people contemporaneous with the events. Fourth, numerous internal claims that Moses did write parts of it and received other parts of it from God are in the Pentateuch. Fifth, the literary references throughout the Bible reflect a long-standing tradition that Moses was responsible for much of the Pentateuch. Sixth, the death and burial of Moses is recorded.

Old Testament scholars, however, have not confined their literary analysis to the Pentateuch. The Former Prophets appear to show evidence of having drawn from many different sources. Several of those are specifically named. However, a unity of theological outlook in these books seems to be based upon Deuteronomy. Thus the Books of Joshua, Judges, 1 and 2 Samuel, and 1 and 2 Kings have come to be called the Deuteronomic History work. They are sometimes identified by the symbol DH.

The same kind of analysis has been carried on in the other prophetic books and among the Writings. Chronicles, along with Ezra and Nehemiah, appear to have used ancient sources, while being guided in their final editorial process by a Priestly Levitical outlook.

Literary criticism has possibly given us an insight into the writing and compilation of the books which make up the Old Testament. The question of how God inspired the Old Testament to be written in no way undermines the belief in the fact that He did it. Furthermore, the evidence for the existence of several major strands to the Pentateuch, as well as for multiple strata behind other books of the Old Testament, says nothing about how the material originated. It merely directs our attention to the fact that the material itself has a history of transmission. The Bible, in addition to being the inspired Word of God, is literature and appears to have a literary history. The study of this history is a valid approach for understanding how the Old Testament got its present shape. The Hebrew people did not invent their history, but they did collect their records and traditions together at various places and times under the inspiration of God. Thus, it has been passed on to us.

Form and Tradition Criticism

In the survey of the history of Old Testament studies, the scholarly world quickly began to recognize that the old Wellhausian approach assuming the creation of Hebrew history just did not stand up to a thorough examination. In addition, scholars recognized that materials dealing with common subjects frequently had a common form, or outline. They assumed that this was not accidental but intentional.

Consider for example, the call narratives of Isaiah, Jeremiah, and Ezekiel (Isa. 6; Jer. 1:4-10; Ezek. 1:4 to 3:27). A simple outline of each of these passages immediately focuses attention upon their similarities. Some of the earlier literary critics declared that this was evidence that none of the calls actually happened but were just the creations of some literary personage (or personages) seeking to authenticate the messages which had been written. The form critics, on the other hand, delved deeper. Recognizing the common elements, such an approach also notes that the first call narrative in the Old Testament is that of Moses, the Old Testament prophet par excellence (Ex. 3:1 to 4:17). The kinds of information which established the credentials of Moses were believed to be the same kinds needed to establish the credentials of any great prophet of God. Thus, the calls of Isaiah, Jeremiah, and Ezekiel were not invented, but the same kinds of information were remembered about each. Furthermore, by using a common outline, it was easier to remember the details of the calls of each of those men.

The form critic also points out that the Old Testament is not first of all a history book but a book of faith. The term used to describe this is the German term, *Heilsgeschichte,* which is usually translated as "salvation history," "holy history," or "the history of redemption." Therefore, form critics begin to look for a place in the ongoing faith and worship of Israel where such traditions or forms may have been preserved, passed on, and used in worship. Such places are identified as the form's *Sitz-im-Leben.* The form critics have demonstrated that such common materials were part of Israel's worship from her earliest days. Thus long before most of the Old Testament was put into written documents, the forms of such material were thoroughly fixed. The form critics, by such analysis, have demonstrated the reliability of such materials. The form into which the information was placed made it easier to remember the details of any particular passage.

Analysis of the common forms of biblical material has led to further assumptions. Among these are the concept that the major religious festivals called for common forms to be used in each of them. Thus hymns or psalms with similar messages were put into common forms as they were passed on from year to year and from generation to generation.

The study of the forms of Israel's faith, however, developed into what has come to be called tradition criticism. This begins where form criticism leaves off and goes on in the same directions. Since the form critics assumed that the Old Testament forms were used as part of Hebrew worship, the tradition critics assumed that such material would have been preserved at worship centers. Thus each center would have developed its own cycle of traditions, some of which would have been similar or identical to those of other shrines, but some of which would have been quite distinctive, due to the particular interests of the shrine. This may have been due to geographical influences, but it may also have been due to tribal or historical influences. Thus the traditions which were gathered around the Jerusalem Temple have a greater emphasis upon Judah, the major southern tribe in whose territory Jerusalem is located. On the other hand, the priests of Bethel would have preserved material focusing upon Jacob, since so much of his religious experience centered there. Further, as Bethel was the major shrine of the Northern Kingdom whose chief tribe was Ephraim, the narratives in which Ephraim figured prominently would have been especially meaningful to the worshipers there. In such ways, according to this approach, the various narratives which now make up our Old Testament may have been collected and preserved. As such shrines passed out of existence, their traditions would have been carried elsewhere and added to those of other worship centers.

A comparison of Psalms 14 and 53 may illustrate this process. These two psalms are almost identical. However, the name for God in Psalm 14 is Yahweh while the name used in Psalm 53 is Elohim. Since Yahweh was apparently the preferred name at Jerusalem while Elohim was the preferred name at Bethel, these psalms may have originally been the same one. One was probably preserved in the north and the other in the south. Each worship center used the same hymn to worship God, but each was inspired to use the divine name most meaningful to it.

Tradition criticism builds upon the foundation of form criticism, seeking to identify, wherever possible, the particular centers of tradition which existed among the Hebrews and to determine which traditions and narratives were preserved where. Numerous such centers existed throughout Hebrew history. Besides Jerusalem and Bethel, Shiloh, Shechem, Gilgal, Beersheba, Dan, and others were worship centers. The gathering of materials of inspired interest at these centers may have been the major step between the formation of the first independent units and the ultimate compilation of books and of the Old Testament itself.

Form and tradition criticism have made some lasting contributions to the study of the Old Testament. Form criticism has helped us to see that some written materials almost certainly had a long prehistory of oral tradition. Such oral traditions are seen as being historically reliable. The very nature of the forms in which they were preserved aided their accurate transmission. Since they were preserved as a part of worship, and worship is quite traditional, this also further ensured the reliability of the traditions and narratives. Thus, confidence in the reliability of the materials has been vindicated by these approachs.

The second major contribution of these approachs to Old Testament studies has been to demonstrate that most of the larger portions of the Old Testament originally existed in small, independent units. These units appear to be identified by their common forms. They seem to have been the basic building blocks from which the Old Testament was ultimately constructed.

A third major contribution of these approaches to Old Testament studies has been to aid in understanding and identifying the transmission influences upon particular passages or forms. Materials were preserved because they had meaning where they were preserved. These units were kept and built into larger traditions because the people at a particular time and place heard God speak through them. They were not preserved for their antiquarian interest nor for others to know what the ancient Hebrews felt and thought. They were preserved because they were God's Word to a specific, identifiable audience.

However, form and tradition criticism do have major limitations which must be understood. While much has been accomplished using this methodology, the approach is a long way from being an exact science. Sometimes the practictioners of such methods of study get overly enthusiastic and claim more for such studies than they are able to deliver. Thus there is a tendency to force forms upon small units when they do not really fit. There is no basis for altering the biblical text simply because a passage does not have quite the form which an interpreter would desire or which was expected. This is not an adequate tool for "correcting" a text unless some textual evidence otherwise identifies a problem. All such studies are merely an attempt to discover how God spoke to His ancient people, not to say what He should have said to them.

Rhetorical and Structural Criticism

In a real sense, the approach to Old Testament studies which has come to be called rhetorical criticism is an outgrowth of form and tradition criticism. Some scholars do not even classify it as a separate approach. Basically, the rhetorical critic seeks to identify the differences which exist between units which appear to have common forms. Once the differences have been identified, scholars attempt to find an explanation for those differences. While some form critics have sought to emend texts which differ, the rhetorical critics seek to find an explanation for the differences.

The rhetorical critic notes the differences and seeks to determine what historical, geographical, cultural, or religious factors might offer an explanation for those differences. Such an approach frequently strengthens the conclusions of the tradition critic. At other times, it points up the amazing lack of knowledge which we have of the ancient peoples about whom we read and study.

As noted, tradition criticism calls attention to the worshiping communities. Rhetorical criticism sometimes does the same. At other times, however, rhetorical criticism also directs our attention to the individual worshiper. Thus the differences which exist between the call narratives of Isaiah, Jeremiah, and Ezekiel direct our attention to the differences between the individual prophets themselves.

These differences show up in both the nature of the people and the nature of their faith. Through the work of the rhetorical critic, we reaffirm the fact that the people through whom God worked and with whom He spoke in the Old Testament were real people and not just plaster images. Rhetorical criticism puts the final nail in the coffin of the old Wellhausian approach to the literature of the Old Testament. The people about whom the Old Testament speaks and to whom it was addressed are seen to be real people, facing real problems, committing real sin, and finding real forgiveness. They are not simply the figment of someone's imagination.

Perhaps related to rhetorical criticism, yet somewhat different from it, is what has come to be known as structuralism or structural criticism. This approach to the study of the Old Testament has been acclaimed by some as a radically new approach. Yet its adherents have not yet been able even to agree on a clear definition of what they are about.

In some instances, structural critics focus their attention upon the structure of individual sentences. One of the leading practictioners of this approach illustrates this in dealing with the phrase: "Time flies like an arrow." Normally this has been understood as a simple observation that time speeds through our lives as an arrow speeds through the air. But suppose this is not the proper understanding of the structure. Perhaps *time* is an adjective, *flies* is a noun, and *like* is a verb. Then we are noting that time flies (possibly related to house flies and horse flies) like arrows; they just love to cuddle up to arrows. Obviously, we have radically changed the meaning by reassessing the structure. But we are not through. It may be that *time* is a verb and a command. Then we have an order to take out our stopwatches and time those pesky little flies with the speed of an arrow.

Such an approach to the study of the Bible (or of anything else, for that matter) ultimately appears to force us to the conclusion that we can make a passage mean almost anything we wish. However, there is a fallacy to this approach. In the Old Testament, the Hebrew language is generally quite clear as to whether a word is a noun or a verb. There is just no possible way to do the sort of thing seen in our illustration. Thus such an approach becomes utterly meaningless, if this is what is meant by structuralism.

On the other hand, most structuralists seek to probe a passage, hunting for some deep, hidden psychological structure by which the biblical material was arranged. It thus becomes almost a modified kind of form criticism, except that it does not look for simple forms but for very detailed forms which have some kind of hidden pattern which only the initiated can discover. Unfortunately, such approaches have not yet been able to be explained in such a way so that two different interpreters can identify similar patterns in the same passage. When something cannot be communicated clearly enough so that others can duplicate the approach, it is highly questionable whether it has any validity at all.

Canonical Criticism

One of the major weaknesses with each of the foregoing approaches to the study of the Old Testament is that they have focused major attention upon small units and individual paragraphs or sentences. That kind of focus has generally failed to deal with the fact that we have received a completed canon. The Old Testament *is* made up of thirty-nine books. Each book was put together by someone under the inspiration of God. The final edition of each book has a message to proclaim, a faith to share. Each book proclaimed and proclaims something about God.

The books themselves were eventually put together in the collection we now have. In addition, the people who made this collection under God's direction were neither foolish nor faithless. They did not put books in the collection which did not have something in common with one another.

Upon these foundations has been erected the newest approach to the serious study of the Old Testament, canonical criticism. This approach focuses attention upon the unity of each book and of the canon as a whole. Such a study looks for the commonalities which bind Genesis together and then which tie Genesis together with Exodus or Isaiah. In a very real sense, this is a theological approach to the Old

Testament. Canonical criticism also seeks to come to grips with the fact that the Old Testament is the foundation of the New. The strands of the message which bind both Testaments together are also sought, with an attempt to understand the ultimate message of God.

Canonical criticism does not ignore the other approaches which have been made, but it does not stop with them. This approach assumes that the material of the Old Testament is a literature of a people and has a history. It also assumes that there probably were common forms by which such materials were passed on to other generations. The canonical critic appropriates the best features of tradition and rhetorical criticism. To the canonical critic, however, no one of these methods is sufficient in and of itself. Further, to the canonical critic, these methods are not satisfactory when practiced together. They just simply do not go far enough.

We do have an Old Testament. It has been passed on to us by a living community of faith. This needs to be taken seriously and an attempt made to understand what the Old Testament proclaims as a whole.

The biggest difference between the present methodology of canonical criticism and that which was practiced over the years by opponents of one or more of the other methodologies lies in the insistence upon facts and evidence. One cannot argue with positions supported by *biblical* evidence simply on the basis of theology. The only way really to take the Old Testament seriously is to examine it with more thoroughness than has been done before. We must analyze each of its parts, but we must also seek to understand the whole. God was certainly in the inspiration of each small unit of the Old Testament. But our faith insists that He was also in the inspiration of the whole. If we are going to proclaim this with seriousness and conviction, we must do so on the basis of the most thorough search of the evidence and the most critical analysis of the Old Testament text as we have it.

The Present State of Old Testament Studies

The study of the Old Testament has brought us to the place where we can make several assertions with confidence, while acknowledging the limitations of our knowledge in many areas. First of all, we can have confidence in the text of the Old Testament. While we clearly do not possess the original manuscript of any Old Testament book, we can assert with confidence that we have the message which God proclaimed to and through the Hebrew people.

Second, while we have acknowledged the fact that human theories of how we got the Old Testament are subject to change, rejection, or revision, we have learned a great deal about some of the methods by which ancient narratives, traditions, and documents were transmitted. This knowledge has allowed us to have an increasing understanding of the human processes which God used. Our faith led us to believe that the Divine Author would not have allowed His human scribes to have destroyed His revelation. Our study of the evidence has led us to the conclusion that such transmission was performed with care.

Third, critical studies of the Old Testament have led us to a deeper confidence in the belief that the Old Testament is the Word of God. The newer approaches to the Old Testament have led us to focus upon the common faith which binds it together and the common proclamation which it makes about God. At the same time, these studies have allowed us to see the human authors whom the Divine Author inspired and used. We discover both the human side of God's revelation and the divine power behind it.

Fourth, the serious study of the Old Testament has forced us again and again to come to grips with our own finitude and limitations. We do not yet have all the answers. Our knowledge is quite limited. We stand amazed, not at how much we know about this ancient Book but at how much God has communicated to us through our limited knowledge.

Fifth, the study of the Old Testament is exciting and opens up many fascinating new vistas. But we must recognize that we have not arrived at the final point in the process. Scholars continue to direct major effort to the understanding of the Old Testament. We can expect to go onward from here in our pilgrimage of discipleship. We have the tools to do a thorough job in such studies. We have the expectation of new theories and new approaches which will lead to new understanding of old truth.

Part II
Introduction to the Pentateuch and Its Study

6

Issues in Pentateuchal Studies

The first five books of the Old Testament have generally been identified by one of two titles. To the Jews, they were known as the Torah (Hebrew world for *law*). The Jewish people apparently accepted these as having more authority than the rest of the canon. Furthermore, they were accepted as authoritative significantly earlier than other parts of the Old Testament. To the Christians who came along centuries later, these books were simply known as "the Law" in whatever language they were using.

However, quite early in Christian tradition, these books came to be known by the more mundane title of the Pentateuch. This word comes from two Greek words, *pente* (five) and *teuchos* (volume). These were combined into an adjective for the word *biblos* (book), and thus the title was "five-volume book." The expression was eventually shortened to *penteteuchos* and was transliterated into English as *Penteteuch*.

Some scholars have suggested that the division into five separate books was made by the translators of the Septuagint (LXX) since the earliest historical references to "five books of the Law" occur after the time that translation was made. On the other hand, it is quite obvious that Genesis, Leviticus, and Deuteronomy are units in and of themselves, and could stand alone. Since Exodus and Numbers slide into the gaps between these, it would appear that the division into five books is natural and existed from the earliest days.

Although each book is unique, with its own message and unity, they have appeared as a part of this collection from ancient times, and some common issues relate to them which need to be considered.

Literary Issues

At least three literary issues need to be considered in this survey. The first and most basic is the issue of the literary limits of the material itself. The question is whether we should be dealing with a shorter or longer block of material. The second issue deals with authorship and the unity and the diversity of the material. The third issue addresses the literary relationships of these books with other ancient materials. Israel was surrounded by other nations who also had written records, some of which bear a remarkable resemblance to material in the Old Testament. We need to consider what literary relationships may have existed between the records of Israel and those of other ancient peoples.

The Literary Limits

In the Hebrew canon, the Torah is made up of Genesis, Exodus, Leviticus, Numbers, and Deuteronomy. However, for well over a century, many scholars have called attention to the fact that the material in Genesis through Numbers is quite different from that found in Deuteronomy. Thus they have called the first four books the Tetrateuch, based upon the Greek word which means "four." Such scholars have suggested that while Deuteronomy may be a part of the Jewish Torah it should not be studied as a unit with the first four books.

Other scholars have pointed out some significant similarities between the material in Joshua and that in Genesis through Numbers. These have suggested that the real literary unit extends all the way through Joshua and that the basic unit for literary studies should be the Hexateuch, a term derived from the Greek word for "six."

Finally, since the work of Martin Noth in the 1930s, a very strong relationship has been pointed out between Deuteronomy and the material in Joshua, Judges, 1 and 2 Samuel, and 1 and 2 Kings. This relationship appears to be so strong that many scholars now call these latter books the Deuteronomic History. Some followers of this approach find it almost impossible to put any literary limits on the material until they get to the end of 2 Kings.

While each of these approaches appears to have some measure of truth behind it, the reality which we still have to confront is that from the earliest days of the canon the accepted unit was the Torah, Genesis through Deuteronomy. No approach which draws the limits otherwise can adequately account for that fact. Thus, we shall direct our attention to these five books.

Issues of Authorship, Unity, and Diversity

The history of Old Testament critical studies and the overview of the present state of the major methodologies in use in Old Testament studies in the preceding chapter gave a major survey of most of the issues related to the authorship, unity, and diversity of materials within the Pentateuch. Some of these need to be restated and others need to be added.

Insofar as I am concerned, *there is no question but that God inspired this material. It is God-breathed through and through.* This survey is about the human instruments which God used to present His revelation. Serious Bible students who are firmly committed to the inspiration and authority of the Old Testament have raised valid questions based upon the study of the biblical text itself about the processes by which God caused this material to be written.

Seldom do today's scholars question that Moses made significant contributions to the material in these books. The extent of that contribution is the focus of inquiry. Even the most conservative interpreters, such as Edward J. Young and Derek Kidner, acknowledge the evidence for some earlier sources to the Pentateuchal material and for some later additions. The issue the scholars debate is the extent of these sources and additions and with just what precision they can be identified.

Today scholars reject the classical documentary hypothesis as presented by Wellhausen. Its Hegelian philosophy is untenable, and its presuppositions of a series of written documents essentially manufacturing history and being easily identifiable are positions which are no longer possible to maintain.

Any serious study of the question of authorship must deal with the internal evidence that Moses actually wrote some of the material in the Pentateuch (cf. Ex. 17:14; 24:4; 34:27; Num. 33:1-2; Deut. 31:9, 22). Furthermore, substantial evidence is found in the rest of the Bible for attributing major contributions to Moses (cf. Josh. 1:7-8; Judg. 3:4; 1 Kings 2:3; 2 Kings 14:6; 21:8; 2 Chron. 25:4; Ezra 6:16; 7:6; Mal. 4:4; Matt. 8:4; Mark 7:10; 10:5; Luke 20:37; John 5:47; 7:19; Acts 3:22; 15:5-21; and numerous others). Some scholars have suggested, perhaps with legitimacy, that portions or all of these references are literary references, simply acknowledging the fact that the material in these books was assumed to be derived from Moses. But we must at least face the fact that this major tradition was there.

Few scholars would insist that Moses actually inscribed on stone, clay, papyrus, or other material every word (cf. Ex. 34:1 and 34:27). He may have used a scribe to do what writing was done. Yet there does appear to be evidence that there were major oral and written traditions which were utilized in the final editing of the material. However the words were written, God was the ultimate Author and He inspired them from beginning to end throughout the entire process. We turn to the words of the Pentateuch not to hear Moses or some unknown human editor but to hear God speak.

The acknowledgment that God is sovereign over His world and His Word eliminates any question of the impossibility of the supernatural or the miraculous in the Bible. The God who created this world can intervene in it when and how He pleases. When He intervenes, He may use natural as well as supernatural forces. For example, the Bible affirms that when God parted the waters of the Sea for the Hebrews to cross in their exodus from Egypt He did so by means of ''a strong east wind'' (Ex. 14:21).

Any serious study of authorship, unity, and diversity

must deal with the fact that the Pentateuchal material shows a consistent plan throughout. The narrative proceeds in logical development of plan, purpose, faith, and characters from the beginning to the end. Any theory of authorship must also consider the evidence within the biblical material for differing vocabulary, differing linguistic styles in adjacent passages, and differing concerns in passages where similar concerns would have been expected.

The final word has not been said in regard to the human process by which the Penteteuch reached its final form. Studies go on, and new theories will be proposed to account for known and newly discovered facts. But none of that will change the fact of its Divine authorship, its inspiration by God, and its authority over human life in faith and practice.

Issues of Literary Relationships

A last area of literary concern relating to the Pentateuch has to do with its relationship to other ancient literatures from nations which existed in the vicinity of Israel, both geographically and chronologically. In three (possibly four) areas, some kind of literary relationship appears between the biblical material in the Pentateuch and other materials found in the ancient Near East of which Israel was a part. Of several creation accounts, a few show some affinity to the Genesis account. Several flood narratives also show similarities. The law codes of the ancient world show varying degrees of similarities to those found in the Penteteuch. Finally, the form of the covenant in Exodus and Deuteronomy shows some similarity to the form of the ancient suzerainty treaties of the Hittities and other major international powers of the time.

Some scholars have suggested that the literary relationship between the Penteteuch and other writings in the ancient Near East may be nothing more than coincidental. Materials dealing with common subjects may be expected to take similar forms and have similar content. On the surface, this is quite plausible. However, a thorough study of the various sources in their original forms shows significant verbal identity. Such verbal identity makes mere coincidence implausible. If there is a direct literary relationship, three further possibilities exist. First, Israel may have borrowed from some other ancient sources. Second, the other sources may have borrowed from Israel. Third, all of these traditions may go back to some more ancient common source.

The archaeological dating of ancient records other than the Penteteuch makes it abundantly clear that many of these materials significantly predate the Hebrew narratives. Thus, in those instances, the others could not have borrowed from Israel. Of the other two options, evidence is insufficient to draw a general conclusion which would appear to be true in all cases. However, several factors must be considered at this point. If Israel borrowed materials from ancient cultures, it did so under the inspiration of God. This may have been done for one of two reasons. God may have inspired Israel to borrow material because it was correct and it was to use it to proclaim God's revelation. The Bible indicates that other peoples have received some (though not the full) revelation from God. If they have, there is nothing wrong with God inspiring the Hebrews to use some of this early revelation.

Another possibility, at least in some cases, appears to be far more plausible. When Paul went to Athens on his second missionary journey, he took a part of the Greeks' own faith, the altar "To an unknown god," and preached the gospel of Jesus to them (Acts 17:22-31). Israel may have done the same kind of thing, at least in some instances. Perhaps it took ancient narratives which the Canaanites or the Babylonians used and said: "Look, you think that your gods did these things, but we wish to tell you that the God of Israel did them. Our God created the universe. Our God sent the Flood in judgment and started over again with Noah. Our God demands that life be lived in relationship with Him and that our relations with one another must be governed by law." If that is so, the literary relationships of the Pentateuch become essentially missionary and evangelistic instruments by which Israel proclaimed its faith to its world. Even if that were not the purpose for the use of other ancient traditions, it became an effective tool for doing precisely that task. The literary relationships do exist. For whatever purpose, God used them to reveal His truth to Israel.

Historical Issues

The general historical issue related to the entire Pentateuch is determining just what kind of historical and cultural data it gives. We will not discuss those few interpreters who deny any real historicity to the entire narrative. Their approach wholly ignores the concept of revelation and the nature of the documents themselves. However, a significant difference of opinion exists among serious biblical students as to how the information we have in the Penteteuch is to be understood and interpreted.

The narratives of the Pentateuch are very different from modern history. The variety of data makes difficult any consensus as to how it should be evaluated. Cultural references, such as the polygamous marriages of the patriarchs, the substitution of a handmaid for a barren wife, birthrights, and family blessings, are unfamiliar to modern, Western readers.

Some historical data given in these narratives are either confusing or appear to give no concrete basis for establishing an adequate or accurate absolute chronology for the events under consideration. For example, the life spans assigned to the people in the early chapters of Genesis do not relate to modern personal experiences or other historical records. Proposed solutions to these problems frequently are as confusing as the data themselves. Some suggest that the great length of life indicates another method of counting time, such as lunar months instead of years. This offers no help, for such a proposal ends up with Adam becoming a father for the third time when he was ten years old (Gen. 5:3). Others suggest that the length of years assigned to these people relates to the time when their clan or tribe endured. Though this might make sense in some instances, too many persons are clearly presented as individuals. To complete our difficulties, the available data often does not enable us to place these individuals in a historical era. Thus dates proposed for the patriarchs vary considerably from interpreter to interpreter.

When confronted by issues raised by historical and cultural data, we must first admit our limits. We do not know everything, do not need to know everything, do not need to know everything, and cannot know everything. Because of our limits, we will never resolve all the questions surrounding the Penteteuch.

At the same time, we must not be content to know less than is possible. The Christian scholar or student must strive to discover all that it is possible to know. This quest for knowledge drives the scholar to read the ancient documents. In so doing, we discover that the patriarchs were people of their time. Their practices, which often seem strange to us, were usually appropriate within the time period under discussion. Admitting our limits and adopting an expectant stance, we continue to look for new ways of understanding.

Geographical Issues

The study of the geography of the ancient Near East is still a developing science. Some sites and regions mentioned in the Bible have been identified with precision. Such identifications help us to deal with geographical details in the narratives with ease and understanding. However we can hardly identify a site in the entire journey of Israel through the wilderness. Not even Sinai has been identified with certainty. This does not mean that we cannot trust the narrative. It only means that our ignorance is once more seen to be real. We know enough of the geographical references to be able to establish the general nature of the events and the regions in which they occurred. Given the human tendency toward idolatry, more knowledge might even further turn our attention to the place and away from the God who used the place in giving His revelation.

Theological Issues

The ultimate theological question of the Pentateuch is, How important is the faith of the Pentateuch for a Christian? Can a person be a Christian without understanding this part of the Bible? The answer to the latter question is obviously yes. An understanding of the Pentateuch is not necessary for a person to experience the lordship of Jesus Christ. But no one can fully appreciate the richness of the New Testament message without a knowledge of the revelation of God as it is contained within this part of His Word.

The fullness of the New Testament message of redemption cannot be understood without an acquaintance with the various shades of meaning of redemption developed in the Penteteuch. For example, the Book of Hebrews becomes essentially a closed book unless the reader understands the message and content of Leviticus. Sin is most fully understood in light of the rebellions of Genesis, Exodus, and Numbers. Jesus and the New Testament writers made numerous references to that block of material. Those references become wholly meaningless if we are unfamiliar with the faith of the Pentateuch.

While the Pentateuch is of great importance in understanding the faith of the New Testament, the faith of the Pentateuch *is not* identical to the faith of the New Testament. Faith was enlarged and developed between the time of the Pentateuch and the time of Jesus. If the faith of the Pentateuch were exactly that of the Gospels, we would not have needed the Gospels. If the sacrificial system had been adequate, we would not have needed the cross. If we could have understood all about God's demands upon our lives from the Old Testament law, we would not have needed the Sermon on the Mount or the other teachings of Jesus. If the first chapters of Genesis had been adequate for our faith, we would not have needed Paul's magnificant Letter to the Romans.

The Pentateuch is quite important for the understanding of our faith and how it came to us, but it is not God's final word. We cannot sit in judgment upon the Pentateuch as if everything it proclaims must be identical with what we find in the Gospels. The roots for both the faith of Israel and the faith of Christianity are found in these records. But they are the roots only. The full flowering was yet to come.

7

Genesis

In the Hebrew Bible, the individual books are frequently called by the first word(s) found there. Thus Genesis is called *Bereshith*, "In the Beginning" (or more properly, "In Beginning"). The more familiar title of Genesis has come to us from a Latin variation of the Septuagint translation of Genesis 2:4: "This is the book of the *geneseos* [generation, origin] of the heavens and the earth" (author's translation). This word shows up in ten other places in the book (Gen. 5:1; 6:9; 10:1; 11:10, 27; 25:12, 19; 36:1, 9; 37:2), serving apparently as the author's basic marking of the major divisions of the book. In post-New Testament times, the rabbis also called it the "Book of the Creation of the World." The word *Genesis* actually means "generation," "source," or "origin."

Genesis is truly the book of beginnings, of origins. It tells of the origin of the universe, of life, of humanity, of sin, of civilization, and of God's redemptive activities. It also tells of the origin of the nations and of the Hebrew nation, in particular. The narratives of Genesis cover a far greater time span than any other book of the Bible. In fact, Genesis covers more time than all the rest of the Bible.

A careful reading of Genesis brings its purpose into plain sight. The divine Author was setting the stage for all of the rest of the Bible. From the deliverance of Israel from Egypt though the deliverance of humanity from sin at the cross to the ultimate victory of God and the deliverance of His people from the very presence of sin (as seen in Revelation), the story of redemption had its foundation here. God was not wasting His time revealing things which can be found more easily elsewhere. He was revealing what can be found nowhere else: He loves rebellious humans and set as His sovereign purpose their redemption. This is holy history, the history of redemption. As long as we keep that in mind, we shall not wander too far afield in our study.

Analysis of the Book of Genesis is normally done from one of two standpoints. Some authors outline the book in terms of the historical sequence of its narrative. The broad outline of such an approach identifies the successive stages of its history.

1. The Primeval History (1:1 to 11:26)
2. The Life of Abraham (11:27 to 25:18)
3. The Life of Isaac (25:19 to 28:9)
4. The Life of Jacob (28:10 to 35:29)
5. The Life of Esau (36:1-43)
6. The Life of Joseph (37:1 to 50:26)

Other biblical scholars have noted that the author of Genesis apparently followed an outline in structuring the book. The book shows every evidence of very careful planning, with each division of the book being set apart by the Hebrew word *toledhoth* ("generations"). This term introduces each new division of the book. The sections on generations are preceded by a magnificent prose poem introducing the Creator and His creation. This gives us the following outline.

The Content of the Book

Introduction to the book (1:1 to 2:3)
1. The generations of the heavens and the earth (2:4 to 4:26)
2. The generations of Adam (5:1 to 6:8)
3. The generations of Noah (6:9 to 9:29)
4. The generations of the Sons of Noah (10:1 to 11:9)
5. The generations of Shem (11:10-26)
6. The generations of Terah (11:27 to 25:11)
7. The generations of Ishmael (25:12-18)
8. The generations of Isaac (25:19 to 35:29)
9. The generations of Esau (36:1 to 37:1; for some unknown reason, the expression is repeated in 36:9)
10. The generations of Jacob (37:2 to 50:26)

While both approaches are of value in helping grasp the content and the flow of movement within the book, and while each approach calls attention to the careful planning of the book, an approach which also calls attention to the basic message of the book might be more helpful to a contemporary student. Therefore, the outline followed in this book will be a modification of both of these with the deliberate intent of directing attention to the theological development and faith proclamation of the book.

   I. Primeval history: the need for redemption (1:1 to 11:26)
     A. God, the Sovereign Creator (1:1 to 2:3)
       1.   Before God's creation: chaos (1:1-2)
       2.   One day: light in the darkness (1:3-5)
       3.   A second day: the firmament (1:6-8)
       4.   A third day: land and vegetation (1:9-13)
       5.   A fourth day: the stars in their courses (1:14-19)
       6.   A fifth day: first life (1:20-23)
       7.   A sixth day: land creatures, culminating in humanity (1:24-31)
       8.   The seventh day: a sacred day of rest (2:1-3)

Chapters 1 to 11 in Genesis are quite different both in style and content from the rest of the book. They give the appearance of being a prose poem, being very stately and majestic. They serve as an introduction both to the book and to the entire Bible. Here are set forth the foundations for almost all major biblical doctrines. The first part of this block of material (1:1 to 2:3) contains the account of creation and serves primarily to introduce the Creator. Many significant issues are raised in these verses, but two of them require attention at this point: the relationship between this material and other creation accounts of the ancient Near East and the relationship between the creation account and science.

There are obvious relations between the Genesis account of creation and numerous such accounts of the region. However, the most striking relationship is found with the Babylonian account which is known as the *Enuma Elish* ("When Above," or "When on High"). The verbal similarity is too great to be due to mere coincidence. The dating of the two accounts makes it impossible that the Babylonian account is derived from the Hebrew. Some scholars argue that the biblical account is derived from the Babylonian, others that both of these accounts were derived from a still more ancient tradition. The striking differences between the two accounts make the latter suggestion the more likely. The differences direct our attention to the majestic transcendance of God, His awesome power, and the absence of other gods. Israel was probably using the ancient account as a means of proclaiming the true nature of the God who is able to create simply by the power of His spoken word.

The second major issue has to do with the relationship between the creation account and science. The amazing fact is that the narrative of creation was so inspired that people of all ages have sought here the confirmation of the latest scientific theory. But as theories have changed, the majestic truths of Genesis have still remained unaltered. True science and true religion never stand in conflict with one another. Human theories may differ and pass away. God's truth as revealed in nature and in His Word remains unchanged.

The central theme of this unit is God. More than thirty times the name of God appears in its verses. Furthermore, the theme is focused upon the God who acts. He created. Three different times in this narrative the word *bara'* ("create") appears. In the Old Testament, this is a word used only of the activity of God. He created in the beginning (1:1), He created life (1:21), and He created mankind (1:27). The Bible simply affirms that God created, without worrying about all the details of how He created. There is obviously an orderly progression to the origin of the universe and all that is in it. The basic affirmation is that all that is here came from the creative act of God. He is the absolute Sovereign of the universe.

    B. Man, the supreme creation (2:4-25)
        1.   Dust of the earth (2:4-7)
        2.   Eden, the ideal place (2:8-14)
        3.   Labor assigned (2:15-17)
        4.   The search for a companion (2:18-20)
        5.   The ideal relationship (2:21-25)

This block of material is significantly different from that of the preceding section. In Genesis 1:1 to 2:3 the author spoke of God (*'Elohim*), here He is the Lord God (*Yahweh 'Elohim*). There God was majestically transcendant, here He is anthropomorphically immanent. There the beginning stages were a watery waste, here the beginning is an arid desert. There man was a towering figure, created in the image of God, here he is earthy, made of the very dust of the ground. The differences in the accounts have been explained as being due to their original preservation by two different groups within the Hebrew nation or as simple reflections of a difference in subject matter. Either way, Genesis 2:4-25 serves as a distinct complement to Genesis 1:1 to 2:3.

Without question, Genesis 2:4-25 has a radically different focus. In the first section, God was the central figure. While He is clearly sovereign in this section, the focus is upon the crown of His creation: man. The Hebrew word used in both chapters for man is *'adham*, the same word which is later translated as "Adam." The word is used throughout the Old Testament as referring to all of mankind. A translator and an interpreter must make the decision as to when the word is to be understood as one man, the first man, Adam, and when it is to be understood as referring to generic man. In some cases, the word is used with the definite article (translated "the man"). In such cases, it is obviously referring to a specific man, but just as obviously not being used as a proper name (no one speaks of "the Bob" or "the Will").

God in His wisdom sought to provide a companion for His supreme creation, recognizing that "it is not good that the man should be alone" (2:18). When the ultimate mate for man was formed from one of man's own ribs, the man burst forth into the first song found in the Bible (2:23). From the divinely established relationship between the first man and the first woman comes the basic understanding of marriage as God intended it. The reference to unashamed nakedness appears to refer to the absolute openness of the relationship, as well as the full sexual union within it. Such sexual openness is part of the gift and plan of God.

    C. Sin: the creation marred (3:1 to 6:8)
        1.   The first sin and its consequence (3:1-24)
            a. Temptation and rebellion (3:1-7)
            b. Alienation and confrontation (3:8-13)
            c. Judgment and mercy (3:14-24)
        2.   The spread of sin and judgment (4:1 to 6:8)
            a. My brother's keeper (4:1-16)
            b. The spread of sin (4:17-24)
            c. An interlude of worship (4:25-26)
            d. The spread of humanity (5:1-32)
            e. Humanity's evil imagination (6:1-7)
            f. The hint of hope (6:8)

The tragic story of sin's introduction into the world is told in a matchless piece of literature. The serpent, a symbol of pure evil, later in God's revelation properly identified as Satan, came with his subtle temptation, leading the woman and the man to doubt the truthfulness of God. Desiring to be like God instead of sharing His love, the man and the woman rebelled against the express command of God.

The guilt of sin forced the human pair to hide from God. God sought them, they did not go looking for God. Guilt always destroys relationships. God came to them, confronting them with their sin, seeking to lead them to an open acknowledgment of guilt. Being afraid to confess such, each blamed someone else. The man ultimately blamed God, saying, "The woman whom *thou gavest to be with me,* she gave me the fruit of the tree, and I ate" (3:12, author's italics). With great reluctance, however, they both admitted guilt.

God's pronouncement of judgment offered a ray of hope. The seed of woman would ultimately "crush" the head of the serpent. A crushed heel is not fatal; a crushed head is.

By the provision of a better covering for their nakedness than they had devised, God also foreshadowed His ultimate provision for the covering of sin. The awesome difference between God and man is again set forth. The two who sought to be like God were only dust.

In driving the guilty pair from the garden, God acted in both judgment and mercy. The penal dimension was that they could no longer enjoy life as God had intended it. The element of mercy was that God did not want them to live forever in their alienated state. Keeping the tree of life from them provided the opportunity for making them fit to live with Him forever.

The story of sin and its catastrophic consequences proceeds with Cain's murder of Abel. With the arrogant question, "Am I my brother's keeper?" Cain sought to avoid direct confrontation with God by hiding behind theological inquiries. This tactic has been practiced with consummate skill down through the ages. We still seek to avoid doing what God wants us to do by getting involved in arguing theology. Cain was not just his brother's keeper, he was supposed to have been his brother's brother. Even here, God tempered judgment with mercy. The mark of Cain was for protection, not for punishment. As the narrative follows the line of Cain, we see the spread of civilization and the spread of sin. The only bright spot in the narrative focuses upon the line of Seth, where we see that the worship of God began again. With Seth and Enosh, men began to know the name Yahweh for God.

As humanity spread over the earth, a new dimension was added to the sin experience. The "sons of God" (6:2) were not godly men; the expression is an idiom for angelic beings. These apparently were rebellious angels who introduced that strain of rebellion into the world (cf. 2 Pet. 2:4-5). The end result of the tragic spread of sin is described in terms of humanity's evil imagination. Judgment had to come. Yet even in judgment a note of hope was sounded, for "Noah found favor in the eyes of the Lord" (6:8). In the midst of sin's punishment came the expression of grace.

D. Judgment and a new start (6:9 to 10:32)
1. One righteous man and his family (6:9-10)
2. The coming judgment (6:11-13)
3. Provision for deliverance (6:14 to 7:5)
4. The chaos of judgment (7:6-24)
5. The new order (8:1-19)
6. A new hope (8:20-22)
7. A new beginning (9:1-19)
8. Sin's new presence (9:20-28)
9. Racial origins (10:1-32)

From all over the world come stories of ancient floods which were divinely sent to destroy humankind but through which a limited number of persons survived to start civilization over again. Most show no relationship to the Genesis account other than in the broadest outline. However, the Babylonian Gilgamesh Epic shows striking similarities with which we must deal.

In this ancient Babylonian epic, the hero, Gilgamesh, set out to find the secret of eternal life. After many adventures, he found the only man who had ever been given immortality, Utnapishtim. He had been granted immortality because he survived the flood and told its story to Gilgamesh. According to the narrative, Ea (a goddess) warned him that the gods were about to destroy all humanity. There was no reason for the flood other than the whim of the gods and no reason for Ea's warning to Utnapishtim. He was told to make an ark and to take upon it the seed of every living thing. The dimensions of the ark were given, but it was to be deceptively constructed, so that no one would know what he was doing.

Then the flood came. However, the storms got so out of hand that "the gods cowered like dogs and crouched in distress."[1] Not having been wise enough to realize in advance just how great a destruction they were sending, the gods sat down and wept over the destruction of humanity. Finally, the flood abated and the ark rested. Utnapishtim sent forth a dove, but she returned. The he sent forth a swallow, but she also returned. Finally, he sent forth a raven who did not return. Utnapishtim emerged from the ark and offered sacrifice to the gods. The gods, in the meantime, had discovered that without human beings to offer them sacrifices, they were about to starve. However, as the smoke of Utnapishtim's sacrifice ascended,

> The gods smelled the savor,
> the gods smelled the sweet savor.
> The gods gathered like flies over the sacrificer.[2]

The chief god, however, was unhappy that anyone had escaped the flood. The other gods accused him of being unjust. As a result, Utnatpishtim was given partial divinity, being made two-thirds god and one-third man and was granted immortality.

The epic has far more verbal similarities and correspondences in detail with the Genesis flood story than the *Enuma Elish* does with the creation account. There is clearly a direct relationship. However, the differences are very significant. In the Genesis account, there was a moral reason for the Flood, God was always in control, God did not need sacrifices for nourishment, and there was no deception or change of purpose in the process. Furthermore, there is no similarity between the names of Noah and Utnapishtim. Other details also are unlike. Both accounts appear to be variations of some yet more ancient account. The major differences between the stories are theological. Once again, Israel seems to have been proclaiming the sovereignty of its God along with His wisdom, purpose, power, and holiness. The ultimate revelation appears not to be the story itself, which the Hebrew people already possessed, but the nature of the God who was sovereign.

The sad end of the Flood narrative is that sin was still present. Noah exhibited the sins of the flesh (9:21). Ham, on the other hand, exhibited the sin of the mind, the sin of pride, as he went out and ridiculed his father through gossip (v. 22). Ham was not cursed but Canaan, the son of Ham. Further, God did not curse, but Noah. This was not so much a prediction as a statement of fact: Any son is cursed who has a father like Ham.

E. Rebellion, the same old story (11:1-26)
    1.   Babel, a refusal to obey (11:1-9)
    2.   The narrowing focus (11:10-26)

With the Tower of Babel, the stage is fully set for the great history of redemption. The setting for the Babel narrative is clearly the land of Babylon. Probably, the tower has some relation to the great ziggurats of the Babylonian plain. The attempt of mankind was to deliberately disobey the command of God to "fill the earth" (9:1). The people wished to avoid being scattered over the whole earth, while at the same time desiring to make "a name for themselves" (11:4). The Genesis author was actually poking fun at the best which they could do, for when they had built their tallest tower, God had to come down to see it. With the confusion of languages, the people feared one another and scattered abroad. Refusing to cover the earth in loving obedience, they covered it out of fear of one another.

Having failed to purge sin by flood, God set forth to deal with it in another way. At this point, the focus of Genesis narrows from all humanity to the family of Shem (the Semites), to the clan of Terah (the father of Abraham), and ultimately to one man, Abraham (the father of the Hebrew people).

  II. Abraham: faith's response (11:27 to 25:18)
    A. Faith's initial response (11:27 to 12:9)
        1.   Abraham's family (11:27-32)
        2.   God's call and promise (12:1-3)
        3.   Abraham's obedient faith (12:4-9)

The name used for Abraham at this point in Genesis is Abram, but to avoid confusion throughout this section *Abraham* shall be used. The call of Abraham begins the great drama of God's redemption of humanity. God called Abraham to make a journey without knowing the ultimate end of that journey. In point of fact, we can say that the ultimate end of Abraham's journey was not reached until the cross. Archaeological studies appear to show that large numbers of Amorites and other peoples were migrating at the time from the Mesopotamian Valley into the territory of Syria. Abraham made the journey as a venture of faith, going in direct response to his understanding of the call of God.

God promised to do for Abraham what the people of Babel had sought to do for themselves, make his "name great." More importantly, God demanded that Abraham must "be a blessing" wherever he went. Abraham took all of his possessions and his entire family with him. He set out to follow the God who called him. Such is the nature of true faith. "By faith Abraham obeyed when he was called to go out to a place which he was to receive as an inheritance; and he went out, not knowing where he was to go" (Heb. 11:8).

Abraham did not know where he was going until he arrived in the central hill country of Canaan. The time of Abraham's migration is generally assumed to be shortly after 2000 BC. The people of Canaan had not settled in the central hill country, for they were not yet able to build cisterns which could hold enough water for cities to survive the long dry season. When he became aware that he had reached the end of his journey, he established an altar and worshiped God. The building of altars and the establishment of shrines reveal Abraham's deep religiosity, another confirmation of the fact that his pilgrimage was different from that of those around him.

    B. Faith's early trials (12:10 to 14:24)
        1.   Wanderings and fear in Egypt (12:10 to 13:1)
        2.   Confrontation with Lot (13:2-18)
           a. Crowding and conflict (13:2-7)
           b. A generous offer (13:8-13)
           c. God's promise renewed and enlarged (13:14-18)
        3.   Conflict and victory (14:1-24)
           a. Crisis in the plain (14:1-12)
           b. Abraham's act of rescue (14:13-16)
           c. Abraham's worship of God (14:17-24)
    C. God's covenant with Abraham (15:1-21)
        1.   Abraham's anxiety (15:1-6)

2.   Preparation for worship (15:7-11)
3.   God's promises (15:12-16)
4.   Covenant: the gift of land (15:17-21)

The biblical authors never tried to hide their heroes' weaknesses and failings. Abraham, the great father of faith, in his journey to Egypt came off a poor second in comparison with Pharaoh. Abraham's personal fear led him to deal with his wife in a manner for which there was no excuse. For all of his greatness, Abraham was still a man, subject to temptation and the victim of his own selfishness and fear.

In dealing with his nephew Lot, Abraham showed a generous spirit, allowing Lot to choose his pasturing area, when the patriarchal authority plainly gave Abraham that privilege. Further, when Lot's choice caused him to become a captive of the four kings, Abraham risked his life and his possessions to rescue Lot and the people of the plain. That victory was not the source of pride to Abraham but became the basis of a renewed and continued worship of God. Genesis 14 has often been used by scholars as the basis for attempting to determine a specific date in history for Abraham. These attempts have to this time proven quite futile.

At this point, Abraham's faith in God's promise that his descendants would one day be "a great nation" (12:2) was apparently beginning to waver. He was still childless. God repeated His promise and made a covenant with Abraham which included both the promise of offspring and the gift of land (15:5, 18). This was the first of a series of covenants God made with Israel. This one ultimately gave them the most problem because they prided themselves on being descendants of Abraham but forgot their covenant obligations (cf. Luke 3:8).

D. The onward pilgrimage of faith (16:1 to 21:34)
1.   Abraham and Hagar: when faith wavers (16:1-16)
a.   Human connivings (16:1-6)
b.   Divine mercy (16:7-14)
c.   Ishmael's birth (16:15-16)

2. Circumcision: the covenant seal (17:1-27)
   a. The covenant renewed (17:1-8)
   b. The covenant sealed (17:9-14)
   c. God's promise of Isaac (17:15-21)
   d. An obedient response (17:22-27)
3. The Divine visit (18:1 to 19:38)
   a. God's visit to Abraham (18:1-33)
      (1) Renewal of the promise (18:1-15)
      (2) Announcement of judgment on Sodom (18:16-21)
      (3) Abraham's intercession for Sodom (18:22-33)
   b. Destruction of Sodom and Gomorrah (19:1-38)
      (1) Lot welcomes the angels (19:1-11)
      (2) Deliverance offered (19:12-23)
      (3) Lot's escape (19:24-29)
      (4) Origin of the Moabites and the Ammonites (19:30-38)
4. Wanderings and fear in Gerar (20:1-18)
5. Conflict in the family (21:1-21)
   a. Isaac's birth (21:1-21)
   b. Ishmael and Hagar sent forth (21:8-14)
   c. God's mercy on the helpless (21:15-21)
6. The covenant of brotherhood (21:22-34)

Numerous practices reflected in the patriarchal material in Genesis have been identified as normal customs of the era. Many documents from the site of ancient Nuzi (in northeast Mesopotamia) clarify these practices. Provision was made for a childless couple to adopt an heir who would serve them, bury them, and inherit their possessions. However, if a son were born, the adopted son had to give up all claim to the estate. Further, if a woman were barren, she could provide her husband with a female slave to bear a child in her stead. However, that law required that if the natural wife later bore a child, she could not send the handmaid away. That was probably the basis for Abraham's fear recorded in Genesis 21:11-13.

With the introduction of the rite of circumcision, the covenant with Abraham was renewed. At this time Abraham's name was changed from the original *Abram* to the more familiar *Abraham*. In the ancient Near East, a person's name was more than just the title by which he was called. The name was considered to be a revelation of a person's nature and/or character. Furthermore, one who changed a person's name was considered to be sovereign over the person and to have the power or authority to change the person's character. Sarah's name was also changed from the original *Sarai* at the that time.

Some scholars are concerned about the events in Genesis 20:1-18, where Abraham pulls the same stunt with Abimelech of Gerar that he pulled with Pharaoh in Egypt. This is further compounded by Isaac later repeating the same trick on Abimelech (cf. 12:10-20; 20:1-18; 26:1-11). One suggestion has been made that Abraham did it in Egypt and that Isaac tried it with Abimelech and that somewhere along the way the two traditions got interwoven into the Abraham-Abimelech narrative. That is quite possible, but the other could also have happened, particularly if one assumes that there were two Abimelechs, a father and a son by the same name, which was not an uncommon practice in the ancient Near East.

In Genesis 21:15-21, God is portrayed as being very compassionate toward Ishmael, Abraham's child by Hagar. This is a clear evidence for the divine origin of this material, for Hebrew racial pride would not have normally allowed for such concern toward their archrivals, the Ishmaelites.

    E. Faith continues to follow (22:1 to 25:18)
        1.   Faith's greatest test (22:1-24)
            a. The test proposed (22:1-2)
            b. An obedient response (22:3-8)
            c. God's provision (22:9-14)
            d. The promise restated (22:15-19)
            e. Abraham's family (22:20-24)
        2.   Sarah's death (23:1-20)
        3.   A wife for Isaac (24:1-67)
            a. The servant commissioned (24:1-9)

The greatest test for Abraham's faith came with the command to sacrifice Isaac. Those who find a problem with God requiring this kind of test of a man have proposed that this was Abraham's understanding of what God demanded rather than what God actually commanded. Others have found a greater problem with that approach and accept the passage as quite literal, saying that God was not asking of Abraham that which he was not also going to ask of Himself. By getting so involved in the theological controversy, we miss the great human dimension of faith. Either way, Abraham believed that God was asking him to make a human sacrifice of Isaac. Yet through Isaac, Abraham was to have descendants (cf. 15:4; 18:14; 21:1-3). This is the great dilemma of faith, far more difficult to believe than that God commanded the sacrifice. If Abraham had not believed this was God's command, there would have been no test. The whole passage emphasizes that Abraham dared to believe that he could both obey God and trust God.

A second dimension to the thrust of this passage lies with Isaac. Old Abraham could not have bound the strong young Isaac without the son's willful submission. The last minute deliverance of Isaac from Abraham's knife must have made an indelible impression upon Isaac's subsequent walk with God. He had willingly looked death in the face and had been delivered.

Tradition identifies the mountains of Moriah with the Mount Moriah where the Temple was built (2 Chron. 3:1). If this is so, then the place where God did not allow Abraham to offer his only son was the region where He was to later offer His only Son.

In old age, Abraham fulfilled the last responsibility of a

father by providing a wife for Isaac. Not wishing to run the
risk of polluting Isaac's faith by a Canaanite marriage, a
wife was sought from among Abraham's kinsmen in Haran.
Typical marriage customs are reflected with the negotiations being carried out without the son having any part. It
is also typical that the love which developed between Isaac
and Rebekah developed after the marriage rather than
before.

   III. Isaac: a quiet faith (25:19 to 28:9)
      A. The birth of Esau and Jacob (25:19-26)
         1. Prayer for a childless wife (25:19-21)
         2. The birth of twins (25:22-26)
      B. Beginnings of conflict (25:27-34)
         1. The parents' follies (25:27-29)
         2. Attitudes toward the birthright (25:29-34)
      C. Steps in Isaac's pilgrimage (26:1-35)
         1. Fear and deliverance in Gerar (26:1-11)
         2. Days of prosperity (26:12-16)
         3. Searching for peace (26:17-22)
         4. God's promise to Isaac (26:23-25)
         5. A covenant of brotherhood (26:26-33)
         6. Esau's marriage (26:34-35)
      D. Jacob's theft of the patriarchal blessing (27:1 to
         28:9)
         1. Isaac's preparations (27:1-4)
         2. Rebekah's preparations (27:5-17)
         3. Jacob's deception (27:18-25)
         4. The blessing on Jacob (27:26-29)
         5. Esau's heartbreak (27:30-38)
         6. The blessing on Esau (27:39-40)
         7. Esau's hatred (27:41)
         8. Jacob's flight for his life (27:42 to 28:5)
         9. Esau's rebellion (28:6-9)

Isaac had the misfortune to be sandwiched between a great
father and a great son. With less illustrious relatives on
either side, he might have come down to us as a more memorable figure. Throughout the Genesis narratives, he shows
up as a man of quiet faith. It may be that this was the result

of his near sacrifice. We also see him as a man of prayer, interceding for his barren wife. In the Old Testament and in the ancient Near East, for a woman not to have children, especially not to have male children, was considered tragic. The prayer was answered with the births of Jacob and Esau.

The basis of future problems and conflict quickly showed up in parental partiality (25:28). Future conflict was further fueled by Jacob's scheming to obtain the birthright. According to the customs of that time, the birthright carried at least three blessings and responsibilities. First, the eldest son inherited twice as much of the family estate than any other son. With only two sons, the birthright carried with it a two-thirds share of the family property, so the birthright meant wealth. Second, the birthright meant that the eldest son became the leader of the family upon the death of the father, so the birthright meant authority. Third, the birthright carried with it the spiritual headship of the family or clan, so the birthright meant power. Jacob clearly valued these while Esau did not. The material from Nuzi also records a man selling his birthright to his brother. Jacob, however, offered no price of value, simply taking advantage of his brother's weakness and lack of appreciation.

The ongoing narrative reveals Isaac as a man of peace. Again and again he did everything in his power to avoid confrontation with the people of Gerar.

Isaac's great failure, however, rested in his partiality to Esau. Modern readers have a difficult time understanding the theft of the patriarchal blessing. In ancient times, words, once spoken, were considered to have a force and an existence in and of themselves. Thus, when Jacob, with Rebekah's plotting, deceived Isaac and got the blessing, there was no way by which it could be recalled. This was true even though it had been received by deception.

When Esau returned home from hunting, the deception was revealed. With the broad blessing which Isaac had given to Jacob, there was little left to bestow upon Esau. Esau's hatred of Jacob is quite understandable. Rebekah plotted to send Jacob away for a while to spare his life. She died before he returned home. At the same time, realizing that Jacob had been removed from his grasp by the pretense of fear that he should marry a Canaanite, Esau showed his rebellion toward his parents by doing precisely that.

IV. Jacob: the flight which discovers (28:10 to 35:29)
   A. Confronted by God (28:10-22)
      1. The dream at Bethel (28:10-12)
      2. God's promised grace (28:13-15)
      3. Jacob's responses to God (28:16-22)
         a. Awe (28:16-17)
         b. Worship (28:18-19)
         c. Commitment (28:20-22)
   B. Jacob's family affairs (29:1 to 31:55)
      1. Welcome at Laban's home (29:1-14)
      2. Jacob's marriages (29:15-30)
      3. Rivalry between Leah and Rachel (29:31 to 30:24)
      4. Jacob's growing wealth (30:25-43)
      5. Flight from Laban (31:1-55)
         a. Loss of favor (31:1-16)
         b. The secret departure (31:17-21)
         c. Laban's pursuit (31:22-32)
         d. Rachel's theft of the household gods (31:33-35)
         e. The covenant of brotherhood (31:36-54)
         f. A peaceful parting (31:55)

When Jacob fled to Haran, he must have felt like he was going to a foreign country and strange people, even though he was fleeing to his mother's family. He was in terror for his life. In that situation, he was less self-sufficient and more open to a meeting with God. In Jacob's dream at Bethel, the angels were "ascending and descending" upon the ladder (28:12). That is the reverse of what we would have expected. Angels were considered the messengers of God. This probably means Jacob's prayers were ascending to God and divine answers were being returned. This was Jacob's initial experience with God. He established Bethel as a personal shrine. While certainly not a life-changing experience, it was at least a first step toward such.

While sojourning with Laban, Jacob obtained two wives and much wealth. However, he discovered that Laban was also a schemer. In the end, having a new fear for his life, he was forced to flee secretly. At this point, we discover that Jacob's wife Rachel was also cut from the same scheming cloth, for she stole her father's household gods. The material from ancient Nuzi helps us understand that household gods were more than mere idols for worship. The possession of the household gods of a family carried with it the leadership of the family. Thus Rachel's theft was intended to give her husband authority over her brothers. Furthermore, when Rachel's father caught up with them, Rachel again demonstrated her capacity for scheming by hiding the gods so that they were not discovered. Jacob and his family continued their homeward trek. A new danger now confronted him.

2. A return to Bethel (35:16-29)
   a. Purification (35:1-4)
   b. Pilgrimage (35:5-8)
   c. Promise (35:9-13)
   d. Praise (35:14-15)
3. Bethel's aftermath (35:16-29)
   a. Rachel's death (35:16-21)
   b. Jacob's sons (35:22-26)
   c. Reunion and grief over Isaac's death (35:27-29)

One of the more fascinating developments in the Jacob narratives focuses upon Jacob's reunion with Esau. The message brought to Jacob that Esau was coming accompanied by four hundred men frightened him. When Jacob again reached the end of his rope insofar as his own machinations were concerned, he turned to God. We stand on holy ground when we read of Jacob's wrestling with God all night. This was clearly what happened, for at the end he said, "I have seen God face to face, and yet my life is preserved" (32:30). At this time Jacob's name was changed. His wrestling with God finally changed Jacob's nature. That was the time of ultimate transformation for Jacob.

God's blessing upon Jacob did not alter the situation which he faced from Esau, however. Jacob was still forced to face the brother whom he had wronged and whom he feared so greatly. God's transformation of life does not change our history. Suprisingly, when Esau finally came, he greeted Jacob, not with hatred and vengeance, but with forgiveness and mercy. Such an attitude from Esau brought to Jacob's memory his recent experience with God. Forgiveness is an attribute of God.

Jacob's experience with God did not deliver him from the tragedies, cares, and concerns of ordinary life. Following his reconciliation with Esau the Bible tells the tragic story of the rape of his daughter, Dinah. That was followed by the brutal and deceitful vengeance of his sons. Further, there was the death of his beloved Rachel and, ultimately, of his father Isaac. Being properly related to God does not deliver us from the cares of life, it offers the strength to bear them.

The material in the latter section of Genesis (37:1 to 50:26) is considered by many to be the best example of historical narrative in the book. As a literary work, it ranks as one of the greatest of all times. It has frequently been pointed out as an excellent example of the best interweaving of the various strata of tradition within Genesis. The basic framework is usually identified as priestly. The most committed literary critics find it more and more difficult to separate the basic material into the two major strands, the Judean and the north Israelite, however. Much of the normal criteria for making such divisions just do not appear here. The name *Yahweh* occurs very infrequently in these chapters. In those places where it does, the style and theology are indistinguishable from the rest of the material. The normal approach such scholars make in analyzing this material is to stress the so-called contradictions within some of the narratives. Other scholars vehemently deny that there are any contradictions here. Regardless of the analysis which one makes of this material, one must deal with its obvious unity. The narrative was put into the form in which we now have it by a master story teller. Our task is to understand it and to interpret it as it now exists.

One of the more fascinating aspects of this block of material is the forceful emphasis upon the absolute sovereignty of God over the affairs of people. Yet this emphasis is made without the frequent use of the name of God. The emphasis stresses that God can use the acts of people with or without their knowledge and certainly without their approval.

The Joseph narratives bear a significant relation to Hebrew and ancient Near Eastern wisdom materials. (These are discussed in more detail in the chapter on "Wisdom.") This block of material may have been used as an instrument for teaching the value of a life lived under God's moral standards in a world which is basically immoral.

The basic story is one of parental failure (Jacob's partiality), youthful ambition (Joseph's dreams), and sibling rivalry. The immediate result of the interweaving of these plots winds up with Joseph serving as a slave in Egypt. Joseph's faithful service took him to a place of responsibility within his master's house, only to be punished for his own faithfulness to his God and to his master. Moving from the slave quarters to the prison, Joseph's diligence and faithfulness were again rewarded with advancement. He had the opportunity to interpret the dreams of two of the servants of Pharaoh. Yet when his interpretations came true, the one whom he had befriended forgot him. The immediate reaction at this point might be that it doesn't make any difference if a person is good, life is just unfair. But the story wasn't over yet.

The ongoing story of Joseph brought a turn in his fortunes with the dreams of Pharaoh. In the ancient Near East, dreams were considered to be a means by which the gods revealed their plans and purposes to people. Israel was no different from the other nations at this point. When Joseph was able to interpret the dreams of Pharaoh, foretelling years of plenty followed by the years of famine, he was obviously qualified to be placed by Pharaoh in charge of preparation for those years.

The question is sometimes raised as to whether we have any extrabiblical record of Joseph's service as prime minister of Egypt. While there is no direct reference to his ministry there, there is a hint of such. Joseph may have risen to power during the reign of the Hyksos, a Semitic people who ruled over Egypt from about 1750 to about 1550 BC. Since they were Semites like Joseph, such a time would have afforded a good setting for his rise to power. In addition, before the reign of the Hyksos, the Pharaoh ruled over a nation made up of numerous small landholders. After the reign of the Hyksos, the Pharaoh himself owned all of the land of Egypt and the people were essentially his serfs. That would fit in well with the biblical portrait of the Egyptians selling their possessions, their land, and finally themselves to Pharaoh in order to survive the famine.

Throughout the narrative of Joseph's dealings with his brothers, three features stand out. First, the magnificent plea of Judah that he should be allowed to substitute himself for Benjamin reveals a love almost bordering on that which Jesus has shown for us. Second, Joseph's forgiveness of his brothers shows the same kind of love. Perhaps of greatest importance was Joseph's recognition of the hand of God in all that had happened to him. Three times he reaffirmed this belief. "God sent me before you to preserve life" (45:5). "God sent me before you to preserve for you a remnant on earth" (45:7). "You meant evil against me, but God meant it for good" (50:20).

With the reunion between Jacob and Joseph and the settlement of the clan of Jacob in Egypt, the narrative draws to a close. The stage has been consummately set for Israel's great drama of redemption: the Exodus from Egypt. In the fifty chapters of Genesis the stage has been set for all the subsequent development of Israel's faith and for the ultimate development of the faith of the New Testament. Both historically and theologically, the writer has led us to a place of readiness and expectation in an unmatched literary masterpiece.

Notes

1. Alexander Heidel, *The Gilgamesh Epic and Old Testament Parallels*, p. 85.
2. Ibid., p. 87.

8

Exodus

The Hebrews called the Book of Exodus by the opening words, *We'elleh shemoth,* or "And These Are the Names." This was occasionally shortened simply to *Shemoth,* "Names." Our more common English name for the book came to us from the LXX by way of the Latin Vulgate. The LXX based its name upon the Greek word *exodos* which appears in Exodus 19:1.

The book appears to have two purposes, an historical and a theological one. Historically, the book tells how the people of Israel were liberated from their indentured servitude in Egypt and were brought to Sinai, the mountain of God. Theologically, the book sets forth the constitution of Israel as the people of God. It has two focal points: (1) God's redemption of Israel as a result of His free choice of them to be His people, and (2) His uniting Himself to them through the covenant at Sinai. These two themes serve as the basis for all of the rest of Israel's faith. Both of these emphases sprang from God's love. He loved Israel enough to choose them. That was His grace. He also loved them enough to commit Himself to them. That was His loyalty.

The ultimate theme of the book is clearly the sovereignty of Yahweh over His universe. Roy Honeycutt has pointed this out very clearly in his analysis of the four main sections of the book. He describes its contents as follows.

1. Yahweh, Lord of History (1:1 to 7:13)
2. Yahweh, Lord of Creation (7:14 to 18:27)
3. Yahweh, Lord of Man (19:1 to 24:14)
4. Yahweh, Lord of Worship (24:15 to 40:38)

The author of Exodus clearly set forth his faith that God is in ultimate control of everything.

The question of the authorship of the book revolves around the same issues considered in Chapters 5 and 6. Exodus clearly continues the story of Genesis. The fact that it begins with "and" shows that the Genesis narrative was presupposed and that Exodus was going on with it. Those who pursue the identification of traditions see the priestly hand in the legal and worship material of Exodus 25 to 31 and 35 to 40. The rest of the material is considered to be an interweaving of the early northern and southern traditions. On the other hand, here, as in Genesis, those who make this approach find less and less consensus in how to divide this narrative material. Those who oppose the approach maintain that the difference between the narrative material and the legal material requires the literary differences which can be noted and, therefore, reject the whole idea.

There is no question but that much of the material comes directly from Moses and the era which it reflects. On the other hand, there may be some later additions to the material. The book reveals itself as a literary unit and is tied to what went before in Genesis and to what followed after in Leviticus and Numbers. The fact that the basic structure of Genesis, formed around *toledhoth,* is not carried forward into Exodus may be evidence for a different author. At the same time, the final editing of the book places it as a connected part of an ongoing literary work.

The Date of the Exodus Event

The most significant historical problem related to the Book of Exodus is the dating of the Exodus event. Any conclusion must thoroughly consider all the available evidence.

The Exodus event has been tied to the date of the building of the Temple. "In the four hundred and eightieth year after the people of Israel came out of the land of Egypt, in the fourth year of Solomon's reign over Israel, . . . he began to build the house of the Lord" (1 Kings 6:1). The usual assumption based upon historical data from the Old Testament is that Solomon's construction of the Temple began between 966 and 960 BC. This would place the date of the Exodus between 1446 and 1440 BC. This conclusion is made less certain, however, when we note that the LXX version of this verse puts the Exodus 440 years earlier than the Temple.

Before considering other biblical data, archaeological data needs to be added to our considerations. Explorations in the regions of Edom and Moab demonstrate that there were no significant settlements in these regions prior to 1300 BC. Thus before that date Moses and the Israelites would not have had to ask permission to go through those lands; opposition in these regions could only have been faced after 1300 BC (cf. Num. 20:14-21; 21:4,13,21-23). Further, if the Exodus were about 1440 BC, then the entrance into Canaan would have been about 1400 BC, following the forty years in the wilderness. Yet there is no significant evidence of a major influx of people at that time. (The Amarna letters do reflect some problems with insurgents called Habiru' about that time, but there is no evidence of any significant military destructions from that period.) The earlier claim by John Garstang that Jericho fell about that time has been shown by subsequent investigation to have been a misinterpretation of the data. However, there is significant data for a major influx of peoples into Canaan about 1230 to 1210 BC. The new culture, furthermore, was significantly more primitive than the one it replaced. Finally, a victory stela of Pharaoh Merneptah indicates that a group of people called Israel was in western Palestine about 1220 BC. That group was clearly identified as being neither a nation nor a kingdom, but a loosely organized group of people. This is what we might expect if they had just entered the land, but not what we would have expected if they had been in the land more than 150 years.

We are faced with a concern which has been dealt with in at least four different ways. Some have ignored it. Obviously, this does not offer a solution. Others have made the assumption that either the biblical or the archaeological evidence is wrong. Such decisions are often based upon theology rather than upon a serious study of the data. This is not fair either to the biblical material or to the archaeological data. A third proposal has been to suggest that the LXX data as a late version of the Hebrew data is in error and can be disregarded. Ignoring this, then it is suggested that the concern does not lie so much with the data as with our understanding of it. Some scholars have suggested that 480 is 12 times 40. The number 40 is used frequently in the Bible simply as a large, round number. It is also demonstrable that 40 years is sometimes used as a synonym for a generation. Perhaps the biblical author received a tradition that the Temple was begun 12 generations following the Exodus. If a generation were more like 25 years, then the Exodus would be dated about 1260 to 1280 BC and the conquest would have been 40 years later, putting the conquest precisely where it fits the archaeological data.

A fourth solution has been proposed, which is also worthy of consideration. More than one group may have left Egypt and have entered the land at different times. Joshua appears to have found some people already in the land who were related to Israel (cf. Josh. 8:30-35; 24:1-28). The archaeological data could reflect the entrance of one group into Canaan while the dating of the Temple could be based upon a different group which infiltrated the land more peacefully. This interpretation of data is more probable when we consider that the biblical narrative plainly tells only the details which are significant to its main purpose. We would never know, for example, from reading Exodus 2:1-2 that Moses had an older brother and sister. The biblical narrative at that point is only interested in what was happening to Moses.

Tied up with the date of the Exodus is the date of the entrance into the land of Egypt. Exodus simply states: "The time that the people of Israel dwelt in Egypt was four hundred and thirty years" (12:40). This becomes confused by Genesis which says: "They will be oppressed for four hundred years. . . . And they shall come back here in the fourth generation" (15:13-16). Paul made a statement which further clouds the issue when he indicated that the law came 430 years after the promises to Abraham (Gal. 3:17). In addition, the period from Jacob through Eleazar appears to be only seven generations (Ex. 6:13-26). While the data appears to be confusing, our understanding of it may be confused by the possibility that more than one group departed Egypt and, therefore, part of the data may be referring to some departure other than the one under Moses. Any conclusion as to the interpretation of this data must be given with hesitancy and with the acknowledgment that we approach the problem with great gaps in our knowledge.

I think the Exodus from Egypt led by Moses occurred about 1280 to 1260 BC. The entrance into Canaan under Joshua is to be dated forty years thereafter. The descent into Egypt with Jacob, Joseph, and his brothers probably is to be dated about 1710 to 1690 BC. Furthermore, probably more than one group departed from Egypt, which might account for the nature of the confusing chronological data.

Two things must be acknowledged. Our historical interpretations at this point are not absolutely certain. Furthermore, our lack of chronological certainty does not in any way hinder our understanding of the ultimate faith which was proclaimed by Israel in her record of these events.

The Nature of Old Testament Miracles

To some, a major concern in understanding the Old Testament in general and the Book of Exodus in particular has to do with the nature of Old Testament miracles. The most common terms applied to these are *signs* and *wonders*. A sign is something which points to a meaning beyond itself. God's miracles have meaning far beyond the actual event.

It appears in general that three things were needed to have a miracle in the Old Testament. First, an event was necessary. Miracles were not the figment of a writer's imagination or a dream or a vision; they were actual events. Second, the event had to occur at the right time and place. The parting of the sea would have been of no value three days earlier or twenty miles away. Third, an inspired interpreter had to have been present to say that the event was done by God. Some events were open to other interpretations. The Egyptians duplicated the turning of the water into blood, either by sleight of hand or some other means. I, for one, am not willing to grant that the magicians could perform a miracle. But what God did through Moses was a miracle, for it happened at the right time and place and the interpreter was present to point out that it was the hand of God.

The Content of the Book

I. Preparations which point the way (1:1 to 2:25)
   A. A time and a place in history (1:1-22)
      1. Those who descended into Egypt (1:1-6)
      2. Selfish fruitfulness (1:7)
      3. A time of oppression (1:8-22)
         a. Oppression by forced labor (1:8-14)
         b. Oppression by extermination (1:15-22)
   B. The fruits of love (2:1-10)
      1. The love of a man and a woman (2:1-2*a*)
      2. The love of a mother for her child (2:2*b*-3)
      3. The love of a sister for a brother (2:4)
      4. The love of a woman for the helpless (2:5-6)
      5. The love for one's enemy (2:7-9)
      6. The love of an adoptive parent (2:10)
   C. Trying to do God's work man's way (2:11-22)
      1. The wrong way to do right (2:11-15*a*)
      2. Surviving instead of serving (2:15*b*-22)
         a. Flight from punishment (2:15*b*)
         b. The wrong kind of power (2:16-17)
         c. Settling down in the wrong place (2:18-21)
         d. A longing heart (2:22)
   D. God's presence with His people (2:23-25)
      1. Change without change (2:23)
      2. Divine awareness of human need (2:24-25)

The Exodus narrative begins where Genesis left off, with the descent of the family of Jacob into Egypt. The living was easy for the Hebrews in the region of Goshen, located in the fertile delta of the Nile. The people of Israel prospered and multiplied, something which was considered in ancient times (and frequently in modern times) to be a sign of the blessing and approval of God. The only thing wrong was that they had stayed in Egypt where the living was easy instead of returning to Canaan where they were supposed to have been.

Out of fear of potential problems, the Egyptians began a systematic oppression of Israel. Inserted into the narrative of this brutal oppression is a fascinating story of human love, all sorts of tender human love. Although the name of God is not mentioned in 2:1-10, the love of God was undergirding the entire process.

From any approach to the story of the birth of Moses, he appears to have been the first child born to his parents (Ex. 2:2), but we quickly discover that he had both an older sister and a brother (2:4; 4:14; 7:7). Any historian finds it impossible to record every detail of everything which happened. The biblical writers normally appear to deal only with those details which are quite significant to the story which they are telling.

After Moses reached adulthood, he sought to intervene as a deliverer for the Hebrews. He was trying to do the ultimate will of God, but he sought to do it the wrong way. Moses' impetuous act made him a murderer and forced him to flee from Egypt, thus apparently closing a door to any future usefulness in the deliverance of Israel from Egypt. God finally had to overcome Moses' own folly in order to use him as an agent of deliverance.

II. Revelations which transform life (3:1 to 7:13)
    A. When God calls (3:1 to 4:17)
        1. The Divine confrontation (3:1-6)
            a. The burning bush (3:1-3)
            b. The first revelation (3:4-6)
        2. The Divine call (3:7-12)
            a. A statement of purpose (3:7-9)
            b. God's commission (3:10)
            c. Moses' objection (3:11)
            d. The sign of faith (3:12)

3. The Divine nature (3:13-22)
    a. The God who is (3:13-17)
    b. The God who acts (3:18-22)
4. Evidences of God's presence (4:1-9)
5. Excuses which do not excuse (4:10-17)
B. The great mission (4:18 to 5:21)
    1. The journey begun (4:18-26)
    2. Israel's early faith in Moses (4:27-31)
    3. Pharaoh's rejection (5:1-14)
        a. The demand rejected (5:1-4)
        b. Israel's labor increased (5:5-14)
    4. Israel turns on Moses (5:15-21)
C. The call reaffirmed (5:22 to 6:13)
    1. Encouragement for faltering faith (5:22 to 6:1)
    2. The call renewed (6:2-9)
    3. The recommissioning (6:10-13)
D. The mission renewed (6:14 to 7:13)
    1. The religious heritage (6:14-27)
    2. God's purpose in Moses' life (6:28 to 7:7)
    3. God's power in Moses' hand (7:8-13)

The two most significant features of the call of Moses direct attention to the nature of God and the humanity of Moses. Moses does not appear as the great tower of faith here which he later became. In fact, he is seen as a rather weak figure, trying to avoid having his life disturbed by God's intervention. Moses believed that he was a "wanted man" in Egypt. He did not know that the king of Egypt who had sought to execute him was now dead (2:15, 23). Even though he sought every way possible to avoid an affirmative response to God's call, when he finally agreed to return to Egypt, he did so still believing that his life was in real danger.

The major theological truth rests in the revelation of the nature of God. Some scholars wonder whether the name Yahweh was first revealed to Moses or whether it had been known earlier and this was a revelation of the character which the name revealed. Some Bible students have interpreted the occasions when the name *Yahweh* was used in the earlier narratives as anachronisms, a reading back of the divine name into earlier situations. However, the name of Moses' mother, Jochebed, is another matter (Ex. 6:20; Num. 26:59). It is inconceivable that an individual's name would later be modified by the addition of the divine name. *Jochebed* means "Yah [or Yahweh] is glory [or glorious]." Thus Moses was apparently asking for a revelation of what the personal name of God meant, rather than what it was. Yahweh is the God who was, who is, and who always will be.

A minor feature of the call experience has to do with the nature of "the angel of the Lord" (3:2). In the Old Testament, "*the* angel of the Lord" (author's italics) always seems to refer in some way to an extension of God. "The angel of the Lord" appeared to Moses, but God spoke to him.

III. The plagues: confrontations which demand decision (7:14 to 13:22)
   A. God's signs and wonders (7:14 to 10:29)
      1. Victory over the Nile (7:14-24)
      2. Victory over the entire worship system (7:25 to 10:20)
         a. The frogs proliferate (7:25 to 8:15)
         b. The gnats sting (8:16-19)
         c. The flies swarm (8:30-32)
         d. The cattle die (9:1-7)
         e. The boils hurt (9:8-12)
         f. The hail destroys (9:13-35)
         g. The locusts devour (10:1-20)
      3. Victory over the sun: darkness (10:21-29)
      4. Victory over Pharaoh: the Passover (11:1 to 13:22)
         a. A warning issued (11:1-10)
         b. Instructions for the Passover (12:1-13)
         c. The Feast of Unleavened Bread (12:14-20)
         d. The Passover instituted (12:21-28)
         e. The night of death (12:29-42)
         f. Participants in the Passover (12:43-51)
         g. The divine purposes (13:1-16)
         h. The departure from Egypt (13:17-22)

The narrative of the plagues of Egypt is one of the most carefully written in the entire world of literature. It is exciting reading, directing attention to a very basic plot: A series of major catastrophes befell Egypt which resulted ultimately in the freeing of the Hebrew slaves. This plot is presented according to a careful plan. Just as carefully planned are three subplots which are woven into the basic story.

The plagues themselves are described as signs and wonders, as well as being identified by verbs translated "I will plague" (8:2) or "I will strike" (7:17). The former words point beyond the actual events to their meaning, while the verbal designations focus upon the sudden intensity of the events. *Plague* is really not an accurate description of each of these events. On the other hand, the word has become so much a part of our vocabulary that we shall continue to use it. As we do, it is important to remember that the events were far more than plagues.

The account presents the plagues in three series of three events each, followed by the tenth plague which stands by itself. The first plague of each series is introduced by God commanding Moses to rise early in the morning, confront Pharaoh, and demand the release of Israel (cf. 7:15-16; 8:20; 9:13). The second plague of each series is introduced by the divine command to confront Pharaoh with the demand that the people be sent forth to serve Yahweh (8:1; 9:1; 10:1). The first of each series is announced in the early morning by the river, the second is announced in Pharaoh's palace, and the third always comes without warning. As the narrative progresses, the plagues increase in severity. The tenth plague stands out from the others as both different in nature and the most harsh.

The first of the subplots is the actual confrontation of Yahweh, the God of Israel, and the gods of Egypt. The plagues were neither merely demonstrations of God's power nor were they simply God cruelly playing with the Egyptians. They were a direct confrontation between Yahweh and rival gods. The three chief gods of Egypt were the Nile, the sun, and the pharaoh. Each of the other plagues were aimed either at a specific god of Egypt or at a specific religious practice. In every instance, Yahweh was victorious.

The second subplot calls our attention to the changing reactions of the people of Egypt. The Egyptians were able to imitate the first two plagues, but by the third they began to acknowledge that they could not imitate such power. With the fourth plague, a distinction was made between the Egyptians and Israel. By the end of the eighth plague, the Egyptian people were pleading with Pharaoh to send Israel forth from the land. By the end of the tenth plague, Pharaoh himself thrust them forth.

The third subplot relates to the series of compromises which Moses was pressured to accept. Pharaoh sought to get him to settle for less than God had demanded. Yet throughout the narrative, Moses' loyalty to God, his dedication to his task, and his concern for ultimate victory all shine through. Having once yielded to the divine call, Moses would not settle for anything less than God's will.

With the Passover and the Feast of Unleavened Bread, we face the real probability that two ancient spring festivals, one for shepherds and the other for farmers, may have been used by the Hebrews and filled with new meaning. If this were not the case, remarkable similarities exist between those ancient pagan celebrations and Israel's new ones.

IV. Crises which cripple faith (14:1 to 18:27)
    A. Reaffirmation of God's purpose (14:1-4)
    B. The victory at the sea (14:5 to 15:21)
        1. Pharaoh's pursuit (14:5-9)
        2. Faith's frightened failure (14:10-18)
        3. The divine victory (14:19-29)
        4. The people's response (14:30 to 15:21)
            a. Awe and faith (14:30-31)
            b. The song of Israel (15:1-18)
            c. The song of Miriam (15:19-21)
    C. Problems in the wilderness (15:22 to 18:27)
        1. Water that proved unusable (15:22-27)
        2. Hunger which cramped the soul (16:1-36)
            a. Collapsing with hunger (16:1-3)

      b. The response of God (16:4-8)

      c. The revelation of glory (16:9-12)

      d. Quail and manna (16:13-36)

   3. Thirst which dried the spirit (17:1-7)

   4. Enemies which blocked the path (17:8-16)

   5. Troubles which demanded solution (18:1-27)

      a. Family reunion (18:1-9)

      b. Jethro's worship (18:10-12)

      c. Moses' burden (18:13-16)

      d. Jethro's solution (18:17-27)

Shortly after the Israelites had departed from Egypt, Pharaoh decided to pursue them. The Israelites were penned by the Egyptian forces against the *Yam Suph,* the Sea of Reeds. The earlier translation of the Red Sea is not a proper translation of the Hebrew name. However, too much has been made by numerous commentators about this fact. Although the *Yam Suph* does not translate directly into the Red Sea, the term is sometimes used very plainly for the Red Sea. In any case, Israel was penned against a body of water too large for them to go around, too deep to wade, and deep enough to drown the pursuing army once they were in it.

Following Israel's deliverance, a great victory celebration was held. God had acted to deliver His people.

As the Hebrews went deeper into the wilderness, they were faced with recurring problems of thirst, hunger, and opposition to their progress. So short was their memory of God's power in delivering them that they lost all confidence in Him with each new crisis. Yet God in patience continued to lead and deliver, ultimately bringing them to Sinai.

  V. Surrender which calls for cleansing (19:1-25)

     A. The journey's end (19:1)

     B. Commission and response (19:2-9*a*)

     C. Consecration and preparation (19:9*b*-15)

     D. God's descent to the people (19:16-25)

 VI. Demands which call for obedience (20:1-20)

     A. Introductory words (20:1-2)

     B. Commands relating to God (20:3-11)

The block of material from Exodus 19:1 to 24:14 has come to be called the "Book of the Covenant." Most interpreters agree that it is clearly a unit, presenting the essential covenant commitment between Yahweh and Israel. Aside from literary considerations, a major psychological insight is here. Moses had been told that his ultimate assurance that God was with him would come when he and the people of Israel would "serve God upon this mountain" (3:12). In the light of that, imagine the emotions which must have flooded Moses' consciousness as they drew near to Sinai. It must have been an overwhelming experience.

Another nonliterary concern has to do with the location of Sinai. The more traditional site is at the famed Jebel Musa in the heart of the Sinai, Peninsula. A site more to the north or one right up against the Mediterranean has been suggested as the proper location. A volcanic site on to the east in the region of Midian has also been suggested as the correct one. Until other evidence to the contrary is found, I see no reason for rejecting the more traditional location.

Two items of literary significance need to be considered. The first has to do with the form of the covenant and the other with the date of this block of material. A significant similarity in form exists between the Hebrew covenant and those which were common in the ancient Near East shortly before this time. The suzerainty treaties were entered into between a great king and his vassal. The vassal could not negotiate the covenant; he could only accept it or reject it. Such treaties began with the identification of the great king (cf. "I am the Lord your God," 20:2). Next came a recitation of the historical relations between the suzerain and the vassal (cf. "who brought you out of the land of Egypt, out of the house of bondage," v.2). Following that was normally a prohibition against any other treaties for the vassal (cf. "You shall have no other gods before me," v.3). After that came the stipulations of the treaty (the obligations set forth in the other other Commandments). A list of blessings and curses for keeping or breaking the covenant came next. In addition, the gods of the suzerain and the vassal were called upon as witnesses and the place of safekeeping for the document was specified, usually in the sanctuary of the vassal. Since this covenant was between God and Israel, no other witnesses were required. The other two items are missing here, but the blessings and curses are in the Deuteronomic version (cf. Deut. 27:15 to 28:6). The place of safekeeping was left unspecified, but we know that the covenant was ultimately kept in Israel's Temple.

While every detail is not present, there is enough similarity to make it likely that God used this common form to communicate His revelation to Israel. The form itself announced to Israel and to the world that Yahweh was the great King of Israel. The suzerain was frequently called "king of kings and lord of lords," a title which is certainly familiar to all Christians.

The second literary concern has to do with the date of this block of material. In the days of Wellhausen, scholars assumed that this whole unit was from quite late in Israel's history, had no connection with Moses, and was definitely nonhistorical. However, with the scholars from the early 1930s, it became a matter of faith that the material was quite early and of major importance in the development of Israel. Such are the vagaries of scholarship that some scholars are again questioning the historicity of the material.

What does the evidence say? First, the clear claim is that the material was mediated to Israel by Moses at the direct command of God. If that were not sufficient, consider the fact that in the final approach to God, Moses was a leader along with Aaron, Nadab, Abihu, and seventy other elders (24:1-2). If this had been a postexilic creation, Moses would certainly not have been listed along with the others, for in that period, Moses was considered to be the great towering pillar of faith, not just a prime leader among other leaders. Furthermore, in the sealing of the covenant, the sacrifices were offered by "young men" (24:5). Again, if this had been created by the postexilic priests, they would never have ascribed such honor to anyone but themselves. Finally, the narrative describes these leaders as seeing the God of Israel and living (24:9-11). Again, no postexilic writer would have written such a story because they were so wrapped up in the utter unapproachableness of God. The evidence clearly identifies the narrative as a contemporaneous record of the event as it occurred.

VIII. Worship which demands the best (24:15 to 31:18)
   A. The encounter with God (24:15-18)
   B. The design of the tabernacle (25:1 to 27:21)
      1. The required offerings (25:1-9)
      2. The interior furnishings (25:10-40)
      3. The tabernacle itself (26:1-37)
      4. The altar, courtyard, and lamp oil (27:1-21)
   C. The priestly robes (28:1-43)
   D. The consecration of the priests (29:1-46)
   E. Other worship objects (30:1-38)
      1. The altar of incense (30:1-10)
      2. The census tax for support (30:11-16)
      3. The bronze laver (30:17-21)
      4. The anointing oil (30:22-33)
      5. The incense (30:34-38)
   F. God's skilled craftsmen (31:1-11)
   G. The sabbath observance (31:12-17)
   H. The tables of the testimony (31:18)
IX. Renewal which follows rebellion (32:1 to 34:35)
   A. Rebellion in the presence of God (32:1-35)
      1. The demand for a god (32:1-6)
      2. Judgment and mercy (32:7-14)
      3. A time for decision and meditation (32:15-35)
   B. God's grace and glory (33:1-23)
   C. The covenant restored (34:1-35)
      1. The new experience (34:1-10)
      2. The appeal for purity (34:11-28)
      3. The reflected radiance of God (34:29-35)
X. Obedience which thrills the heart (35:1 to 40:38)
   A. Preparations for beginning (35:1 to 36:7)
   B. Building the worship objects (36:8 to 38:31)
   C. The priestly garments (39:1-31)
   D. Completing the work of God (39:32 to 40:33)
   E. God leads while the people follow (40:34-38)

From a literary standpoint, the most significant feature of this section is that Exodus 35:1 to 40:38 duplicates the material found in Exodus 24:15 to 31:18 with only a slight variations. The first section gives the commands for the worship material and the tabernacle while the latter section describes the actual construction. The verbal identity appears to have been intended to demonstrate that God's commands are to be obeyed precisely as He gives them. This is especially significant when contrasted with Israel's response to His other commands.

What is sandwiched between these two sections is the record of how Israel radically disobeyed God's commands regarding worship of idols. In a very real sense, this demonstrated at the outset of Israel's covenant relationship with God that it would neglect the weightier matters of the law. That was a problem for all of its history.

The book ends with the assurance that God was with Israel to lead and guide it. As long as it would follow and obey, all would be well. Thus the description of Israel's faithfulness in regard to the tabernacle also serves as an introduction to its future with God. It was expected to be obedient and faithful in its future relationship with God. With this note of expectancy and hope, the book draws to a close.

9

Leviticus

The third book of the Pentateuch has come to us with the name of *Leviticus*. This name is derived from the Latin Vulgate, which in turn was a variation of the name found in the LXX, *Levitikon*. The name refers to the fact that the book is a list of codes and regulations governing the Levitical priesthood, its worship, and leadership in Israel. The Hebrew name of the book, as usual, comes from the first word of the book, *wayyiqra'*, "And He Called." In the time of the Talmud, the book was called by the rabbis *torath kohanim*, "The Law of the Priests."

The Book of Leviticus is probably the least read and the least understood book of the Old Testament, for the sacrificial system which is its central feature is wholly foreign to most people in the contemporary world. At the same time, it is one of the very important books in the Old Testament, for the forms of Israel's worship were central to their faith. A serious student of the Old Testament, who wants to understand the worship of ancient Israel, would read Leviticus and Psalms jointly. Psalms sets forth the content of Hebrew worship while Leviticus sets forth a major part of the form of it. The study of either book without the other will leave a distorted view of Israel's worship and its meaning.

The Book of Leviticus also sets the foundation for much of the Book of Hebrews in the New Testament. It is quite difficult to understand most of Hebrews' proclamation of Jesus as both High Priest and sacrifice without having first studied the teaching of Leviticus related to these concepts.

The purpose of Leviticus seems to focus upon two very significant ideas. First, the worship of God is important and must be done properly. An inadequate approach to God was understood to indicate an inadequate understanding of God and an inadequate reverence of Him. God is holy and must be approached in a holy manner. The second purpose of the book appears to build upon the first one, for Leviticus proclaims that since God is holy His people must be holy. Israel was expected to be a holy people in the presence of the holy God.

The first-time student who makes a serious approach to Leviticus must recognize that the book falls short of the typical New Testament understanding of God and of worship. However, when read against the background of the ancient Near East, the world of which Israel was a part, the major thrust of its message can be discovered. God was holy. Israel was to be holy. Although the Levitical understanding of holiness was not as exalted as that which Jesus proclaimed, the basic fact of God's holiness remains the same. Even though Israelite worship might seem quite bloody and anything but worshipful to a contemporary audience, it was appropriate for that day. Jesus added new content to the message of Leviticus, but its message is still a viable one. Its strangeness must not keep students from hearing what it proclaims about God and His people.

An overview of the content of the book can be grasped through the following outline.

The Content of the Book

I. The worship of the people (1:1 to 7:38)
   A. The burnt offering (1:1-17)
   B. The cereal offering (2:1-16)
   C. The peace offering (3:1-17)
   D. The sin offering (4:1 to 5:13)
   E. The trespass offering (5:14 to 6:7)
   F. Instructions for the priests (6:8 to 7:38)
II. The ministry of the priests (8:1 to 10:20)
   A. The ceremony of consecration (8:1-36)
      1. Gathering the congregation (8:1-3)
      2. Robing the priests (8:4-9)

3. The anointing (8:10-13)
4. The sacrifices (8:14-29)
    a. The sin offering (8:14-17)
    b. The burnt offering (8:18-21)
    c. The ordination (8:22-29)
5. The consecration (8:30)
6. The week of ordination (8:31-36)
  B. The installation ceremony (9:1-24)
  C. The sin of ignoring God's holiness (10:1-20)
III. The dedication of life (11:1 to 16:34)
  A. Clean and unclean animals (11:1-47)
  B. Purification following childbirth (12:1-8)
  C. Diagnosis of leprosy (13:1-59)
  D. Treatment of leprosy (14:1-32)
  E. Leprosy in houses (14:33-57)
  F. Sexual purity (15:1-33)
  G. The great ritual of atonement (16:1-34)
1. Preparation for the Day of Atonement (16:1-5)
2. Personal atonement for the high priest (16:6-14)
3. Atonement for the people (16:15-19)
4. The bearing away of guilt (16:20-22)
5. Final cleansing (16:23-28)
6. Ongoing observance of the ceremony (16:29-34)
IV. The laws of holiness (17:1 to 26:46)
  A. The sacredness of life (17:1-16)
  B. Unlawful sexual acts (18:1-30)
  C. The nature of holy living (19:1-37)
  D. Condemnation of pagan practices (20:1-27)
  E. Regulations for the priests (21:1-24)
  F. More priestly regulations (22:1-33)
  G. The holy times and seasons (23:1-44)
1. The sabbath (23:1-3)
2. The Feast of Unleavened Bread (23:4-8)
3. The Feast of First Fruits (23:9-14)
4. The Feast of Pentecost (23:15-22)
5. The Day of Atonement (23:23-32)

The Book of Leviticus faces the fact that sinful people need a way by which God can be approached for fellowship and worship. The point of the sacrificial system was to accomplish just that.

The book nowhere claims to have been written by Moses. On the other hand, it claims again and again to have been the revelation of God to Moses, for the expression "and the Lord said to Moses" occurs frequently, along with other phrases such as "the Lord called Moses, and spoke to him" (4:1, *et al;* 1:1). In the ancient Near East, it was a common practice to take the words of an ancient authority and enlarge them as new situations presented themselves. Some scholars have suggested that such may have been the case with some of the material in Leviticus, but the student must consider the evidence and make a personal decision. Clearly the material had its start with God's revelation to Moses, regardless of when or how it was written.

Two blocks of material within the book deserve more attention. They are the laws governing the great Day of Atonement (16:1-34) and the Holiness Code (17:1 to 26:46).

The ritual of the Day of Atonement has come to be considered as the high point of the Old Testament sacrificial system. In a very real sense, Hebrews 9:6-28 is a New Testament commentary upon this passage from a Christological standpoint.

On the Day of Atonement, all of the sins which had not been dealt with in any of the other sacrifices throughout the year were supposed to be confessed and atoned for. The purpose, of course, was that a right relationship to God might be maintained by the people of Israel. That was the only day of the year the high priest was allowed to enter into the "holy place within the veil" (16:2-3). The Day of Atonement was the only day of fasting set aside as a regular worship time within the Old Testament. Of all the special days and seasons, it was considered the most significant. It was actually called a "sabbath of solemn rest," literally a "sabbath of sabbaths" (16:31). It was the highest and holiest of all the high and holy days, as it has remained for the Jews.

Many Old Testament scholars have long believed that the Holiness Code (17:1 to 26:46) probably had a separate existence from Leviticus. The reasons for this suggestion are the following. (1) Some of material found in it is also found elsewhere in Leviticus and in the rest of the Pentateuch. This duplication might be an indication of a separate circulation. (2) The phrase "I am the Lord [Yahweh]" occurs nearly fifty times in this block of material and not at all in the rest of the book. (3) The reason given for the expected holiness of the people is set forth by the frequent use of the phrase, "You shall be holy, for I the Lord your God am holy." This expression does not occur in the rest of the book. (4) Finally, this section appears to be more involved with life and less with ritual than the rest of the book. Those who disagree with this conclusion point out that a different theme requires different vocabulary and emphases.

Regardless of whether the material known as the Holiness Code had a separate identity apart from Leviticus, the nature of its theme is unquestionable. The people of Israel were expected to be a holy people because the God who had delivered them and who led them was the holy God. This awareness identifies one of the major differences between Hebrew religion and those of the rest of the ancient Near Eastern nations. Their gods were frequently undependable, capricious, and often downright immoral. The God of Israel was holy. He expected Israel to be a holy people. Thus the designation of this section as the Holiness Code is quite appropriate.

At first glance, little unity of content appears within this section. However, reading all of the block at one time brings to the fore that the emphasis upon holiness holds it together. This emphasis upon holiness has within itself the temptation to descend to an extreme legalism. The New Testament demonstrates that for some Jews, at least, it did just that. At the same time, just because the emphasis upon holiness could be abused does not mean that it is unimportant or insignificant. The external signs of holiness need to demonstrate that inner holiness is present.

10

Numbers

The fourth book of the Pentateuch is called Numbers, the English translation of the title assigned by the translators of the LXX who called it *Arithmoi*. This title was apparently given to the book because of the three recorded censuses (numberings, chs. 1, 4, and 26) as well as the book's significant interest in numbers and statistics. The Hebrew title, *bemidhbar* ("in the wilderness"), is found in the first verse and is far more appropriate to the actual content of the book.

Insofar as that content is concerned, Numbers forms a natural bridge between the legislation of Leviticus and Israel's final preparation for entering the land of Canaan while encamped upon the plains of Moab. Numbers begins with a large block of material which is statistical and legislative in nature and then picks up the narrative from Exodus as the tribes moved from Sinai to Kadesh and on to a thirty-eight-year period of wanderings in the wilderness before they finally arrived in the plains of Moab, on the doorstep of the land of Canaan.

From a literary standpoint, no book in the Pentateuch and probably no other in the entire Bible has such a diverse character. It has census lists, descriptions of territorial boundaries, cultic and ritualistic material, festal calendars, gripping narrative, magnificent poetry, reports of divination, and prophetic oracles.

The diverse character of the material, the varied styles and vocabulary, and the changing points of interest have led many scholars to continue the kinds of literary analysis into sources which are done on the earlier books of the Old

173

Testament. In general, such analyses have assigned the censuses, legal and cultic materials to the P cycle of traditions and the narrative portions to the JE strata. Other scholars continue to question whether such analyses can be justified or defended.

The ultimate source for the material in this book is God. The constant emphasis upon God's speaking to Moses and through him to the people leaves no question as to the divine authorship. Various groups within Israel, under the inspiration of God, possibly preserved the parts of the tradition which were of most interest and concern to them. Further, the final editor drew those traditions together under God's guidance so that people who came later would have the whole story.

The human author is nowhere identified in the book. The only place where any literary activity is recorded of Moses is found in Numbers 33:2: "Moses wrote down their starting places, stage by stage." Throughout the book Moses is spoken of in the third person, not in the first person as if he were writing himself.

The major critical issue in Numbers has to to with the numbers of the Hebrews who were of fighting age (cf. 1:20-46). Several approaches have been made in dealing with this issue. First, the numbers can be taken literally. That is all right as long as the problems which this approach raises are seriously considered and evaluated. The biblical narrative states, "The descendants of Israel were fruitful and increased greatly . . . so that the land was filled with them" (Ex. 1:7). For the Hebrews to have increased from 70 persons to a population of about 2.5 million (the approximate number of people necessary to have had 603,550 fighting men, cf. 1:46) is a staggering idea. They are portrayed as being enslaved by Egypt, frightened by Edom, and terrified by the Canaanites, yet none of those nations had an army even remotely approaching this size. In fact, in Canaan the Hebrews were to face seven nations greater than they were (cf. Deut. 7:1), yet the archaeological evidence would indicate that Canaan *never* had such a population. Furthermore, the tribes were to be controlled by only two trumpets (10:1-2), their births had been attended by only two midwives (Ex. 1:15).

The second approach to the statistics is that they are from a misplaced census list, probably from the time of David. That, however, offers no solution. An army of that size in the time of David offers just as many problems plus the difficulty of how the list was misplaced in the first place.

A third approach was first suggested by Sir Flinders Petrie. Though it has been developed and modified over the years, it retains same basic form. Petrie suggested that the Hebrew word 'eleph which is normally translated as "thousand" has been misinterpreted. Intensive investigation has shown that the word was frequently used for the number "thousand," but it was also used for a clan, a tribe, or a fighting unit. He suggested that it should have the latter meaning in the census list. If that were so, the size of the forces of Israel would have been dramatically reduced and this particular problem eliminated. This does not solve all of the difficulties, however. For example, the numbers of the firstborn males cannot be so easily explained away (3:43). Petrie's approach may be the first step toward a solution, but we cannot claim more for it at this time.

The fourth solution is to frankly admit that there is a problem and also to admit that we do not know enough to understand fully this ancient data and how it was handled. We do not have to be able to answer every question we have to be able to hear God speak through His Word. If the difficulty with the numbers distracts us, we may miss the message of the passage. The primary purpose of Numbers is not simply to record historical detail and epic narrative; it is to point out the divine message which was proclaimed through such events.

The Content of the Book

I. Israel in the plains of Sinai (1:1 to 10:10)
    A. Preparation for military service (1:1-46)
        1. Arrangements for taking a census (1:1-16)
        2. The numbering of the tribes (1:17-46)

B. Preparations for the tabernacle service (1:47-54)
C. Preparations for Israel's camp (2:1-34)
D. Preparations for the service of the priests and Levites (3:1 to 4:49)
    1.   Background: Moses, Aaron, and the Levites (3:1-13)
    2.   The families of the Levites (3:14-39)
    3.   The "setting apart" of the Levites (3:40-51)
    4.   Census of the Levites fit for service (4:1-49)
E. Preparations for the camp (5:1 to 10:10)
    1.   Cleansing the camp (5:1 to 6:27)
        a. Those exluded from the camp (5:1-4)
        b. Confessions and restitutions (5:5-10)
        c. The ordeal of jealousy (5:11-31)
        d. The Nazarite vow (6:1-21)
        e. The Mosaic benediction and God's blessing (6:22-27)
    2.   The dedication of the altar (7:1-89)
    3.   The lampstand for the tabernacle (8:1-4)
    4.   The consecration of the Levites (8:5-26)
    5.   The second Passover celebration (9:1-14)
    6.   The cloud and fire over the tabernacle (9:15-23)
    7.   The making and the use of the silver trumpets (10:1-10)

This block of material is most often ignored by contemporary readers, due to its long, involved lists and its overwhelming concern with the details of an ancient cultus (system of worship). It is so foreign as to be almost meaningless. However, it was important to Israel and it was preserved by God because it has a message for us. This material is a proclamation that the manner and means of serving God, both in worship and in the rest of life, are important. It also proclaims that the preparations for obeying the Lord are important. Those who serve God must do so fully prepared for the tasks and responsibilities which are to come.

II. Israel's journey from Sinai to Kadesh (10:11 to 14:45)
- A. The stages to Kadesh (10:11 to 12:16)
  1. The journey begun (10:11-36)
  2. Complaint over misfortunes (11:1-3)
  3. Complaint over lack of meat (11:4-35)
  4. Complaint over Moses' marriage (12:1-16)
- B. Israel's failure at Kadesh (13:1 to 14:45)
  1. Spying out the land of Canaan (13:1-33)
     - a. Selecting the spies (13:1-16)
     - b. Commissioning the spies (13:17-20)
     - c. Carrying out the task (13:21-24)
     - d. The report of the difficulties (13:25-29)
     - e. The recommendation to attack (13:30)
     - f. The recommendation to withdraw (13:31-33)
  2. A decision based on lack of faith (14:1-10a)
  3. God's anger and Moses' intercession (14:10b-19)
  4. The judgment announced (14:20-38)
     - a. Pardon (14:20)
     - b. Punishment (14:21-35)
     - c. Special provision for the spies (14:36-38)
  5. Punishment for attempting to avoid God's judgment (14:39-45)

The journey from Sinai to Kadesh was almost a replica of the one from Egypt to Sinai. At each difficulty, the people turned against God and Moses with bitter complaint. Once they arrived at Kadesh, they faced the land from the south with great expectations. But when the spies reported the difficulties which they would face, the people accepted the majority report and decided not to obey God and invade the land. Such faithlessness aroused the wrath of God; but upon Moses' intercession, God offered pardon to His faithless people. Even though the faithless would not be allowed to enter the land, the nation would still be allowed ultimately to do so. Seeking to avoid this judgment, however, the people foolishly decided to try to take the land. They had already lost their opportunity and suffered a bitter defeat. The whole episode is a magnificent contrast between faith and faithlessness, obedience and disobedience.

   III. Wanderings in the wilderness (15:1 to 20:13)
      A. A variety of laws (15:1-41)
         1. Laws regarding offerings (15:1-21)
         2. Laws for offerings for unwitting sins (15:22-29)
         3. Sins with a high hand (15:30-36)
         4. Fringes for remembrance (15:37-41)
      B. Issues of authority and responsibility (16:1 to 18:32)
         1. Rebellions against Moses' leadership (16:1-50)
         2. The confirmation of Aaron as high priest (17:1-13)
         3. Responsibilities and rewards of priests and Levites (18:1-32)
      C. Special rites for cleansing (19:1-22)
         1. The rite for the water of impurity (the red heifer) (19:1-10)
         2. The rite for defilement by a corpse (19:11-22)
      D. The death of Miriam (20:1)
      E. Bitterness over lack of water (20:2-13)
         1. The bitterness of the people (20:2-9)
         2. The bitterness of Moses and Aaron (20:10-13)

The main period of the wanderings in the wilderness is covered in this section. Numerous issues were supposedly settled for Israel during this period. One thing which is presupposed throughout the Old Testament, but which is clearly spelled out at this time, is that the entire sacrificial system had no provision for the cleansing of the guilt of "sin with a high hand" (15:30-31). In the Old Testament as in the New, such sin found forgiveness only through the sinner throwing himself upon the mercy of God, not by any ritual observance.

    IV. The journey from Kadesh to the Transjordan (20:14 to 21:35)
        A. Israel's request to pass through Edom denied (20:14-21)
        B. The death of Aaron (20:22-29)
        C. Encounters along the way (21:1-35)
           1. Encounter with the king of Arad (21:1-3)
           2. Encounter with fiery serpents (21:4-9)
           3. The journey to Pisgah (21:10-20)
           4. Encounter with Sihon and the Amorites (21:21-30)
           5. Encounter with Og of Bashan (21:31-35)
    V. Encamped upon the plains of Moab (22:1 to 36:13)
        A. Confrontation with Balak and Balaam (22:1 to 24:25)
           1. Israel's arrival on the plains of Moab (22:1)
           2. Balak's appeal to Balaam (22:2-10)
           3. Balaam's journey to Moab (22:21-35)
           4. The meeting between Balak and Balaam (22:36-40)
           5. Balaam's blessing of Israel and Balak's distress (22:41 to 23:12)
           6. Balaam's second blessing and Balak's greater distress (23:13-26)
           7. Balaam's third blessing and Balak's anger (23:27 to 24:11)
        B. The danger of pagan relationships (25:1-18)
        C. An additional numbering of Israel (26:1-65)
        D. Laws of inheritance (27:1-11)
        E. Announcement of Joshua as the new leader (27:12-23)
           1. The announcement of Moses' death (27:12-14)
           2. Moses' concern for his people (27:15-17)
           3. Joshua designated as Moses' successor (27:18-23)

F. Laws governing religious observances (28:1 to 30:16)
1. Introduction (28:1-2)
2. Daily offerings (28:3-8)
3. Sabbath offerings (28:9-10)
4. New moon offerings (28:11-15)
5. The Feast of Unleavened Bread (28:16-25)
6. The Feast of Weeks (28:26-31)
7. The Feast of the Seventh Month, New Year (29:1-6)
8. The Day of Atonement (29:7-11)
9. The Feast of Booths (29:12-38)
10. Summary statement (29:39-40)
11. Vows of men (30:1-2)
12. Vows of women (30:3-16)
G. Vengeance upon Midian (31:1-54)
H. The Transjordan region settled (32:1-42)
I. Summary of the journey from Egypt to Moab (33:1-49)
1. Introduction (33:1-4)
2. From Egypt to Sinai (33:5-15)
3. From Sinai to Mount Hor (33:16-40)
4. From Mount Hor to the Plains of Moab (33:41-49)
J. Final instructions (33:50 to 36:13)
1. The elimination of paganism (33:50-56)
2. Boundaries of the land established (34:1-29)
3. The cities for the Levites (35:1-8)
4. The cities of refuge (35:9-34)
5. Issues of inheritance (36:1-12)
6. The divine source for Israel's laws (36:13)

The journey and the experiences which Israel had when it turned from the wilderness south of Kadesh are recorded in this last block of material. There were many experiences of significance, but two appear to carry special importance. First the episode of Balaam and Balak is fascinating. Prophecy, particularly the kind known as divination, was a common phenomena throughout the ancient Near East.

When Balaam blessed Israel, it was going to be blessed. That shows the acceptance of power of the spoken word at that time. The frustration of King Balak is quite understandable and adds a major dimension of human interest.

The second feature which shows up here, as well as earlier in the book, is that much of Israel's legislation came about in direct response to specific need. Rulings were issued and became law when problems arose which brought forth the need to know the right and proper thing to do. This obviously does not apply to all of Israel's laws, but it just as obviously does apply to many of them. Israel's relation with God is seen as a living experience which was able to meet new situations when they arose.

Any thorough reader of the Book of Numbers will also see that much of the material is a repetition of that which is found elsewhere. In many ways, the legal materials serve as a summary of much that has gone before. It is a handy reference book, especially as regards the times of religious observances. Of significance is the fact that provision was made for the celebration of the Feast of the New Moon (28:11-15) even though that festival was never commanded. Rather, it appears to have been a regular part of Israel's common heritage with those peoples of their world. In a real sense, it was a part which was sanctified and regulated, even though it was not specifically commanded.

The Book of Numbers shows how and why Israel took so long to move from Sinai to the plains of Moab. Depending upon the actual location of Sinai, the journey could have at the shortest lasted for no more than a few days possibly up to three or four weeks, yet it lasted thirty-eight years. The book follows Israel's trek into the plains of Moab, in the Transjordan region. It leaves the people there, facing the land of promise. God was in control all the way, being clearly presented as sovereign over the affairs of men and nations, including foreign nations.

11

Deuteronomy

The fifth and final book of the Pentateuch is Deuteronomy. This name came from a mistranslation the LXX made of an expression found in Deuteronomy 17:18 in which future kings were commanded to make a "copy of this law." The LXX translators mistakenly translated this as *to deuteronomium touto,* which literally means "this second law." The Latin Vulgate then translated this title merely as *deuteronomium,* a second law. The Hebrews as usual named the book after its first words, *'elleh haddebharim,* "These Are the Words." This was occasionally shortened simply to *haddebharim,* "words." Though the present title is derived from a mistranslation, it is quite descriptive, for the Book of Deuteronomy is a restatement of many of the laws found in the preceding books.

The Nature of the Book

The Book of Deuteronomy makes easier reading than any of the other legal material in the Old Testament. For anyone who has seriously labored through the legal materials of Exodus, Leviticus, Numbers, and Deuteronomy, this ease in reading is quite striking and raises the issue of why it should be so. The answer is really quite simple. The Book of Deuteronomy is primarily exhortation, preaching. Instead of being simply a set of laws, it is preaching about the Hebrew laws. It claims to be three sermons which Moses preached to the people of Israel while they were encamped upon the plains of Moab immediately before their entrance into the land of Canaan. A single theme runs throughout the book. *Yahweh is the one sovereign God who is active in*

183

history and Israel is His one holy people, chosen by His sovereign grace to live in a covenant relation with Him. In addition to the three sermons, three short appendixes are found at the end.

Deuteronomy was apparently a favorite book of Jesus. He turned to it when He was tempted by Satan, using it as His basic weapon in resisting that temptation (cf. 6:13-16; 8:3; Matt. 4:4,7,10; Luke 4:8,12). He also turned to it for His answer when asked which of the Commandments was the greatest (cf. 6:5; Matt. 22:37-38; Mark 12:29-33; Luke 10:27). It is also possible that a key thrust of the Sermon on the Mount comes from this book (cf. 18:13; Matt. 5:48). The book had some impact upon Paul and the rest of the New Testament writers and continues to have a real impact upon contemporary Christians. Some concerns in Deuteronomy cause many people to shy away from it. These should be seriously considered.

Major Concerns Related to Deuteronomy and Its Study

Perhaps the greatest concern which contemporary Christians have with the Book of Deuteronomy relate to its concept of "holy war" (cf. 7:1-26). Many people today are quite willing to be involved in the kind of holy war which Deuteronomy proposes but show little or no leaning toward Jesus' way of love. Other people seek the way of peace or are committed to Christ's way of love and are totally shocked by the kind of destruction proposed by the words of Deuteronomy. We should not stand on this side of the cross with the full teachings of Jesus before us and pass judgment upon the laws of Deuteronomy which came centuries before Jesus. Rather, we must seek to understand this material in the light of its own times.

The very foundation of the concept of holy war was the idea of devoting or dedicating something to one's God. In ancient times when anything was dedicated to God no individual or nation could possess it or be enriched by it. Rather, such an object had to be totally destroyed. In fact, the verb which is translated as "utterly destroy" (7:2) literally means "to consecrate" or "to dedicate." This kind of warfare was actually viewed as a kind of sacrifice, an actual act of worship. Certainly this is a far cry from the love of one's enemies which was proclaimed by Jesus. But it was a stumbling step in the direction of devoting all one has or touches to God.

Two additional explanations are sometimes given for the kind of holy war proposed by Deuteronomy. One points to the wickedness of the Canaanites. The biblical picture of their paganism and sexual license has been affirmed and heightened by the archaeological discoveries at Ugarit. The Canaanites' whole religious system was morally degrading, appealing to the basest part of human personality. The people of Israel were intended to be God's executioners upon such a life-style. Certainly God has the right to make such a choice. If He could use pagan nations as instruments of His judgment upon Israel, as all the prophets proclaimed, surely He could use Israel as His instrument of judgment upon pagans.

A second proposed reason for the holy war concept of Deuteronomy has to do with Israel's own weakness. Israel was not a people, as some have suggested, with a religious genius. They were chosen for no qualities of their own but simply because God loved them (7:7-8). They had to destroy the temptations of pagan sensualism before those temptations invaded their lives and destroyed them. The whole course of Israel's subsequent history points up the truth of this argument. They did not destroy the Canaanites and their religion. Consequently, the great crises of the Hebrew kingdom which were addressed in the eighth century by Amos, Hosea, Isaiah, and Micah, and in the seventh century by Jeremiah, stemmed in a large part form Israel's involvement with the immorality of the Canaanites.

At the foundation of all of this is the basic Old Testament conception of Yahweh. He was not the God who sat far above in the heavens. On the contrary, Israel met Him in the daily affairs of life. Whatever work was to be done, it was to be done on earth and Yahweh was involved in it. Moses, Joshua, and Israel understood God's commands in terms of the world in which they lived. The world as it is at any time must be faced by people as they are at that time. God is steadily transforming life, but the teachings of Jesus would not have been comprehended by the Israelites on the plains of Moab. For that matter, it is doubtful if we have fully comprehended them either.

A second major concern in the interpretation of Deuteronomy has to do with date and authorship. Foundational to any answer to this question is the relationship of the Book of Deuteronomy to the reform of King Josiah as recorded in 2 Kings 22:1 to 23:30. During that reform, "the book of the law" was found in the Temple in 621 BC. It served as the basis for the greatest effort at religious reformation that the Hebrews ever experienced. Jerome, the translator of the Latin Vulgate, identified this law book with Deuteronomy. Centuries later, that same suggestion was proposed by W. M. L. DeWette. From the late nineteenth century, there has been no serious disagreement. The reasons for this conclusion can be seen by comparing the actions taken by Josiah after the discovery of the book with the teachings of Deuteronomy. While some of the reforms which he made are found in several different books of the Torah, Deuteronomy appears to have them all.

Action, 2 Kings	Teaching, Deuteronomy	Subject
23:2-3, 21	17:2; 28:6, 9	Covenant
23:3	11:1; 13:6	Keeping commands
23:3	13:4	Heart and soul
22:13	18:19	Warning to heed
22:17b; 23:4, 13	6:14; 8:19; 11:28	No foreign gods
23:4-5, 11-12	4:19; 17:3	No star worship
23:5b, 8b, 10	7:16	No Canaanite gods
23:5a, 8a, 13	7:5; 12:2	No high places
23:24	7:5,25; 12:3	No idols
23:14	7:5; 12:3	No standing stones
23:6, 14	7:5; 12:3	No asherim
23:24	18:11	No necromancy
23:10	12:31; 18:10	No child sacrifice
23:7	23:17	No Temple prostitutes
23:5, 8, 13, 15, 17	12:5-14	Central sanctuary
23:8a-9	18:6-8	Priest at high places
23:21-23	16:5-7	Passover
22:13, 17	11:17	Kindling of wrath
22:13	29:20	Curses

| 22:16 | 31:17, 21, 29*a* | Bringing of evil |
| 22:17 | 31:29*b* | Provoking anger |

Thus it appears that the Book of Deuteronomy was essentially, if not completely, in its final form by 621 BC. With this as a basis, we can ask, Who wrote Deuteronomy and when it was written? There have been essentially four answers given to this by biblical scholars.

Mosaic Authorship

The general assumption from the earliest times has been that Moses was the author of the book. There are numerous references in Deuteronomy to Moses speaking and at least two to his writing (31:9,24-26):

> "And Moses wrote this law and gave it to the priests the sons of Levi" (31:9)
> "When Moses had finished writing the words of this law in a book, to the very end, Moses commanded the Levites, . . . 'Take this book of the law, and put it by the side of the ark of the covenant of the Lord your God, that it may be there for a witness against you' " (vv. 24-26).

However, at least two issues must be considered further. Exactly what was intended by the phrases "this law" and "this book of the law"? There is no indication as to what the references are to be identified with. Further, the death and burial of Moses are recorded in the book (34:5-6). Generally, those who hold to a Mosaic authorship propose that "this law" refers to most of the book, or at least to chapters 12 through 26. Further, they usually acknowledge that there were later additions to the book, including a few earlier glosses and the final description of Moses' death and the mourning following it.

Authorship Around 621 BC

A second set of suggestions about authorship say the book was written shortly before it was "found" in the Temple in 621 BC. These generally suggest that the writing took one of two forms. The Wellhausian approach suggested that the book was written at that time and was in a real sense a pious fraud, the product of religious leaders who were seeking to give an authority to the reform of Josiah. Almost no one holds to this concept any longer.

Another view is that some of the earlier Mosaic sermons and traditions had been preserved by the people of Israel up to the time of the division of the kingdom after the death of Solomon. At that time, those traditions were carried northward by the Levites and priests and preserved by them until the fall of the Northern Kingdom in 722 BC. Refugees fleeing southward brought the traditions with them. Fearing the loss of those traditions, they were written down at that time and hidden in the Temple. Some propose that these traditions had been preserved by Levites while others suggest that they had been preserved by disciples of the prophets. Either way, the document was discovered during the early days of Josiah's reform and served as the basis for his subsequent efforts. This proposal usually grants the essential historicity of the Deuteronomic material while acknowledging its modification over the centuries to make the message applicable to new historical situations.

Authorship Around 950 BC

A major variation on the foregoing theory was proposed in the early part of the twentieth century and still finds significant support. This proposal suggests that the basic writing of Deuteronomy was done during the reign of Solomon. The essential historicity of the traditions, coming directly from Moses but with some enlargement to meet new situations is assumed. According to this proposal, a written scroll was carried northward after the division of the kingdom. When Israel fell, refugees carried that scroll southward, hiding it in the Jerusalem Temple. However, shortly thereafter, the Jerusalem Temple fell into disuse during the evil days under wicked Manasseh. During the reform of Josiah, the book was discovered and recognized for what it was.

Authorship after the Exile

Some twentieth-century scholars have suggested that Deuteronomy is not to be identified with the law book found during the reign of Josiah. They suggest that Deuteronomy is the product of that reform, rather than its source. According to these scholars, the book was finally written during or after the Exile, reflecting the things which Josiah had tried to accomplish in the Hebrew kingdom. The book was written not as the conclusion to the Pentateuch but as the introduction to the Deuteronomic histories: Joshua, Judges, 1 and 2 Samuel, and 1 and 2 Kings.

Obviously, the present state of Deuteronomic studies is in a very unsettled condition. It appears impossible to deny a major part of the book to Moses and to Mosaic influence. To deny that he wrote anything is to deny an explicit statement of Scripture. On the other hand, it also appears quite likely that part of the material was passed on through oral tradition for a significant period of time. I believe that it was essentially written during the time of Solomon, but I make this statement very tentatively. It does appear to have had some editorial additions and glosses made later. However, there is no question as to its divine authorship and inspiration. The book as we have it is as God has sent it. Conscientious biblical scholars who take the biblical message seriously disagree as to how God has brought Deuteronomy to us. There is no question but that He has done it. Israel heard trumpets in it once. We can hear them again.

The Content of the Book

To the Jewish people, the greatest and most significant verse in the entire Bible is Deuteronomy 6:4, with its enlargement in verse 5 and its importance set forth in verses 6-9.

Hear, O Israel: The Lord our God is one Lord; and you shall love the Lord your God with all your heart, and with all your soul, and with all your might. And these words which I command you this day shall be upon your heart; and you shall teach them diligently to your children, and shall talk of them when you sit in your house, and when you walk by the way, and when you lie down, and when you rise. And you shall bind them as a sign upon your hand, and they shall be as frontlets between your eyes. And you shall write them on the doorposts of your house and on your gates.

These verses are recited daily by many Jews and every sabbath by worshiping Jews. Many have literally bound them on their wrists and foreheads at times of prayer and most have them on the doorposts of their homes. The passage is called by them the *Shema'*, from the first word in the verse, "Hear." The singleness of the theme—one Lord, one love, one loyalty—is expanded throughout the entire book.

I. Moses' first sermon: Yahweh, Lord of history (1:1 to 4:43)
   A. Introduction and setting (1:1-5)
   B. Yahweh's mighty acts from Horeb to Beth-peor (1:6 to 3:29)
      1. Leaving the place of past experienced (1:6-8)
      2. Organizing for effectiveness (1:9-18)
      3. The double failure of Kadesh-barnea (1:19-46)
      4. Through the wilderness to Transjordan (2:1-25)
      5. Victory over Sihon (2:26-37)
      6. Victory over Og (3:1-11)
      7. Division of the Transjordan region (3:12-17)
      8. Preparations for conquest (3:18-22)
      9. Moses' pleas to Yahweh (3:23-29)
   C. Israel's obligations in consequence of Yahweh's acts (4:1-40)
      1. Exhortation to obey God's commands (4:1-8)
      2. Exhortation not to forget (4:9-14)
      3. The dangers of idolatry (4:15-28)
      4. The mercy of Yahweh (4:29-31)

> 5. Israel's special blessing: being Yahweh's chosen ones (4:32-40)
> D. Cities of refuge established (4:41-43)

The Hebrews with Moses on the plains of Moab did not really remember the Exodus, for at the best they had merely been children or youth at that time. The adults who would have remembered that great experience had all (with the exceptions of Moses, Joshua, and Caleb) died in the wilderness. All that the people who were with Moses would have remembered were the years of wandering in the wilderness. From Moses' standpoint, it was imperative that the people learn one of the major tenets of faith: Yahweh is the Lord of history. Thus Moses set forth in the first of his final messages to the people a resumé of the history which they had experienced and would remember, carefully pointing out that what had happened to them had been due to the sovereign control of Yahweh their God.

The point behind the recital of God's great acts was that the mighty acts of God on behalf of Israel laid a special obligation and responsibility upon Israel. Being God's chosen people was a distinct and significant blessing. But it also carried with it distinct and significant consequences. It still does. Unfortunately for Israel all too often the responsibility which came with being the chosen ones was forgotten.

> II. Moses' second sermon: Yahweh, Lord of the covenant (4:44 to 26:19)
> A. Introduction and setting (4:44-49)
> B. The demands of the covenant faith (5:1 to 11:32)
> > 1. Restatement of the Ten Commandments (5:1-21)
> > 2. Warning to love and fear Yahweh (6:1-19)
> > 3. The responsibility of training children (6:20-25)
> > 4. Responsibilities, opportunities, and dangers in Canaan; the holy war (7:1-26)
> > 5. Lessons from the past and warnings for the future (8:1 to 10:11)

     6.   A call to obey the demands of God (10:12 to 11:32)

        a. The requirements of God (10:12-22)

        b. The demand to love God (11:1-7)

        c. The demand to obey the Commandments (11:8-17)

        d. Treasuring the Commandments (11:18-25)

        e. The blessing and the curse (11:26-32)

Moses clearly set forth the expectations which God had for His people. Over and over the emphasis was upon obedience. Faith was to be demonstrated in concrete action. Furthermore, the keeping of the Commandments included teaching them to their descendants. A faith which is not passed on will die out in only one generation.

Israel's loyalty to the covenant of God was predicated upon the fact that God had already demonstrated His loyalty to them in His redemptive acts and in His acts of deliverance and guidance through the wilderness. Deuteronomy describes both the loyalty of God and the loyalty of Israel in terms of love. Those who would say that the Old Testament is a book of law have not considered this block of material. The constant emphasis upon love is both striking and emphatic.

Moses also set forth with great vividness the awesome dangers of prosperity. It was easy for the Israelites, as it is for us, to forget that they had been slaves as they enjoyed the freedom they had by the grace of God. The Hebrews were exhorted never to forget their past and to demonstrate their remembrance by loving the sojourner (10:19).

    C. The demands expanded into covenant law (12:1 to 26:19)

        1.   One sanctuary, no other places of worship (12:1-31)

        2.   One God, no apostasy (13:1-18)

        3.   One Chosen People, to be different from others (14:1 to 25:19)

           a. Difference in diet (14:1-21)

We find it difficult to conceive of ritualistic legal materials

serving as the basis for such a sermon. However, we need
to recognize that Israel's ritual was designed to demonstrate that it was a unique people in the service of the
unique Lord. The covenant which Yahweh had offered it
and into which it had willingly entered had set it apart from
all peoples on earth. Through that covenant it had become
"the sons of the Lord your God; . . . a people for his own
possession" (14:1-2). Its life and worship were to be visible
demonstrations of that unique position.

The final summary of this sermon presents two major
confessions, the first setting forth Israel's faith in what God
had done for it and the second setting forth its proclamation
of obedience to God. The first one is a key concept in any
understanding of Israel's faith in the mighty acts of God.
There proclaimed:

> A wandering Aramean was my father; and he went down
> into Egypt and sojourned there, few in number; and there he
> became a nation, great, mighty, and populous. And the Egyp-
> tians treated us harshly, and afflicted us, and laid upon us
> hard bondage. Then we cried to the Lord, the God of our
> fathers, and the Lord heard our voice, and saw our affliction,
> our toil and our oppression; and the Lord brought us out of
> Egypt with a mighty hand and an outstretched arm, and
> with great terror, with signs and wonders; and he brought us
> into this place and gave us this land, a land flowing with milk
> and honey (26:5-9).

Israel's major confession was not what she had done but
what God had done for her.

III. Moses' third sermon: Yahweh, Lord of the future (27:1 to 31:29)
A. Covenant renewal upon entrance into Canaan (27:1-10)
B. Blessings and curses for faithfulness and un-faithfulness (27:11 to 28:68)

Commentators disagree as to whether chapters 27 and 28
serve as the conclusion of Moses' second sermon or the introduction of his third. These words are presented as com-

ing from *Moses and the elders* and may simply be an interlude between the second and third sermon. Although I have included them as a part of the third sermon, the idea of their being an interlude has great merit.

C. Exhortation to covenant commitment (29:1 to 30:14)
   1. Recitation of the past (29:1-9)
   2. Invitation to present and future commitment (29:10-15)
   3. Warnings of disobedience (29:16-28)
   4. Affirmation of God's mercy (29:29 to 30:14)
D. Present decisions with future consequences: the way of life and death (30:15-20)
E. Encouragement for the future (31:1-7)
F. Final preparations for Moses' death (31:8-29)

The note of pathos and sadness sounds throughout this section. The final days of Moses had come. He felt deeply Israel's need for guidance and sustenance as it faced what lay ahead. The one certainty which Moses had was that the God who had led thus far would lead after his death. Though Moses could not lead the people into the future, God could—and would.

One of the great texts affirming the task of sharing one's relationship with God is set forth in this message. It should serve as a reminder to every church and to every person of faith.

Assemble the people, men, women, and little ones, and the sojourner within your towns, that they may hear and learn to fear the Lord your God, and be careful to do all the words of this law, and that their children, who have not known it, may hear and learn to fear the Lord your God, as long as you live in the land which you are going over the Jordan to possess (31:12-13).

IV. Final appendixes on Yahweh's lordship (31:30 to 34:12)
   A. Moses' song: Yahweh, Lord of all (31:30 to 32:52)

1.   Introduction (31:30)
2.   The song itself, praising Yahweh (32:1-43)
3.   A final warning (32:44-47)
4.   The command for Moses to ascend Mount Nebo (32:48-52)
   B. Moses' blessing, Yahweh, Lord of love (33:1-29)
   C. Yahweh, Lord of life and death (34:1-12)
1.   Moses viewed the Promised Land (34:1-4)
2.   Moses' death and burial (34:5-8)
3.   Final evaluation of Moses (34:9-12)

The Book of Deuteronomy draws to a close with both a backward look and a forward view, with both sadness and joy. The backward look directs attention to the towering human figure of Moses and his part in the great drama of the mighty acts of God in choice and deliverance. But the forward look calls into view the rising figure of Joshua. God buried the worker, but the work went on. One leader passed away, but God had a new servant already prepared. The mighty acts of God do not stop just because a human worker dies.

The note of sadness was sounded with the death of Moses, the mighty man of God. Israel mourned the passing of that leader and rightly so. He had led the people, instructed them, interceded for them, and carried them on his heart and mind. But the sadness was tempered by joy at the view of the Promised Land which was just over the Jordan. Israel under Joshua was ready for the next step of the journey.

From a literary standpoint, the narrative of the Pentateuch has drawn to a close. At the same time, the stage has been set for Israel's great adventure in Canaan. No book ever accomplished its literary purpose so well.

From a theological standpoint Deuteronomy towers high. Its emphasis upon one God, the sovereign Lord who is active in history and who has called His one holy people through His sovereign grace to live in a covenant relation with Him sets the stage for all the future development of Israel's faith. In its highest view of God, the Book of Deuteronomy points the way for a life of service and devotion.

Part III
Introduction to the Study
of the Former Prophets

12

Issues in the Study
of the Former Prophets

Most contemporary Christians who participate in Bible study approach the Books of Joshua, Judges, Ruth, 1 and 2 Samuel, 1 and 2 Kings, 1 and 2 Chronicles, Ezra, Nehemiah, and Esther from the general standpoint that they are histories and should be studied as such. This approach is adequate for an initial study. Subsequent study of this Old Testament material will raise the question of whether this is really the best approach to make to these books.

The Hebrew Old Testament does not identify any of these books as histories. In fact, Ruth and Esther are identified as a part of the Megilloth, which in turn is classified as a part of the Kethubim or the Writings. Furthermore, 1 and 2 Chronicles, Ezra, and Nehemiah are also identified as a part of the Writings. Now whatever else may be said about this classification, the other materials within it are far from being histories in any sense of the word. (For example, consider Psalms, Proverbs, the Song of Songs, or Ecclesiastes.)

In the Hebrew canon Joshua, Judges, 1 and 2 Samuel, and 1 and 2 Kings are classified under the title of the "Former Prophets." The "Latter Prophets" include those books generally associated with biblical prophecy: Isaiah, Jeremiah, Ezekiel, and the Twelve (Minor Prophets). The Hebrew people apparently saw both sets of books as being similar in some way. The immediate conclusion might be that the two titles indicate chronology, the Former Prophets preceding the Latter Prophets. However, a quick look at the books included eliminates this possibility, for most of the men represented in the Latter Prophets ministered during the time covered by 1 and 2 Kings, before the Hebrew kingdom came to an end.

Another suggestion is that the two divisions referred to the times in which the books were written. The conclusion is less certain here, but a serious literary-historical study of the books would indicate that this is not the case either. In point of fact, it appears that the titles of "Former" and "Latter" have no more significance than pointing out that the books of the Former Prophets were placed first in the canon.

The very fact that all of these books were classified as Prophets would indicate that they had something of significance in common. On the other hand, the fact that they were subdivided into two separate collections would indicate that there was also a difference between these sets of books.

If the books of the Former Prophets were truly prophetic, they should primarily be understood as proclaiming messages about what God was doing in Israel's world. Since they were separated from the other prophetic books something about the nature or method of their proclamation must be different. Both of these things turn out to be quite true.

The Hebrew people were quite aware that *what* had happened to them on the way from Egypt to the plains of Moab was not nearly as important as *what God was doing* through those events. In the great confession of Deuteronomy 26:5-9, what Israel had done or what had happened to her was not as important as the fact that "the Lord heard our voice, and saw our affliction, our toil, and our oppression; and the Lord brought us out of Egypt with a mighty hand and an outstretched arm, with great terror, with signs and wonders; and he brought us into this place and gave us this land" (vv. 7-9). *What was important to them was not history, but significant history and its meaning.*

If we want to know what happened at any point in these records, we have to probe behind the meaning to the event itself. Great events may have occurred which were not recorded since the prophetic authors were not inspired to see God at work in those events. This offers a clear explanation why events which were viewed by Egyptian, Assyrian, or Babylonian writers as of great significance were either not mentioned or were only briefly considered by the biblical writers. It also offers an explanation as to why events given major treatment in the Old Testament are not mentioned in the records of other ancient Near Eastern nations. The first and overwhelming emphasis in the Old Testament is always the message for Israel, not the event.

The Issue of Relationship and Authorship

From the very early days of the literary critical movement, attempts were made to identify the sources which may (or may not) have been used in writing Joshua, Judges, 1 and 2 Samuel, and 1 and 2 Kings and to determine what relationships, if any, existed between the Former Prophets and the Pentateuch. Some scholars have suggested that Joshua actually completed the Pentateuch and that we, therefore, have a Hexateuch. Others suggested that Deuteronomy was so different from the other books of the Pentateuch that we actually had a Tetrateuch and that Deuteronomy was the introduction to the Former Prophets. However, no one was ever able to present an argument convincing enough to gain a consensus among scholars.

However, with the work of Martin Noth in the 1940s and Gerhard von Rad in the 1950s, a new approach to these materials has been made which has found a more general acceptance. Recognizing that there is both a relatedness between the Former Prophets and Deuteronomy as well as a close tie between Deuteronomy and the rest of the Pentateuch, they have accepted the basic collections just as they are. They have proposed that the six books of the Former Prophets were written, edited, and collected over the centuries by a group of people who were particularly disciples of the Book of Deuteronomy. The judgments which were passed on Israel's failures in these books were primarily Deuteronomic in tone and content.

Joshua through Samuel were probably originally written by one person and later edited by disciples of the Deuteronomic school. That would explain some of the differences as

well as the similarities in the books. The Books of 1 and 2
Kings appear to have been compiled from earlier materials
with editing and possibly re-editing by the students of the
Deuteronomic proclamation and tradition. Scholars have
proposed an ongoing group of Deuteronomic historians
which was primarily prophetic in nature. Some of the
prophets themselves may have come from that group. The
term which has come to be applied to the group is the
Deuteronomic Historians. The books of the Former Prophets themselves have come to be called the Deuteronomic
Histories or the Deuteronomic History Work.

The proclamation made by these books is that the Word
of the Lord is active in history. It is seen as law and coming
with power, judgment, and destruction. It is also seen as
gospel, where God's Word is saving, fulfilling, loving, and
forgiving. An ongoing theme of responsibility to God is coupled with the theme of His love and loyalty, ultimately
focusing upon His promise to David. It is from this, of
course, that the messianic hope springs. What God had done
and would do is presented in such a way that the contemporary audience at any point was called upon to repent, turn
from their evil ways, and trust Yahweh's promises which
would not fail.

The proclamation of these books offers an explanation for
the various catastrophes that fell upon the Hebrew people.
They were punished because they had forsaken Yahweh,
the God who had brought them out of Egypt, and had turned
to other gods. The end of such actions was death and destruction. Within these books, the law and the covenant are
presented as good gifts of God. The covenant established the
relationship with Yahweh and laid upon Israel the obligation of obeying the law. But the issue of obedience and
disobedience was primarily one of trust and distrust, of believing God or not. Either way, the Israelites experienced
the consequences of their own choices.

The Issues of Authorship and Date

The Book of Joshua continues the narrative of the Pentateuch. Picking up with the death of Moses, it follows the

Hebrew people over the Jordan River and on to the conquest of Canaan. The latter part of the book with its details of tribal allotments sounds like similar passages in Exodus, Leviticus, and Numbers. Because of these similarities, much effort has been spent seeking to trace the same strands of tradition in Joshua that are supposedly identified in the Pentateuch, but all to no avail. Joshua still stands apart from the Pentateuchal traditions insofar as literary identification is concerned.

Judges has significant literary differences from the books which precede and follow it, although there are also major similarities. The differences have caused scholars to propose that Joshua and Judges probably had separate independent existences from the rest of the Deuteronomic Histories. The Bible itself lists several sources which were or may have been used in compiling the material recorded in the Former Prophets. Among these are the following.

The Book of Jashar (cf. Josh. 10:13; 2 Sam. 1:18)

The Chronicles of Samuel the seer, the Chronicles of Nathan the prophet, and the Chronicles of Gad the seer (cf. 1 Chron. 29:29; could they possibly have also been used here?)

The official court records of King David (cf. 1 Chron. 27:24; possibly?)

Samuel's description of the kingdom (cf. 1 Sam. 10:25)

The Book of the acts of Solomon (cf. 1 Kings 11:41)

The Book of the Chronicles of the Kings of Judah (cf. 1 Kings 14:29, et al; this is not the biblical Books of Chronicles.)

The Book of the Chronicles of the Kings of Israel (cf. 1 Kings 14:19; et al; not our Chronicles)

The eyewitness accounts of other prophets were also used (cf. 2 Chron. 9:29; 13:22, Ahijah and Iddo; 12:15, Shemaiah; 20:34, Jehu; 26:22, Isaiah; some or all possibly were used here). In addition to the sources which are cited, other records were probably used. Obviously, the final editing and compilation of this material could not have been done until after the last events had occurred, in the exilic period of the sixth century BC. To have written of events in the sixth century which occurred as far back as the tenth century, the writers must have used some kind of earlier sources.

Granting that the final compilation of these books took place no earlier than the sixth century, the immediate reason for drawing the material together is presented. The great catastrophe of the destruction of the land, Jerusalem, and the Temple, as well as the Exile had just occurred (586 BC). Many people, both Jews and outsiders, must have been asking, "Where was God when all this happened?" In the light of Israel being God's chosen people and Canaan being their Promised Land, how were they to understand all the tragedies which had befallen them? Throughout the rest of the ancient Near East, the defeat of a people or a nation was an indication that the god of the defeated people was weaker than the god of the victors. The proclamation of the Deuteronomic Historians was aimed precisely at that point. By illustrating that Yahweh was sovereign over history, punishing His people for unfaithfulness and disobedience in the past, the historians were also defined what had happened to the people in their present. God had not been defeated by the armies of Babylon. Only Israel had been defeated. God in His sovereign power had used the historical forces of Babylon to effect His work of judgment upon His own people. Even though the great defeat had come, God's promises still held. He was faithful and loyal even when His people were not.

Even as the Book of Deuteronomy had closed upon the theme of the death of Moses (God buries the worker but God's work goes on) so the Deuteronomic Histories end on the same note. God buried Israel in the Exile, but His work was going on. God was not the victim of history but the victor over history. That proclamation fully set the stage for the cross. Jesus was not the victim of Satan, Rome, Judas, or a conniving priesthood. Rather, He was the victor! Of all the religions in the world, only Judaism developed a theology of exile under the inspiration of God. That was a major step on the way to the cross. The themes of judgment and hope were proclaimed through these books to a people in despair.

The summary of the probable date and authorship of the Former Prophets is just that, a summary. Almost certainly these books were prophetic in outlook and reached their final form in the Exile. The Books of 1 and 2 Chronicles appear to be priestly and Levitical in outlook and seem to have been completed somewhat later. Even as the four Gospels give us a full picture of the life of Jesus, these two different approaches to the understanding of Israel's history provide a full and balanced understanding of the full meaning and message of Israel's history.

13

Joshua

Joshua is the first book of the Former Prophets in the Prophets of the Jewish canon. Although it serves as the beginning of the second part of the Jewish canon, it continues the story of Israel after the death of Moses. Specifically, it tells of Israel's entrance into Canaan, the land's essential capture under the leadership of Joshua, and its division into tribal allotments. The focal points, however, appear to be the great ceremonies of covenant renewal (8:30-35; 24:1-28). The title of the book in both the Hebrew and the Greek (LXX) comes from the name of its hero, Joshua.

Date and Authorship

Traditionally, the book has been ascribed to Joshua's authorship, although it makes no claim of authorship. In 8:32, Joshua is said to have written "a copy of the law of Moses," but that was recorded on stones and is clearly not the Book of Joshua. The statement in 24:26 that "Joshua wrote these words in the book of the law of God" appears to refer only to the covenant "statutes and ordinances" (cf. v. 25) and not to the book as a whole. The information in the book clearly had to come from Joshua or someone who was present at the events recorded there. Much of the historical and geographical detail appear to come from an eyewitness. Indications that the book was put into its final form long after the time of Joshua include statements that things were still in existence "to this day" (cf. 4:9; 7:26; 8:28; et al). Such explanations clearly point to a time of final writing well after the events recorded.

The material in Joshua has a decidedly Deuteronomic

flavor to it, particularly its emphasis upon the covenant and
its renewal. The book appears to have been placed in its
final form some time after the days of Joshua by the
Deuteronomic Historians, probably during the time of the
monarchy.

Critical Issues in the Book

At least five significant issues have been raised by scholars who have sought to understand and interpret the book
of Joshua. The first of these has to do with the nature of the
sources which were used in the book's final compilation. At
least one source is clearly identified, the "Book of Jasher"
(10:13). Other than that this book is quoted elsewhere in the
Former Prophets, we know nothing about it. This book
would appear to have been some kind of anthology of ancient Hebrew poetry dealing with the great events of Israel's past. Many scholars believe that the same basic sources
which they felt were found in the Pentateuch are carried
over into Joshua. However, they have reached no consensus
in the identification of any of these sources. It does appear,
however, that there were significant materials which the
author/editor of Joshua used in the final compilation. These
probably included oral, written, and eyewitness account
sources.

The question about which tribes and who among the people of Israel were involved in the conquest under Joshua is
the second issue of importance. A first reading of the book
might not raise such a question, but a thorough analysis of
its material clearly does. Immediately after the conquest of
Ai-Bethel, Joshua and the people turned northward and
marched about twenty-five miles through what is supposed
to have been the heart of enemy (Canaanite) territory. On
the slopes of Mount Ebal and Mount Gerizim they apparently held a covenant festival. (8:30-35). Situated in the valley
between those two mountains was Shechem, a major Canaanite city-state. Why was that location chosen when it
would have been far more logical to have selected an al-
ready-conquered site? How could that have been done without conflict with the inhabitants of Shechem or the region?

Many serious biblical scholars have suggested that not all of Israel remained in Egypt for the entire period of oppression. Joshua may have found the region of Shechem already under the control of Hebrew people, people who had experienced neither the great deliverance of the Exodus nor the covenant ceremony at Sinai. If that were true, the covenant ceremony would have been intended to include them in the redemptive experience, making them one nation under God. That would also explain how Joshua and his army could move through the region without opposition.

The third critical issue in the study of the Book of Joshua has to do with the nature of the conquest itself. Again, a first and hurried reading of the book leaves the impression that the victory was sudden, overwhelming, and total. That impression is undergirded by such statements as "Joshua defeated the whole land" (10:40), "Joshua took all that land" (11:16), and "they put to the sword all who were in it" (v. 11). On the other hand, the Book of Judges and all the subsequent history of the monarchy would indicate that many Canaanites and their city-states were left untouched, for they created problems for Israel for centuries. Even the Book of Joshua acknowledges that state of affairs, for the Lord said to Joshua at the end of his days, "There remains yet very much land to be possessed" (13:1).

Some scholars have proposed that the Bible preserves two conflicting traditions. More to the point is the suggestion that the history writers, in looking back to the conquest of Joshua, had idealized the conquest (as people are prone to do), while acknowledging that Joshua left an unfinished task which his successors were forced to deal with both immediately and over the centuries. An even more appropriate proposal appears to be that, for all practical purposes, Joshua had captured the land. He had isolated it from the outside. What was left to do, even though extensive, was primarily a mopping-up operation. From that standpoint, both concepts are true. Anyone who has ever been involved in a military conquest can clearly understand this approach. The land had been taken. Yet many sites were still under Canaanite control and remained yet to be overcome.

The issue of the total decimation of the population of cities is the fourth critical issue which must be considered. This was also a concern in the Book of Deuteronomy, perhaps one more indication of the common background or relationship of these two books. We must acknowledge that fundamental to the Hebrews understanding was the concept of *cherem*, "the devoted [or sanctified] thing." In the thinking of that day, that which was *cherem* belonged to God. Israel was not allowed to appropriate such to itself, it was to be offered to God. The total destruction of all which was *cherem* accomplished that.

The fifth major issue has to do with the date of the conquest. It must be closely tied with the date of the Exodus event, for the wilderness experience and the time at Sinai lasted for a total of forty years. Thus the conquest has to be dated forty years after the Exodus. The biblical evidence can be interpreted to indicate a date for the Exodus in the fifteenth or in the thirteenth century BC. It is possible that we actually have two different traditions, which would put a group of Hebrews coming into Canaan in the latter part of each of these two centuries. The Joshua account might indicate that other Hebrews were present when he and his armies arrived, so his conquest could be dated in the last half of the thirteenth century BC. This is further underscored by the victory stela of Pharoah Merneptah. This stela, dated sometime around 1220 BC, identifies a people in Canaan at that time by the name of Israel. They are identified not as a nation, nor as a city-state, but as a loosely organized group. That would have been the case if they were still involved in the process of conquest. On the other hand, if the entire group had been in control for two centuries, it should have been otherwise identified.

Archaeology and the Conquest Under Joshua

The biblical account of the conquest gives little detail. At this point the science of archaeology is helpful. Archaeology neither proves nor disproves the Bible. Belief or disbelief in the Bible is a matter of faith. On the other hand, archaeology helps in visualizing the events that Joshua records.

The biblical narrative of the conquest under Joshua divides it into three distinct phases. First, there was the push across Jordan and into the central hill country. That involved the miraculous defeat of Jericho (6:1-21), the initial defeat by and ultimate victory over Ai and Bethel (7:2-5; 8:1-29), and the trickery and surrender of the people of Gibeon, accomplished without the defeat of their city (9:3-18). The second phase of the conquest involved the encirclement of the hill country of southern Judah, capturing the cities of Makkedah, Libnah, Lachish, Eglon, Hebron, and Debir (10:28-38). The third major phase was the Galilean campaign, which focused upon the city of Hazor (11:1-15). In addition to these specific territorial conquests, Joshua is also said to have had several other victories over armies in the field which apparently did not involve the conquest of specific cities (10:1 *ff.*). He is also given credit for the conquest of major areas without specific cities being listed (10:40-43; 11:16-20). With this biblical material in mind, we must consider and evaluate the data from the excavations of these ancient sites.

Jericho

The site of ancient Jericho has been excavated frequently, with significant excavations having been carried out periodically from 1930 to the present. The earlier excavations of John Garstang were thought to have identified the ruins of the wall destroyed in Joshua's campaign, with its destruction being dated to about 1400 BC. Subsequent excavations have led to a reassessment of that evidence. The ruins which Garstang found are more properly dated about four centuries earlier. At the present time, no ruins possibly datable to the time of Joshua have been identified. Such ruins may have been missed due to the fact that the city may have been smaller than at first expected. Weathering, erosion, and plundering of this mound for building stone by later inhabitants of other nearby sites may have eliminated or significantly reduced the available evidence.

Ai

The Hebrew name for Ai literally means "the ruin." The modern location of the site is not absolutely certain. It most probably is to be identified with the modern et-Tell, slightly east of Bethel and about ten miles north of Jerusalem. The evidence seems to indicate no significant occupation at all during the time of Joshua. More than likely it was a military outpost of Bethel. The defeat of Joshua's army by such an outpost would have been even more startling. His ultimate victory and slaughter of all the inhabitants would have then probably included both the outpost and the city it guarded.

Bethel

Excavations at Bethel show a massive overthrow and the burning of everything combustible around 1230 to 1220 BC. The fact that the Bible does not mention the overthrow of Bethel makes it even more probable that Bethel and Ai were two parts of the same campaign. Evidence exists for new settlements at both Bethel and Ai immediately following this period.

Gibeon

The Bible records no overthrow of Gibeon, but a peace made by subterfuge. Excavations of this site, the modern el-Jib, show no sign of destruction. Instead, the cultural occupation remains the same throughout the period, exactly as would have been expected.

The invasion of the central hill country effectively cut the land in two. A direct attack upon the southern hill country would probably have produced a long, drawnout campaign of slow attrition characterized by long seiges and guerrilla-type warfare. To avoid that, Joshua devised a brilliant military strategy and surrounded the region. He took, in turn, each major fortification along the access routes into the region. The southern campaign effectively isolated the region from all outside help.

Makkedah

Makkedah is probably to be identified as either the modern Khirbet el-Kneism or Khirbet Maqdum. Neither site has been excavated. Makkedah was apparently a fortress on one side of a valley controlled on the other side by Libnah.

Libnah

Libnah is located at the entrance of the Valley of Elah (where David later killed Goliath, 1 Sam. 17:2). It is presently identified with the modern site of Tell es-Safi. If this identification is correct, the city guarded both the entrance into the hill country by the Valley of Elah and the main north-south highway in the Shephelah. Due to current occupation of the site, the area available for excavation is quite limited. It appears to have been quite a significant city in pre-Israelite times and was settled during Israelite times as well. Due to the very limited excavations, all conclusions, including its actual identification, are quite tentative.

Lachish

Lachish was a Canaanite royal city. It was used regularly by the various peoples of Palestine as a major fortress guarding one of the valley entrances into the central hill country. It has been identified as the modern site of Tell ed-Duweir. It had massive walls for defense prior to the time of Joshua. W. F. Albright dated its almost total destruction to the fourth year of Pharaoh Merneptah, thus placing its fall at about 1230 BC.

Eglon

Early archaeologists identified Eglon with the modern Tell 'Atun, although most scholars today prefer the identification of Tell el-Hesi. It was also a fortress city, guarding a major valley entrance into the southern highlands. The city appears to have undergone a massive destruction sometime during the late twelve hundreds. A considerable ash layer, which varies from one to two-and-a-half meters thick, has been found in every pit sunk on the mound. Though some

have suggested that this was due to a major smelting industry, it appears more likely to have been the result of a
massive destruction of the city.

Hebron

With all of the major valleys from the coastal plain being
cut off from the highlands, the next logical step on the part
of an invading army would have been to actually enter the
highlands in the south to cut off the southern entrance into
the land. That is precisely what Joshua did. Hebron is located at the modern site of el-Kalil, on a major route about
twenty miles south of Jerusalem. It also had a more ancient
name, Kiriath-Arba. When the Hebrew spies had first entered the land from Kadesh in the time of Moses, Hebron
was one of the cities they investigated (Num. 13:22). Archaeological evidence suggests a major destruction at about the
time of Joshua with no immediate resettlement.

Debir

Having closed off the highlands from the south, Joshua
then turned the army further southward and came upon
the last southern fortress city in an attack from the rear.
Debir was earlier known as Kiriath-sepher. Archaeologists
long identified this city with Tell Beit Mirsim. More recent
excavations have shown that it is more likely to be identified with Khirbet Rabud, located about seven miles southwest of Hebron. It was a strong fortress and shows evidence
of a massive overthrow near the end of the thirteenth century BC. The settlements which followed are somewhat
more primitive in culture than that which preceded it,
which is precisely what would be expected.

With the completion of the isolation of the southern highlands, Joshua had several options opened to him. He could
have marched into the highlands, beginning a long war
designed to overthrow all of the inhabitants in that region,
city by city and village by village. The nature of the geography would have made that both difficult and costly. On the
other hand, with all access to the region cut off, he could
have simply sat back and waited for the eventual weaken-

ing of the inhabitants and their will to resist, making conquest more easily attainable. Choosing the latter alternative, he turned to the north to cut it off also. He already had the northern highlands isolated from the south. All that remained was to isolate it from the north.

Hazor

Hazor was the major fortress city on the main entrance of the northern highway into the region of Canaan. This is located as the modern Tell ed-Qedah, a city about ten miles north of the Sea of Galilee. Judging from the size of its ruins, it was one of the largest cities in ancient Canaan. Its population is generally estimated to have been about forty thousand people at the time of its violent overthrow near the end of the thirteenth century BC. That victory was almost certainly Joshua's greatest feat of arms. With the fall of that major city, Joshua had essentially completed his task, for the land of Canaan was completely isolated from outside help. Further, all of its major border fortresses had been overthrown.

In a thorough examination of the archaeological evidence of the cities which Joshua overthrew, along with other excavations in the land, several features stand out. (1) In no way does archaeology "prove" the Hebrew conquest of Canaan. No discovery names either Joshua or Israel as the conqueror of any site. (2) Where there is evidence from archaeological excavations, the cities which have been identified suffered a violent overthrow near the end of the thirteenth century BC, around 1230 BC or later. (3) Examining the location of the cities appears to demonstrate that they were not selected at random but were carefully chosen as a part of one unified military strategy for isolating the land from outside help. (4) Where evidence is available, the culture of the settlers who followed the violent overthrow was somewhat more primitive than that which preceded it. This makes it easy to believe that a long-established city culture was replaced by that of a group of nomads or freed slaves. (5) Those cities which were not overthrown, according to the narrative, such as Gibeon, added through subterfuge, Shechem, assimilated through covenant, and Jerusalem by merely bypassing it do not show any archaeological evidence of a violent overthrow. (6) Those sites which had no settlement prior to the latter part of the thirteenth century but which were occupied immediately thereafter show a culture similar to the replacement culture of the overthrown cities. (7) Some other cities, unmentioned in the Book of Joshua, also show evidence of a violent overthrow in the latter part of the thirteenth century BC. All of this lends credance to the biblical portrait of the overthrow of Canaan under Joshua and also appears to confirm the basic chronological conclusions about the date of Israel's entrance into Canaan under Joshua.

Joshua, the Man

The hero of the narrative is Joshua, one of the two courageous and faithful spies from Kadesh (Num. 14:6-9). He had served as one of Moses' main associates throughout the Exodus experience (cf. Ex. 24:13; 32:15-17). Joshua's name is given once as Hoseha (Num. 13:8, meaning "salvation") but was apparently changed by Moses to Joshua (Num. 13:16, meaning "Yahweh is salvation," or "Yahweh saves"). The Greek form of his name is *Iesous,* Jesus. He was designated as Moses' successor, apparently accepting that fact with some fear and trepidation, as he had to be encouraged at least four times when he was actually forced to take command of Israel (Josh. 1:6-7,9,18). He appears as a brilliant military strategist, a man of faith, and an able leader and administrator. He ably fulfilled the responsibility of stepping from a position of second place into the vacant shoes of a great leader.

The Content of the Book

I. The conquest of western Palestine (1:1 to 12:24)
  A. The commission of Joshua (1:1-9)
  B. Preparation for the invasion (1:10 to 2:24)
    1. Joshua's challenge to prepare (1:10-15)

2. The people's response (1:16 to 2:11)
3. Spies sent into Canaan (2:12-24)

Joshua's sending of the spies into Canaan prior to the invasion had to have brought back memories of his own earlier trip into the land as a spy. He had to have had some reluctance because of the earlier experience at Kadesh. Yet, as a military commander, he needed accurate information concerning what he and the army were going to have to face when they actually invaded.

To the modern mind, the idea of a house built upon the wall of a city sounds quite strange (2:15). Excavations have uncovered such, however, demonstrating not merely the validity of such a feature but also its relatively common practice. It was apparently a means of increasing the number of dwellings inside a city when its territory had already been set by the construction of the city wall.

C. Entry into the land (3:1 to 5:12)
    1. Miraculous crossing of the Jordan (3:1 to 4:18)
    2. Establishment of the camp at Gilgal (4:19 to 5:12)
D. The invasion of central Canaan (5:13 to 10:15)
    1. The Jericho campaign (5:13 to 6:27)
        a. Joshua's experience with an angelic visitor (5:13-15)
        b. The army encircling the city (6:1-14)
        c. Jericho's fall (6:15-21)
        d. The deliverance of Rahab (6:22-25)
        e. The curse over the ruins (6:26)
        f. God's presence with Joshua (6:27)

The miraculous fall of Jericho is quite familiar to most students of the Bible. What is not so familiar is the fact that Rahab's incorporation into Israel provided the offspring from which David ultimately descended and thus from which great David's greater Son was descended (Matt. 1:15-16). Such was the wisdom of God that a prostitute might find a place in His ultimate plan of redemption. Joshua's curse upon those who might rebuild Jericho found its fulfillment in 1 Kings 16:34.

The ultimate victory over Jericho brought fame to Joshua. But there was to be no question as to whom the ultimate victory belonged, for it was Yahweh who "was with Joshua" (6:27).

    2.   The Ai-Bethel campaign (7:1 to 8:29)
        a. Failure in the first attempt (7:1-26)
           (*1*) Achan's theft of devoted things (7:1-26)
           (*2*) Defeat in the attempt (7:2-5)
           (*3*) The sin set forth (7:6-21)
           (*4*) The punishment of Achan (7:22-26)
        b. Victory in the second attempt (8:1-29)
           (*1*) Yahweh's announcement of victory (8:1-2)
           (*2*) The stragetic plan (8:3-9)
           (*3*) The victory (8:10-29)

Much more important from a theological standpoint, than whether Ai was a military outpost for Bethel, is the concept set forth in the passage dealing with Achan's sin. The Old Testament has a strong concept of corporate personality. Every individual was aware of being a part of the entire nation and of how individuals' acts bore fruit in the entire congregation. Modern individualism is quite foreign to the Old Testament. When Achan sinned, all Israel was guilty. Thus the nation was defeated. Carried to its ultimate dimension, when the specific guilt of Achan was identified, not only was he punished but also his "sons and daughters, and his oxen and asses and sheep, and his tent, and all that he had" were also held responsible (7:24).

The idea of the casting of lots was a common part of Israel's ancient Near Eastern heritage. The high priest carried such lots in the pockets on his vestments. The casting of lots was used to identify the sinful person when Israel was defeated.

To fully appreciate the strategic planning which went into Joshua's military victories, you need to locate the sites described in these accounts on a good map. The careful planning of the entire attack becomes obvious. The major roads were cut, and the valley entrances into the central highlands were controlled. Furthermore, the conquest of those cities was an amazing feat of arms. While not all of the fortresses were that significant, Hazor was one of the major cities in that region of the world. Its defeat and destruction would have been a significant military accomplishment for anyone. For it to have been accomplished by a group wandering in from the desert is even more amazing. It was not attempted until Joshua's army had gained significant experience. Yet, even then, it was still a major military accomplishment.

The recurring theme through the entire narrative is that the accomplishments were not really due to Joshua's military genius or to Israel's military prowess. The victories are clearly ascribed to the God of Israel (10:42).

    2.   The request of Caleb (14:6-15)
    3.   Judah (15:1-63)
    4.   Manasseh and Ephraim (16:1 to 17:18)
    5.   Benjamin, Simon, Zebulun, Issachar, Asher, Naphtali, and Dan (18:1 to 19:51)
  D. The cities of refuge (20:1-9)
  E. The Levitical cities (21:1-42)

At one time scholars suggested that the allotment of the land was not really done in the time of Joshua. They said this was simply an idealized priestly reconstruction of what might have been or should have been. However, a thorough study of these lists by modern historians and archaeologists appears to demonstrate that the places listed were under Hebrew control during the time of Israel's greatest territorial expansion, the time of David. There is no reason to date them to the exilic era.

    The request which Caleb made to Joshua is quite fascinating. He and Joshua were the two spies among those Moses sent into Canaan from Kadesh who believed that they should attack the land then. Only he and Joshua survived of that generation, thus he had to be quite an old man. Yet he requested of Joshua the most difficult part of the central hill country as his allotment of land, saying, "I am this day eighty-five years old. I am still as strong to this day as I was in the day that Moses sent me; my strength now is as my strength was then, for war, and for going and coming. So now give me this hill country" (14:10-12). He was a man of courage and action to the end of his life.

    III. A time of commitment and covenant renewal (21:43 to 24:33)
      A. Statement of God's faithfulness (21:43-45)
      B. Departure of the Transjordan tribes (22:1-34)
        1.   Joshua sends them away (22:1-9)
        2.   The altar by the Jordan (22:10-34)
      C. Joshua's address at Shechem (23:1-16)
      D. A second address and the covenant renewal (24:1-28)
        1.   Joshua's challenge (24:1-24)

One of the great pieces of the world's oratory is Joshua's final address as he led the people of Israel to a new commitment to Yahweh's covenant. Through the recitation of God's mighty acts and his own commitment, Joshua carefully led the people Israel to the point of their own commitment. No great leader ever asks his people to go further than he is willing to go himself. Joshua had his people clamoring to be allowed to serve God with their whole being.

The Book of Joshua sets forth over and over again in specific historical situations its basic theological proposition. God can be depended upon. He keeps His promises. He did in Joshua's day. He still does.

14

Judges

The second book of the Former Prophets is Judges, whose name is derived from the heroes whom Yahweh raised up to deliver the Israelites in times of crisis. While serving as the narrative bridge between the conquest under Joshua and the rise of the kingdom in the time of Samuel, Judges is strangely unlike either book in structure. At the same time, it clearly has a Deuteronomic outlook: God is in sovereign control and Israel's sinful rebellion will be punished. The theme acknowledges that God's purposes cannot ultimately be thwarted. Judges has some of the most fascinating stories in the Old Testament, vivid in description and fast in action. Once read, the stories of Ehud, Deborah, Gideon, Jephthah, and Samson are not soon forgotten. One of the world's earliest folk songs, the Song of Deborah, is found in Judges. The book deserves study for its literature alone; but God speaks through its pages, and that is our basic reason for studying Judges.

Date and Authorship of the Book

Judges nowhere gives any clue as to the author. The earliest Jewish tradition identifies Samuel as the author, but no one today takes this claim seriously. Its ultimate outlook on faith makes it likely that it is a product of the Deuteronomic Historians.

The date of Judges is difficult to establish. It obviously contains some very ancient material from eyewitnesses. Other expressions are from a later time than the events themselves. For example, "In those days there was no king in Israel" appears to come from a time after the kingship had been established (see 18:1; 19:1). Judges 18:31 indicates that Shiloh had already been destroyed, but that did not occur until at least the time of Eli and Samuel (1 Sam. 4:12-18). Some have suggested that the statement in 18:30 that the priests of Dan served "until the day of the captivity of the land" indicates that the final writing of the book did not take place either until the fall of Israel in 722 BC or the fall of Judah in 586 BC. However, the next verse makes it appear that the reference was to the captivity of the ark and the ultimate fall of Shiloh. The book was probably written during the days of the united monarchy or shortly thereafter.

Major Issues in the Study of the Book

Among the basic issues which interpreters usually consider in the study of the Book of Judges, seven are worthy of consideration: the structure of the book, the nature of the Canaanite religion, the nature of a judge, the chronology of the period, the oppressions themselves, the issue of amphictyony, and the emotional impact of the judges.

The Structure of the Book

The major part of the Book of Judges begins with chapter 3 and continues through chapter 16. This block tells of the activities of twelve deliverers (thirteen, if you include Abimelech, Gideon's son). This is followed by two units of rather extraneous material, the Danite migration and Micah's graven image (chs. 17—18) and the almost total destruction of the tribe of Benjamin (chs. 19—21). The main part of the book is introduced by a section (chs. 1—2) connecting Judges with Joshua and setting forth the basic philosophy of history behind the book. The basic outline of the philosophy goes through several specific steps.

1. "And the people of Israel did what was evil in the sight of the Lord and served the Baals; . . . They forsook the Lord and served the Baals and the Ashtaroth" (2:11-13).
2. "So the anger of the Lord was kindled against Israel" (v.14).

3. "He gave them over to plunderers, who plundered them; and he sold them into the power of their enemies round about, so that they could no longer withstand their enemies . . . as the Lord had warned, and as the Lord had sworn to them" (vv.14b-15).

4. "Then the Lord raised up judges, who saved them out of the power of those who plundered them" (v.16).

5. And yet they did not listen to their judges; for they played the harlot after other gods" (v.17).

6. "Whenever the Lord raised up judges for them, the Lord was with the judge, and he saved them from the hand of their enemies all of the days of the judge; for the Lord was moved to pity by their groaning because of those who afflicted and oppressed them" (v.18).

7. "But whenever the judge died, they turned back and behaved worse than their fathers" (v.19).

8. "So the anger of the Lord was kindled against Israel" (v.20).

The author clearly saw the history of Israel, as moving through the specific steps of apostasy, Yahweh's anger, oppression, the groaning of Israel, Yahweh's pity, the raising up of a deliverer, and deliverance. After the Israelites were delivered, they became apostate and the whole process began again. At first glance, this view of history appears to be identical to the cyclical view of history which Israel's neighbors (particularly the Canaanites) held. A more thorough reading reveals that the Hebrew view of history differs in two ways from the cyclical view. First of all, the cycle was not automatic. It happened as a result of Israel's deliberate choices. Second, it differs because the responses of God are the fulfillment of His promises in the covenant. He promised judgment upon apostasy and, at the same time, set forth the basic teachings of His love and mercy. In spite of the repeating cycles which Israel experienced, God was sovereign over history, not the reverse. History was ultimately under God's control and was moving toward the ultimate fulfillment of His purposes.

Those who compiled the material did so under the inspiration of God from a Deuteronomic viewpoint. Israel was

responsible to God as His covenant people. As such, they
had to face the responsibilities of their own choices and
actions. The main part of the book is a narrative cycle adding the details of each oppression and deliverance.

The Nature of the Canaanite Religion

Possibly related to the original demand that the Canaanites be destroyed, and certainly related to the constant problem which Israel had with apostasy, is the nature of the
Canaanite religion itself. The details of the Canaanite religion are known because of the discovery and translation of
a large number of clay tablets from ancient Ugarit (the
modern Ras Shamra). Several hundred such tablets were
found in northern Syria beginning in 1929. They date from
the earlier part of the fourteenth century BC and set forth
in ritual, myth, and epic the religion of Canaan.

Canaanite religion was a fertility cult, intended to guar-
antee the fertility of the land, the crops, the flocks, and the
people of Canaan. The Baals ("Lords") were the rulers of
each of the various territories of the land and were worshiped upon the hilltops, the "high places" of the Old Testament. Baal worship was highly sexual in nature. The priests
and priestesses were little more than sacred prostitutes,
and worship involved having sexual intercourse at the high
places. Such was supposed to ensure the fertility of everything about which the people were concerned. The appeal
that such worship would have upon the physical lusts of
people is quite understandable.

People of the ancient Near East believed that gods had
control over a specific territory or a specific function. Thus
the Hebrews found it easy to believe that Yahweh was a
"god" of the wilderness and/or of victorious warfare. They
also found it easy to believe that the Baals of Canaan knew
more about successful agriculture and the specific needs of
running farms in Canaan. This belief coupled with the sen-
sual appeal of the Canaanite cults made it quite easy for
Israel to justify worshiping the Baals of the land. (Note:
Baalim is simply a transliteration of the Hebrew plural
form of Baal. Thus Baalim and Baals are the same word.

The -*im* ending in Hebrew is the normal masculine plural. Thus, seraphim is the plural of seraph.)

Israel's problem with the worship of the Baals was not just confined to its early period in the land. Clearly, it did have much trouble with that temptation in the period of the judges. But it was still having a major problem with Baal worship in the great days of the Northern Kingdom, during the eighth century when Amos and Hosea prophesied.

The Nature of a Judge

The title of *judge* when applied to the deliverers in the Book of Judges is misleading to modern readers. The judges usually did not render judgments upon disputes or complaints brought before them for consideration. Only a very few of the judges may have had such a function. Furthermore, the Bible does not often even call any of these leaders or deliverers by the title of judge. They are more often described as having "judged" Israel.

The basic function of the judges is best described as savior or deliverer. They frequently, though not always, furnished some sort of military leadership to overthrow the oppressors of the land. They were obviously in their positions by virtue of the native gifts which they possessed and because God had elected to use those gifts to accomplish His purposes. In that sense, modern commentators frequently call them "charismatic leaders." When the basic need was over, they generally seem to have faded into the background.

The judges themselves came from varied stations and occupations. Deborah was a woman and a prophetess (4:4). Gideon was a farmer (6:11), Jephthah was a soldier (11:1), and Samson was apparently a rural playboy (13:9,24; 16:1,4,). Each of these, along with the others, was raised up by God at a particular time and place to deliver the people of Israel from an oppressing enemy. Regardless of their individual backgrounds and abilities, they were instruments of God's deliverance for Israel.

The judges are usually classified as either major or minor judges, depending upon the amount of detail given to each. The major judges are Ehud (3:15-30), Deborah (4:4 to 5:31),

Gideon (6:11 to 6:35), Jephthah (11:1 to 12:7), and Samson (13:2 to 16:31). The minor judges are Shamgar (3:31), Tola (10:1-2), Jair (vv.3-5), Ibzan (12:8-10), Elon (vv.11-12), and Abdon (vv.13-15). Interpreters disagree about whether Othniel (3:7-11) ought to be classified as a major or minor judge. I personally consider him a major judge. Finally, there is disagreement as to whether Abimelech, Gideon's son, should be called a judge at all (cf. 9:1-57). I do not think his abortive attempt at kingship should qualify him as a judge. We have enough information to study the major judges. Any suggestions concerning the functions or accomplishments of the minor judges is wholly speculative.

The Chronology of the Period

The chronology of the judges may not be as simple as it first appears. The judges' various periods of service and the times of peace between add up to 410 years. First Kings 6:1 says that Solomon began to build the Temple 480 years after the Exodus. That would allow only 70 years to cover the 40 years in the wilderness, Joshua's conquest of Canaan, the judgeships of Eli and Samuel, and the reigns of Saul, David, and the first four years of Solomon.

The Bible comes to the rescue. A more thorough reading of the data in Judges shows that in most instances, three or fewer tribes were involved in each oppression. In the instance of Deborah, only ten tribes are mentioned and two of those, Machir and Gilead, may only have been clans from a tribe instead of the entire tribe (5:14-18). The following table illustrates this point.

Oppressions of the Time of the Judges		
Judge	*Tribe(s) Involved*	*Reference*
Othniel	??(Caleb of Judah?)	3:7-11
Ehud	Benjamin, Ephraim	3:12-30
Shamgar	??	3:31
Deborah	Ephraim, Benjamin, Machir, Zebulun, Issachar, Reuben, Gilead, Dan, Asher, Naphtali	4:1 to 5:31
Gideon	Manasseh, Asher, Zebulun, Naphtali, Ephraim	6:1 to 8:35
Tola	Issachar, Ephraim	10:1-2

Jair	Gilead (?)	10:3-5
Jephthah	Judah, Benjamin, Ephraim	10:6 to 12:7
Ibzan	?? (Judah?)	12:8-10
Elon	Zebulun (?)	12:11-12
Abdon	Ephraim (?)	12:13-15
Samson	Dan, Judah	13:1 to 16:31

Even a hurried look at this table leaves the impression that most, if not all, of the oppressions involved were rather limited in scope. Reading the biblical material and locating the territory of the oppressors also confirms this.

The conclusion that most of the oppressions were limited in scope leads to the realization that two or more oppressions may have been going on at the same time. When two events are going on at the same time, they have to be written about one after the other. This theory, which the Bible itself makes probable, allows the total number of years necessary for the period covered by the Book of Judges to be less than 410 years.

One other feature of the narratives may shrink the total number of years a bit further. A significant number of references to chronological data in Judges appear as a multiple of forty. The peace after Othniel, Deborah, and Gideon, as well as the oppression of the Philistines, is stated as forty years (3:11; 5:31; 8:28; 13:1). Further, the oppression by Jabin and Samson's judgeship are both given at twenty years (one-half of forty; 4:3; 15:20; 16:31). Finally, the peace after Ehud is given as eighty years (two times forty; 3:30). Some numbers appear to have a special meaning to the Hebrews and may sometimes have been used as symbols or figures of speech rather than literal numbers. Among these are three, seven, ten, and twelve. Forty sometimes appears to have been so used, either referring to a long, indefinite time or, when coupled with years, to a generation. If that is so in Judges, the references may be to a generation, a half-generation, or two generations. If this interpretation of the use of forty is accepted, the period of the judges can be further reduced.

At the very least, the period of judges must be fitted in to that block of time between 1220 and about 1020 BC. At the longest, it must fit from about 1400 to about 1020 BC. Either way, acknowledging the probability of two or more oppressions occurring at the same time eliminates any problem with the chronological data.

The Oppressions Themselves

The various oppressors Israel faced during this period were after different things. The Canaanites appear to have been seeking to reestablish control over the territory which Israel had conquered upon entering the land. The Philistines landed upon the coastal plain shortly after Israel entered the central highland. Originally, scholars thought the Philistine invasion was made after having been defeated in an attempt to land on the coast of Egypt. It now appears that the Philistines may have been employed by the Egyptians as mercenaries to try to harrass the Hebrews. The Philistines were the first people in the region to know how to smelt iron. That gave them a major advantage in the ancient arms race (cf. 1 Sam. 13:19-22). The Philistines' pressure upon the Hebrews from the Shephelah almost led to the end of the Hebrew kingdom.

The Midanites and Amelekites made no attempt to conquer territory. Instead, their incursions into the land appear to have been primarily for plunder. They were willing for the Hebrews to possess the land and grow crops. They merely sought to steal Israel's produce at harvesttime. Finally, the Transjordan peoples, Edom, Moab, and Ammon, apparently did not see themselves as capable actually of taking territory from Israel. They appear, however, to have made an attack every time Israel was under pressure from some other source. They apparently wanted to create as many problems for Israel as possible.

The major feature of the oppressions, however, was not what the external enemy was doing. From the standpoint of the Hebrews, the oppressors were viewed as God's agents of punishment for Israel's apostasy and rebellion. In this period, God's inspired writers began to realize that He used men and nations without their own knowledge as agents of temporal judgment. This dimension of their faith had a major impact upon the later preaching of the prophets.

The Issue of the Amphictyony

Martin Noth in the first half of the twentieth century picked up a term from early Greek history and applied it to Israel: *amphictyony*. The term applies to a loose organization of peoples, bound together around a central sanctuary by a common cultus or worship form. He insisted that was precisely the situation in Israel during the period of the judges. A closer examination of the biblical material suggests numerous differences between the Greek structure and that which existed in Israel. Most books written on the period for the past thirty or forty years have made a great deal over the term *amphictyony* and its contribution toward understanding what was happening in Israel during this era. However, recent scholarship has largely abandoned both the term and the concept.

The Emotional Impact of the Judges

One last issue in understanding the Book of Judges has to do with the emotional impact which the inspired author created with his narratives. The narratives of the judges may bring us to the point of revulsion. Deborah's song of the gruesome slaughter of Sisera (5:24-27), Jephthah's slaying of his daughter, and Samson's dalliance with Delilah often repell the reader (11:30-39; 16:4-21). The biblical author seems to have gone out of the way to create this emotional response on our part. Perhaps he did. Could it be that a message is contained in our emotional response? Just as God could accomplish something with someone or something so revolting, so He could ultimately accomplish His purposes with rebellious Israel. The message appears to be that in spite of Israel's actions, Yahweh is still sovereign. If God could use Samson, He could also use Israel. If He could use Israel, He can use you and me.

The Content of the Book

I. The failure to complete the conquest of Canaan
(1:1 to 2:5)
   A. Successes and failures of Judah and Simeon
(1:1-21)
   B. Successes and failures of the house of Joseph
(1:22-28)
   C. Failures of the other tribes (1:29-36)
   D. Curse upon Israel's disobedience (2:1-5)
II. The work of the judges (2:6 to 16:31)
   A. Introduction to the era (2:6 to 3:6)
      1. The end of the work of Joshua (2:6-10)
      2. Israel's cycles of rebellion (2:11-23)
      3. The nations left in Canaan (3:1-6)

Part of this material overlaps with the end of the Book of
Joshua. This appears to indicate that even though many
scholars consider Judges to be a part of the Deuteronomic
Histories, it also had a separate existence prior to its final
inclusion.

   B. The judgeship of Othniel (3:7-11)
   C. The judgeship of Ehud (3:12-30)
      1. The oppression of Eglon, king of Moab
(3:12-14)
      2. Ehud's subterfuge and murder of Eglon
(3:15-23)
      3. The quandary of Eglon's servants (3:24-25)
      4. Israel's victory over Moab (3:26-30)

Ehud's secret message for Eglon at the time of the bringing
of tribute seems to have aroused the king's greed, as he
apparently expected a special gift or bribe. Ehud's being
left-handed caught the king by surprise, for at best he would
have been watching Ehud's right hand, the normal hand for
using a weapon. The vivid description of Eglon's death is
another of those gruesome touches characteristic of Judges.

   D. The judgeship of Shamgar (3:31)
   E. The judgeship of Deborah (4:1 to 5:31)

1. The oppression of Jabin, king of Hazor (4:1-3)
2. Deborah's message to Barak (4:4-7)
3. Barak's cowardice and final agreement (4:8-10)
4. Introduction of Heber the Kenite (4:11)
5. Victory over Sisera's army (4:12-16)
6. Treachery and murder of Sisera by Jael (4:17-22)
7. The ultimate defeat of Jabin (4:23-24)
8. The Song of Deborah (5:1-31)

Deborah served Yahweh both as a prophetess and as a judge. She was far more heroic than Barak, the military leader. The Song of Deborah is certainly one of the older songs, if not the oldest, in the Bible. Its reference to Taanach near Megiddo places the song earlier than 1125 BC, for the fortress was totally destroyed then and never reconstructed. The listing of the various tribes and clans would indicate that although many should have had a part, only a few responded with any significant number of troops. The description of the anxiety of Sisera's mother, awaiting the return of her son from battle, touches the heart of anyone who has awaited news of loved ones who have gone forth to war.

F. The judgeship of Gideon (6:1 to 8:35)
   1. The crisis of the Midianite oppression (6:1-10)
   2. The call of Gideon (6:11-40)
      a. Gideon confronted while hiding (6:11-16)
      b. Gideon's act of sacrifice (6:17-24)
      c. The destruction of the altar to Baal (6:25-32)
      d. The call to battle (6:33-35)
      e. Putting out the fleece, a final confirmation (6:36-40)
   3. Reducing the size of the army (7:1-8)
   4. Spying out the camp of Midian (7:9-15)

     5.   The initial victory (7:16-23)
     6.   The final victory (7:24 to 8:21)
     7.   Gideon's rejection of the offer of kingship
        (8:22-28)
     8.   Gideon's death and Israel's apostasy
        (8:29-35)

The author included a great deal of humor, possibly to relieve the tension, in introducing the story of Gideon. Gideon was addressed as a brave man while hiding in the wine vat trying to thresh his wheat. The whole episode with the fleece is presented as an attempt by Gideon to escape doing God's will. He already knew what God wanted and sought to propose such an impossible situation that he could avoid it. When God miraculously responded, Gideon was so taken aback that he reversed the test, only to have his call confirmed again. With no other path left, he finally submitted and became the leader God intended him to be. He was so successful as a general and as a leader that the people sought to crown him king. He resisted, but one of his sons was not so loyal to Yahweh.

     G. Interlude with Abimelech's abortive kingship
        (9:1-57)
     H. The judgeship of Tola (10:1-2)
     I. The judgeship of Jair (10:3-5)
     J. The judgeship of Jephthah (10:6 to 12:7)
        1.   Israel's rebellion and oppression (10:6-18)
        2.   Jephthah called to serve (11:1-11)
        3.   Jephthah's victory and rash vow (11:12-33)
        4.   The death of his daughter (11:34-40)
        5.   The rebellion of the Ephraimites (12:1-7)
     K. The judgeship of Ibzan (12:8-10)
     L. The judgeship of Elon (12:11-12)
     M. The judgeship of Abdon (12:13-15)
     N. The judgeship of Samson (13:1 to 16:31)
        1.   The Philistine oppression (13:1)
        2.   The miraculous birth of Samson (13:2-25)
        3.   Samson's love for a Philistine woman (14:1
           to 15:8)

       a. The arrangement of the marriage (14:1-4)

       b. The slaughter of the lion (14:5-9)

       c. Samson's riddle and its outcome (14:10-20)

       d. Samson's anger at being deprived of his bride (15:1-8)

    4. Samson's victory over the Philistines (15:9-20)

    5. Samson's weakness for women (16:1-22)

       a. The harlot at Gaza (16:1-3)

       b. Delilah's treachery (16:4-19)

       c. The tragic consequences (16:20-22)

    6. Samson's vengeance and self-sacrifice (16:23-31)

The story of Samson is familiar. Two features stand out. He is shown as a selfish playboy throughout most of the story. Even so, he was used of God to bring respite to Israel from the Philistines. Perhaps the most tragic verse in the Old Testament is found in his statement after Delilah's treachery. When she awoke him from his slumber, he said, "I will go out as at other times, and shake myself free. *And he did not know that the Lord had left him*" (16:20, author's italics). Samson had played around with sin so long that he did not even miss God when He departed from him.

  III. Final appendixes (17:1 to 21:25)

    A. The migration of the tribe of Dan (17:1 to 18:31)

      1. Micah's graven image (17:1-13)

      2. Dan's involvements (18:1-31)

       a. The spies' expedition (18:1-10)

       b. The theft of the image and the Levite (18:11-20)

       c. Dan's relocation (18:21-31)

    B. Benjamin's near destruction (19:1 to 21:25)

      1. The outrage at Gibeah (19:1-21)

      2. The war with Benjamin (20:1-18)

       a. The inquest of the crime (20:1-11)

       b. The battles against Benjamin (20:12-48)

3. Israel's concern over Benjamin (21:1-7)
4. Provision of wives for the survivors (21:8-25)

The last two appendixes bring the book to a close with renewed violence. The whole narrative has struck the emotions of the reader, a masterpiece of a style of writing which communicates theological concepts. Even though the acts of Israelites and others turn the stomach, God used such people. From an historical standpoint, the writing is equally as effective, for the stage is set for the other books of the Deuteronomic History. This is done by the use of the recurring phrase, "there was no king in Israel" (18:1; 19:1; 21:25). The final verse of the book states: "Every man did what was right in his own eyes." The chaotic times had almost produced a state of anarchy. Without some form of centralized government, the nation might destroy itself. Upon this carefully laid foundation, the Books of Samuel and Kings were constructed.

15

1 and 2 Samuel

The Books of 1 and 2 Samuel were originally one book in Hebrew and were divided into two books for convenience. The division was probably made simply because one long scroll was too unhandy. The actual division into two books may have been done by the translators of the LXX. They treated both the Books of Samuel and the Books of Kings as a unified work, which they designated as 1, 2, 3, and 4 Kingdoms. When Jerome translated these titles into the Latin Vulgate, they were shortened to 1, 2, 3, and 4 Kings. The artificial division of 1 and 2 Samuel can be seen by reading the conclusion of 1 Samuel and the beginning of 2 Samuel. The Book of 1 Samuel draws to an end with the death of Saul. David's response to Saul's death is presented in 2 Samuel 1.

Date, Authorship, and Unity of the Books

Jewish tradition has ascribed the authorship of these books to Samuel; but since Samuel died early in the books (1 Sam. 25:1; 28:3), this tradition is clearly impossible. More likely, Samuel's name was given to the work because he was the dominant figure in the establishment of the kingdom. He was probably responsible for some of the material in 1 Samuel. The author of Chronicles clearly identified part of his sources for this period as having come from Samuel, along with records from Nathan and Gad.

> Now the acts of King David, from first to last, are written in the Chronicles of Samuel the seer, and in the Chronicles of Nathan the prophet, and in the Chronicles of Gad the seer,

with accounts of all his rule and his might and the circumstances that came upon him and upon Israel, and upon all the kingdoms of the countries (1 Chron. 29:29-30).

If these sources were available to the author of 1 and 2 Chronicles, they were certainly available to the author of 1 and 2 Samuel. In addition, 2 Samuel clearly indicates that David's great elegy over the deaths of Saul and Jonathan was quoted from the Book of Jashar, a source noted in our study of the Book of Joshua (2 Sam. 1:18; cf. Josh. 10:13).

Some scholars have suggested that abundant evidence exists, especially when reading these books in Hebrew, that at least two basic sources were drawn together in compiling the final forms of 1 and 2 Samuel. The contention is made that one older, probably eyewitness source always presents the founding of the kingship in a favorable light and that a later source is highly critical of the kingship, since most of the kings were absolute failures, at least insofar as their obedience to the teachings of Deuteronomy were concerned. Further, the Hebrew and the style of writing is much more vivid and graphic in the early source, while the later source is far less beautiful. Some of the passages in 1 and 2 Samuel are in the best prose Hebrew of the Old Testament, while others are in very inept Hebrew. Even if there were dual sources for the material in 1 and 2 Samuel, both may have been early. Those who accept such a proposal believe that the source with the better Hebrew was probably an eyewitness.

The proponents of this suggestion also point to what appear to them to be numerous duplicate accounts of identical events. Consider the following list as a sample of this approach.

1. The sudden end of Eli's house was announced twice (1 Sam. 2:31-36; 3:11-14).

2. Saul was anointed king once privately and twice publicly (1 Sam 9:26 to 10:1; 10:17-24; 11:15).

3. Saul was twice deposed from the throne but continuted to rule until his death (1 Sam. 13:14; 15:26-29).

4. David was twice introduced to Saul (1 Sam. 16:14-23; 17:55-58).

5. David was three times offered a daughter of Saul in marriage (1 Sam. 18:17-19, 20-21*a*, 22*b*-29*a*).

6. David twice escaped from Saul's court never to return (1 Sam. 19:12; 20:42*b*).

7. Saul was at once aware of David's first flight but later wondered why David was not present at dinner (1 Sam. 19:17; 20:25-29).

8. David twice had Saul in his power and spared his life (1 Sam. 24:3-7; 26:5-12).

9. David made a covenant with Jonathan three times (1 Sam. 18:3; 20:16-42; 23:18).

10. David sought refuge from Achish, king of Gath twice (1 Sam. 21:10-15; 27:1-4).

11. Goliath was slain both by David and by Elhanan, one of David's heroes. This was later corrected by the Chronicler (1 Sam 17; 19:5; 21:9; 22:10*b*, 13; 2 Sam. 21:19; 1 Chron. 20:5).

12. The origin of the proverb, "Is Saul among the prophets?" is given twice (1 Sam 10:11; 19:24).

13. The treason of the Ziphites is twice recorded (1 Sam. 23:19-28; 26:1).

14. Absalom is said to have had three sons, yet later is said to have no son (2 Sam. 14:27; 18:18).

15. Two accounts of the circumstances of Saul's death are given (1 Sam. 31:4; 2 Sam. 1:6-10).

Each of the supposed dual accounts can be explained. On the other hand, the multiplicity of these things when coupled with the other evidence of possible sources behind the Books of Samuel make such a suggestion at least plausible. That two sources may have existed creates no problem. The Gospels of the New Testament present four sources for information on the life of Jesus. Each writer reported on the events of the life of Jesus from his own perspective. We may have a similar case in the Books of Samuel.

The date of the final compilation of Samuel also concerns students of the Old Testament. The explanation of archaic expressions indicates that the final editing took place long after such terms were in use in Israel (1 Sam. 9:9). The need to explain ancient customs indicates the same thing (2 Sam. 13:18). The repeated use of the expression, "Unto this day," suggests that the writer, in referring to events, the consequence of which were still being felt, was living some considerable time after those events (1 Sam. 5:5; 6:18; 27:6; 30:25; 2 Sam. 4:3; 6:8; 18:18). Since the entire length of David's reign is given in 2 Samuel 5:5, the editor or compiler had to have lived after the death of David, which is recorded in 1 Kings 2:10. Finally, the reference to the kings of Judah would indicate that the final writing took place after the division of the kingdom (1 Sam. 27:6). Thus it appears that the earliest possible date for the writing of the book is sometime after the death of Solomon and at least late enough for more than one king to have ruled in the Southern Kingdom.

The way the narrative ties in with Judges on the one side and with Kings on the other appear to confirm that 1 and 2 Samuel are part of one ongoing narrative, even though it was compiled from sources other than those found in the other books. The judgments passed upon the people of Israel and its leaders during this period appear to be essentially prophetic and Deuteronomic in character. Clearly, the Books of Samuel are a unit. The structure of the book is held together by the common theme of the sovereign lordship of Yahweh and Israel's responsibility for faithfulness to Him and loyalty to His covenant.

The Content of the Books

Since 1 and 2 Samuel were originally a unit, the analysis of the content will be done in one ongoing outline. The only place in this outline where I shall specifically identify the books as 1 Samuel or 2 Samuel is in those outline sections where the two books actually touch.

I. The end of the era of Israel's judges (1:1 to 7:17)
   A. Birth and commitment of Samuel (1:1 to 2:11)
      1. Hannah's grief over her childlessness (1:1-8)
      2. Hannah's prayer and vow (1:9-11)
      3. Eli's confrontation of Hannah (1:12-18)

4. Samuel's birth and commitment by his
   mother (1:19-28)
5. Hannah's song of praise (2:1-10)
6. Samuel left at Shiloh (2:11)

The heartache of Hannah at her childlessness and her overwhelming joy at the birth of her son is one of the great
moments of tenderness in the Old Testament. Eli's surprising reaction at her prayer may be an indication of the kinds
of women his sons were bringing to the shrine of Shiloh (cf.
1 Sam. 2:12-17; 3:13). Childlessness was considered almost a
curse. At this time in Israel the people appear had little
hope of life after death. Rather, they expected to live on in
their offspring. They thought they were without a future
with God's people or with God when they had no children.

B. The early ministry of Samuel (2:12 to 7:17)
   1. The rejection of the house of Eli (2:12-36)
      a. The sin of Eli's sons (2:12-17)
      b. Samuel and his family (2:18-21)
      c. Judgment upon Eli's house contrasted
         with Samuel's blessing (2:22-36)
   2. Samuel's call and ministry (3:1 to 4:1a)
      a. The call of Samuel (3:1-14)
      b. Eli's submission to Samuel's word
         (3:15-18)
      c. God's Word through Samuel's words
         (3:19 to 4:1a)
   3. The Philistine conflict (4:1b to 7:14)
      a. The ark captured (4:1b-11)
      b. Consequences of its capture in Israel
         (4:12-22)
      c. Philistine problems with the ark (5:1-12)
      d. The ark returned to Israel (6:1 to 7:2)
      e. Victory over the Philistines (7:3-14)
   4. Samuel's ministry as judge and priest
      (7:15-17)

Among the many tragic figures of the biblical narratives,
Eli is one of the more pathetic. He was a failure as a father,
yet he served as spiritual tutor and guide for young Samuel.

Eli's submissiveness to the judgment of God was admirable. Finally, his death in grief at the capture of the ark of God brought him to his grave with a sense of total failure. He did fail at many points, but his training and influence upon Samuel left him with a significant memorial in Israel.

In this first major section of the book, Samuel is clearly identified as prophet, priest, and judge. In his function as a judge, he served both as the charismatic judge, like those in the Book of Judges, as well as the kind of a judge who actually heard cases and rendered decisions.

Many interpreters of the Old Testament speak and write as if the prophets and priests were always in conflict with one another. Such was sometimes the case, but often the prophets and priests worked toward the same goals. In Samuel, the roles were combined in one person. He served as the example par excellence of the happy combination of these two offices in the service of God.

Israel's taking the ark to the field of battle arose from a popular belief that God was localized over the ark. Their view of God was too small. In the ancient Near East, people believed that a victory over a people was a victory over their gods. The Philistines discovered that was not so. They had defeated Israel and captured the ark, but their gods were powerless before Yahweh.

The fact that the Philistines sent golden tumors and mice back with the ark may be an indication that the plague they were afflicted with was the bubonic plague. The fleas on mice are carriers and the disease causes an outbreak of tumors.

II. The founding of the Hebrew kingdom: Samuel and Saul (8:1 to 15:35)
    A. Samuel's decline as a leader (8:1-22)
        1. Samuel's failure as a father (8:1-3)
        2. Israel's plea for a king (8:4-9)
        3. Description of the nature of a king (8:10-16)
        4. Israel still insists (8:19-20)
        5. God's granting of Israel's request (8:21-22)

One major thing Samuel did not learn from Eli was how to

be a good father. He failed with his sons just as Eli had done. It is always a real possibility that those involved in ministering to others may fail in ministering to their own families.

Israel's plea for a king was based on the desire to be "like all the nations" (1 Sam. 8:5). When the prophet tried to talk the people out of it, they became more specific, saying, "No! but we will have a king over us, that we may also be like all the nations, and that our king may govern us and go out before us and *fight our battles*" (1 Sam. 8:19-20; author's italics). What they really wanted was a leader who would defeat their enemies, specifically the Philistines.

Samuel was deeply distressed at Israel's request for a king. God's response to Samuel's prayer would indicate that Samuel saw Israel's request as a rejection of his leadership. God pointed out to Samuel that the people of Israel were not rejecting their human leader but their divine Leader (1 Sam. 8:7). As in the long days at Sinai, the Israelites were still having trouble accepting a king whom they could not see. The Israelites wanted a king nearer by.

    B. Saul designated as Israel's king (9:1 to 10:27)
        1. Saul introduced and described (9:1-2)
        2. Saul seeking for his lost asses (9:3-14)
        3. Saul's meeting with Samuel (9:15-26)
        4. Samuel's private anointing of Saul (9:27 to 10:8)
        5. Saul's homecoming (10:9-16)
        6. Saul's public anointing (10:17-27)
           a. Samuel's warning about the kingship (10:17-19)
           b. Saul's public accession (10:20-24)
           c. Saul's mixed acceptance (20:25-27)

Saul is introduced as an outstanding young man, one gifted with those qualities of leadership which the nation needed. He is also shown as being patient with those who objected to his new place of leadership. Two features stand out, however, which were to bear bitter fruit for Saul and Israel in the years to come. First, Saul's joining with the band of the prophets may have been an indication of an unstable nature. In the ancient Near East, including Israel, bands of roving prophets were involved in ecstatic frenzy. Saul apparently joined such a group. Saul's actions later showed him to be unstable. The second feature was Saul's hiding when the time of public coronation came. If he was that timid, being thrust into such a position of leadership would have been a great strain upon him. He may have hidden for another reason. Samuel, with great drama, had prepared Israel for the introduction of the king, only to discover that he was not present. When he was found, unassumedly tending the baggage, he clearly upstaged the dramatic moment which Samuel had planned. That certainly would not have pleased Samuel and may have been part of the basis for the later problems between the two.

       C. Saul's early days as king (11:1 to 12:25)
          1.   Saul's defeat of the Ammonites (11:1-11)
          2.   Saul's renewed accession to the throne
               (11:12-15)
          3.   Samuel's final warning to Israel (12:1-25)

The early days of Saul's kingship produced two events of major significance. First, following Saul's deliverance of the men of Jabesh-gilead, the people were greatly excited, for Saul had given them victory in battle. The crowd wished to execute those who had been opposed to Saul's kingship (1 Sam. 11:12). Saul, on the other hand was both gracious and merciful toward his enemies and expressed gratitude to God for his victory. However, after the second public ceremony of crowning, Samuel rehearsed Israel's history and announced in no uncertain terms that Israel's demand for a king had been wrong and would bring judgment upon them. Such an announcement, even coupled with the final offer of mercy, surely left Saul with a very shaky foundation from which to rule. Saul's failure was entirely the result of his own choices, but Samuel may not have done all that he could to help Saul get off to a good start.

D. Saul's successes and failures (13:1 to 15:35)
   1. The incomplete summary (13:1)
   2. Conflict with the Philistines (13:2 to 14:52)
      a. Saul's army gathered for battle (13:2-7)
      b. The disobedience of Saul (13:8-15a)
      c. Iron weapons, the Philistine advantage (13:15b-23);
      d. Victory over the Philistines (14:1-46)
         (1) Jonathan's leadership (14:1-23)
         (2) Saul's foolish oath (14:24-30)
         (3) Saul's victory worship (14:31-35)
         (4) Jonathan spared from Saul's judgment (14:36-46)
      e. Saul's other enemies (14:47-48)
      f. Saul's family (14:49-51)
      g. The ongoing Philistine conflict (14:52)

The incomplete summary of Saul's reign is an indication of the reverent care with which the scribes copied the Word of God. Obviously, something is missing from the text. Perhaps a mouse or an insect ate a hole in the ancient scroll. In spite of the need for some additional numbers, no scribe ever inserted made-up figures. The scribes continued to copy just what they had.

Saul gathered his army and waited for Samuel to come offer the sacrifice before they went to battle. When Samuel delayed, the army began to scatter, as any volunteer army will do in the face of inactivity. Saul, in desperation, offered the sacrifice himself, at which point Samuel immediately appeared, almost as if he had been hiding nearby, waiting to see what Saul would do. Samuel castigated Saul for assuming priestly functions. We do not know all that was implied here, for at a later time both David and Solomon appear to have done similar things with no such priestly opposition (2 Sam. 6:12-19; 24:25; 1 Kings 3:15). This is clearly an indication of the continuing opposition between Samuel and Saul. Samuel's announcement that God had already selected someone to succeed Saul in the kingship was a major push toward the final dissolution of Saul's personality.

The announcement that the Philistines had discovered the process of smelting iron which Israel did not know is a declaration that they had a clear advantage over Israel in the arms race. This is confirmed by the discoveries of archaeology.

The episode with Jonathan over Saul's foolish oath is just one more indication of the seriousness with which Israel regarded the spoken word. Only through redemption by the people of Israel was Jonathan spared from Saul's verdict.

3. Conflict with the Amelekites (15:1-33)
   a. Saul's disobedience with regard to the Amelekites (15:1-9)
   b. Yahweh's rejection of Saul (15:10-11)
   c. Samuel's confrontation with Saul (15:12-33)
4. Samuel and Saul part forever (15:34-35)

In conflict with the Amelekites, Saul's disobedience to God was flagrant and without excuse. Samuel made one of the great proclamations of the Old Testament when he confronted Saul for the last time.

> Has the Lord as great delight in burnt offerings and
>   sacrifices,
>   as in obeying the voice of the Lord?
> Behold, to obey is better than sacrifice,
>   and to hearken than the fat of rams.
> For rebellion is as the sin of divination,
>   and stubbornness is as iniquity and idolatry.
> Because you have rejected the word of the Lord,
>   he has also rejected you from being king
>   (1 Sam. 15:22-23)

In spite of the fact that Samuel apparently never thought very much of Saul, when Yahweh finally announced His rejection of Saul, Samuel pleaded with Him all night (1 Sam. 15:11). From beginning to end, the relationship between Samuel and Saul was quite complex. Although there was no excuse for Saul's disobedience to God, Samuel appears not to have offered all of the support and encouragement along the way which he might have done. Saul, who may never have been very sure of himself, was forced to face the end of his reign without the support of Samuel. This breach would have been obvious to the people and could have made Saul's final days even more insecure.

III. Saul's reign with David in his shadow (1 Sam. 16:1 to 2 Sam. 1:27)
   A. David anointed as future king (16:1-13)
   B. David joined with Saul's court (16:14-23)
      1. Saul's torment of spirit (16:14-17)
      2. David's entrance into Saul's service (16:18-23)
   C. David's victory over Goliath (17:1-58)
      1. Israel terrified of Goliath (17:1-11)
      2. David sent to visit his brothers (17:12-22)
      3. David's offer to combat Goliath (17:23-40)
      4. David's and Goliath's taunts (17:41-47)
      5. Goliath killed by David (17:48-54)
      6. Saul's inquiry about David (17:55-58)

In Saul's early days, he had been led by the Spirit of Yahweh. The writer now declared that "an evil spirit from the Lord tormented him" (1 Sam. 16:14). This concerns many interpreters, for the idea of God sending an evil spirit is quite foreign to the modern concept of God. However, in ancient Israel, their belief in the ultimate sovereignty of God was such that anything which happened came from God. Only later did they begin to describe such evil visitations as coming from Satan (cf. 2 Sam. 24:1 and 1 Chron. 21:1).

David's confrontation with Goliath is generally well-known, however, one feature is occasionally abused by interpreters. David was certainly no little boy at this time. He was a competent shepherd who had successfully confronted wild animals. Saul offered David his own armor. Saul himself was head and shoulders taller than most Hebrews (1 Sam. 8:2). He was not trying to make David look ridiculous, he was trying to help him fight Goliath. Thus it is highly likely that David was about the size of Saul. David did not

put aside the armor because it did not fit but because he was
not used to it (1 Sam. 17:39).

    D. Conflict between David and Saul (16:1 to 24:22)
       1.   Friendship between David and Jonathan
          (18:1-5)
       2.   Saul's jealousy aroused against David
          (18:6-9)
       3.   Attempts to kill David (18:10-29)
          a. With a spear (18:10-11)
          b. By sending him to battle (18:12-16)
          c. By demanding an unusual marriage
             present (18:17-29)
       4.   David's successes (18:30)
       5.   Renewed attempts to kill David (19:1-24)
          a. Jonathan's aid to David (19:1-7)
          b. The spear again (19:8-10)
          c. During David's sleep (19:11-17)
          d. Pursuit to Ramah (19:18-24)
       6.   Jonathan aids David's escape again (20:1-
          42)
       7.   David's flight from Saul (21:1 to 22:5)
          a. To the priest at Nob (21:1-9)
          b. To Achish, king of Gath (21:10-15)
          c. To the cave of Adullam (22:1-2)
          d. To the wilderness of Judah (22:3-5)
       8.   Saul's vengeful slaughter at Nob (22:6-23)
       9.   The conflict's intensification (23:1 to 24:22)
          a. David's rescue of the people of Keilah
             (23:1-6)
          b. David's flight from Keilah (23:7-14)
          c. Jonathan's covenant with David (23:15-
             18)
          d. Betrayal by the Ziphites (23:19-24*a*)
          e. David's escape in the wilderness
             (23:24*b*-29)
          f. David's mercy to Saul in Engedi (24:1-
             22)

These narratives contain some of the most exciting events

in the Books of Samuel. Numerous features stand out and capture the imagination. Jonathan's love for and loyalty to David is most striking. David was Jonathan's chief rival to succeed Saul as king, yet he loved him. Jonathan was aware that David was to be king. He said to David, "Fear not; for the hand of Saul my father shall not find you; you shall be king over Israel, and I shall be next to you; Saul my father also knows this" (1 Sam. 23:17).

A second feature which stands out is that in spite of all of Saul's attempts to kill David, David did not kill Saul when he had the opportunity. That was clearly an act of magnimity, as well as mercy. It was also a politically expedient act. David knew that he was one day going to be king. If his followers had seen him kill the king, they might someday have been tempted to kill him. Instead, David's followers saw the great reverence which he had for "the Lord's anointed" (1 Sam. 24:6).

Furthermore, countless phrases from this block of material capture our attention and ring responsive chords within our minds and hearts. As David's popularity grew, we are told that "Saul eyed David from that day on" (1 Sam. 18:9). Another such expression is found where David was explaining his weaponless condition; he said, "the king's business required haste" (1 Sam. 21:8).

> E. The final days of Saul's reign (25:1 to 30:31)
>   1. David's marriage with Abigail (25:1-43)
>   *a.* His threat to Nabal (25:1-13)
>   *b.* Abigail's presents to David (25:14-35)
>   *c.* Nabal's death (25:36-38)
>   *d.* David's marriage (25:39-42)
>   *e.* David's other marriages (25:43)
>   2. David spares Saul again (26:1-25)
>   3. David's flight to the Philistines (27:1 to 30:31)
>   *a.* Achish's acceptance of David (27:1-8)
>   *b.* David's subterfuge (27:9-12)
>   *c.* Advancement under Achish (28:1-2)
>   *d.* Saul and the witch of Endor (28:3-25)

> e. The Philistine lords reject David's help
> (29:1-11)
> f. David's victory over the Amelekites
> (30:1-31)

The final days of Saul's reign and the final conflicts between Saul and David show David at his best and worst. In dealing with Nabal, David was apparently doing little more than running a protection racket. At this time, David's weakness for women began to show.

Some of the greatest examples of David's wisdom also appear in his dealings with Achish, king of Gath. First of all, to hide from Saul in the Philistine territory was a masterpiece of genius. That was one place where David was absolutely secure from Saul's wrath and jealousy. The way he kept the Philistines happy and at the same time delivered the people of Judah from peoples who were troubling them was also an act of political statesmanship. David's dealings with those of his soldiers who had not fought against the Amelekites after their attack on Ziklag by allowing them a share in the booty won their loyalty forever.

Certainly God's providence kept the Philistines from allowing David to go with them in their battle against Israel. If David had fought against Israel at that time, he almost certainly would never have been allowed to be king in Israel.

Throughout this whole period, David was faced with Saul's hostility and with his own knowledge that he would one day be king in Israel. It is a measure of the greatness of the man that he was able to wait for that outcome with patience. In this period David prepared himself for that reign which was to come by winning the loyalty of his people. By spending time with the Philistines, he led them to believe that he was their protégé, thus probably ensuring initial days of peace when he finally came to Israel's throne. Also, during the time among the Philistines, David's men learned the art of smelting iron, so that the arms race was made equal. During those days of waiting, David honed and developed his skills in political statesmanship which stood him in such good stead when the time of waiting was over.

F. The end of Saul's reign (1 Sam. 31:1 to 2 Sam. 1:27)
    1. Jonathan's death (1 Sam. 31:1-2)
    2. Saul's death (1 Sam. 31:3-6)
    3. The Philistine victory (1 Sam. 31:7)
    4. The abuse and rescue of Saul's body (1 Sam. 31:8-13)
    5. David's vengence upon the Amalekite (2 Sam. 1:1-16)
    6. David's lament over Saul and Jonathan (2 Sam. 1:17-27)

The end of Saul's reign was marked by tragedy, grief, and greatness. The tragedy of Saul's and Jonathan's deaths and the exposure of their bodies by the Philistines was horrible. On the other hand, the grief of the men of Jabesh-gilead and their heroism in rescuing the body of their beloved king brings a deep sense of amazement and gratitude. Finally, David himself stands tall in the entire episode. David's punishment of the Amalekite who had claimed to kill Saul is one more example of his respect for anyone who was the Lord's anointed. David's magnificent lament and elegy over the deaths of Saul and Jonathan stands as one of the great pieces of world literature. David's personal grief is unquestionable. He did not look upon Saul's death as his opportunity to become king at last. Rather, he showed a genuine love for his friend, Jonathan, and respect for his king, Saul.

IV. David as king of Judah (2:1 to 4:12)
    A. David anointed king of Judah (2:1-4a)
    B. His blessing of Jabesh-gilead (2:4b-7)
    C. Ishbosheth's reign over Israel (2:8-10)
    D. War between south and north (2:12 to 3:1)
        1. The victory of David's army (2:12-17)
        2. The death of Asahel (2:18-32)
        3. The extended period of warfare (3:1)
    E. David's family (3:2-5)
    F. Abner's negotiations with David (3:6-21)
    G. Joab's murder of Abner (3:22-30)

Once again, David demonstrated his political genius as he assumed the kingship over Judah. David began to reign over the south from Hebron, again waiting with patience until the Lord delivered the whole kingdom to him. His reward of the men of Jabesh-gilead would certainly have been noted and appreciated by those tribes which still followed the house of Saul. The war between the south and the north seems to have been more intended by the north to keep Judah in line than intended by David to gain control over Israel. The Philistines apparently stayed out of this conflict. That may have been due to their belief that David was "their" man. It may also have been due to the fact that such intertribal war could do nothing but weaken Israel and make it easier for ultimate Philistine conquest.

The negotiations opened by Abner, the military leader of the north, were probably intended to gain for himself the military leadership of the whole nation if he delivered the allegiance of the northern tribes to David. Joab prevented that by murdering Abner. It was passed off as blood revenge, but it was likely to have been just as much motivated by Joab's desire to maintain control of David's army. In any case, David's obvious grief over Abner's death would have convinced the northern tribes that David had nothing to do with it. Finally, David's punishment of the murderers of Ishbosheth, Saul's son, would have ingratiated him with the northern tribes.

2. God's message for David (7:4-17)
3. David's commitment to Yahweh (7:18-29)

One significant feature of Hebrew kingship was the idea of the people having a voice as to who their king would be. That was apparently a holdover from the old days of the charismatic leadership of the judges. The kingship was never wholly automatic in Israel, for it appears that the people always assumed that they had a voice in the kingly succession.

David's decision to move his capital to Jerusalem was a stroke of political genius. To have remained with his court in Hebron would have risked alienating the northern tribes. However, to have moved his court to one of the northern cities would have had the same effect upon his southern supporters. So David chose Jerusalem, a city which was near the border of the two regions and which had never been captured by the Israelites after their invasion of the land, thus it was neither southern nor northern. Upon its capture, Jerusalem truly became the City of David.

When the ark of Yahweh was brought to Jerusalem, David's excesses in celebration caused his wife, Michal, to despise him (2 Sam. 6:16). She may have been all too familiar with the end result of her own father's excesses. When Michal greeted David with sarcasm, David responded with the reminder that God "chose me above your father" (v.21), the kind of remark which cuts deep. Their marriage effectively ended with that dispute, for "Michal . . . had no child to the day of her death" (v.23). David never showed the same genius in dealing with his family that he exhibited in ruling his people.

    D. David's victories (8:1 to 10:19)
      1. His conquests (8:1-14)
      2. His government (8:15-17)
      3. David's kindness to Saul's son, Mephibosheth (9:1-13)
      4. David's victories over the Ammonite and the Syrians (10:1-19)
    E. David's sin with Bathsheba (11:1 to 12:31)

1. The setting (11:1)
2. His surrender to lust (11:2-5)
3. Attempts to deceive Uriah (11:6-13)
4. The murder of Uriah (11:14-25)
5. David's marriage (11:26-27)
6. Nathan's confrontation (12:1-15*a*)
7. The child's death (12:15*b*-23)
8. Solomon's birth (12:24-25)
9. Joab's victory over Rabbah (12:26-31)

David's sin with Bathsheba is one of the darkest spots in the great king's life. He had moved from victory to victory in his military achievements. The territory of Israel had reached the point of its greatest enlargement. But the pressures of administering such a kingdom made it necessary for David to send his armies forth without him. "In the spring of the year, the time when kings go forth to battle" (11:1), David remained behind in Jerusalem. His heart was with his troops. Then he saw Bathsheba and lust took over. When she became pregnant and their sin was about to be known, he did everything possible to try to get Uriah to go home and stay with Bathsheba, hoping that he would later think the child was his. When all else failed, David in desperation took advantage of Uriah's bravery and had him placed so that he would be killed in battle. When this had been accomplished, David then took Bathsheba as his wife.

At that point, Nathan spoke his famous parable. The wrath of David was aroused at the crime of the man in Nathan's story. At that point, the prophet's "you are the man" came stabbing into David's conscience (2 Sam. 12:7). It took courage for Nathan to do that; for in any other nation of the ancient Near East, the king was above the law and a prophet who so confronted a king could expect swift punishment. It was not so with David. David's acknowledgment of his sin was immediately forthcoming. For David, the confession brought forgiveness. But the historical consequences of David's sin were still there. His actions would bear bitter fruit throughout the rest of his life.

David had announced a fourfold judgment upon the rich man in Nathan's parable. In David's life the four-for-one judgment appears to have been carried out. He had murdered Uriah. The first child of Bathsheba died immediately. His son Amnon was killed by Absalom (2 Sam. 13:28-29). Absalom was killed by Joab during the rebellion (2 Sam. 18:15). Finally, his son Adonijah was murdered by Solomon (1 Kings 2:23-25).

- F. Problems within David's family (13:1 to 18:33)
  - 1. Amnon's rape of Tamar (13:1-29)
    - a. Amnon's love and lust (13:1-6)
    - b. Tamar's rape (13:7-19)
    - c. Absalom's vengeance upon Amnon (13:20-29)
  - 2. Absalom's banishment (13:30 to 14:33)
    - a. Absalom's flight (13:30-39)
    - b. A wise woman of Tekoa urges Absalom's return (14:1-20)
    - c. Absalom's return to Jerusalem (14:21-27)
    - d. Absalom's return to court (14:28-33)
  - 3. Absalom's rebellion (15:1 to 18:33)
    - a. The initial stages (15:1-12)
    - b. David's flight from Jerusalem (15:13-30)
    - c. Hushai sent back to confound Ahithophel (15:31-37)
    - d. David's difficulties (16:1-14)
    - e. Absalom's entrance into Jerusalem (16:15-22)
    - f. Hushai's advice followed (16:23 to 17:23)
    - g. Absalom's death (17:24 to 18:15)
    - h. David's grief over Absalom (18:16-33)

The plant of David's sin quickly began to bear its bitter fruit. David's son Amnon lusted after and raped his half-sister Tamar. In retaliation, Absalom murdered Amnon. When Absalom's banishment was finally ended, he plotted against David, finally moving into open rebellion. As a part of that rebellion, Absalom "went in to his father's concubines in the sight of all Israel" (2 Sam. 16:22). In that time, whoever possessed the king's concubines was the king.

David was obviously disturbed when he discovered that his chief adviser, Ahithophel, was the mainstay in his son's rebellion. He sent another adviser, Hushai, back to confound the advice of Ahithophel. When it turned out that Absalom decided to follow Hushai's advice, Ahithophel realized that the rebellion would fail, so he committed suicide.

An interesting sidelight to the rebellion has to do with Ahithophel's part in it. Why would the king's chief adviser join, much less take a lead, in such a plot? Some of the genealogical lists of the Old Testament offer an answer. Ahithophel was the father of one Eliam, one of David's mighty men (2 Sam. 23:34). Bathsheba was the daughter of Eliam (2 Sam. 11:2). Ahithophel was apparently participating in the rebellion in vengeance upon David for the seduction of his granddaughter.

In spite of the rebellion of Absalom, David was overcome with grief at Absalom's death. David's heartbreak shows vividly through his outcry: "O my son Absalom, my son, my son Absalom! Would I had died instead of you, O Absalom, my son, my son!" (2 Sam. 18:33). A major part of David's grief had to be due to the fact that he had failed to show Absalom the right example.

G. David's final days as king (19:1 to 24:25)
1. Joab's rebuke of David's excessive grief (19:1-8a)
2. David's return to the throne (19:8b-15)
3. Mercy toward enemies (19:16-43)
4. The abortive revolt of Sheba (20:1-22)
5. David's administrators (20:23-26)
6. The execution of Saul's sons (21:1-14)
7. War renewed with the Philistines (21:15-22)
8. Gratitude in the song of David (22:1-51)
9. David's last words (23:1-7)
10. David's mighty men (23:8-39)
11. David's census (24:1-17)
12. David's altar to Yahweh (24:18-25)

The Books of Samuel draw to a close with a sad whimper. The great events of the earlier days of the kingdom gave way to the mundane affairs of an old man whose life had slowly crumbled away. The greatest moment of these latter days was David's expression of mercy toward those who had taken advantage of his misfortune in the days of Absalom's rebellion. At that point, David once again showed his greatness and the great lesson he had learned from God's own mercy toward him at the time of his sin with Bathsheba.

This passage shows Israel's early belief that everything had to come from the hand of God. The incitement of David in 2 Samuel 24:1 which is ascribed to God was later ascribed by the Chronicler to Satan (1 Chron. 21:1). The ancient Hebrews did not use the modern theological concepts of God's permissive will and His active or causitive will. To them, everything was direct. Whatever happened, it had to have come from God.

Two major features of the Books of Samuel are the rise of the monarchy and the rise of prophetism. The latter was of ultimately more significance. From the beginning, the prophets felt an authority over the kings insofar as God's will was concerned. The fact that Saul and David were submissive to the words of the prophets set the stage for a development which was unique to Israel. Only in Israel were the kings expected to be submissive to the will and word of God. Later, as the people of Israel looked back to greatness of David's kingdom, they also began to look forward to the coming of great David's greater Son, who would one day establish and even greater kingdom.

16

1 and 2 Kings

Like the Books of Samuel, the Books of Kings were originally one book. The division into two books was merely a matter of convenience and was apparently done by the LXX translators. The original unity of the book shows up very clearly in that 1 Kings ends with the beginning of the reign of Ahaziah of Israel and 2 Kings begins with the end of his reign. However, one feature of the Books of Samuel and Kings which is not often noticed is that the same sort of thing also occurs at the end of 2 Samuel and the beginning of 1 Kings. Second Samuel ends right after the last words of David and 1 Kings begins with his last days and his death. Therefore, Samuel and Kings may have been originally one unit. That might explain why the LXX translators first called the four books 1, 2, 3, and 4 Kingdoms.

The Date, Authorship, and Unity of the Books

The date of the final composition of the Books of Kings is fairly easy to identify. They had to have been compiled after the beginning of the reign of Evil-merodach, king of Babylon (known in the Babylonian records as Amel-Marduk), who began to reign about 561 BC because we are told that

> in the thirty-seventh year of the exile of Jehoiachin king of Judah, in the twelfth month, on the twenty-seventh day of the month, Evil-merodach king of Babylon, in the year that he began to reign, graciously freed Jehoiachin king of Judah from prison (2 Kings 25:27).

Furthermore, the author appears to have known a bit about the way in which King Jehoiachin was treated after his release from prison (2 Kings 25:28-30). On the other hand, the author of the material apparently knew nothing of the Hebrews' ultimate release from captivity in 539 BC. Such a significant event could hardly have escaped comment. The Books of Kings, therefore, were most likely put into their final form sometime during the period between 561 and 539 BC, probably during the early part of that period.

The entire composition appears to have been done by some of the ongoing school of Deuteronomic Historians. The influence of Deuteronomy on the evaluation of the kings of both Israel and Judah is nowhere more clearly seen than in 1 and 2 Kings. The author's use of earlier sources is also quite clear. At least three major sources are specifically cited. (1) "The book of the acts of Solomon" is listed as the place where additional information concerning the reign of Solomon may be found (1 Kings 11:41). (2) "The Book of the Chronicles of the Kings of Judah" is also cited (1 Kings 14:29; 15:7; *et al*). That is obviously not the Books of 1 and 2 Chronicles of the Old Testament. (3) Finally, "The Book of the Chronicles of the Kings of Israel" is given as the source of information for the reigns of the northern kings (1 King 14:19; 15:31; *et al*). That, too, is obviously not the Old Testament Books of 1 and 2 Chronicles. All of these sources appear to have been official court records which were kept by the scribes of the kingdoms.

In addition to these three sources which the author identified, scholars have suggested at least three other collections of material which the final author used in his compilation. The first of these is usually identified as "the succession narrative," that block of material which tells how it was determined that Solomon should succeed David upon the throne. The succession narrative was probably a part of the original court history of David and can be found in 2 Samuel 23:1 through 1 Kings 2:46. That material could also have come from one of the participants in the events and may have been a part of "The Chronicles of Nathan the Prophet" (1 Chron. 29:29) which was later used by the author of Chronicles.

Another additional source suggested by many scholars is

more favorable to the reign of Ahab of Israel than the rest of the biblical material. Found in 1 Kings 20 and 22, this material includes the story of the prophet Micaiah son of Imlah and shows significant appreciation for Ahab's ability as a ruler.

A third source or collection of materials has been suggested for the stories of the prophets, with particular reference to Elijah, Elisha, and Isaiah. The Elijah and Elisha materials sound different from the rest of the material around them. The Isaiah material (2 Kings 18:13 to 20:19) is almost identical to that found in Isaiah 36:1 to 39:8. This material speaks of Isaiah in the third person. Most likely all of this material was originally preserved by the disciples of the prophets and later used by the editor or author of Kings as part of his source material.

With the conclusion of the Books of Kings, the final process of compiling the Former Prophets appears to have been completed. If scholars are correct in their proposal of an ongoing Deuteronomic History, it came to an end at this point. Apparently God raised up a new group of historians from among the Levites. At least the rest of the Hebrew's history appears to have been written from that standpoint.

The Structure of the Books

Nowhere else in the Bible, either in the Old or the New Testament, did an author present material in such a distinct and obvious framework as in the Books of Kings. The final compilation of 1 and 2 Kings appears to have been the work of one person, for no committee could have maintained such a standard consistency.

First, there is a standard introduction and conclusion for each of the kings. For the kings of Judah, the framework usually uses the following pattern.

Introduction: "In the _____ year of _____ king of Israel, began _____ to the son of _____ the king of Judah to reign. He was _____ years old when he began to reign and he reigned _____ years in Jerusalem. And his mother's name was _____ from _____."

*(The actual wording of this formula may vary. How-
ever, many apparent variations are frequently due to
the translators.)*

Then follows the history of the king's reign.

Conclusion: "And the rest of his acts, and all that he
did, are they not written in the Book of the Chronicles of the Kings of Judah? So he slept with his fathers, and they buried him with his fathers in the
city of David, and _____ his son reigned in his
stead."

For the kings of Israel, the framework is shorter. The name
of the king's mother and the age of the king upon his accession to the throne is omitted.

In both forms, however, judgment is passed upon each
king. Of all the kings, only Hezekiah and Josiah are praised
unconditionally. The others are absolutely rebuked for
their idolatry, or their loyalty to Yahweh is praised but
limited by the information that they did not abolish the
bamoth (the high places). Further, concerning the kings of
Israel, we are consistently told of each that "he walked in
the way of Jeroboam the son of Nebat [or "he departed not
from the sins of Jeroboam the son of Nebat"], who made
Israel to sin." Whenever the formulaic approach to the
reign of a king is not followed, the reason for its omission
is easily identified.

Another feature which stands out is the process by which
the author handled the reign of kings who were upon the
throne of the two kingdoms at the same time. When he
began to tell the story of the reign of a king of Israel, for
example, and a new king began to reign in Judah, he told
the entire story of the reign of Judah's new king before
returning to his basic narrative. This system, though
straightforward, presents major problems for the interpreter. The author may have been (and frequently was) telling
of events which occurred in the reign of the new king but
which actually followed the death of the king whose basic
story he had first begun.

The Nature of the Material in the Books

In covering such a large block of material, the human author had to be quite selective. As he made his choices under the inspiration of God as to what to include and what to omit, he regularly referred his readers to sources he had apparently used which contained much more detail and which were probably readily available to contemporary readers. These sources, however, are not available to us. This leaves the modern historian frequently longing for additional information.

The choice of the materials to be included was apparently not made upon the basis of historical significance. Rather, those choices were made upon the basis of the meaning of the events. The author's purpose was to tell what God was doing through what happened. Events of significance for faith were recorded, often only partially recorded, giving just enough facts to form a foundation for setting forth the meaning of the message.

The Chronological Concerns of Kings

No other concern in Old Testament studies has been as complex and difficult as the chronology and the chronological data in Kings. This is true both in matters of absolute chronology and in those of relative chronology. Relative chronology is the relationship between the data for the two parallel kingdoms as well as with that of the other kingdoms with whom Israel and Judah came in contact.

The overall concern of absolute chronology is really outside the bounds of this book. Insofar as this material is concerned, one absolute date is of major significance. An eclipse of the sun is recorded in the Assyrian annals which modern astronomers can date as having occurred in 763 BC. From that information a major Assyrian battle, the battle of Qarqar, can be dated at 853 BC. Ahab of Israel fought in that battle and so an absolute chronology for the period of the Hebrew kingdom by working forward and backward can be established.

The major chronological concern of Kings has to do with

the relative chronology between the two kingdoms. Nonspecialists in Old Testament studies frequently ignore the concern raised by the relative chronology between the two kingdoms. The reason for such an approach probably lies in the fact that so much chronological data are given that most people assume that everything ought to fit. Unfortunately, this is not the case. In fact, the contrary is true. So much is data given that assimilating it becomes quite chaotic. Consider the following data.

When the kingdom divided after Solomon's death, his son Rehoboam began to reign in Judah and Jeroboam began to reign in Israel. Let us call that "year zero" in both kingdoms. In the Southern Kingdom, Rehoboam reigned 17 years (1 Kings 14:21), Abijam reigned 3 years (15:2), and Asa reigned 41 years (v.10). During that time in the north, Jeroboam reigned 22 years (14:20), Nadab reigned 2 years (15:25), Baasha reigned 24 years (v.33), Elah reigned 2 years (16:8), Zimri reigned 7 days (v.15), Omri reigned 12 years (v.23) and was succeeded by his son Ahab "in the thirty-eighth year of Asa king of Judah" (v.29).

In Judah, Rehoboam had reigned 17 years and Abijam 3 for a total of 20 years, thus the thirty-eighth year of Asa would have been year 58 in Judah's history. If we add the years of the reigns which preceded Ahab in Israel (22 + 2 + 24 + 2 + 12), we discover that 62 years would have elapsed. How can we possibly make any sense out of the fact that four more years elapsed in the north than in the south? If this chronology were carried throughout the entire period, the problem gets worse.

As interpreters have tried to understand the data, several solutions have been proposed. Some have suggested that the synchronisms are late additions and wholly inaccurate. Others have suggested that the synchronisms are accurate and the lengths of reign are to be ignored. Some have tried to develop a system of accepting some of each and assuming inaccuracies in others. Yet still other interpreters have essentially ignored all biblical data and reconstructed the history of this period wholly from archaeological materials.

Since the entire period has to fit within some rather definite limits, the various reconstructions do not differ from one another very much. However, the one essential feature which all of these approaches have in common is the assumption that the biblical writers who drew this material together could not do addition.

In the mid-twentieth century, Edwin R. Thiele made a wholly new approach to the problem. Thiele's first assumption was that the biblical authors knew precisely what they were doing and that the fault is not with their data but with lack of understanding. He made a study of the methods of keeping chronological data among the writers of the ancient Near East. He discovered that some nations began their new year in the fall while others did so in the spring. Further, in some nations the years of a king's reign were only counted from the New Year's celebration following his accession while others counted that part of the year before that celebration as a whole year in a king's reign. In this latter approach, the year of one king's death and another's accession was counted for both kings, thus adding one year to the total. Thiele also noted several times when an aging father associated his son with him on the throne for a period of a coregency. In such times, the overlapping years were included in the reigns of both kings.

With this information as a background, Thiele proposed that when either of the Hebrew kingdoms were under the domination of Assyria, they were forced to use the Assyrian system of reckoning. At times of independence, he suggested that they expressed such independence by breaking away from that system. Finally, by a study of the biblical text, he also proposed that there were a number of coregencies in both kingdoms.

By applying these assumptions to the chronological data of Kings, Thiele was able to make sense out of the data and to demonstrate that the major problem with biblical chronology was not the inaccuracies of the data but with our lack of understanding of what that data meant. Thus with this approach, the major concern of biblical chronology has been essentially solved.

The Content of the Books

I. The end of the united monarchy (1 Kings 1:1 to
   11:43)
   A. The final days of David (1:1 to 2:11)
      1. Competition over the succession (1:1-27)
      2. The choice of Solomon (1:28-53)
      3. David's final charge to Solomon (2:1-9)
      4. David's death (2:10-11)

As the days of David drew to a close, an intense intercourt
struggle broke out over whether Adonijah or Solomon
would succeed him. Adonijah was supported by Joab, David's general, and Abiathar, one of David's priests. Solomon,
on the other hand, was supported by Nathan the prophet
and Zadok, another of David's priests. However, the end
result was David's proclaiming Solomon as his successor. At
that point, Adonijah fled to the "horns of the altar" for
sanctuary, fearing Solomon's wrath (1:50). The horns of the
altar were four upright projections on the corners of the
altar. They were especially sacred and holding onto them
was supposed to grant one special protection. Solomon offered peace of a sort to Adonijah, and he returned to his own
home.

David's final words do not show the great king in the best
light. His command to Solomon to execute both Joab and
Shimei reveal the dying king as an embittered old man. The
Bible never seeks to cover over the weaknesses of its heroes.
It was not David's greatness which made him great but
God's.

   B. Solomon's consolidation of power (2:12-46)
      1. Solomon's kingdom established (2:12)
      2. Adonijah's execution (2:13-25)
      3. The banishment of Abiathar (2:26-27)
      4. Joab's murder (2:28-35)
      5. Shimei's house arrest and execution (2:36-
         46a)
      6. The firm establishment of Solomon (2:46b)

The differences between the early days of Solomon's reign

and those of David are quite striking. Solomon moved onto
the throne in the manner of a typical Oriental despot. He
immediately eliminated those who might threaten his kingdom.

Adonijah's request for the concubine of David offered a
direct threat to Solomon, for in the ancient Near East, the
possession of the king's harem was a claim to be the king.
Solomon recognized that the presence of his older brother
was an ongoing problem, so he had him executed. Knowing
of Joab's opposition to his kingship and of his own father's
wish, Solomon had Joab executed, even though he clung to
the horns of the altar. Solomon had also recognized that as
long as Joab lived, the army might be more loyal to him
than to the new king. Solomon merely banished Abiathar,
the other leader of the opposition. That may have been
because Abiathar was a priest. With the execution of Shimei, the last potential threat to his kingdom was eliminated
and thus "the kingdom was established in the hand of Solomon" (2:46). David had patiently waited for God to confirm
him in the kingship. But Solomon brought about his own
confirmation upon the throne in Jerusalem. Those high-
handed methods were to be a characteristic of the new king.

C. Solomon's kingship (3:1 to 11:43)
    1.   The wisdom and wealth of Solomon (3:1 to
        4:34)
        a. A marriage alliance with Egypt (3:1-2)
        b. Solomon's dream of God (3:3-15)
        c. Judgment in the harlots' case (3:16-28)
        d. Government administrators (4:1-19)
        e. Solomon's wealth (4:20-28)
        f. Solomon's reputation for wisdom (4:29-
          34)

Most of the nations of the ancient Near East developed what
has been called a "wisdom movement," with an emphasis
upon what constitutes the good life. Solomon was the founder of such a movement in Israel and is always remembered
as Israel's wise man without equal.

In those ancient days, treaties between nations were frequently sealed by the marriage of the daughter of one king with the second king, or with his son. This was what happened in Solomon's alliance with Egypt. The novel dimension here is that this was a new procedure for Egypt.

    2.   The Temple built and dedicated (5:1 to 9:9)
        a. The treaty with Hiram, king of Tyre (5:1-12)
        b. The forced levy (5:13-18)
        c. Building the Temple (6:1-38)
        d. Solomon's other projects (7:1-12)
        e. The Temple's metalwork (7:13-51)
        f. Dedication of the Temple (8:1 to 9:9)
            (*1*) Procession with the ark (8:1-11)
            (*2*) The blessing of Israel (8:12-21)
            (*3*) Prayer of dedication (8:22-53)
            (*4*) Blessing and consecration (8:54-66)
            (*5*) God's response and warning (9:1-9)

Of all of Solomon's activities and accomplishments, the building of the Temple was his greatest and most memorable. It was certainly a magnificent building. Numerous artists and model builders have attempted to draw or to build a replica of that sanctuary. No one is certain precisely how it looked. The most significant thing about it, however, was not how it looked but that it was finally done. Israel at last truly had a national shrine and sanctuary for the worship of Yahweh. Its building and its dedication was clearly extravagant. For Israel and Solomon, that was the very nature of their worship and adoration of God—extravagant.

    3.   Solomon's commercial ventures (9:10 to 10:29)
        a. The sale of cities (9:10-14)
        b. His forced labor battalions (9:15-25)
        c. His deep sea fleet (9:26-28)
        d. Admiration of the queen of Sheba (10:1-13)
        e. Solomon in all his glory (10:14-29)

4. The decline and fall of Solomon (11:1-43)
   a. Worship of other gods (11:1-8)
   b. God's displeasure (11:9-13)
   c. External adversaries (11:9-13)
   d. Internal adversary (11:26-40)
   e. The death of Solomon (11:41-43)

From the standpoint of economic ventures, Solomon was one of the greatest, if not the greatest, of Israel's kings. Unfortunately, that was also a major part of his downfall. To accomplish all which he did, he forced the Hebrews into labor battalions. That was a source of great unrest and ultimately produced the opposition which sundered the kingdom after Solomon's death. Beyond his wealth, however, he apparently became utterly self-satisfied, turning to the gods of his foreign wives. Those wives had apparently been added to his harem through many treaties. His idolatry aroused the divine displeasure which furnished the power to split the kingdom. Solomon's wisdom in affairs of government did not extend to the affairs of his own life. The same desire to do everything in his own way and by his own power which had led him to consolidate his kingdom through violence, ultimately led him to lose his kingdom through his apostasy. He sought to do things his way instead of God's.

The prophet Ahijah played a part in the division of the kingdom. As with Samuel and Nathan, the prophets clearly felt that they had a significant part to play in the Hebrew kingdom. The kings were responsible to God. Thus God's spokesmen carried God's message to those in power. Ahijah's act of tearing his robe was typical of the symbolic act of the prophets. The symbolic acts of the prophets actually appear to have released power to make the acts which had been dramatized come true. That did not happen by magic but by the power of God who sent them to perform the act.

II. The divided monarchy: Israel and Judah together
   (1 Kings 12:1 to 2 Kings 17:41)
   A. A time of separation and conflict (1 Kings 12:1
      to 16:20)

1. The kingdom divided (12:1-33)
   a. Rehoboam's harshness (12:1-15)
   b. Israel's rebellion (12:16-20)
   c. Rehoboam's acceptance of the revolt (12:21-24)
   d. Jeroboam's consolidation of his rule in Israel (12:25-33)
2. Prophetic attack on Jeroboam (13:1 to 14:20)
   a. The attack on Bethel (13:1-34)
   b. Ahijah's word from Shiloh (14:1-20)
3. Rehoboam's reign in Judah (14:21-31)
   a. The high places of Judah (14:21-24)
   b. Defeat before Egypt (14:25-31)
4. The reign of Abijam in Judah (15:1-8)
5. The reign of Asa in Judah (15:9-24)
   a. Asa's limited reform (15:9-15)
   b. War with Israel (15:16-24)
6. Troubles in Israel (15:25 to 16:20)
   a. Nadab's reign (15:25-26)
   b. Nadab's assassination (15:27-31)
   c. Baasha's reign (15:32 to 16:5)
   d. Elah's reign and assassination (16:6-10)
   e. Zimri's reign and suicide (16:11-20)

No strong tie ever existed between the north and the south in Israel. The united monarchy was less a union of commonality than it was an allegiance to a charismatic leader. Thus the division of the kingdom upon the death of Solomon was not so much a new development as it was a return to an older way. The unrest of Israel had been produced by the harsh policies of Solomon. When Rehoboam offered an even harsher policy instead of relief, the relationship cracked. Throughout the days of early separation, the the two nations struggled with each other. Israel, the Northern Kingdom, was larger and generally able to dominate Judah, the Southern Kingdom. Since Jeroboam had found refuge in Egypt during Solomon's latter days, the Egyptians were apparently concerned with Jeroboam's success. Anything which weakened and troubled the Hebrews was to the advantage of Egypt. Thus Shishak's invasion of Judah was probably designed to give Jeroboam of Israel time to consolidate his kingdom.

The prophets continued to take a major part in the ongoing affairs of the kingdoms. Jeroboam's establishment of two ancient sanctuaries as the shrines of Israel were designed to keep his people from going to Jerusalem to worship. He feared that if his people went to the capital of the Southern Kingdom to worship he might loose control over them. He was almost certainly right.

Jeroboam's establishment of the two calves of gold may have had a different meaning from that which appears on the surface. Representations from Canaan show Baal standing upon the back of a calf. Jeroboam may have been intending to represent Yahweh, the invisible God, as being upon the backs of his calves. Be that as it may, the people obviously began to worship the calves themselves.

The inherent instability of the Northern Kingdom showed up even in those early days. David had set an example for the south of reverence toward the anointed king. That apparently carried on through all of the days of the Southern Kingdom. Such an attitude, however, was never found in the north. In the early period of Israel's history, two of its kings were assassinated and a third committed suicide rather than face assassination.

B. The time of Israelite supremacy (1 Kings 16:21 to 2 Kings 8:29)
  1. The reign of Omri of Israel (1 Kings 16:21-28)
  2. The reign of Ahab of Israel (16:29 to 22:40)
    a. Ahab's accession and marriage (16:29-34)
    b. Elijah and the famine (17:1 to 18:19)
    c. The contest with the Baal prophets (18:20-40)
    d. Elijah's flight from Jezebel (18:41 to 19:3)

     e. Confrontation with Yahweh at Horeb (Sinai; 19:4-21)

     f. Ahab's victories over Syria (20:1-34)

     g. A prophetic rebuke of Ahab (20:35-43)

     h. Ahab, Elijah, and Naboth's vineyard (21:1-29)

     i. Ahab's death at war with Syria (22:1-40)

3.   Jehoshaphat's reign in Judah (22:41-50)

4.   Ahaziah's reign in Israel (1 Kings 22:51 to 2 Kings 1:18)

5.   Elijah's mantle passed on to Elisha (2 Kings 2:1-25)

     a. Elisha's request (2:1-9)

     b. Elisha's new status (2:10-18)

     c. Elisha's first acts (2:19-25)

6.   The beginning of Jehoram's reign in Israel (3:1-27)

7.   The Elisha stories (4:1 to 8:15)

     a. A series of miracles (4:1 to 6:7)

        (*1*) The vessel of oil (4:1-7)

        (*2*) The child of the Shunammite (4:8-37)

        (*3*) Miracles with food (4:38-44)

        (*4*) The healing of Naaman (5:1-27)

        (*5*) The floating axe head (6:1-7)

     b. Victory over the Syrians (6:8-23)

     c. The Syrians' flight (6:24 to 7:20)

     d. Testimony of the Shunammite (8:1-6)

     e. Hazael's elevation in Syria (8:7-15)

8.   Jehoram's reign in Judah (8:16-24)

9.   The beginning of Ahaziah's reign in Judah (8:25-29)

The reign of Omri in Israel initiated a time of significant strength on the part of the Northern Kingdom. Throughout this entire period, Judah appears to have been little more than a vassal of the north. Omri was so significant and made such an impression on his world that the Assyrians would regularly refer to Israel as "the land of Omri." When Ahab fought against Assyria at the battle of Qarqar in 853 BC, he had more chariots present than any other king, indicating Israel's strength.

Yet the kings did not really make this period important. The prophets Elijah and Elisha did. What the kings did was not nearly as important as what God was doing. This entire period is a demonstration of the fact that the prophets exercised significant leadership in Israel throughout the period of the monarchy.

Jezebel of Phoenicia who married Ahab was to be the source of much trouble for the Hebrew kingdoms. She imported the worship of the Phoenician Baal. Although they had the same name, the Baal of Phoenicia is not to be identified with the Baals of Canaan. Jezebel, coming from a non-Hebrew background, was not at all understanding of the influence which the Hebrew prophets had over their lands. Neither was she aware that in Israel kings were subject to a higher law than their own.

Joram is a contraction of the name Jehoram. Thus, for a time, both Hebrew kingdoms were ruled by kings with the same name. This coupled with the two Ahaziahs affords an opportunity for some confusion on the part of interpreters.

C. The time of the prophetic revolution (9:1 to 14:20)
1. Jehu's revolution (9:1 to 10:36)
a. Jehu acclaimed king (9:1-16)
b. The assassination of Joram (9:17-26)
c. The assassination of Ahaziah (9:27-29)
d. The murder of Jezebel (9:30-37)
e. Jehu's blood bath in Israel (10:1-27)
f. Israel's losses (10:28-36)
2. Athaliah's usurpation in Judah (11:1-20)
3. Jehoash's reign in Judah (11:21 to 12:21)
4. Jehoahaz's reign in Israel (13:1-9)
5. Jehoash's reign in Israel (13:10-13)
6. The death of Elisha (13:14-21)
7. Victory over Syria (13:22-25)
8. Amaziah's reign in Judah (14:1-20)

Two major features stand out in this period. The first of

these is the part played by the prophets in the revolution of Jehu. Jehu's means of consolidating his kingdom were so bloody, however, that almost a century later the prophet Hosea called the nation to account for those excesses (Hos. 1:4-5). The second feature of importance was the abortive seizure of the throne of Judah by Athaliah.

In this period two kings had the same names. Jehoash and Joash are variations of the same name, a potential source of further confusion.

    D. The period of Israelite revival (14:21 to 15:15)
        1. The beginning of Azariah's reign in Judah (14:21-22)
        2. Jeroboam's reign in Israel (14:23-29)
        3. The rest of Azriah's reign (15:1-7)
        4. Zechariah's reign and assassination in Israel (15:8-12)
        5. Shallum's reign and assassination in Israel (15:13-15)

The real understanding of the accomplishments of this era are found in the books of Amos and Hosea. For the Northern Kingdom, it was a time of great peace and prosperity. Jeroboam (usually known as Jeroboam II) expanded his nation's territory until it was almost as extensive as at the time of David. It was also a time of intense assimilation of the worship of the Canaanite Baals. Archaeological excavations reveal that a large number of Israelite names from this era were made of compounds with Baal. Not a single such name has been uncovered in Judah. Two more assassinations in Israel point to the unstable nature of the throne in the north. Azariah in the south is also known by the name of Uzziah. Leprosy forced him to take his son upon the throne with him as a coregent.

    E. Israel's ultimate collapse (15:16 to 17:41)
        1. The reign of Menahem in Israel (15:16-22)
        2. The reign and assassination of Pekahiah in Israel (15:23-26)

From the prosperous days of Jeroboam II to the final collapse of Israel was only a brief time. The main feature of this period was the Syro-Ephraimitic crisis, which is also addressed in the preaching of Isaiah the prophet. In 735 BC, Pekah of Israel and Rezin sought to overthrow Ahaz, with the intent of putting their own puppet on the throne of Judah. Ahaz, however, against the advice of Isaiah, sent to Assyria for help. The end result of that request was the fall of Damascus, capital of Syria in 732 BC and the fall of Samaria in 722 BC. Although Judah at that time did not face the military might of Assyria, she became a vassal of the Assyrian king in return for being delivered from her enemies. This involved the payment of tribute and the worship of the Assyrian gods. The strength of Samaria is indicated by the fact that it took Assyria three years to take the city.

The Assyrians had adopted a policy of systematic deportation of those whom they conquered. They removed many Hebrews and imported people from other conquered nations. The people could not easily communicate with one another since they spoke different languages. Such a policy inhibited future rebellions. From Israel's standpoint, it also ultimately meant that her remaining citizens would intermarry with those who had been resettled. This eventually produced the people known as Samaritans in late Old Testament times and in the New Testament.

      1.   Hezekiah's reign (18:1 to 20:21)
         a. Initial accomplishments (18:1-12)
         b. Sennacherib's invasion (18:13 to 19:37)
            (*1*) The tribute paid to Assyria (18:13-16)
            (*2*) The Assyrians' taunts (18:17-37)
            (*3*) Isaiah's encouragement (19:1-7)
            (*4*) Sennacherib's defeat (19:8-37)
         c. Hezekiah's illness (20:1-11)
         d. Hezekiah's death (20:12-21)
      2.   Manasseh's evil reign (21:1-18)
      3.   Amon's reign and assassination (21:19-26)

The two major features of this era are the invasion of Sennacherib and the wicked reign of Manasseh. King Hezekiah rebelled against Assyria and withheld tribute. Eventually, the armies of Assyria invaded and seemed about to destroy the people of Judah just as they had earlier destroyed Israel. God intervened as a result of the taunts of the Rabshakeh, the chief officer of the Assyrian army. Isaiah sent King Hezekiah a message of hope, and Sennacherib's army was miraculously defeated. Egyptian records tell of the Assyrian army being overrun by a horde of mice which even ate the bowstrings of the Assyrian soldiers. God may have used an outbreak of bubonic plague to drive the Assyrian army back to their own land; in the Assyrian's own records (where they just do not record defeats), they claim to have shut Hezekiah up like a bird in a cage, but they never took Jerusalem.

Hezekiah was succeeded by the most evil king ever to sit upon the throne of David. Manasseh apparently imported Assyrian worship and allowed the Temple in Jerusalem to be abused and to fall into disuse. Tradition has it that he had Isaiah tied up in a hollow tree and sawed asunder. That tradition may be reflected in the New Testament (Heb. 11:37).

    B. The great reform (22:1 to 23:30)
      1.   The beginning of Josiah's reign (22:1-2)
      2.   The finding of the book of the law (22:3-20)

The Books of Kings draw to a close quickly. Josiah's great reform of Hebrew life and faith was a case of too little, too late, and too superficial. Jeremiah's ministry overlapped all of the kings from Josiah to the end of the nation and his book adds significant details to the understanding of this era.

To understand the history of this period fully, we need to put what was happending in Judah against the backdrop of Assyrian, Egyptian, and Babylonia conflict. The changing of the names of Eliakim to Jehoiakim by Pharaoh Neco of Egypt anad of Mattaniah to Zedekiah by Nebuchadnezzar of Babylon are significant. Names were supposed to reveal something of a person's nature or character. Anyone who changed a person's name was considered to have the authority to change the way a person lived. Thus the changing of Judah's kings' names by foreign kings indicates how weak the nation of Judah had become and how helpless her kings were.

Jehoiachin's self-sacrifice in order to spare Jerusalem the destruction at the hands of Babylon is one of the high points of the period. The deportations by Nebuchadnezzar were aimed at eliminating Judah's power to fight. When the first deportation did not accomplish that, a second and more extensive one was instigated following the fall of Jerusalem. For all practical purposes, the curses of the Book of Deuteronomy had borne their bitter fruit. Judah's rebellion and apostasy had led her away from God, but God had the last word. Israel's kingdom had come to an end. Her only hope lay in the hands of God to send another King, great David's greater Son.

Part IV
Introduction to the Study
of the Latter Prophets

17

Issues in the Study
of the Latter Prophets

The Hebrew prophets were some of the most disturbing men who ever lived. Anyone who would seriously seek to come to grips with the message of these men must take into account not only what they said but also who they were. Except for Jesus of Nazareth and His disciples, probably no single group of men made as great an impact upon the world as the Old Testament prophets. In introducing the study of canonical prophets, we must come to grips with four basic issues. (1) Who are the canonical prophets? How shall we limit and define those men and/or books which we shall consider? (2) What manner of person was a canonical prophet? What did it take to be a prophet? (3) What is the historical background of the prophetic movement in Israel? How and why did the phenomenon of prophetism come about and take the shape it did in Hebrew society? (4) What are the common forms of the messages of the prophets? Are there identifiable molds into which the prophets poured and by which they proclaimed their messages? Only when we have dealt with each of these issues in general will we be ready to consider the prophets individually.

Identification of the Canonical Prophets

The term *canonical prophet* is not wholly appropriate, for people like Deborah, Nathan, Gad, and Elijah are clearly within the canon yet are not included in those to whom we refer here. Others have sought to identify those intended by the term *writing prophets*. But this also falls far short, for we have no real indication that many of those included actually wrote anything. On the other hand, we have clear

281

references to Samuel, Nathan, and Gad having written; but they are not included. Further, we also know quite well that Jeremiah used a scribe, Baruch, to record his sermons for him. Probably the best term used to identify those to whom we refer is that used in the Hebrew Bible itself, the *Latter Prophets*. It is at least specific, including precisely those to whom we refer and no others. Unfortunately, that term has never achieved anything like a uniform acceptance among Christians.

The men with whom we are concerned in this part of our study are those who were considered to be prophets in the Old Testament and whose sermons were collected into separate books in the Old Testament. Furthermore, each book that contains the record of their ministries and their sermons must also have been identified as a book that belonged in the section of the Old Testament canon identified as the Books of the Prophets. This includes Isaiah, Jeremiah, Ezekiel, Hosea, Joel, Amos, Obadiah, Jonah, Micah, Nahum, Habakkuk, Zephaniah, Haggai, Zechariah, and Malachi. Although Daniel is included among the prophets in the arrangement of the books in most English translations of the Bible, it was not so identified by the Hebrew Old Testament. We shall consider the reasons for this when we study the Book of Daniel itself.

The Nature and Character of an Old Testament Prophet

The prophets were essentially people whose minds were able to comprehend both God and man at the same time. Their hearts and minds were sensitized by the voice and Spirit of God. They proclaimed not general truths but God's special word to a specific historical situation. Unfortunately, too many times we have thought of them primarily as foretellers of what was going to happen. To the contrary, they were primarily forthtellers, pouring forth God's awareness and understanding of what was happening at that moment. In so doing, they announced what was going to happen if God's people did not change their ways, repent, and turn back to His way.

The prophets were not dealing with a world that had no meaning but with one that was deaf to the meaning of what was going on. The words of the prophets were stern, rebuking, and castigating. To read those words even today is a wrench on the emotions, a strain on the imagination. The prophets were people who felt deeply. They agonized over the heartbreak of God and suffered with the oppressed of their people. They bluntly announced that their society was on the road to utter destruction. They were not unafraid of the people with power, but they were so afraid of what was going to happen that they faced them with audacity.

The acts which shocked the prophets are all too often the kinds of things which occur daily in our world. The events recorded in contemporary newspapers, which are accepted as the normal results of social dynamics, were precisely the kinds of things that sent the prophets into tirades. Modern people would call the prophets hysterical. But the prophets would say that our insensitivity to what is happening around us is far worse. The prophets were not philosophers, exploring the issues of human thought; they were activists, concerned with the actuality of life, the plight of humanity, the blindness which never saw God at work and the deafness which never heard Him.

Abraham Heschel has well said that two fundamental issues frightened the prophets: A people may be dying without being aware of it; a people may be able to survive yet refuse to make use of that ability. This raised the messages of the prophets to their highest levels. Perhaps the most amazing feature of the prophets is that they were tolerated at all by the Hebrew people. This very fact is a testimony that Israel recognized the voice of God in the prophets' proclamations.

The prophets did look to the future. However, they were concerned not so much with predicting what would happen as what had to happen. Yet even their concern with the future was always aimed at having meaning for the audience whom they addressed. Their prime concern was always those to whom they spoke.

Concern for the people also made the prophets intercessors. They saw themselves as members of the heavenly council, seeking to advise God in His dealings with His people. They sought to delay judgment, to lay hold of God's merciful nature in order to give their people one more chance.

Ultimately, however, the prophets' relationship to God and to Israel kept them constantly under tension. The revelation of God was a constant demand rather than a comfort. It challenged, exhorted, transformed, and forced decision. The prophets heard God's word and sensed His heart. But they also sensed the hurt and the agony, the stubbornness and the rebellion of their people. This dual tension under which they lived is like rewiring an old house with the power turned on. Any moment could be the last. Every moment had to be taken seriously. There was no place for carelessness and no time for levity. There was only time for the message of the moment in the hope that this next moment might be better.

The Rise of Hebrew Prophetism

Prophets were a part of the society of most of the nations in the ancient Near East. In almost every nation, there were those who announced the will of the deity to their people. Generally, however, this was done only upon request. Those ancient prophets officiated at a shrine and if people wished to know the will of their god, they went to the prophet, paid a fee, asked their question, and received the answer in the form of an oracle. The prophets cast lots, practiced some form of divination, or went into trances or states of ecstasy, in order to communicate with their god and get his message.

That kind of prophet was also found in Israel. Saul was going to see Samuel to find out the location of his lost donkeys at the time he was crowned Israel's first king (1 Sam. 9:6). Saul also joined in with roving bands of ecstatic prophets on at least two occasions (1 Sam. 10:9; 19:24). Furthermore, the professional prophets many of the kings kept at their court were apparently of this sort, giving the king guidance only when he asked for it.

In Israel, however, prophecy developed a unique dimension, not due to anything different in Israel, but to a difference in the God of Israel. There the prophets became spokesmen for Yahweh because God had a message for His people. The prophets of Israel did not wait until their people had a question, they proclaimed God's message when God spoke. We see evidence of this transition in the biblical description of Saul's visit to Samuel. "Formerly in Israel, when a man went to inquire of God, he said, 'Come, let us go to the seer'; for he who is now called a *prophet* was formerly called a *seer*" (1 Sam. 9:9, author's italics). The earlier prophets had been "seers," those who dreamed dreams, saw visions, and otherwise "saw" what God wished. Israel's prophets became something else. They became *nabhi'*, prophets. This word apparently refers to one who pours out God's message unbidden. This peculiar function of the Hebrew prophet is also seen in the description of the relationship which existed between Moses, Aaron, and Pharaoh. "See, I make you as God to Pharaoh; and Aaron your brother shall be your prophet. You shall speak all that I command you; and Aaron your brother shall tell Pharaoh" (Ex. 7:1-2). The point is that the prophet in Israel did not initiate the message. The prophetic message was initiated by God. The prophet was the mouthpiece through whom God spoke.

The Hebrew prophets, *nabhi'*, were described in other ways. Two of the more descriptive titles are "the man of God" (1 Sam. 9:6; 1 Kings 12:22; Jer. 35:4) and the "servant of Yahweh" (1 Kings 14:18; 18:36; 2 Kings 9:7). Such terms indicate the special relationship which existed between Yahweh and His prophet.

This special relationship is probably more clearly seen in the *call* of the prophets than anywhere else. In general, the prophets were not people who were involved in religion in any professional way. Even when they were, their vocation was involved with the priesthood. Yet, whatever their vocation, a time came when they were confronted by God. Amos descibed it vividly when he said, "The Lord took me from following the flock, and the Lord said to me, 'Go, prophesy to my people Israel' " (Amos 7:15). From whatever walk of life they came, after that initial confrontation with Yahweh, they became spokesmen to their nation and its leaders.

The first and great prophet of Israel was Moses. Following him others were scattered along, such as Deborah, Samuel, Nathan, Gad, Elijah, and Elisha. With the eighth century, however, something new happened. That was the time of the rise of some of the most influential prophets Israel ever had: Amos, Hosea, Isaiah, and Micah. The latter part of the sixth and the early part of the fifth centuries produced Jeremiah and Ezekiel, along with several minor prophets. There were a few prophets after the Exile, but none ever seem to have reached the great stature of earlier prophets. Gradually, Hebrew prophetism died out. Many reasons have been offered, but none are convincing. It simply appears that prophetism had filled its place on the stage of God's revelation and then given way to other means of proclaiming God's Word. Perhaps the best suggestion is that with the rise of the scribes, Israel had a written revelation from God and needed less the proclamation by inspired spokesmen.

The Common Forms of the Prophetic Books

The books of the prophets, upon a close examination, can be seen to have a number of common forms. These can be divided first of all into prose and Hebrew poetry. (For the basic characteristics of Hebrew poetry, see Chapter 34, "Hebrew Poetry.") The prose falls into two divisions, autobiographical forms and biographical forms.

Autobiographical forms are always in the first person and share information only the prophet himself could know. The call narrative, where the prophet tells how he came to be God's prophet, is obviously the primary example of this form. It usually includes a report of the Divine confrontation, a commission, some kind of objection or response from the prophet, a reassurance on the part of God, and frequently a sign confirming the reality of the experience. In addition to this, the prophets also regularly gave autobiographical vision reports. In such reports, they either saw something with their eyes or with their minds; through those visions, God gave them special revelation. The prophets also gave autobiographical reports of their symbolic acts. These reports usually included the Divine command to perform a particular act, a report of the fact that they had done what God commanded, and a sermon interpreting the meaning of their act to their people.

The biographical forms found in the prose material of the prophetic narratives are always in the third person. Thus they are being told about the prophet by someone else. These are usually classified under two headings. Prophetic biography describes events that happened to a prophet, usually inserted as the introduction or conclusion to a sermon or a collection of sermons. A second category has been called the prophetic legend. This is an unfortunate choice of terms, but if *legend* is properly understood, the term is acceptable. Technically, a legend is an edifying and pious story relating an event, episode, or life of a holy man, with emphasis upon the miraculous. I prefer to call all biographical forms prophetic biography.

Most prophetic sermons appear to be in poetry. There are common forms frequently used with common kinds of sermons. The major ones have been identified as follows:

1. The prophecy of disaster.
   a. Usually begins with some kind of introductory word, such as the commissioning of the prophet to speak.
   b. Added to this, or standing by itself, is some kind of appeal for attention.
   c. Then the situation is described, setting forth the nature of the problem the prophet sees.
   d. This is accompanied by a prediction of disaster, an announcement of judgment.
   e. Some concluding characterization may be given, either of the prophet or of his audience.

The basic structure of this form is fairly consistent, especially when the message is addressed to an individual. If the message is addressed to a group, the structure appears to be less rigid, though the content is essentially consistent.

2. The prophecy of salvation. This form is identical to that

of the prophecy of disaster, except for a prediction of deliverance instead of the announcement of disaster.

3. An oracle of salvation. This appears to be a word of assurance issued by a prophet to a person or persons who have been lamenting over a tragedy or crisis which confront them.

    a. It begins with a promise of God's intervention on on behalf of those in need.

    b. This is usually followed by a statement of the results which can be expected by His intervention.

    c. The conclusion usually indicates the Divine purpose in intervening.

Some scholars also identify a separate form as a proclamation of salvation, saying that the oracle is oriented to the present while the proclamation is oriented to the future.

In addition to these major forms, other forms have been identified which occur less frequently and with less uniformity. Among these are the woe oracles, so called because they begin with the word, *Woe* or *Alas*. They usually conclude with an announcement of intense judgment. Also there are two kinds of trial speeches. The first of these is set in the form of a courtroom scene, with a summons, a trial, and ultimately the sentencing. Related to this is what has been called the *rib* or covenant lawsuit. The Hebrew word *rib* is usually translated as "controversy" and is apparently used either exclusively or primarily in cases accusing Israel of violating their covenant with Yahweh. Another minor form is the disputation speech, where the prophet was engaged in an actual or rhetorical disputation with his audience. In addition to these, other even more minor forms have been suggested as being present. For most students, these basic ones are sufficient.

18

The Eighth-Century Prophets

In introducing the books included in the Former Prophets, I am departing from the procedure I have followed in introducing the books of each section in the order in which they are found in the Hebrew canon. While I am still limiting myself to the books in this specific section of the canon, I am rearranging the order into one that is essentially chronological, insofar as the ministry of each prophet is concerned. As I note in dealing with each book, there is disagreement on the date of the ministry of some of these men. Further, insofar as the Book of Jonah is concerned, I am not placing it at the time of his ministry but rather at what seems to me to be the most likely time of its writing. By following this arrangement, I will not have to be repeating the historical backgrounds for the ministry of each prophet and will be able to devote more attention to the contents of each book and to each prophet's ministry.

Prophets had been among the people of Israel and Judah before the eighth century and had participated significantly in national life. In the eighth-century, a new phenomenon appeared on the stage of the national life of the two kingdoms. Four major prophetic figures appeared on the scene, all overlapping with one or more of the others. Furthermore, the messages of these men were remembered and recorded in separate books, probably by the prophets' disciples or followers. Their messages may have been written down and circulated in order to get them before as many people as possible, seeking to lead the Hebrew kingdoms to repentance to avoid the disaster these prophets saw on the horizon. On the other hand, their messages may have been treasured among their followers and then written down when catastrophe came, in order to serve as a warning to future generations. For whatever reason, the messages and the ministries of Amos, Hosea, Isaiah, and Micah were all preserved and recorded in separate books. In a profound sense, these men were the shapers of the peculiar form the prophetic tradition took among the Hebrews. They were certainly the greatest of all the prophetic figures who walked upon the stage of Israel's national life. In order to better understand both the ministries and messages of these men, as well as the crises which called them forth, we need briefly to examine the history of Israel and Judah in the eighth century BC.

The first half of the eighth century BC was a time of relative peace for the Hebrew kingdoms. Jeroboam II came to the throne of Israel about 782 BC and Azariah (Uzziah) came to the throne of Judah about fifteen years later. At the time of Jeroboam's accession, Egypt was very weak, Assyria was in a time of national decline and impotence, and Syria and Judah were essentially insignificant threats insofar as Israel was concerned.

Jeroboam II faced an opportunity for territorial expansion such as no Hebrew king since David had enjoyed. Furthermore, Jeroboam had the ability to take advantage of that opportunity. "He restored the border of Israel from the entrance of Hamath as far as the Sea of the Arabah, . . . and he recovered for Israel Damascus and Hamath" (2 Kings 14:25-28). A look at a good map will reveal that the territory controlled by Israel and Judah at this time was almost as great as that controlled by David at the time of his greatest conquests.

A further examination of the map will show that, along with additional territory, Jeroboam II now controlled every major highway which came through Canaan in a north-south direction. Canaan was a land bridge, bordered on the east by the great Arabian Desert and on the west by the Mediterranean; therefore, Israel was in a position to control all of the commerce between Egypt and the regions of Syria, Assyria, and the Mesopotamian Valley. Control of commerce ensured both prosperity for the merchants of the north and major income for the government from taxes imposed upon trade caravans which passed through the land.

If there is anything designed to keep a people happy, it is territorial expansion with little risk and great national and personal prosperity. Jeroboam II brought precisely that to his land. Unfortunately, prosperity breeds greed. Those in prospering Israel sought by every means at hand, both just and unjust, to further expand their prosperity. By the middle of the eighth century, the great middle class of Israel had virtually disappeared. The wealthy had exploited them to the extent that they had been impoverished, driven into debt, and then forced to sell their lands and frequently even themselves into indentured servitude. Furthermore, this process had been accelerated through the bribing of judges and through the acquiescence of priests and prophets (cf. Amos 8:4-6; Hos. 4:1-2,4-8; 5:1-2). Although some have accused the prophets of exaggeration concerning these conditions, archaeological excavations offer abundant support. At that time in Samaria, one small section of the city had very large, luxurious homes; the rest of the city was made up of hovels.

Added to the political, military, and economic successes of Jeroboam II, the religious shrines in the north were being thronged with people. Sadly, however, the worship at the shrines was either pure Baal worship or an assimilation of Baal worship into that of Yahweh. The fertility cult of Canaan, with its sacred prostitutes and utter sensuality, had led astray the people of Israel.

Those who visited Samaria or Bethel in those days might have praised the magnificent buildings which were being built or been enthralled with the prosperity which was evident. The general tone of happiness and the great revival of religion would have made even the most skeptical believe that things were all right in Israel.

Amos and Hosea, however, saw otherwise. They saw the great cracks in the facade of national existence. They saw the oppressions and injustices, felt the heartaches and guilt, and were aware that no national existence built on such a foundation could long endure.

Meanwhile, in the south, Judah was experiencing a lesser degree of prosperity. Azariah (Uzziah) is credited with expanding Judah's territorial borders. He is also remembered as a great builder. However, Judah did not experience the same overwhelming prosperity as Israel, probably because it controlled but one major north-south highway. The rise of Baalism was not nearly as pronounced and the worship of Yahweh at the Temple of Jerusalem remained relatively pure. Possibly because of these two features, immorality and injustice in the south did not rise as it did in the north. Finally, throughout this period, Judah was also in a position of being a vassal to Israel. That in itself may have served to keep Judah more stable. It is difficult to become too proud from a position of vassalage.

As the century passed its midpoint and moved toward its end, the visions and warnings of Hosea and Amos began to come true. Zechariah, Jeroboam's son, had ruled only six months when he was assassinated by Shallum. He in turn was assassinated only one month later by Menahem. This was the beginning of the end for Israel. Instability in government breeds instability in everything. The great kingdom of Jeroboam II was not just tottering; it was collapsing. Thirty years after his death it had ceased to exist.

In 745 BC, an event occurred which brought trouble to Judah and death to Israel: Tiglath-pileser III ascended to the throne of Assyria. His enthronement brought the real beginning of the days of Assyria's empire. He forced Menahem of Israel to pay a massive tribute (2 Kings 15:19). In order to pay that tribute, Israel's king had to levy a major tax upon the wealthy, an act that destroyed his only real base of support. Upon Menahem's death, he was succeeded by his son, Pekahiah, who was shortly assassinated by Pekah.

Pekah's accession was immediately characterized by an anti-Assyrian policy. It was this which produced the Syro-Ephraimitic crisis of 735 BC. In order to deal with the Assyrian threat, Pekah sought to form a coalition of Israel

(Ephraim), Syria, and Judah, with the avowed purpose of overthrowing Assyria. When Ahaz (Judah's new king) refused to join the coalition, Pekah realized that he dare not face Assyria with a nonaligned Judah at his back, so Israel and Syria sought to attack Judah with the purpose of dethroning Ahaz and placing a puppet upon the throne there.

At this point, Ahaz of Judah sent to Tiglath-pileser III, asking for aid. Isaiah of Jerusalem intervened, seeking to talk Ahaz out of this foolish policy; Ahaz refused to listen, having already worked everything out for himself, or so he thought. Assyrian armies began to march against Damascus, the capital of Syria. That brought immediate relief to Judah from the threat of Syria and Israel. Unfortunately, it also made Judah into an Assyrian vassal, a situation that endured for more than a century.

The Assyrians defeated Syria by capturing Damascus in 732 BC. Syria, for all practical purposes, ceased to exist as a nation at that point. Also at that time, Hoshea (not to be confused with Hosea the prophet) assassinated Pekah and seized the throne of Israel. Hoshea's immediate submission to the authority of Assyria preserved a part of Israel for a few more years. However, a subsequent rebellion on his part brought the Assyrian armies back. Following a three-year siege, Samaria fell to the Assyrians and Israel ceased to exist as an independent kingdom. There was a major deportation of Hebrews and a resettlement of large numbers of captives from other parts of Assyria's empire.

In the Southern Kingdom, Hezekiah succeeded Ahaz upon the throne of Judah about 715 BC. He began his reign with a great religious reform. This may have been motivated by the earlier preaching of Isaiah and Micah. It may also have been influenced by a period of weakness in Assyria. At this time a number of small kingdoms rebelled, including a coalition which centered around Ashdod. This city was attacked in 711 BC by the Assyrian armies, bringing the Ashdod rebellion to an end. Hezekiah stayed out of that rebellion, following the graphic advice of Isaiah (Isa. 20:1-6).

However, Hezekiah apparently allowed himself to become involved in a Babylonian-supported rebellion in

705-704 BC. Knowing Assyria could not ignore such an act, Hezekiah began preparing Judah for a siege, building his famous Siloam tunnel in order to furnish water to Jerusalem. As a consequence of that revolt, Sennacherib invaded Judah in 701 BC. As noted in Chapter 16, although Sennacherib did not capture Jerusalem at this time, he did devastate much of the land of Judah. The end result was that Judah was once again made an Assyrian vassal. This apparently lasted until the great reform of Josiah, more than three-quarters of a century later.

Against this chaotic eighth-century political situation, we must place the ministries and understand the messages of Amos and Hosea in the north and Isaiah and Micah in the south. It began as a time of peace and prosperity and ended as a time of defeat and enslavement. Into those days, which began with light and laughter and ended with gloom and misery, God thrust four of His greatest messengers. Their words echo through the corridors of history to ring within our ears the Divine warning:

> Woe to those who are at ease in Zion,
> and to those who feel secure on the mountain of Samaria,
> the notable men of the first of the nations,
>   to whom the house of Israel come! (Amos 6:1).

> Hear, O heavens, and give ear, O earth;
>   for the Lord has spoken:
> "Sons have I reared and brought up,
>   but they have rebelled against me.
> The ox knows its owner,
>   and the ass its master's crib;
> but Israel does not know,
>   my people does not understand" (Isa. 1:2-3).

Therefore because of you
    Zion shall be plowed as a field;
Jerusalem shall become a heap of ruins,
    and the mountain of the house a wooded height (Mic.
3:12).

The deeds of Israel and Judah were known to God. They were going to be punished said the prophets. As we have seen, they were.

19

Amos

Amos was the first of the four great prophets to appear upon the stage of eighth-century Israel. He was a citizen of the Southern Kingdom who was sent to the Northern Kingdom with the message of Yahweh for that part of God's people. His lot was to lead the rebellion of God's spokesmen against the crimes of the day at a time when almost no one but God's prophets saw anything wrong with what was happening among the Hebrew people. To understand fully the impact his ministry and message had upon Israel, we need to remember that it was a time that seemed from most outward appearances to be happy, prosperous, and characterized by a religious revival. Into that setting, God thrust this shepherd from Judah. His name means "Sustained"; if anyone ever needed to be sustained, he did. And he obviously was sustained by the God who sent him.

The Date of Amos's Ministry

The ministry of Amos is given a firm historical footing in the title verse: "In the days of Uzziah king of Judah and in the days of Jeroboam the son of Joash, king of Israel, two years before the earthquake" (1:1). The time when both of these kings were upon the thrones of their kingdoms began approximately 767 BC, so Amos's ministry could not have begun any earlier. At the same time, the conditions Amos described in Israel were relatively early in the reign of Jeroboam; therefore, most interpreters seek to date Amos fairly close to the beginning of these kings combined reigns.

If we could date "*the* earthquake," we could have a precise time for Amos's ministry. It would appear to be clear that the final editor of the book was referring to an earthquake with which he assumed his readers would be familiar. Although the entire Jordan Valley is a major earthquake fault and there is abundant evidence of numerous earthquakes in the region, archaeologists have turned up no evidence of a major earthquake anywhere near the appropriate time and place. Further, the Hebrew can be translated as "two years before the shaking." Some commentators have suggested some other kind of shaking, such as a major international threat or even the assassination of Jeroboam's son Zechariah (2 Kings 15:8-10). That was surely a "shaking"·of Israel's government. At the same time, if Amos's ministry is to be dated by that, it would appear that the problems he saw in the land would not have been nearly so surprising, for many of them would have been fairly visible.

Some have suggested that "*the* earthquake" may have been made significant not by the violence of the earthquake but by an accompanying event. In one of the prophet's sermons, he may have described an earthquake that was to be accompanied by an eclipse of the sun.

> The Lord has sworn by the pride of Jacob:
>   "Surely I will never forget any of their deeds.
> Shall not the land tremble on this account,
>   and everyone mourn who dwells in it,
> and all of it rise like the Nile,
>   and be tossed about and sink again, the Nile of
>   Egypt?"
> "And on that day," says the Lord God,
>   "I will make the sun go down at noon,
>   and darken the earth in broad daylight" (8:7-9).

There was as eclipse of the sun in Assyria on June 15, 763 BC. While not a full eclipse in Palestine, it would have been visible and would have significantly darkened the day. Suppose at such a time there had been a minor earthquake; it would surely have been long remembered as "*the* earthquake." It would also have called to mind Amos's words that described just such an event. If this theory identifies "*the* earthquake" for us, the ministry of Amos would be dated two years earlier, in 765 BC. This would be two years after the earliest possible date and would fit in well with the times the prophet described. Whether we are correct in identifying "*the* earthquake," most scholars date Amos's ministry about 765 BC. His ministry appears to have been quite brief, almost certainly no more than two years and probably less than one. If he had still been preaching when "*the* earthquake" occurred, he would certainly have made some reference to such an event having happened as he predicted.

The Nature and Character of the Man

We know very little about Amos. Brief biographical material is given in 1:1, indicating that he was a shepherd from Tekoa. A further bit of autobiographical material is contained in Amos's report of his call in 7:14-15. To this we can add a few other items deduced from some of the sermons.

Amos was certainly a man of rural, pastoral background, with abundant time to think as he followed his sheep around the region of Tekoa, on the rough arid slopes above the western side of the Dead Sea. Being a "pincher," or pruner, of the trees which produced the sycamore figs was a second vocation, apparently one needed in order to sustain his meager existence. However, being a rural person did not make Amos the "country bumpkin" some people have portrayed him as being. He was quite aware of the events going on in his world, both in Judah and in neighboring Israel, and also knew of events in the nations which surrounded his land. Further, he was quite aware of the history of many of these people.

Tekoa was in that region of Judah near the territory of Edom. Edom was one of the centers of the wisdom movement in the ancient Near East. Amos's preaching indicates he was quite familiar with that wisdom movement and easily could have been classed as a wise man himself. Many commentators have assumed that his background precludes personal wisdom; therefore, anything in his book which sounds like a product of ancient wisdom had to have come from someone else as a later addition to the book. Hans W. Wolff has pointed out that Amos's natural background would have made it quite easy for him to be familiar with Edomite wisdom. No adequate reason any longer exists for denying wisdom-sounding materials to the prophet from Tekoa.

Furthermore, Amos's preaching shows that he was a master of oratory. His sermons show as much and probably more oratorical skill than those of any other Old Testament prophet. He knew how to approach a hostile audience and get them on his side before he began to attack them directly.

Amos also was a man of great courage. He faced the actual threat of the high priest of Bethel and the implied threat of King Jeroboam II without flinching. He also took his message to a hostile audience, knowing that there was a real possibility of martyrdom. But he who had faced the lion in the wilderness was not afraid of the jackals in Bethel.

Finally, Amos was overwhelmingly aware of his sense of call from Yahweh. Amaziah, the priest of Bethel, accused Amos of preaching only for the purpose of making a living, assuring him that he would get no "bread" by preaching his message in Israel (7:12). At this, Amos disassociated himself from the professional prophets who preached only for the living they made. Not all such professional prophets in the Old Testament were bad. Remember Nathan. On the other hand, the movement had clearly degenerated.

Amos also separated himself from the "sons of the prophets." These were the prophetic guilds or groups of disciples who associated themselves with a leader in order to develop the skills needed for the ministry. Such groups appear frequently to have been ecstatics. These were not always bad, but they never seem to have become very significant in the Old Testament prophetic movement. At the same time that he was putting distance between himself and the kinds of prophets with which Amaziah was familiar, Amos acknowledged that he had been sent by Yahweh as His prophet to Israel. It was that simple for Amos. He was a shepherd who had been sent as a prophet of God.

The Book of Amos

The Book of Amos is classified as a Minor Prophet. However, it is minor in length only. The structure of the book is carefully planned and its message is among the more significant in the Old Testament. It was apparently not written by Amos, although much of it obviously comes directly from him or from someone who was an eyewitness of his ministry. The messages of Amos were apparently remembered by friends and enemies. However, whenever "the earthquake" occurred, some of his disciples apparently decided that since part of Amos's messages could be demonstrated to have happened, the rest should be written down with the purpose of trying to give Israel one last chance to hear and repent. The Hebrew of the book is some of the purest and most classical found anywhere in the Old Testament. The book may have had some minor editing late in Israel's history, but its essential form clearly was set very shortly after the sermons were preached.

The Content of the Book

I. Prologue: the man and his time (1:1)
II. The book of sermons (1:2 to 6:14)
    A. Sermon of judgment upon the nations (1:2 to 2:16)
        1. The text: Yahweh's message from Zion (1:2)
        2. Judgment on sins against humanity (1:3 to 2:3)
            a. Judgment on Syria for cruelty (1:3-5)
            b. Judgment on Philistia for treachery (1:6-8)
            c. Judgment on Phoenicia for covenant breaking (1:9-10)
            d. Judgment on Edom for disloyalty (1:11-12)
            e. Judgment on Ammon for atrocities (1:13-15)
            f. Judgment on Moab for sacrilege (2:1-3)

 3. Judgment on Judah for sins against God's
     law (2:4-5)
 4. Judgment on Israel for sins against God's
     love (2:6-16)
     a. Description of the sins (2:6-8)
     b. God's mighty acts (2:9-11)
     c. Israel's rebellious acts (2:12)
     d. The coming judgment (2:13-16)

This first sermon is a masterpiece of the indirect approach as a means of addressing a hostile audience. Amos began by attacking the sins of Israel's neighbors, all of whom the people hated. People always seem to enjoy hearing the sins of those they dislike being attacked. In fact, the sins of our neighbors make us comfortable. Amos, a southerner addressing a northern audience, probably near the temple precincts in Bethel, probably was viewed either with suspicion or hostility. By beginning his sermon as he did, the crowds on the street stopped to listen and liked what they heard. Even when he attacked his own people of Judah, they approved, for there was little love lost between the nations. When he finally attacked Israel, they were hooked. They already recognized his wisdom and insight and, thus, were compelled to listen.

This sermon shows a great deal of Amos's familiarity with current events and with history. A number of typical wisdom forms used in this sermon further underscore Amos's probable relationship to that movement.

The sins of which Amos accused Israel were the oppression of the poor and its careless involvement in the Baal worship of Canaan. The people had become involved in that worship in spite of what God had done for them in His mighty acts of love. The Israelites had turned away not only from God but also from those whom God had sent to them in loving ministry.

 B. A sermon of judgment upon the people of Israel
     (3:1 to 4:5)
     1. The responsibility of privilege (3:1-2)
     2. The Divine warning (3:3-8)

3. Israel's enemies called to view Israel's distress (3:9-11)
4. The coming punishment (3:12 to 4:3)
   a. Utter destruction (3:12)
   b. Destruction of the pagan shrine (3:13-14)
   c. Destruction of the luxurious homes (3:15)
   d. Debasement for the luxurious women (4:1-3)
5. The folly of false worship (4:4-5)

The vivid portrayal of the coming destruction was enough to strike fear in the hearts of anyone who would listen. Some have questioned Amos's accuracy here, but the uncovering of multitudes of ivory inlays have shown that the wealthy in his time were truly living in luxury. The demands of the idle and alcoholic wives of Samaria are described as a major part of the problem. Their captivity was to be degrading and painful.

C. A sermon of the evangelistic purpose of judgment (4:6-13)
   1. Five occasions of futile judgment (4:6-11)
      a. Famine (4:6)
      b. Drought (4:7-8)
      c. Blight, mildew, and locusts (4:9)
      d. Plague (4:10)
      e. Devastation (4:11)
   2. The final confrontation (4:12-13)
      a. The coming of God in judgment (4:12)
      b. The power of the God who comes (4:13)

In one of the more significant theological passages in the entire book, Amos pointed out that the primary purpose of the temporal judgments which God had sent had been to lead Israel back to Him in repentance. The thundering echo of the refrain, "yet you did not return to me" on five separate occasions stabs us awake. Far too often we view judgment primarily as penal. To Amos, it was primarily redemptive. However, God's offer of redemption could be rejected too long. The warning, "prepare to meet your God," was a proclamation that the people were about to face God in a final confrontation.

> D. Lament over Israel's doom (5:1-27)
>   1. The portrait of doom (5:1-3)
>   2. Threefold invitation (5:4-15)
>   a. Seek God instead of idols (5:4-5)
>   b. Seek God by doing justice (5:6-7)
>   c. Digression: contrast between God and Israel (5:8-13)
>   d. Seek God by doing good (5:14-15)
>   3. Grief to come (5:16-17)
>   4. The inescapable day of darkness (5:18-20)
>   5. Israel's empty worship (5:21-23)
>   6. Demand for practical righteousness (5:24)
>   7. Past, present, and future in a nutshell (5:25-27)

The threefold invitation of Amos further underscores that he saw his primary purpose to be that of bringing Israel to God. However, he minced no words in describing the results if they did not make the proper choice. His demand for demonstrating their choice of serving Yahweh by living lives of practical righteousness is set forth in one of the great passages of the book,

> But let justice roll down like waters,
>   and righteousness like an ever-flowing stream (5:24).

Amos's words about the Day of the Lord are the first mention of this concept in the Old Testament. However, the way in which he referred to it clearly show that it was an idea already widespread in Israel. Here is graphically demonstrated the difference between much popular theology and true biblical theology. The people looked for the Day of the Lord as a day of light, a time of vindication upon God's enemies which Israel assumed were its enemies as well. To the contrary, Amos pointed out that Israel, God's chosen people, was the enemy of God. The Day of the Lord would be darkness instead of the light for which the people longed.

E. A sermon against false comfort (6:1-14)
  1. Judgment upon false security (6:1-3)
  2. Judgment upon luxurious idleness (6:4-7)
  3. Judgment upon false strengths (6:8-10)
  4. Judgment, because God commands it (6:11-14)

In case the people had any doubt or uncertainty, Amos announced that an enemy was coming at the express command of God. Further, the enemy was coming because Israel had placed its trust in the strength of Samaria instead of in God. Military strength is nothing when there is no righteousness and justice in the nation.

III. The book of visions (7:1 to 9:15)
  A. The vision of locusts (7:1-3)
    1. The vision (7:1)
    2. Amos's intercession (7:2)
    3. The judgment avoided (7:3)
  B. The vision of fire (drought? 7:4-6)
    1. The vision (7:4)
    2. Amos's intercession (7:5)
    3. The judgment avoided (7:6)
  C. The vision of the plumb line (7:7-9)
    1. The vision (7:7-8a)
    2 The inescapable judgment (7:8b-9)

Two things need to be noted about these vision reports. First, the repentance of God is a different word from that used of the repentance of man. It refers to deep emotions but has nothing to do with a moral change. Second, we need to note that eventually Amos realized that the time of intercession had passed. Should this be a warning to us?

  D. Biographical interlude: Amos's call (7:10-17)
    1. Amaziah's report to the king (7:10-11)
    2. Amaziah's warning to Amos (7:12-13)
    3. Amos's response (7:14-17)
      a. His call (7:14-15)
      b. His warning to Amaziah (7:16-17)

Although we have already considered Amos's call, we need

to question why it was recorded here rather than at the beginning. Note that Amaziah addressed Amos as a "seer." This probably caused the editor to place the episode in the middle of the things Amos was "seeing."

    E. The vision of the summer fruit (8:1-14)
        1. The vision (8:1-2a)
        2. The meaning (8:2b-3)
        3. Israel's atrocious behavior (8:4-6)
        4. The coming judgment (8:7-14)
    F. The vision of God (9:1-15)
        1. The coming catastrophe (9:1-4)
        2. The power of God (9:5-6)
        3. The God of all men (9:7-10)
        4. The epilogue of hope (9:11-15)

Amos's final visions bring us back to the theme of absolute destruction. Once again Israel was warned that it could not and should not presume upon its special relationship.

Some have suggested that the epilogue of hope came from a later editor rather than from the eighth century. The reasons for this are usually summed up as its being a message of hope when Amos had not offered any hope and its proclaiming a restoration of the throne of David and a restoration of Jerusalem when Amos had not predicted that the house of David would come to an end or that Jerusalem would be destroyed and Judah go into exile. Those who disagree point out that just because a man had not preached any hope was no reason that he could not. Further, one can occasionally see glimpses of hope in Amos's preaching. Some have also suggested that Amos was predicting a restoration of the house of David over all of Israel. Either way, whether a late addition or from Amos himself, the inspired author brought the book to a close with a forward look to God's ultimate redemption beyond temporal judgment.

Amos's message to the world was and is that a religion which does not produce practical righteousness is of no value. In fact, it is the source of ultimate destruction. Further, Amos proclaimed that God's judgment was redemptive in purpose, that even when we experience the wrath of God, we are still inside His love. Finally, Amos acknowledged that both our present and our future are in the hands of God. On that we can rely with confidence.

20

Hosea

The second of the four great eighth-century prophets was
Hosea. His name means "Salvation" and is in form similar
to Joshua or its Greek equivalent, Jesus. Like Amos, Hosea
also was a prophet to the Northern Kingdom of Israel. Unlike Amos, he was a northerner and had no problems with
being considered an outsider. However, as a northerner, he
apparently felt more deeply than Amos the personal tragedies which were about to befall his people and his beloved
land. The Book of Hosea has well been called the Gospel of
John in the Old Testament, for his theme is quite similar,
the unswerving love of God. Hosea has also been called the
first evangelist of the Old Testament, seeking to lead people
to respond to that overwhelming love.

The Book of Hosea

The Book of Hosea has the most corrupt text of any Old
Testament book. There are many differences between the
Hebrew text and that of the LXX. Further, recent manuscript discoveries have only confirmed the problems in the
text. However, as noted in the discussion in Old Testament
textual studies, even though the corruptions in Hosea give
countless difficulties in translation, they do not affect our
understanding of the basic message of the book.

Furthermore, the book is very difficult to outline. No
really logical development appears to exist between the
various messages or oracles within the book. Two suggestions have been made to explain this. Professor A. B. David-
son long ago described the contents of the book as a series
of sobs torn from the heart of the agonized prophet. Obvi-

ously, one does not sob in logical outline. Emotions are seldom logical. On the other hand, it has also been noted that normally we do not find a logical consistency of plan in the order of sermons any person preaches. Rather, they are called forth as the situation and changing circumstances demand. What we may have is simply the collection of Hosea's sermons, in a sense just as they were tossed into a file drawer. Again, our understanding of his basic themes is not hindered by our failure to find a tight structure within the book. However, in order to deal with his preaching in any consistent way, the interpreter is forced to deal with passages that are separated from one another in the book.

The Date of Hosea's Ministry

As is usual in the prophetic books, the date of Hosea's ministry is given in the title verse. "The word of the Lord that came to Hosea the son of Beeri, in the days of Uzziah, Jotham, Ahaz, and Hezekiah, kings of Judah, and in the days of Jeroboam, the son of Joash, king of Israel" (1:1). It is intriguing to speculate as to why the author did not also list the kings of Israel who reigned after Jeroboam II and during the time of the southern kings whom he named, particularly since Hosea was a northern prophet. It may have been due to the fact that, with all of the assassinations and the chaotic conditions during the last days of Israel, the prophet or the editor did not really consider those men kings. It may also have been due to the fact that the book was not written until well after the fall of the Northern Kingdom and Jeroboam II was the only one mentioned because he was king when Hosea's ministry began.

In order to cover the reigns listed, the ministry of Hosea would have had to extend from the mid-750s to about 715 BC, a period of almost forty years. That would give him one of the longest ministries of any Old Testament prophet. Since the sermons of the prophet apparently know nothing of the fall of Samaria in 722 BC, it has been suggested that his ministry was somewhat shorter than the title would indicate. Furthermore, it would appear that Gilead was still an Israelite territory (based on 6:8) during Hosea's ministry, yet Gilead fell to Assyria in 732 BC. Therefore, Hosea's actual ministry must have come to an end before this, possibly around 735 BC. The listing of the later kings in Judah may have been given to describe the period when the effects or predictions of Hosea were still being felt.

Be that as it may, it is obvious that Hosea was preaching after the decline of Israel had begun and the effects of the rising empire of Assyria were being felt. This would place his ministry sometime after that of Amos. Serious and reverent students of the Bible date his ministry either as having lasted from around 755 to around 735 BC, or as extending from about 755 to about 715 BC.

Hosea as a Man

Even less is known about Hosea as an individual than is known about Amos. Based upon various implications from Hosea's messages, some scholars have suggested that he was a priest, a professional prophet, or a member of Israel's upper classes. If any of these were true, he was also one whose conscience had been stabbed awake by the abuses of the group of which he was a part. However, we have no conclusive evidence for any of these suggestions. All that we know for certain is that he was an Israelite and was apparently a city dweller since he appears to have been quite familiar with the affairs of both Samaria and Bethel.

He was also quite aware of what was going on upon both the national and the international scene of the day. Hosea's knowledge of history and geography, as well as the religious traditions and rituals of his day, was quite extensive, far more than we would assume that the ordinary Israelite possessed.

Some insights can be gained by contrasting what we know of Amos and Hosea. Both were prophets to Israel, but Hosea was the native while Amos was the "foreign missionary." Hosea was a man of deep emotions, preaching from the heart. Amos, on the other hand, seldom exposed his heart, revealing primarily his intellect and his deep convictions.

Amos *saw* Israel's injustices and unrighteousness, but Hosea appears to have *felt* them as well. He suffered when his people suffered. Both men were fully dedicated to trying to lead Israel to repentance and a new relationship with Yahweh, turning away from the Baals. Amos saw God as the God of wrath and justice. Hosea saw God supremely as the Lord of love. To Hosea, all other aspects of God were subordinate to His overwhelming love. Hosea also saw God as feeling very deeply the sins of His people. For centuries, Christians have preached as if the only time God suffered for sin was at the cross. To this, the Book of Hosea responds with a, "Not so!" For the prophet Hosea, God suffered for sin throughout all time.

Hosea's Marriage

From the standpoint of interpretation, Hosea's marriage offers the most difficult problem. Through marriage Hosea received his call to prophetic service and also discovered (had revealed to him) the deeper awareness of God's redemptive love. The entire experience is recorded in the first three chapters.

In summary, the story states simply that Hosea was commanded to marry "a wife of harlotry," so he married Gomer (1:2-3). Over the years, three children were born in their home (1:3-9). Eventually, however, tragedy struck. Gomer left Hosea, going off with her lovers. Finally God commanded Hosea to seek for Gomer. He found her for sale as a slave, so he bought her and took her home. However, he did not force himself upon her. Rather, he sought to woo her again, to win back her loyal love (3:1-3). It is a tragic story, all too familiar in the ongoing problems of human life. Through this experience, Hosea learned the lesson of a heart broken by the betrayal of one he loved. He also learned that love does not necessarily end with such betrayal. The greatest lesson he learned, however, was that real love seeks the faithless lover, restoring the betrayed relationship if possible. Hosea proclaimed this new insight into Yahweh's love for faithless Israel.

The problem with understanding this whole episode has arisen over the difficulty of understanding God commanding His prophet to marry an immoral woman. The issue is not merely academic, for the entire message of Hosea is based upon this experience. Further, the law required the stoning of an adulteress (Lev. 20:10; Deut. 22:22; John 8:5). Various interpretations are offered.

Some interpreters suggest that the story should be understood literally, as I have summarized it. However, others object on the grounds of the moral and ethical problem of conceiving of God ordering a prophet to marry such a woman. Further, the Hebrew description of her is literally a "wife of harlotries"; the singular form of the word would have normally been expected if this were to be understood literally.

Seeking to avoid this problem, interpreters have suggested that the entire story is an allegory, having no basis in fact. According to this approach, Hosea was inspired with an awareness of the love of God and created the whole story as an allegory on the human level of what God was doing with Israel on the Divine level. Three major objections are raised to this interpretation. First, the narrative gives no indication that this is to be understood in any way other than as fact. Second, such an allegory would have been an extremely cruel thing to have said about Hosea's own wife. The ethical problem of telling such a story about his wife is no less serious than the one such an interpretation was trying to avoid. Third, the "first" word of Yahweh to Hosea involved his marriage (1:2). This would indicate that there had been no previous revelation about the love of God. It would further imply that God spoke to Hosea through the tragedy of his broken marriage and broken heart.

A further interpretation of the passage suggests that the woman in chapter 1 and the one in chapter 3 are not the same. This, however, really offers no solution to the original problem and raises others. If the woman in chapter 3 is different, the whole case breaks down, for there is no parallel between Hosea's experience and that of Yahweh's love for Israel. The whole point of the message is that God still loved unfaithful Israel.

A different approach notes that the plural form of the word *harlotries* is normally used in the Old Testament to refer to idolatry, rather than to physical adultery (cf. 2 Kings 9:22). This would then state that Gomer was an idolatress, although physically chaste at the time of Hosea's marriage. This approach also calls attention to the fact that we are told that she bore "him" a son in regards to the first child, while this is not said of the other two children. According to this, Gomer only became an adulteress after their marriage. This may find further confirmation in the names of the last two children. The second child was named "Not Pitied" (Hebrew: *Lo-ruhamah,* literally, "Unloved") and the third was "Not My People" (Hebrew: *Lo-'ammi*). The names may actually reflect Hosea's growing awareness of Gomer's unfaithfulness. Finally, Gomer left for her lovers, only to be sought by Hosea and eventually brought back to his love.

A variation on this latter approach is made by those who suggest that Gomer was a follower of Baal and that, although she was chaste at the time of betrothal, she had participated in Baal rites of sexual initiation with a sacred priest at the time of her marriage. A further variation also suggests that she herself was a cultic prostitute. Neither of these really solve any existing problems but raise others.

A final approach offers variations to several of those already stated. This suggests that Hosea's awareness of God's call and involvement in his marriage only came after the fact. That is, after he became aware of Gomer's infidelity and of his own ongoing love for her, he realized that God had been guiding him all along. Thus, looking back at his marriage, he could say that it was done at the command of God.

Whatever approach we take to the problem of Hosea's marriage, it is quite obvious that through his own heartache and personal tragedy he became aware of God's abiding love for His unfaithful people. Further, he also became aware that God took the pain of sinful infidelity into Himself and in His love sought again to win the love of His faithless people.

The Content of the Book

I. The setting of the prophet's ministry (1:1)
II. The prophet's marriage and its lessons (1:2 to 3:5)
    A. Hosea's marriage (1:2-9)
        1. The command of God (1:2)
        2. The first child: Jezreel (1:3-5)
        3. The second child: Lo-ruhamah (1:6-7)
        4. The third child: Lo-'ammi (1:8-9)
    B. A message of hope (1:10 to 2:1)
    C. Punishment for infidelity (2:2-13)
        1. The tragedy of infidelity (2:2-5)
            a. The heartbreak of being forsaken (2:2a)
            b. Wrath (2:2b-3)
            c. The heartbreak of forsaken children (2:4)
            d. The folly of infidelity (2:5)
        2. The judgment announced (2:6-13)
    D. Pursuing love (2:14-23)
        1. Back to the wilderness (2:14-15)
        2. A new relationship (2:16-17)
        3. A new covenant (2:18-20)
        4. A new commitment (2:21-23)
    E. Unending love (3:1-5)
        1. The command of God (3:1)
        2. The wife brought home (3:2-3)
        3. The lesson for Israel (3:4-5)

The whole process of naming children in Israel, as well as in the ancient Near East, is relatively strange to us. A name was more than just a title, it was generally descriptive of either a person's character or of the faith and hope of the parents. Insofar as the children of prophets were concerned, it was quite common to give them the names of major sermons or themes. This is also related to the kinds of word play frequently found among the prophets. More than a century after Jehu's blood bath in the valley of Jezreel (2 Kings 10:1-27), Hosea was announcing judgment upon the excesses perpetrated there.

The message of hope inserted in 1:10 to 2:21 was probably

not preached at that time in Hosea's life, but sometime later, possibly at the end of 2:23. However, its inclusion at this point in the book was based upon a reversal of the word play found in the names of Hosea's children. Chapter 2 moves from the personal experience of the prophet to that of Yahweh and Israel.

The Baal worshipers of Israel apparently wore some kind of identifying pendants on their foreheads attached to a headband, as well as amulets on a chain around the neck which hung between the breasts (cf. 2:2). The Baal worship was intended to bring fertility, so Israel did not realize that Yahweh gave her all of the produce. Hosea promised two things which were intended to demonstrate to Israel the futility of such worship. First, the produce of the land was going to be stopped (vv. 11-12). Far more dramatic, however, Hosea announced that Israel was going to experience a new time in the wilderness to discover what Yahweh could really do. There is another intriguing word play here, for the Valley of Achor was where Achan was stoned for his sin in the time of Joshua (Josh. 7:26). In Israel's history, the valley had stood as a symbol of failure and frustration, but God was going to transform it into a "door of hope" (2:15).

Obviously Israel had assimilated Baal worship into Yahweh worship, even calling Yahweh by the title of Baal (v. 16). That, too, was going to be changed, with Israel entering into a new love relationship with God because He was making it possible (vv. 16-20).

Further, Hosea clearly saw that Israel's infidelity made a time of punishment and exile necessary. At the same time, he saw that the judgment was not the end of the story, for the people would return to Yahweh.

III. Selections from the messages of Hosea (4:1 to 14:9)
    A. The moral and spiritual decay (4:1 to 7:7)
        1. Yahweh's controversy with the people (4:1-3)
        2. Infidelity of religious leaders (4:4-10)
        3. The spirit of apostasy (4:11-13*a*)

Yahweh's "controversy" is the Hebrew word *rib*, which seems to imply an attack upon covenant breaking (4:1*a*). What was missing among the people of God was faithfulness, kindness, and the knowledge of God (v. 1*b*). In the Old Testament, "the knowledge of God" appears to be an idiomatic expression for God's revealed will, His law. Since Israel had rejected God's revelation, becoming unfaithful to Him and unkind to others, the end result was a national life characterized by "swearing, lying, killing, stealing, and committing adultery" (v. 2).

Taken at face value, Israel's words of penitence in 5:15*b* to 6:3 would sound quite sincere. But God saw them as insincere, as His response shows: "Your love is like a morning cloud, like the dew that goes early away" (6:4). Israel was very religious, but God looked for something deeper than the outward forms of religion (v. 6). Furthermore, the problem in Israel was one which went through every strata of society, including priests, prophets, kings, and people. All were involved.

5. The harlotry of Israel's worship (9:1-6)
6. The coming judgment (9:7-9)
7. God's love and Israel's faithlessness (9:10-15)
8. The judgment viewed again (9:16-17)
9. The folly of Israel's kingship (10:1-10)
10. A punishment to fit the crime (10:11-15)

Bethel was the major shrine of the Northern Kingdom, the center of most of Israel's worship. Since the people had devoted it to Baal worship, it had become a path to sin. The Hebrew name for this place literally means "the house of God." Hosea characteristically modified its name to Beth-aven, which means "the house of iniquity" (cf. 10:5), which it had become in Israel.

In this section, several very vivid phrases describe the folly of Israel's worship of the calf at Bethel. Equally as descriptive are Hosea's phrases referring to Israel's foolish national and international policies.

One of the more beautiful images of this section is the description of God's love for Israel.

> Like grapes in the wilderness,
>   I found Israel.
> Like the first fruit on a fig tree,
>   in its first season,
>   I saw your fathers (9:10).

Imagine one wandering in the barren wilderness, hungry and thirsty, and then stumbling across a luxurious vine, loaded with grapes. What joy was experienced! Or imagine the husbandman, planting a fig tree, caring for it, nurturing it, and then rejoicing over the very first luxurious fruit. Again, the image is one of overwhelming joy. This was what God felt for the people of Israel, but they spurned Him and His love. Instead, they turned to Baal, the fertility god. As punishment, they were going to lose that for which they had turned to Baal, as Yahweh announced; "No birth, no pregnancy, no conception!" (v. 11).

C. The compassion of Yahweh (11:1-11)
   1.   The Father's love (11:1-3)
   2.   The coming judgment (11:4-7)
   3.   Overwhelming love (11:8-9)
   4.   The promised redemption (11:10-11)

No passage in the Old Testament is more descriptive of God's love than the beautiful images here. Even as He pronounced judgment upon their unfaithfulness, God also proclaimed His unswerving love.

> How can I give you up, O Ephraim!
>   How can I hand you over, O Israel!
> ....
> My heart recoils within me,
>   my compassion grows warm and tender.
> I will not execute my fierce anger,
>   I will not again destroy Ephraim;
> for I am God and not man,
>   the Holy One in your midst,
>   and I will not come to destroy (vv. 8-9).

Yet God's love for Ephraim had not changed the people's commitment to Baal. This was still present.

D. The final appeal to repent, the inevitability of doom (11:12 to 13:16)
   1.   The sin of Ephraim remained (11:12 to 12:1)
   2.   Ephraim's self-sufficient pride (12:2-9)
   3.   The prophets among them (12:10-14)
   4.   The high cost of sin (13:1-3)
   5.   Judgment for infidelity (13:4-16)

The final proclamation of judgment by Hosea was couched in terms designed to get Israel to repent. He pointed out the greatness Israel had experienced in days past, even in its very immediate past. Yet the people had thrown it all away with their apostasy. You can almost hear him snort with sarcasm as he said of their idolatrous worship: "Men kiss calves!" (13:2). He pointed out again that God was the only God they had ever experienced, that He was the only Savior (v. 4). As the only One who could redeem them, Yahweh was certainly able to punish them. "Samaria shall bear her guilt" (v. 16).

>   E. Final restoration after repentance (14:1-9)
>   1.   The invitation to repent (14:1-3)
>   2.   The promise of restoration (14:4-7)
>   3.   A final admonition (14:8-9)

Many interpreters have denied these verses to Hosea, claiming that anyone who preached such judgment could not also proclaim hope. Hope is offered, however, in the section dealing with Hosea's marriage (chs. 1 to 3). Those are obviously integral to that section. Further, anyone who was so aware of God's love had to be able to see hope beyond judgment.

Hosea's great discovery was that all that Israel could really offer to God was words, asking Him to "take away all iniquity" and promising to "accept that which is good," that which comes from the hand of the One who loved them (14:2). Furthermore, God promised,

> I will heal their faithlessness;
> I will love them freely (v. 4).

Israel had been unable to do anything about its own faithlessness, but God could do something with it. He could heal it as the outpouring of His love. From Hosea's personal tragedy had come one of Israel's greatest revelations about the nature of God. Thus God can use that evil which happens for His own redemptive purposes. The love of God can even transform a broken heart into an avenue of ultimate blessing.

21

Isaiah

Most superlatives that could be applied either to a book or to a man have been applied to Isaiah the prophet and to the book which bears his name. The book itself is one of the longest in the Bible, along with Jeremiah and Psalms. It is clearly one of the more significant books in the Old Testament. Its impact upon Jewish thought of the late Old Testament and early New Testament era can be measured by the fact that more copies of it have been found among the Dead Sea Scrolls than any other book with the exception of Deuteronomy. Its impact upon Jesus and the writers of the New Testament is demonstrated by the fact that it is quoted more than any other book, with more than four hundred different references to it having been identified. Its appeal lies in its portrayal in the first part of the book of the Messiah as King and in the second part of the book of the Messiah as Suffering Servant. The poetry of the book is exalted and its literary genius is unquestioned.

The Authorship and Unity of the Book

No book in the Bible has had its authorship and unity as seriously questioned as Isaiah. Before considering this, however, let us remind ourselves that such questions have been seriously raised by people who love the Bible, are devoted to its study and preaching, and serve Jesus Christ with their whole being. Further, such questions have nothing to do with issues of inspiration. God can (and does) inspire whomever He pleases to record what He pleases. The basic issue is not whether the book is inspired but how God inspired His human spokesmen to record and pass on this specific book.

As far as we know, Jesus never wrote a word, but we do not doubt His words because of this. We have no idea who wrote the Epistle to the Hebrews, but that has nothing to do with its authority or its inspiration. This issue is basically an academic question, not an issue of theology. The book as we now have it is as God inspired it for us to have. Our task at this moment is to try to find out, insofar as is possible, how God led His servants in accomplishing this task.

The overwhelming majority of biblical scholars today contend that the sixty-six chapters of this book are not all by the same author. While such things are not settled by majority vote, the overwhelming agreement on this issue should at least cause us to give serious consideration to it. Among those sections most generally questioned as having come from Isaiah are the following:

1. The lyric psalm following the vision of the messianic kingdom (12:1-6)
2. The oracle against Babylon (13:1 to 14:23)
3. The oracle against Moab (15:1 to 16:14)
4. Oracles against Babylon, Edom, and Arabia (21:1-17)
5. The so-called "little apocalypse" of Isaiah (24:1 to 27:13)
6. The oracle to Jerusalem (33:1-24)
7. The oracle of judgment and restoration (34:1 to 35:10)
8. The historical appendix, generally parallel to 2 Kings 18:13 to 20:19 (36:1 to 39:8)
9. The great complex of 40:1 to 66:24, frequently subdivided into two sections
   a. That section frequently called Deutero-Isaiah, whose theme is the great redemption by God (40:1 to 55:13)
   b. That section frequently called Trito-Isaiah whose theme is the new people of God (56:1 to 66:24)
10. In addition to these major blocks of material, other less lengthy and less significant passages are also frequently questioned.

A detailed discussion of all of these questioned passages can be found in any contemporary commentary. However,

some discussion of the major arguments presented is in
order at this point.

Isaiah 40:1 to 66:24

Since most of the arguments suggested for any of the
other passages are dealt with in this block of material, we
shall begin here. The question is usually asked in one of two
ways. Did these chapters come from the hand (or at least
from the mouth) of Isaiah of Jerusalem? Are these chapters
the product of a later hand or hands? In order to deal with
these issues, we must consider the differences and similarities between this section and the first part of the book.

Those who argue for a disunity point out that nowhere in
chapters 40 to 66 is there is a claim that Isaiah is the author.
They also point out a distinct change in attitude in the
second half of the book. In the first part of the book the
message is primarily one of confrontation and rebuke, while
in the second part is a message of comfort and assurance.
Further, the destruction of Jerusalem is not predicted in the
second half; it is presupposed as an accomplished fact. Not
only that, in the second part of the book the Jewish people
were in exile, as was the prophet himself. Even more striking, Cyrus, king of Persia is mentioned by name twice
(44:28; 45:1) without any introduction or explanation, although he clearly lived at least one hundred and fifty years
after Isaiah of Jerusalem and would not have been known
at all by the prophet's hearers in Jerusalem. In addition, the
fall of Babylon is seen in the immediate future in chapters
40 to 55, in the past in chapters 56 to 66, with both being
a matter of joy, yet the Babylonians were not even a threat
during the life of Isaiah. These latter items are not questioning whether God could inspire a man to know this kind of
future information. Of course He could! The issue is
whether He did it, and if He did it, would it have been
recorded with no words of explanation to the contemporary
hearers.

Furthermore, supporters of this view point to the fact
that the Bible itself twice refers to the decree of Cyrus
allowing the Jews to go home from the Exile as being in

fulfillment of the prophecy of Jeremiah (2 Chron. 36:22-23; Ezra 1:1-4). Why should those authors have looked to Jeremiah's prediction of a return from the Exile in seventy years if material actually naming Cyrus had been available to them? Also, Jeremiah was almost lynched for predicting the destruction of the Temple (Jer. 26:18), and barely escaped when someone found a passage in Micah predicting its destruction (Mic. 3:12). Yet this part of Isaiah presupposed the destruction of Jerusalem and its Temple (44:26, 28; 49:19; 51:17-20; 52:9; 60:10; 63:18; 64:10-11). Surely if so many references to its destruction had come from Isaiah of Jerusalem, no one would have been so upset with Jeremiah or turned to one minor passage in Micah.

Finally, those who believe that chapters 40 to 66 are by a different author point out the major differences in style and theology. No poetry in the Bible is as high and exalted as that found in this latter section. It is clearly different from the poetry in the first part. Numerous words or phrases found in chapters 1 to 39 do not even appear in chapters 40 to 66, such as "the Lord, Yahweh of Hosts," "remnant," "to stretch out the hand," and "in that day" (about thirty times in 1 to 39, only once in 40 to 66). The reverse is also true, with the following appearing only in 40 to 66: "all flesh," "to choose," "chosen," "I, Yahweh [or other names for God]," and "redeem" (more than twenty times in 40 to 66, only once in 1 to 39). The theological differences are reflected in that in 1 to 39 the majesty of God is emphasized while in 40 to 66 His infinity is the focal point. In 1 to 39, the Messiah is King, while in 40 to 66 He is the Suffering Servant; in 1 to 39, Yahweh is related to Israel through covenant commitment, while in 40 to 66 the relationship is based upon Yahweh's choice.

On the other hand, those who argue for unity point out that the Bible has always treated the book as a unity. It is further noted that the Dead Sea Scrolls show no division between chapters 39 and 40. (There is a division between chapters 33 and 34, to which we shall return later.) They also note that a different purpose requires different styles and different emphases. They note that Isaiah could have been put forward under inspiration and produced a message for those people at that time.

While it goes without question that God could have inspired Isaiah of Jerusalem to produce the material in 40 to 66, my opinion is that the evidence, particularly that of the Cyrus decree and Jeremiah's Temple sermon, make it unlikely that He did so. Rather, it appears that this material was probably produced by some of the ongoing group of Isaiah disciples who had preserved his sermons and were seeking, under the inspiration of God, to offer a new message to God's people in the Exile and in these early days following the return in 539 BC. It appears that chapters 40 to 55 are to be dated shortly before the return, while chapters 56 to 66 were likely produced in Jerusalem in the period following that return. References in the New Testament to material in this section as coming from Isaiah were, therefore, probably literary references only, indicating the book and not the man.

If by using the terms *Deutero-Isaiah* and *Trito-Isaiah*, we are referring to those particular blocks of material, I find no problem with them. If by those terms we are indicating that the sections were produced wholly independently of each other, I have a distinct problem, for I believe that the same group or individual produced both. There just does not appear to be the kinds of differences between them that exist between the first and second half of the book.

While serious biblical students maintain separateness here, other serious students maintain the basic unity of the entire book, although even these usually grant that there was a significant amount of later editing done to the book to bring it into the form in which we now find it. However, there is no disagreement as to the basic setting of the three sections. The first of the book has Judah and Jerusalem in the eighth century BC as its basic setting. Chapters 40 to 55 have as their setting the Exile of the Hebrew people in Babylon, shortly before 539 BC. Chapters 56 to 66 are set in Jerusalem following the return from the Exile in 539 BC. Whether these settings were achieved by inspiration or by actual presence of the speaker does not alter the fact of the settings.

Isaiah 34:1 to 35:10 and 36:1 to 39:8

Those interpreters who have maintained that an un-known prophet of the Exile produced chapters 40 to 66 have also pointed out that chapters 34 and 35 have a remarkable similarity to the so-called Deutero-Isaiah. Although there is not sufficient material here to prove an identity with Deutero-Isaiah, there appears to be more similarity than with the unquestioned material produced by Isaiah of Jerusalem. However, the similarity of 34 to 35 (which is in the first part of the book) with 40 to 66 has been used by supporters of Isaianic unity as evidence for that unity.

On the other hand, the fact that Isaiah 36:1 to 39:8 is almost identical to 2 Kings 18:13 to 20:19 has also created a significant amount of discussion. In general, those who have maintained that Deutero-Isaiah was produced by a separate author have suggested that these four chapters were copied from Kings, edited, and placed here to give the historical details of the last significant events of Isaiah's ministry, thus serving as an introduction to chapters 40 through 66. However, with the discovery in the Dead Sea Scrolls that there is a break between chapters 33 and 34, some supporters of a separate authorship for Deutero-Isaiah have suggested that this section actually begins with chapter 34, rather than with chapter 40. They now main-tain that this unknown prophet began his material with an oracle of judgment and restoration, prepared an historical summary of the end of the ministry of Isaiah of Jerusalem as the background for understanding Judah's ultimate hope for deliverance, and then added the major message, chap-ters 40 to 66. According to this approach, the author of 2 Kings borrowed the historical material and edited it for his purposes.

The final situation regarding these chapters appears to be that those who hold to a separate authorship of 40 to 66, also hold to a separate authorship for chapters 34 to 39. There is some disagreement among them as to whether this entire block is a unit or not. On the other hand, those who maintain that the entire book is a unit are forced to admit that there is obviously a literary relationship between Isaiah and Kings. Although these usually suggest that the author of Isaiah borrowed from Kings, no really satisfactory explanation has been offered to explain why the borrowed material was inserted at this place.

The Oracles Against Babylon and Related Material (13:1 to 14:23; 21:1-17)

The issue of whether this material was produced by Isaiah of Jerusalem or by some later disciple relates to the conclusion one has reached regarding the authorship of Isaiah 40 to 66. The problem here is that Babylon was no threat to the people of Judah and Jerusalem during the eighth century BC. The bitterness expressed toward Babylon (as well as Edom and Arabia) in this material presupposed the Babylonian destruction of Jerusalem and the captivity of the Hebrew people following that destruction. This material is presented with no explanation and, therefore, would have been essentially meaningless to the people of Isaiah's day; it would have carried a significant message to the people in exile in the mid-sixth century BC. Some have suggested that these were originally preached by Isaiah to Assyria and other contemporary enemies and then reedited in the Babylonian era.

In general, then, those who deny that Isaiah produced chapters 40 to 66 also deny that Isaiah produced these oracles for the same reasons. On the other hand, those who find no problem in the unity of the two major sections of the book certainly have no problem with these chapters.

The "Little Apocalypse" of Isaiah (24:1 to 27:13)

This block of material is frequently denied to Isaiah for significantly different reasons than those which have been suggested in dealing with the other materials. The primary problem here has to do with the fact that these chapters have some characteristics of apocalyptic literature, such as a universal judgment, the shutting up of members of the heavenly host, and the resurrection of the dead. However, many of the characteristics of full-blown apocalypses, such as Daniel and Revelation, are missing. Obviously apocalyptic literature has to have a beginning somewhere, and this may have been the first halting steps toward it. But there are enough differences from real apocalyptic to deny that it is necessary to date this material anywhere near the end of the Old Testament era. If this material did come from Isaiah of Jerusalem, we must wonder why no other material like it showed up for more than a century and a half, and possibly longer, depending upon when we date the writing of the Book of Daniel. It may, therefore, come from the exilic period or the postexilic period, although there is no universal agreement among Bible scholars. If it does come from Isaiah of Jerusalem, it is different from anything else he produced and made no known impact upon Hebrew thought or writing for an extended period of time.

The Oracle Against Moab (15:1 to 16:14)

Because so much of this oracle is similar to that found in Jeremiah 48:28-39, some interpreters have denied it to Isaiah, saying that it was originally preached by Jeremiah and a later editor added it to the Book of Isaiah. However, it could just as easily have been preached by Isaiah and later reinterpreted by Jeremiah. A few interpreters have suggested that it was an earlier anonymous prophecy both Isaiah and Jeremiah later used with modifications. The fact is, we know very little of Moabite history and find it quite difficult to identify one specific occasion where it would fit better than any other. There is no legitimate reason for denying this oracle to Isaiah of Jerusalem. He may have been inspired to use an earlier oracle or to create this one himself.

The Lyric Psalm and the Oracle to Jerusalem (12:1-6; 33:1-24)

Because these two chapters do not sound at all like what we have come to know as the preaching of Isaiah of Jerusalem, many scholars have also denied these two chapters to

Isaiah. They argue that the poetry is more like that of the latter part of the book than that which is undoubtedly from Isaiah. However, the material is too brief to allow a great deal of evidence to be gathered for the discussion. The differences between chapter 12 and the rest of Isaiah do not appear to be great enough to deny chapter 12 to the eighth-century prophet. Further, since the break in the Dead Sea Scrolls comes after chapter 33 and the evidence regarding this chapter is also scant, it appears unjustified to deny this chapter to Isaiah also.

Summary

While some very legitimate questions have been raised about the authorship of parts of Isaiah, no serious question have been raised as to the fact that the entire book is a part of the Word of God which will stand forever (Isa. 40:8). Thus, we will consider the book as a whole, while recognizing that, regardless of its unity and authorship, it has at least three basic historical settings for the three major sections of the book. These settings may have been the actual settings of different authors or the inspired settings viewed by an author transported into new situations by God.

Isaiah of Jerusalem

The name Isaiah means "Salvation of Yahweh" and probably expressed the faith, hope, or dream of Isaiah's parents that he would be an instrument of Yahweh's salvation for his nation. It also clearly described the way of Yahweh's salvation which Isaiah preached to the people of Jerusalem. According to a Jewish tradition recorded in the Talmud, Isaiah was a nephew of Amaziah and a cousin of Uzziah, kings of Judah. He was the son of Amoz (not to be confused with the prophet Amos).

Isaiah's ministry extended from the end of the life of Uzziah through the reigns of Jotham, Ahaz, and Hezekiah. Although the last datable oracle in his book comes from 701 BC, the time of Sennacherib's invasion, another tradition holds that he was martyred by being placed in a hollow log and then sawed in two by the wicked Manasseh. Since his call is specifically dated to "the year that King Uzziah died" (6:1), it must have lasted from about 742 BC to the early 600s BC, a period of more than forty years.

Although Isaiah's being a part of the royal family is only based upon a tradition, he apparently had easier access to the palace than any of his contemporaries and was always aware of the intrigues of court life and national and international politics. According to 2 Chronicles 26:22, Isaiah was the author of "the acts of Uzziah," thus possibly identifying him as an official court scribe. He was probably born about the time Amos began his ministry in Israel, was married to a prophetess (8:3), and had two children. The names of his children, Maher-shalal-hashbaz ("The spoil speeds, the prey hastes") and Shear-jashub ("A remnant shall return") reflect the two main themes of his early proclamation. He warned his people that the crisis of temporal judgment was immediately upon them and that, while the destruction would be great, ultimately God would spare a remnant of His people, bringing them back from exile and destruction.

As is true with most of the prophets, Isaiah's ministry was but the lengthened shadow of his call. He had apparently been overcome with grief and anger toward God at the death of his beloved Uzziah. In the Temple at a time of worship, as the smoke of incense and sacrifice filled the precinct, he received a vision of Yahweh, revealing His awesome holiness. From that time on, the most common phrase he used to describe Yahweh was "the Holy One of Israel." Seeing this aspect of the Divine Presence, Isaiah was overcome by his own sinfulness in even daring to question God's wisdom. Confessing his sin, he was cleansed by God. Although his sins were forgiven, the terms used to describe the experience reflect that it was painful.

Once aware of being forgiven, Isaiah became aware that Yahweh was seeking someone to carry His message of purging judgment, awesome holiness, and ultimate redemption to His people. Isaiah became an eager volunteer, crying "Here am I! Send me" (6:8). There was no reluctance on his part here, nor do we ever find it in his ministry. In openness, Yahweh revealed to Isaiah that his ministry would be essentially fruitless (vv. 9-10), although at the end a few people would hear and respond (v. 13).

Throughout his long ministry, Isaiah was a towering figure in Jerusalem. Confronting kings, priests, and people, he eagerly and faithfully proclaimed the divine message. He interferred with military preparations, involved himself in international diplomacy, intervened in Temple worship and importuned the people in the marketplace. Ultimately, he gave his life in proclaiming the "Salvation of Yahweh." No other prophet saw as clearly the ultimate portrait of the Messiah as King as did this princely prophet of eighth-century Jerusalem.

The Content of the Book

Whether one grants all of this book to the prophet Isaiah or whether it is assumed that major (or minor) parts of it may have been produced by his disciples, it has come to us as one book. We shall deal with it as such.

I. Selections from sermons dealing with Judah and Israel (1:1 to 12:6)
   A. The setting (1:1)
   B. The indictment of Judah (1:2-31)
      1. The sin of Judah (1:2-6)
      2. God's judgment (1:7-9)
      3. Judah's empty worship (1:10-15)
      4. God's great invitation (1:16-20)
      5. Their sin restated (1:21-23)
      6. Judgment and redemption (1:24-31)
   C. Contrast between Jerusalem's present and future (2:1 to 4:6)
      1. The exaltation of Jerusalem (2:1-5; vv. 2-5 are parallel to Mic. 4:1-4)
      2. The Lord's great day of judgment (2:6-22)
      3. The folly of Judah's life (3:1-12)
      4. The oppression of the poor (3:13-15)
      5. The humbling of the haughty women (3:16 to 4:1)
      6. Restoration of Jerusalem (4:2-6)

    D. Awesome sin and terrible judgment (5:1-30)
       1.   The Song of the Vineyard (5:1-7)
       2.   Woes over Jerusalem's sin (5:8-25)
       3.   The coming judgment (5:26-30)
    E. Isaiah's call (6:1-13)
       1.   Isaiah's vision of Yahweh (6:1-4)
       2.   Isaiah's vision of his sin (6:5)
       3.   Isaiah's cleansing from sin (6:6-7)
       4.   Yahweh's call (6:8*a*)
       5.   Isaiah's surrender (6:8*b*)
       6.   Yahweh's commission (6:9-10)
       7.   Isaiah's questioning response (6:11*a*)
       8.   His ultimate ministry (6:11*b*-13)

These first six chapters give a good sampling of the types of preaching Isaiah of Jerusalem produced. His blunt attacks upon the sinfulness of his people were not intended to win friends and influence people. To call them "rulers of Sodom" and "people of Gomorrah" was the height of insult (1:10). He did that to awaken them to their condition. At the same time, he offered to them God's opportunity for transformation.

> Wash yourselves; make yourselves clean;
>   remove the evil of your doings
>   from before my eyes;
> cease to do evil,
>   learn to do good;
> seek justice,
>   correct oppression;
> defend the fatherless,
>   plead for the widow.
> Come now, let us reason together,
>   says the Lord:
> though your sins are like scarlet,
>   they shall be as white as snow;
> though they are red like crimson,
>   they shall become like wool (1:16-18).

    Isaiah was also able to contrast vividly the present conditions in Jerusalem with the future which God intended for the city. The literary relationship between Isaiah 2:2-5 and

Micah 4:1-4 raises the question of dependency. There is just no way of knowing whether Isaiah borrowed from Micah or Micah from Isaiah, or both from some anonymous prophet.

Isaiah's Song of the Vineyard was designed to set forth in a parable the contrast between God's care for His people and their evil deeds. In this song we find one of the typically prophetic play on words. Isaiah proclaimed:

> and he looked for justice [*mishpat*],
>> but behold, bloodshed [*mispach*];
> for righteousness [*tsedhakah*],
>> but behold, a cry [*tse'aqah*] (5:7).

F. The prophecy of Immanuel (7:1 to 8:22)
  1. The Syro-Ephraimitic crisis (7:1-9)
  2. The sign of Immanuel (7:10-17)
  3. The oppressor called for (7:18-25)
  4. The sign of Isaiah's son (8:1-4)
  5. The fear of God (8:5-15)
  6. The written Word (8:16-22)
G. The messianic names and nature (9:1-7)
H. The anger of God (9:8 to 10:34)
  1. Coming adversaries (9:8 to 10:4)
  2. Assyria as the rod of God (10:5-11)
  3. Judgment on Assyria (10:12-19)
  4. God's ultimate deliverance (10:20-27*a*)
  5. Advancing enemies (10:27*b*-34)
I. The Shoot of Jesse (11:1-16)
  1. The messianic nature (11:1-5)
  2. The messianic kingdom (11:6-16)
J. Praise for God's salvation (12:1-6)

The most significant focus of these chapters from a Christian's standpoint are the three messianic prophecies: the sign of Immanuel (7:1 to 8:22), the messianic names and nature (9:1-7), and the shoot of Jesse (David's father, 11:1-16). Each of these obviously had meaning to the people of Isaiah's day, but they also looked forward to the Coming One.

The Immanuel prophecy was spoken during the Syro-

Ephraimitic crisis of 735 BC. (See Chapter 18 which gives the historical background of the eighth-century prophets.) At that time, Isaiah offered a sign to Ahaz that God was going to deliver His people. That sign was Immanuel. Isaiah obviously expected the birth of the child to be in the near future, but he did place it in the future. This is an example of the foreshortened future which appears frequently in the Bible. When God's spokesmen view an event in the future, it frequently appears to be closer than it actually is.

Interpreters have different opinions as to whether Isaiah 7:14 predicted a virgin birth. (This has nothing to do with whether Jesus was born of a virgin; the New Testament clearly teaches this. Rather, the issue is whether Isaiah foresaw such a birth.) The Hebrew word here is 'almah, which literally means a young women who is sexually mature. The Hebrew does have a word for *virgin*, which is *bethulah*. This word is normally translated in the LXX by *parthenos*, a Greek word which also means "virgin." The fascinating thing is that the LXX writers translated 'almah in 7:14 with *parthenos*. The question is, Why?

'Almah occurs nine times in the Old Testament (Gen. 24:43; Ex. 2:8; Prov. 30:19; Ps. 46:1; 68:25; Song of Songs 1:3; 6:8; 1 Chron. 15:20; Isa. 7:14). In some instances the woman referred to is clearly not a virgin. But in Genesis 24:43, she is clearly a virgin and the LXX translators again translated the word by *parthenos*. Thus there must have been something in the context which made them use this word. It may have been due to the fact that the woman named the child and that there was no man in the oracle. However, we must at least acknowledge that they saw something more than just what is found in 'almah itself. Certainly, if the LXX had not made this translation, there would have been no passage in the Old Testament to encourage Joseph when he faced the issue of Mary's pregnancy. It is also possible that God was trying to reveal the virgin birth to Isaiah but that it was so unbelievable that he chose a word which would allow such but not require it. This becomes more likely when we consider the second messianic prophecy.

There is no way of dating Isaiah 9:1-7, but it obviously

came later than chapter 7. The names of the Messiah given here are both titles and descriptive of His character. Among the terms used is the word "Wonderful." This word is used many times in the Old Testament in referring to something miraculous. In at least two places, it used in a context of a miraculous birth (cf. Gen. 18:14, where the word is translated as "hard"; Judg. 13:18). Could it carry anything of that meaning here? Further, the Hebrew expression translated as "Mighty God" is *'El Gibbor. Gibbor* occurs over seventy times, and in every instance except the few places where it is connected with *'El,* the word for God, it is understood as a mighty man. Could it be that we are again being confronted with a new truth beyond all of Isaiah's comprehension, that the Coming One was to be the product of a miraculous birth and was to be the combination of God and man? Even if these verses do not teach this, they allow for the possibility Jesus fulfilled.

In both the second and the third messianic prophecies, the Coming One was to be of the house of David, great David's greater Son. His kingdom would be forever and would initiate a reign of ultimate peace, and He would be filled with the Spirit of the Lord. Although this was far distant insofar as Isaiah was concerned, it offered a message of hope to God's people that God was in control of this world and would one day firmly establish His kingdom, just as He had promised.

II. The foreign prophecies (13:1 to 23:18)

The prophets regularly addressed major messages to the nations around them. In general, these are not as meaningful to us for we know little or nothing of the historical situations which called them forth. The major thrust is that God was the God of all the nations, they were ultimately responsible to Him. This is another reflection of the fact that the prophets felt commissioned to a ministry which was not limited to their own people.

III. The little apocalypse (24:1 to 27:13)
A. The doom of this present world (24:1-23)

B. The Lord's great victory (25:1-12)

C. God's provision for the future (26:1-21)

D. Ultimate redemption (27:1-13)

This passage is not apocalyptic but may be a step on the way from typical prophecy to a full-grown apocalyptic, such as Daniel. Its emphasis is upon the utter sovereignty of Yahweh and upon the full confidence which can be had in His ultimate victory over His enemies, as well as in His ultimate redemption of His people. The first clear teaching of a resurrection from the dead in the Old Testament is found here. However, the view here is of a limited resurrection of the righteous only (cf. 26:13-14, 19).

IV. God's wisdom contrasted with human stupidity (28:1 to 33:24)

A. God's wisdom contrasted with human stupidity (28:1-29)

B. Attack upon empty rituals and secret uprighteousness (29:1-24)

C. Divine revelation to a rebellious people (30:1-33)

D. The folly of foreign alliances (31:1-9)

E. The righteous King (32:1-20)

F. Praise for God's exaltation (33:1-24)

This section is generally understood as being preached in the latter part of Isaiah's ministry, being addressed to King Hezekiah in the midst of the Assyrian crisis. It is frequently called "The Book of Hezekiah" or "The Assyrian Cycle." There is another messianic oracle here, pointing to the nature of the messianic kingdom as a time of righteousness, justice, and protection from enemies. While God was using Assyria as His instrument to chastise Judah, it was also going to be held responsible for its own injustices.

V. The fury and blessing of Yahweh (34:1 to 35:10)

A. Yahweh's day of vengeance (34:1-17)

B. The wilderness highway (35:1-10)

VI. Historical interlude (36:1 to 39:8)
   A. Sennacherib's abortive attack on Jerusalem (36:1 to 37:38)
   B. Hezekiah's sickness (38:1-22)
   C. Isaiah's response to the Babylonian envoys (39:1-8)

This section is more and more assumed to be the historical introduction to the change in emphasis of the latter portion of the book. The stage is here set for God's judgment and the return of His people from the Exile. Following this, the historical crises of Hezekiah are described, along with Isaiah's part in them. This further sets the stage for the ultimate captivity in Babylon and the Hebrews' return from it. Hezekiah's utter shortsightedness is described in terms which can apply to many people. As long as there was peace in his time, he did not really appear to care what might happen later. How tragic!

VII. God's great redemption of His people (40:1 to 55:13)
   A. The good news to Zion (40:1-11)
   B. The majesty of God (40:12-31)
   C. The God who helps (41:1-29)
   D. The song of the Servant (42:1-9)
   E. The new song of God's people (42:10-25)
   F. God's redemption (43:1 to 44:8)
   G. The folly of idolatry (44:9-20)
   H. The great Redeemer (44:21 to 47:4)
   I. Judgment upon Babylon (47:5-15)
   J. Foretold redemption and judgment fulfilled (48:1-22)
   K. The second song of the Servant (49:1-13)
   L.. God's abundant blessing (49:14-26)
   M. The third song of the Servant (50:1-9)
   N. Invitation to share in Yahweh's redemption (50:10 to 51:23)
   O. Those who bring good tidings (52:1-12)
   P. The fourth song of the Servant (52:13 to 53:12)
   Q. Vindication of God's servants (54:1-17)
   R. The fifth (?) song of the Servant (55:1-13)

The setting for this section is clearly among the Hebrew people who were in Babylonian Exile. It thus has to be addressed to the period between 586 BC and 539 BC, and probably was nearer that latter date. It was a message of hope and comfort, directing the Hebrews' attention to the coming redemption by God. Not really a development of one thought to another, it is more a repetition of the basic themes of deliverance and vindication over and over again.

The most significant issue of this section is the identity of the Servant who was to be Yahweh's instrument in delivering His people. Numerous suggestions have been made over the centuries ranging from Israel, to the remnant, to some form of an idealized Israel, to an individual, to the Messiah Himself. In the New Testament, Jesus is clearly the fulfillment of this hope. The basic issue here is, who did the prophet think the Servant was to be? If, as some suggest, the Servant was corporate Israel, it is strange that never again after Isaiah 48:20 is Israel called a servant of Yahweh. On the other hand, if the prophet clearly identified the Servant as the Messiah, it is strange that no other Old Testament writer ever seems to have picked up this connection. It is even more strange that the disciples of Jesus did not make this identification. It is far too technical an issue to go into in detail here, but it appears that the prophet was expecting an ideal individual who would ultimately effect the spiritual salvation of God's people. However, I do not believe that the actual connection between the Davidic Messiah and the Suffering Servant was made until Jesus did it Himself in His own life and ministry. He was both King and Servant.

Most scholars identify only four songs of the Servant in this section. However, even though chapter 55 is not usually so identified, it appears to me to be both the climax of this section and the climax of the Servant Songs.

VIII. God's new people (56:1 to 66:24)
    A. Judgment and redemption (56:1 to 59:21)
        1. Outsiders becoming insiders (56:1-8)

2. Difficulties in the new community (56:9 to 57:13)
3. Peace for God's people and its absence for the wicked (57:14-21)
4. Alienation and redemption (58:1-14)
5. Rebellion, judgment and redemption (59:1-21)
B. The shining glory of God (60:1 to 66:24)
   1. The restored people (60:1-22)
   2. A further song of the Servant (61:1-4)
   3. The vindication of Zion (61:5 to 62:12)
   4. The steadfast love of Yahweh (63:1-19)
   5. The wrath of God (64:1-12)
   6. God's eagerness to be found (65:1-7)
   7. Blessings and wrath contrasted (65:8-16)
   8. The new heavens and the new earth (65:17 to 66:24)

Note that the setting of this section is in Palestine after the return from exile. The emphasis is upon the humanity of God's people, who found that life in the restored community was less than ideal. However, there was still to be an ideal future for them. This would ultimately be found in God's new heavens and new earth. The prophet proclaimed that before the ideal future could be realized something more had to be done for God's people. They had to be a new people, living on a new earth. God Himself would be the light within that new world. Jesus began His ministry by quoting words form this section.

> The Spirit of the Lord God is upon me,
>   because the Lord has anointed me
> to bring good tidings to the afflicted;
>   he has sent me to bind up the brokenhearted,
> to proclaim liberty to the captives,
>   and the opening of the prison to those who are bound;
> to proclaim the year of the Lord's favor,
>   . . . (61:1-2; cf. Luke 4:16-19).

On this theme of good tidings, the Book of Isaiah closes, having proclaimed some of the most profound words ever uttered. Their height and depth still tantalizes us as we seek to probe ever deeper into their prophetic insights.

22

Micah

The fourth of the eighth-century prophets was Micah. If he had had the good fortune to preach in almost any other time, he would be far better remembered and studied. However, standing in the shadows of Amos and Hosea in Israel and Isaiah in Judah, he gets overlooked in most studies. This is unfortunate, for his book has some of the most significant teachings in the Old Testament.

The State of the Text

Fascinating disagreement has arisen among scholars concerning the state of the Hebrew text of Micah. Some have suggested that the text of Micah is in the best state of preservation of any of the eighth-century prophets. Others suggest that the text is the most corrupt prophetic text we have, other than that of Hosea. Those who consider the text corrupt usually do so based upon their own opinion of what the Hebrew should say rather than upon actual divergences in manuscripts and versions. Although Micah did not use the best Hebrew found in the Old Testament (to put it mildly), no really objective evidence has been found to question the essential accuracy of the best Hebrew manuscripts.

Authorship, Unity, and Date of the Book

As in the study of the text, there has been a disagreement concerning the unity of the Book of Micah. Most scholars have agreed that the material in chapters 1 through 3 comes from Micah himself. Chapters 4 and 5 have frequently been denied to him because of the general message of comfort. The steady belief among some interpreters that a prophet who preached doom could not also preach messages of hope and promises of restoration continues to haunt us. Further, others have denied chapters 6 and 7 to Micah, as they are addressed primarily to the nation rather than to its leaders, as were the first three chapters.

However, other scholars disagree with these suggestions. There appears to be little doubt but that chapters 1 through 3 and 6 and 7 were essentially addressed to different audiences, but neither is there any sufficient reason for thinking that they did not come from Micah. They clearly come from the same historical period, and to invent an unknown prophet to preach these latter chapters when the major difference has to do with the audience rather than with the vocabulary or the theology is to create a bigger problem than the one we are trying to solve. Further, although there may be a few late editorial additions, there is no reason to deny chapters 4 and 5 to Micah, just because their theme is hope for the future. The general consensus among scholars today is that the book is essentially a unit, coming from the tongue of Micah himself.

We have no way of knowing whether the actual author was Micah or some follower of his. It is unlikely that a country man of his day would have been able to write, yet it is not impossible. More than likely, some scribe became a follower of Micah and recorded his words, probably very shortly after they were uttered. Certainly the book was written and available by the time of the ministry of Jeremiah, less than a century later, for a quotation from Micah actually saved Jeremiah's life (cf. Jer. 26:18-19; Mic. 3:12).

The author dates Micah's ministry to "the days of Jotham, Ahaz, and Hezekiah, kings of Judah" (1:1). This would extend his ministry from shortly after Isaiah began his ministry to shortly before he ended it. However, the only passage that can certainly be dated before the fall of Samaria is the polemic against Samaria in 1:5b-9. The major part of his ministry appears to have centered around the Assyrian threat, probably at the time of the Ashdod rebellion in 711 BC and the Sennacherib crisis in 701 BC. If, as it appears, his ministry ended shortly after 701 BC and the book was known and available at the time of Jeremiah's crisis involving his attack upon the Temple in 609 BC (cf. Jer. 26:1), its writing must fit into this period. As I have indicated, there is no reason for not dating it at the early part of this era, possibly in the early days of wicked Manasseh, at a time when Judah so desperately needed to hear Micah's warning again.

Micah, the Prophet

The name *Micah* means "Who is like Yahweh?" It occurs in the Old Testament in several variations and was applied to numerous individuals. However, with the possible exception of Micaiah, who confronted King Ahab of Israel in the ninth century BC (1 Kings 22:1-28), no one ever demonstrated commitment to such a name as did this prophet of the eighth century BC.

Micah's home was in Moresheth, near Gath (1:1, 14). Although the site has not been identified with certainty, it clearly was in the Shephelah, about twenty-five miles southwest of Jerusalem and obviously in the vicinity of the Philistine territory. Other than his home and his time, we are told nothing directly about him. What we know, we have to infer from his preaching.

He was a rural person, with the healthy skepticism that comes from being a "son of the soil." He was not taken in and deceived by the pomp of the great city of Jerusalem; nor was he overawed by great and influential leaders. However, he apparently had no access to the so-called great of the land, although he clearly knew of the nature of their deeds.

Micah had a suspicion of anything connected with life in the big cities and saw the civilization and social structures there as a major cause of the sin and wrong in his land. Although he and Isaiah ministered in the same nation and at approximately the same time, neither ever referred to the other. They have one oracle in common (Mic. 4:1-4; Isa. 2:2-5). It is not likely that Micah would have deliberately copied the preaching of a city prophet, such as Isaiah. It is even less likely that Isaiah would have copied the words of someone as relatively unimportant as Micah. It appears far more likely that each used, with slight modifications, an anonymous oracle that was circulating in their time.

Micah's preaching was stern, blunt, and to the point. He was not one to mince words, being even more direct than most prophets appear to have been. He was incensed at the injustice he saw in his land and pronounced an unequivocal message of judgment upon those who practiced such. Yet he was also a man with time to reflect upon the ultimate purposes of God. Indicative of the time he spent in the presence of God is the fact that he viewed the future more clearly than any other Old Testament prophet. Among the things which he foretold were the destruction of Samaria in 722 BC and of Jerusalem in 586 BC (1:6-8a; 3:12). He also saw the Exile in Babylon and the return from the Exile in 539 BC (4:6-7,10). Finally he foresaw the birth of the Messiah in Bethlehem, the vision which made it possible centuries later for the Wise Men to find the Child they sought (Mic. 5:2; Matt. 2:1-11).

Micah fearlessly attacked the sins he saw. He attacked the powerful and the wealthy, the false prophets, the unrighteous judges, the greedy priests, and many others who were in positions of power. He drew his strength for such blunt confrontations from the Lord, declaring:

> But as for me, I will look to the Lord,
> I will wait for the God of my salvation;
> my God will hear me (7:7).

Micah was not only a stern denouncer of sin but also a man of infinite confidence and hope. He knew that Yahweh alone was the One who could forgive sin "because he delights in steadfast love" (v. 18). He knew that God would ultimately bring in a time of peace for all people, although that time would not ultimately be ushered in until the reign of the Messiah (4:3-4; 5:4).

The Content of the Book

I. Setting of Micah's ministry (1:1)
II. The coming judgment upon Israel and Judah (1:2 to 3:12)
   A. The coming of Yahweh in wrath (1:2-8*a*)
   B. Micah's personal grief (1:8*b*-9)
   C. The judgment of exile (1:10-16)
   D. Attack upon society's evils (2:1 to 3:12)
      1. Greed for massive land holdings (2:1-5)
      2. Verbal attack upon the prophet (2:6)
      3. Oppression of the helpless (2:7-10)
      4. The problem of alcohol (2:11)
      5. An interlude of ultimate hope (2:12-13)
      6. The rulers' perverted sense of justice (3:1-4)
      7. Prophets who preach only for money (3:5-7)
      8. Micah's strength in God's Spirit (3:8)
      9. Religious and political rulers who lead wrongly (3:9-12)

The book opens with the sternest denunciation of sinful oppression. Micah, while a master at identifying sin, did not enjoy doing so. Instead, he was deeply distressed over the sin of his people and the judgment that was to come upon it.

Many of the prophets were masters at word play, or puns. However, nowhere in the entire Old Testament is there such a sustained play on words as in Micah 1:10-16. Drawing upon Hebrew town names, which are translatable, Micah proclaimed his message of coming judgment with one pun after another. There is no adequate way to show this in English, but the following modified paraphrase, based upon one originally prepared by Dr. Clyde Francisco for a graduate seminar at The Southern Baptist Theological Seminary, will partially demonstrate this technique.

Tell it not in Gath,
in Weepville, do not weep;
in Duston, roll in the dust.

Pass over Beautytown in nakedness and shame,
The people of Rescueville have not rescued;
the lamentation of Helpvillehouse has taken from you its
    help.
The people of Bittertown are longing for sweet,
for evil from Yahweh has come to the gate of Jerusalem.
Hitch your chariots to a *reckish* (horse), people of
    Lachish.
The beginning of sin to the daughter of Zion,
for in you has been found the apostasy of Israel.
Therefore you shall give a parting dowry to Bridesburg.
The houses of Snaretown are a snare to the kings of
    Israel.
Therefore the owner has come to you, Ownapolis.
The glory of Israel shall go into oblivion (1:10-15)

Micah was incensed by the greed of people who spent all
night plotting their next business moves, who oppressed the
most helpless people in the community. Further, he was
angered by prophets who preached only for money and attacked those who did not pay them. To him, there was only
one possible end for such a society. Both Israel and Judah
would be destroyed and go into exile. The punishment simply had to come.

   III. The glorious future of Yahweh's faithfulness (4:1 to
      5:15)
      A. The exaltation of the Temple of the Lord and the
         Lord of the Temple (4:1-4)
      B. The outcasts brought in (4:5-8)
      C. Judgment upon enemies (4:9 to 5:1)
         1.   Exile and rescue (4:9-10)
         2.   The destruction of their enemies (4:11 to
            5:1)
      D. The Messiah and His Kingdom (5:2-4)
      E. Deliverance from Assyria (5:5-6)
      F. Exaltation of the remnant (5:7-15)

The most magnificent part of the future Micah saw was the
coming of the Messiah and His kingdom. The reference to

Bethlehem has been interpreted by some as simply pointing to David's hometown, thus identifying the Messiah as coming from the line of David. That is surely a possibility. However, the specific identification of Bethlehem was interpreted by New Testament writers as being the fulfillment of Micah's prophecy. Whether Micah fully understood his words is not certain. However, there appears to be little doubt about what God intended.

The prophecy further predicted a birth, "when she who is in travail has brought forth" (5:3) in Bethlehem. The Messiah was not coming into the world as a conquering king but as a helpless baby. But He was to become the Ruler who would stand in the strength of Yahweh and bring security to His people.

IV. Present crisis and future deliverance (6:1 to 7:20)
    A. Yahweh's controversy with His people (6:1-8)
        1. The courtroom scene (6:1-2)
        2. His mighty acts (6:3-5)
        3. The divine demands (6:6-8)
    B. The sins of God's people (6:9-16)
    C. Despair over the present (7:1-6)
    D. Confidence in the future (7:7-20)
        1. The prophet's hope (7:7)
        2. Vindication before all the earth (7:8-17)
        3. The forgiving God (7:18-20)

The courtroom setting for Micah's final attack upon his people is in the form of a *rib*, a covenant lawsuit. The Hebrews' infidelity is contrasted with God's mighty acts in the past in choosing them as His people. Yet God's people had presumed upon that relationship, assuming that all that was required of them was the proper ritual, bringing all the right sacrifices at the proper time and adding to them in abundance. They were wrong. Micah thundered at them:

> He has showed you, O man, what is good;
>   and what does the Lord require of you
> but to do justice, and to love kindness,
>   and to walk humbly with your God? (6:8).

In one of the greatest passages of the Old Testament, Micah set forth the teaching that a religion which does not produce acts of ethical righteousness as well as a spiritual relationship with God is of no value.

Micah's final proclamation sounds almost like a gospel proclamation of the New Testament. His people's only hope rested not in their faithfulness but in God's forgiveness.

> Who is a God like thee, pardoning iniquity
>> and passing over transgression
>> for the remnant of his inheritance?
> ....
> He will again have compassion upon us,
>> he will tread our iniquities under foot.
> Thou wilt cast all our sins
>> into the depths of the sea (7:18-19).

That was Micah's hope. He proclaimed it as Judah's only hope. It is still our hope.

23

The Seventh-Century Prophets

Following the end of the ministries of Micah and Isaiah, almost three-quarters of a century of prophetic silence descended upon the Hebrew people. Their national identity was now located in Judah with its major focus in Jerusalem. During this era of silence we pass through the latter part of the reign of Hezekiah, the long reign of wicked Manasseh, the brief reign of Amon, and the beginning of the reign of youthful Josiah. In this night of darkened spirituality for Judah, the Lord gave no fresh word. Then, about 626 BC, the prophetic silence was not simply broken, it was shattered by the piercing words of Jeremiah and Zephaniah. They were soon joined by Habakkuk, Nahum, and Obadiah. The ministries and messages of these men attain a richer meaning within the historical framework in which they served.

The seventh-century BC arrived in the final days of the reign of good King Hezekiah. As is all too frequently the case, a good father was followed upon the throne of Jerusalem by a son remembered primarily for evil. Manasseh (ca. 696-642 BC) was apparently a loyal vassal of Assyria for the entire period of his reign. He restored the worship of the Assyrian gods, as well as that of some of the old Canaanite gods. He actually brought idols into the Temple in Jerusalem and introduced human sacrifice, burning his own sons as offerings. His evil policies were opposed by many of the people of Judah, but he finally put down that opposition with bloodshed. He is credited with a minor attempt at religious reform late in his reign. However, it was neither thorough nor long lasting. It was his evil which lived after him and for which he is remembered.

Upon the death of Manasseh, his son Amon (642-640 BC) succeeded to the throne, apparently following in his father's evil steps. Opposition to idolatrous policies was still present and his own servants rose up and assassinated him. The assassins were immediately executed and his son Josiah (640-609 BC), who was only eight years old, came to the throne. From the earliest days of Josiah's reign, he sought to lead his people back to God. By the time he was sixteen (632 BC), Josiah proclaimed that he was determined to seek the way of Yahweh. Five years later (627 BC) Ashurbanipal, king of Assyria, died. This gave Josiah the opportunity he needed; he cast off the Assyrian yoke, purging the Temple of Assyrian worship. The upheaval in Assyria also gave Babylon an opportunity for independence, as its new king, Nabopolassar, rebelled in the year of his accession, 626 BC. At the same time, the barbaric Scythians from the steppes of Russia began making major raids into the heart of the Assyrian Empire, reaching as far south as Egypt. With Assyrian attention devoted to these major forces, their control of western Palestine began to slip badly.

These national and international events, both religious and political, had the whole land of Judah in an uproar, as the people wondered what God was doing around them and in their midst. At this time both Jeremiah and Zephaniah began their ministries. Jeremiah's call is dated precisely to the thirteenth year of Josiah (626 BC). As God was moving through the nations, He sent forth His spokesmen to interpret to His people what He was doing.

The growing weakness of Assyria gave Josiah the opportunity he needed. It was the first time since the reign of Tiglath-pileser III began in 745 BC that Assyria had been too weak to deal with Hebrew rebellion. Josiah moved rapidly with religious reform, a part of which was the refurbishing and restoration of the Temple. During this work, a copy of the "book of the law of the Lord given through Moses" was found (2 Chron. 34:8-15). When King Josiah heard its words, he was deeply stricken and led his people into an even more thorough religious reform, using the book as the basis for his actions. Almost certainly, this book was

Deuteronomy. Josiah also sought advice from Huldah, a prophetess in Judah, as to what course of action he should take. The end result was that Josiah led the nation into a renewal of their covenant commitment to Yahweh, a thorough purging of their religion, and a great Passover celebration.

While apparently Jeremiah did not preach about Josiah's reform, he clearly proclaimed the new commitment to the old covenant. As a part of Josiah's reform, the shrines throughout the land were closed, putting countless priests out of work. Many of them apparently blamed Jeremiah and sought to kill him (Jer. 11:18-23).

The remaining years of Josiah's reign were apparently fairly peaceful. He continued his labors aimed at the purification of the faith of Judah. Assyria was growing ever weaker, being drained by the increasing pressure of the Babylonians who were joined by the Medians. During this time Habakkuk seems to have begun his ministry. Assyria's capital, Nineveh, fell before the attack of the Medo-Babylonian coalition in 612 BC. Assyria removed its government to Haran, but it fell in 610 BC. About this time, Nahum rejoiced over Assyria's fall.

In 610 BC, Pharaoh Neco II ascended the throne of Egypt. Fearing the rising power of Babylon, Neco decided that it was to Egypt's benefit to maintain a weak Assyria as a buffer zone between his nation and the might of Babylon. Thus he set forth to aid Assyria in 609 BC in an attempt to retake Haran. However, this was directly opposite to what Josiah and Judah desired. They had suffered so much from Assyria that any resurgence of its power would have been experienced with fear and trembling. The small armies of Judah could in no way have hoped to defeat the armies of Egypt, which were moving up the coastal highway. However, Josiah apparently felt that if he could delay Egypt the Assyrians would in the meanwhile have been totally and thoroughly defeated by Babylon.

Thus Josiah and his pitiful army ambushed the overwhelmingly larger forces of Egypt at the pass of Megiddo. The geographic features there are such that, for a time at least, a small force can hold off a large one. That was precisely what happened. Josiah literally offered himself as a sacrifice for his people, seeking to punish their enemies and ultimately to deliver Judah from Assyrian domination. Josiah was killed in the battle, but the Egyptians had been so delayed that Assyria was defeated by the time Egypt's forces arrived.

Josiah's death was like the life he lived—given for his people. He was remembered by Judah for his great reform of religion. Unfortunately, Judah's last real chance for a national survival was lost because the reform was essentially superficial, making no real change within the hearts of the Hebrew people.

Upon Josiah's death, his son Jehoahaz ascended to the throne of David. There is no way of knowing what kind of king he would have made for he only reigned three months. Neco returned from his abortive attempt to aid Assyria in a very hostile mood. The Pharaoh deposed Jehoahaz and installed his older brother Eliakim upon the throne, changing his name to Jehoiakim (609 to 598 BC). Such a change of name indicated Neco's absolute authority over the Hebrew king and his kingdom. Jehoahaz was carried captive to Egypt, where he was either executed or died. Jehoiakim, as Neco's vassal, established a pro-Egyptian policy in Judah, much to the chagrin of men like Jeremiah.

The new king of Judah made a reversal of the religious policies of his father, Josiah. Much of the paganism of Manasseh was brought back. The ease with which this was done indicates how superficial the earlier religious reform had been. For a few years, affairs in Judah moved along smoothly. However, with the ultimate defeat of Assyria and their Egyptian allies by the armies of Babylon at the battle of Carchemish (605 BC), a major change came to the international scene. It was precisely at that point that Nabolpolassar, the king of Babylon, died. Nebuchadnezzar, the victorious general at Carchemish, hurriedly withdrew his armies, racing for Babylon to consolidate his claim to the throne. This left a power vacuum in western Palestine, of which Jehoiakim sought to take advantage.

The Hebrew king declared his independence of Egypt and refused to submit to the rising Babylonian power. At this time Jeremiah was inspired to record all of his earlier sermons (Jer. 36:1-3, 605 BC). This was apparently done with the hope that seeing all of his words of warning at one time might cause the people and the king to turn back to God. However, his words of stern rebuke were not only ignored by Jehoiakim but also the scroll was burned.

In the winter of 604-603 BC, Nebuchadnezzar, having consolidated his control of Babylon, marched his armies into the Philistine Plain, defeating Askelon. Jehoiakim apparently pledged his subservience to Babylon at that time, remaining loyal to them until 601 BC. However, at that time the Babylonian armies were amazingly defeated by the armies of Egypt at the borders of Egypt. This afforded Jehoiakim with the opportunity of rebelling against his Babylonian masters. Although Nebuchadnezzar had to have time to rebuild his army, he employed bands of mercenaries from Judah's traditional enemies to harass the Hebrew kingdom. After a period of military rebuilding, Nebuchadnezzar at last marched on Judah and Jerusalem. Fortunately for Jehoiakim, he died just before the armies of Babylon arrived at Jerusalem. It is possible that he was assassinated in an attempt to appease the Babylonians. Jehoiakim's death occurred near the end of 597 BC.

The eighteen-year-old son of Jehoiakim ascended the throne under the name of Jehoiachin. He reigned for three months and ten days, surrendering himself and his city to Nebuchadnezzar when the Babylonian armies arrived at Jerusalem. He sacrificed himself in an attempt to save his land from the devastation of war. His magnificent act only postponed Judah's ultimate destruction. Jehoiachin and the leaders of Jerusalem were deported to Babylon as captives (597 BC). This deportation was intended to remove Judah's possibilities of waging war. Unfortunately, it also removed all those experienced in government, ultimately dooming Judah to destruction.

Upon the deportation, Jehoiachin's uncle, Mattaniah, was placed upon the throne and his name was changed to

Zedekiah (597-586 BC). Zedekiah was expected to adopt a pro-Babylonian stance in his government. Sadly, there was still a large pro-Egyptian party in Jerusalem and Zedekiah was too weak to resist it. He, on occasion, sought advice from the prophet Jeremiah but was usually too weak and indecisive to follow it. Jeremiah insisted that Judah's only hope for national survival lay in her submission to Babylon. However, Zedekiah allowed himself to be controlled by his pro-Egyptian advisers, sending to Egypt for help. As a result, he was called to Babylon in 593 BC to give an account of his activities. There he was apparently able to convince Nebuchadnezzar of his loyalty. However, in 588 BC, Zedekiah publicly rebelled against Babylon, the victim of his anti-Babylonian advisers. Nebuchadnezzar's reaction was swift and direct. By January 587 BC, Babylonian armies were surrounding Jerusalem and devastating the surrounding countryside. The Lachish letters clearly reveal the tragic state of affairs in the land at this time.

The people of Jerusalem were enheartened when Babylon lifted the siege momentarily to do battle with an Egyptian army ostensibly coming to Judah's rescue. Egypt was quickly defeated, and the armies of Babylon renewed the attack on Jerusalem with vigor. In July 586 BC, as the food supplies of Jerusalem were giving out, the armies of Babylon broke through the wall and took the city. Zedekiah attempted to escape but was captured and taken to Nebuchadnezzar at Riblah. There the sons of Zedekiah were executed and the king's eyes were put out. He was then carried captive to Babylon, along with a large number of the people of the land and all of the Temple treasures. The city was utterly devastated.

Jeremiah, given a choice of going to Babylon or remaining with his people, chose to stay in Judah. Nebuchadnezzar appointed Gedaliah as governor, bringing the Hebrew kingdom to an end.

Some of the chronology becomes hazy at this point, but shortly thereafter, Gedaliah was assassinated through the intrigue of the Ammonites. Fearing, properly so, the retribution of Nebuchadnezzar, the leaders of Judah who remained fled to Egypt, carrying Jeremiah with them. Thus he died in Egypt, an exile and captive of his own people. During these last chaotic days of Judah, Obadiah apparently carried on his brief ministry.

For all practical purposes, Israel's attempt at kingship had come to an end. Seeking its own way, it had come to its own end. But God had not been defeated. His work continued.

24

Jeremiah

Few men have made the impact upon the world which Jeremiah did. It is impossible to write a history of ancient prophetism or even of ancient Israel without becoming aware of his influence. Almost seven centuries after his ministry, people looked at Jesus of Nazareth and thought of Jeremiah (Matt. 16:14). At the last meal with the disciples, Jesus spoke of His blood as the new covenant, identifying Himself as the fulfillment of Jeremiah's preaching on the new covenant (31:31-34). Living in extremely critical times, Jeremiah heard the voice of God and allowed God to use him as a catalytic agent. Reluctant to the point of seeking to quit, overcome by the awareness of his own limitations and the awesomeness of his task, he was a man who did what God called Him to do. Counting the cost with accuracy, entering his ministry with no illusions of either greatness or success, he announced to a people who rejected him and his message, "Thus said the Lord!"

The Text of Jeremiah

No book in the Old Testament has such massive textual divergences as the Book of Jeremiah. The Hebrew Text (MT) is one-seventh again as long as is the text of the Greek (LXX). Approximately twenty-seven hundred words which occur in the MT have no corollary in the LXX, while only about one hundred words of the LXX show no correspondence with the MT. In general, textual critics normally assume (with demonstrable justification) that a longer text has been enlarged from a shorter one. In the case of Jeremiah, however, the longer Hebrew text gives every evidence of careful transmission. The readings which differ are not contradictory but appear to add more of the same kinds of material. Further, significant differences exist in the arrangement of passages. In the MT, for example, the foreign prophecies are found in chapters 46 to 51. But in the LXX these prophecies are found between 25:13 and 25:15. In addition, those oracles are found there in a different order.

Scholars have long debated which version is the original. The discovery of the Dead Sea Scrolls was greeted with excitement by Jeremiah scholars, for they hoped that at long last the argument would be settled. To the contrary, two different Hebrew versions of Jeremiah were found, one corresponding with the MT and the other with the LXX. Thus the Qumran community had two versions of Jeremiah and were content to leave it at that. Furthermore, among the scrolls at Qumran, three versions of some books were found. This has given rise to a theory that some of the books were collected by the Hebrews in exile in Babylon, others were collected by those who fled as refugees to Egypt, and some were put together by the people of the land who remained behind in Judah. This may offer an explanation for the divergent versions of Jeremiah and the fact that both were accepted as part of God's revelation with no attempt at reconciliation. The English text of Jeremiah that appears in most Bibles is based upon the MT.

The Unity and Authorship of the Book of Jeremiah

In approaching the discussion of the unity of Jeremiah, interpreters have raised one major issue and several minor ones. The major issue is related to the intermixture of prose and poetry within the book. Prophetic oracles are normally assumed to be in poetry, but in Jeremiah the prose and poetry are intermingled in greater proportions than normal. This has caused a number of interpreters to conclude that the prose sections of Jeremiah were added by a later editor or disciple and do not come from the prophet himself. The following table shows the extent of the problem.

Prose and Poetry Verses in Jeremiah

	Prose	Poetry
Introductory phrases	45 vv.	—
Narrative	302.5 vv.	—
Sermons	457 vv.	499 vv.
Prayers, etc.	25.5 vv.	6 vv.

As would be expected, introductions and narratives are all in prose. The sermons and prayers, however, are almost equally divided. Further, the prose and poetry are so interwoven with one another it appears impossible to build a clear case for the poetry having come directly from Jeremiah while the prose came from traditions and reinterpretations through his disciples or a later editor. They may be later insertions, but their content is not sufficiently different from the original poetic material to deny that Jeremiah was the basic human source for both the prose and poetic oracles.

Among the minor issues of unity, the one most often considered is the historical appendix of chapter 52, which is apparently based upon 2 Kings 24:18 to 25:30. Chapter 51 in Jeremiah ends with the words, "Thus far are the words of Jeremiah" (51:64b). It appears that the book originally ended at that point then an editor added the historical appendix to demonstrate just how tragically and literally the prophet's predictions of destruction had been fulfilled.

The origin of some of the foreign prophecies are also questioned. There may be some valid questions here, but our knowledge of the historical events of some of those nations is too limited to allow us to pass judgment with certainty on most of them.

The sermon on sabbath observance (17:19-27) has also been denied to the prophet since the extreme legalism appears to be so out of character with the rest of his preaching. That is quite true. During the time of the reform of Josiah, Jeremiah may have tried to lead his people to a renewed covenant observance through sermons based upon keeping the Ten Commandments. He did proclaim that *mere* legal observance of the law was insufficient. There is value in such an outward testimony of inward faith. But when people fail to develop the inner relation, the outward observance becomes a stumbling block rather than a stepping-stone.

The book itself bears some testimony to its writing. "In the fourth year of Jehoiakim" (36:1; 605 BC, the time of the rebellion after Carchemish), Jeremiah was commanded to record his messages from the preceding two decades. He employed Baruch, a scribe, to do this for him (v.4). A year later, the scroll was read in the presence of the people and finally in the king's court. In cold fury the king cut the scroll to pieces and burned it. Undaunted, Jeremiah did the task all over again, adding a number of things he had omitted at first (vv.28,32). From this time onward, Baruch became the friend and companion of Jeremiah. We can safely assume that he collected, correlated, and edited the material from the rest of Jeremiah's life.

Since there is such divergence between the MT and LXX versions of the Jeremiah book, we may reconstruct the basic history of the book as follows. The original scroll of Baruch appears to have been added to and enlarged over the years and may have come to us as the section found in 1:1 to 25:13a. If this is so, numerous later insertions can be identified, for they refer to events in Jeremiah's ministry after the time of the original writing.

The foreign prophecies obviously had a separate existence, for they are found in two different orders and are placed in two different positions within the versions of the book. This material (46:1 to 51:64) seems to have had an independent, oral existence before it was put into written form.

A third section also appears to have had a separate existence, the so-called book of consolation (30:1 to 33:26). Jeremiah's basic messages of hope are found in this block of material. Almost all of these messages come from the latter years of the prophet's ministry and may have been some of the last oracles collected.

The biographical material in 26:1 to 29:32 was obviously prepared by someone other than Jeremiah. The prophet is always referred to in the third person in this section, something a person seldom does about himself. This was most likely put together by Baruch (or some other disciple) and may have served as an introduction to the book of consolation, the two sections circulating as one unit.

A fifth section of the book, 34:1 to 45:5, is also basically biographical material. This had to have been compiled by someone very familiar with the Jeremiah-Baruch relationship. Several things are recorded here which only the two of them knew. The most likely candidate for this compilation is Baruch himself, although we cannot rule out a close friend of either or both of the two men.

The historical appendix (ch. 52), which we have already considered, was obviously added last. The various collections of Jeremiah material apparently had separate and independent existences. These may have been gathered together and edited by the Hebrews who were carried captive to Babylon, seeking to remember both the warnings and the hope the great prophet of Anathoth had offered them. The other collection was most likely compiled by Baruch or a later disciple after he and Jeremiah had been carried captive to Egypt by the fleeing Hebrew refugees. In summary, the book appears to be a unit, made up of separate collections. The hands of a later editor are obvious but not of great significance.

The Date of the Ministry and Book

At first glance, dating the life and ministry of Jeremiah would appear to be more simple than that of any of the prophets. Numerous very specific dating references are given throughout the book, dating both the beginning of Jeremiah's ministry and specific events within his ministry. The beginning of his ministry is dated as:

> The words of Jeremiah . . . to whom the word of the Lord came in the days of Josiah . . ., in the thirteenth year of his reign. It came also in the days of Jehoiakim . . . and until the end of the eleventh year of Zedekiah . . . until the captivity of Jerusalem in the fifth month (1:1-3).

This would place the call of Jeremiah in 626 BC. He served not just until the fall of Jerusalem but until the assassination of Gedaliah, Nebuchadnezzar's governor. This had to have occurred at least after 586 BC and may have occurred as late as 582 BC. Therefore, Jeremiah's ministry extended forty to forty-four years. By any reckoning, he would have had one of the longest ministries of any Old Testament prophet and would have been quite an old man at the time of his death.

However, the dating of Jeremiah's ministry has been seriously questioned. No single event or sermon in the book is given a specific date until the beginning of the reign of Jehoiakim in 609 BC. Scholars have been surprised that Jeremiah did not make a single specific reference to the great reform of Josiah, the most significant religious event for Judah in the entire century. Finally, since Jeremiah related his call to his conception and birth, some scholars have concluded that he actually began his ministry in 609 BC and that his call was later assumed to go back to his birth, which they place in 626 BC. While the issues are significant, the arguments for this position do not appear to be conclusive. Though the prophet made no mention of Josiah's reform as such, he clearly referred to the proclamation of the covenant upon which the reform was based. Recognizing the futility of mere outward reform, he apparently sought to deal with the deeper issues of personal and national commitment. In this book, I shall stick with the more traditional dates for the prophet's life.

The date of the book is less certain. The Baruch recension is clearly to be placed in 604 BC (36:9-32). The final compilation must have occurred after the restoration of Jehoiachin in the Babylonian captivity (52:31-34; 560 BC) However, the various scrolls from which the final compilation was made appear to have been drawn together shortly after the time of the Exile.

Jeremiah as a Man

We know more of Jeremiah as an individual than any other person in the Old Testament. Not only do we have an extensive book reporting his ministry but in that report the prophet also opened up the innermost recesses of his being, showing us his fears and anxieties, as well as his devotion and commitment to his God.

The basic facts of Jeremiah's home and heritage are given in 1:1. Born in Anathoth, a small town about four miles northeast of Jerusalem, he was of a priestly family. Almost certainly, this means that he was a descendant of Abiathar, a priest who was banished to Anathoth by Solomon (1 Kings 2:26-27). This would explain Jeremiah's intimate knowledge of things related to the priesthood. It would also offer a potential explanation for his hostility toward the Jerusalem priesthood, descendants of the unbanished Zadok. Further, if he were a descendant of Abiathar, Eli and ultimately Aaron were among Jeremiah's ancestors. This would root Jeremiah's heritage firmly in the priestly, legal traditions of his people.

On the other hand, his call placed him squarely in the prophetic traditions (1:1-10). More than any other figure in the Old Testament, Jeremiah had a firm sense of his foreordination to the prophetic ministry (v.5). At the same time, he had serious objections to his call, pleading his immaturity (v.6). This sense of being inadequate for the task haunted Jeremiah for most of his life. On the other hand, God assured the prophet of divine companionship and strength (vv.7-8). Yahweh also empowered the prophet by assuring him of the divine source of his message and of his authority (1:9-10). Much of Jeremiah's ministry was devoted to negative, destructive tasks before he was allowed to build and to plant. Further, he was aware from the earliest days that he had a responsibility for a larger ministry than simply to his own people, bearing responsibility for nations and kingdoms beyond his own.

Jeremiah's objections to his call continued through a major part of his ministry. His "confessions" reveal just how angry he became with God over being thrust into a ministry he did not seek and for which he felt utterly inadequate (cf. 14:17-18; 20:7,9,14-18). His attacks on God verged on blasphemy. At the same time, he showed a relationship with God that was wholly open and honest. Jeremiah never pretended to be anything with God other than what he was.

Insofar as his relationship with other prophets, Jeremiah revealed an intimate knowledge of the text of Hosea. Further, he was familiar with at least the earlier parts of Isaiah. In addition, he was acquainted with Amos and Micah. In regard to his contemporaries, Jeremiah maintained a running battle with false prophets, foolish priests, and wise men. However, he made no direct reference to any of his canonical contemporaries, such as Zephaniah, Habakkuk, Nahum, or Obadiah. He did deal with the same issues with which they dealt.

Essentially, Jeremiah's message was quite simple. For the major part of his life, he called his people to repent and turn to God, for there might still be hope that the nation might survive. He also proclaimed a coming judgment which they could not stop but which they might be able to survive. Related to this, he told his people that if they submitted to God's judgment, they might find hope beyond, but submission was the only path to that hope. Ultimately, when the catastrophe struck, he did offer a hope beyond which was rooted in the new covenant, a new relationship which God would establish with His people.

In regard to his personal life, Jeremiah revealed more of himself than any other prophet. He deeply loved Anathoth and his family. This increased both his shock and his heartbreak when he discovered that his friends and his family were plotting to kill him (11:21; 12:6). Jeremiah showed that he desperately needed human companionship, yet was denied the consolation and companionship of marriage (16:1-2). This not only left him lonely but also left him childless. In his day, childlessness meant that he had no hope for a future existence among his people or with God; for the basic future hope of the Hebrews was rooted and grounded in living on in their children. Like Paul, he was willing to be cast away for his love of his people. Further, Jeremiah was denied the normal social outlets of his day, such as weddings, funerals, and feasts (15:17; 16:5,8). He was called to demonstrate by his life that he really believed what he proclaimed. He did finally find both a friend and companion in Baruch, who served him as a scribe and accompanied him even into exile.

In his self-image, Jeremiah appears to have viewed himself as God's spokesman and as Judah's conscience. He would not be silenced either by imprisonment or the threat of death. However, he clearly did not enjoy imprisonment and certainly had no wish to become a martyr.

The most obvious contributions of Jeremiah's ministry lay in his preaching. In his preaching many great truths shone forth. Two basic issues are almost unique to him. One of his major concerns had to do with the nature of prophetic authority. Jeremiah proclaimed that he had no authority except as his words came from God, becoming the word of the Lord. He was not overly confident of his own message but was utterly sure of God's. His other major contribution is in the nature of his prayers. He was more honest with God than most of us would dare to be. He had discovered early that God knew how he felt, so he laid it all out before Him, even accusing God of spiritual seduction (20:7*a*). These prayers became a part of his total proclamation, but they are generally confined to the first half of the book, being found in chapters 11, 12, 15, 17, 18, and 20. Jeremiah approached God as a person, speaking as one individual to another. Jeremiah also discovered that God was not threatened by his hostility. In his prayers, Jeremiah let people who were hurting know that he hurt too. What he learned from his prayers was that God hurt also. He discovered that God was teaching him lessons of individual responsibility. Through their prayer relationship, God said, in essence, "Why are you so upset? I never said it would be easy."

It never was. But Jeremiah learned to live with the absence of ease by living with God.

Approaches to the Study of the Book of Jeremiah

No book in the Old Testament is as difficult to read with understanding as Jeremiah. Neither a chronological nor a theological order is apparent in the book. Many people who have sought to read the Bible through have survived the genealogies of Genesis, the laws of Leviticus, and the lists of Numbers only to become bogged down in the disorder of Jeremiah. It is easy to understand the absence of order, particularly when you remember that the first draft of the book was done all at one time, following twenty years of ministry. This absence of order, however, makes study quite difficult. At least four basic approaches to the book have been made by those who seek to interpret the book.

A Verse-by-Verse, Chapter-by-Chapter Approach

The most obvious approach is to begin at the first verse and proceed through to the end. This is generally done by attempting to develop a logical outline from the Jeremiah materials. Unfortunately this is quite difficult, for the Jeremiah materials are generally not logical in their movement from one oracle to another. Further, they are clearly not chronological.

A variation on this approach, showing at least an openness to this problem, was done by Fred Wood. He concluded that the book was originally made up of seven Jeremiah scrolls that had an existence independent of each other. When they were finally united into the Jeremiah book, the scrolls were connected to one another by historical anecdotes, marking the beginning and ending of each scroll. Wood suggested this arrangement for the book:

1. Scroll 1 (1:1 to 6:30), earlier prophecies of Jeremiah, dated before 621 BC
2. Temple anecdote (7:1 to 8:3)
3. Scroll 2 (8:4 to 10:25), the nature of true wisdom
4. Covenant anecdote (11:1-8)
5. Scroll 3 (11:9 to 20:18), pessimistic passages
6. Siege anecdote (21:1-14)
7. Scroll 4 (22:1 to 29:32), polemics against kings and prophets

(Note: There is no anecdote here, the very change in mood being sufficient to mark the break.)

8. Scroll 5 (30:1 to 33:26), passages of hope
9. Three anecdotes: convenient religion (34:1-22); un-

wavering conviction (35:1-19); the indestructible word (36:1-32)

10. Scroll 6 (37:1 to 44:30) a historical section, in chronological order
11. Baruch anecdote (45:1-5)
12. Scroll 7 (46:1 to 51:64) foreign prophecies
13. Historical anecdote (52:1-34)

A third variation in this approach is based upon the theory that the major sections of the book were divided from one another by the phrase "the word that came from the Lord," or some similar expression. Each expression used both the terms "the word" and "from the Lord." These occur in 7:1; 11:1; 18:1; 21:1; 25:1; 27:1; 30:1; 32:1; 34:1; 35:1; 36:1; 40:1; 47:1.

Each of these approaches is basically simple and does move through the book, one verse after another. However, in seeking to try to understand Jeremiah's life or the development of his thought, these approaches simply leave us confused.

Development of Jeremiah's Teachings

A second approach to unlocking the ministry and message of Jeremiah has been to deal with the book on the basis of the common themes which run throughout. Perhaps the best example of this approach is that done by John Skinner in *Prophecy and Religion.* This kind of approach avoids the confusion of moving through the book directly. Unfortunately, this approach simply deals with those passages the interpreter deems to be central to Jeremiah. It can become utterly subjective, dealing only with what the interpreter wishes, omitting some things about which Jeremiah spoke.

Consideration of Literary Types

A third approach deals only with a particular literary type. E.W. Nicholson in *Preaching to the Exiles* demonstrated this approach by dealing only with the prose passages in the Book of Jeremiah. Such an approach may have value in doing exactly what it proposes. However, its very limits make it not applicable toward a full understanding of the book as a whole.

The Chronological or Biographical Approach

The fourth manner in which the Jeremiah material is frequently studied is by attempting to arrange all of the Jeremiah material in its chronological order. Many of the oracles and events in Jeremiah's book can be dated quite precisely. The other passages can frequently be related to those events which can be dated. This leaves a few passages which must be assigned on the basis of an educated guess, acknowledging the possibility of error in location. Such an approach gives a better understanding of the developing life and ministry of Jeremiah while assuring that every passage is considered. John Bright's *Jeremiah* and Fred Wood's *Fire in My Bones* both take this approach.

The Content of the Book

In seeking to survey the ministry of Jeremiah, the chronological or biographical approach will be used. Other commentaries or introductions can be used to explore the other approaches. (Note: This chronological outline is based upon one by Fred Wood, with modifications made as a result of my own study.)

I. Introduction and setting (1:1-3)
II. Messages and events from the reign of Josiah (626-609 BC)
    A. From before the reform of 622 BC
        1.   Jeremiah's call and commission (1:4-19)
        2.   A call for national repentance (2:1 to 4:4)
        3.   The foe from the north (4:5 to 6:15,22-30)

Jeremiah's call, like that of the other prophets, cast its shadow throughout his ministry. The six key words in his assigned tasks, "to pluck up and to break down, to destroy and to overthrow, to build and to plant" (1:10), are found in messages throughout his ministry. Further, the word play seen in the reaffirmation of his call also became characteristic of his preaching. Viewing an almond (*shaqedh*) tree, so named because it was the first tree to "wake up" and bloom in the spring, Jeremiah was reminded that God was awake (*shoqedh*) and would accomplish what He had said.

Jeremiah was also a master of sarcastic ridicule. He pointed out that the pagan nations were loyal to their gods who did not even exist, while the Hebrew were faithless to the one God who actually lived.

> For cross to the coasts of Cyprus and see,
>   or send to Kedar and examine with care;
>   see if there has been such a thing.
> Has a nation changed its gods,
>   even though they are no gods?
> But my people have changed their glory
>   for that which does not profit (2:10-11).

Jeremiah was also a master of vivid description. Consider the image of a man turning away from a cool, swift-flowing spring to dig out a cistern in the limestone rock, only to discover that it was cracked and, therefore, utterly worthless (v.13).

Among Jeremiah's many images, one of the more threatening is his "foe from the north." Warned about this foe from the very beginning of his ministry, he directed his people's attention to their ultimate danger (1:13-15; 4:6 to 6:15,22-30). The identity of the foe is unclear from the beginning. It appears in places to be the Scythians, the Assyrians, and finally the Babylonians. Jeremiah may have left it intentionally ambiguous. Each of them may have been used as God's instruments of judgment at one time or another. He was quite sure of the ultimate outcome of God's judgment. Drawing upon the images of the chaos in Genesis 1:2, Jeremiah proclaimed that the end result for Judah would be exactly the same (4:23). Further, the prophet was quite clear that the rebellion, which was calling for such judgment, was the direct result of the failure of Judah's religious leaders.

> An appalling and horrible thing
>   has happened in the land:
> the prophets prophesy falsely,

and the priests rule at their direction;
my people love to have it so,
but what will you do when the end comes? (5:30-31).

B. Following Josiah's reform
1. The preaching of the covenant (11:1-8)
2. A sabbath message (17:19-27)
3. A plot against Jeremiah (11:18 to 12:6)
4. The perils of legalism (8:4-13)

By closing down all the shrines in the land, the reform of
Josiah put priests out of work. Since Jeremiah was preaching the Book of Deuteronomy (11:1-8), he was perceived as
the one responsible; therefore, his neighbors and family
plotted to kill him. Jeremiah was utterly dismayed by such
opposition, at which point God confronted him with the
immensity of his task.

If you have raced with men on foot, and they have
wearied you,
how will you compete with horses?
And if in a safe land you fall down,
how will you do in the jungle of the Jordan? (12:5).

In essence, God said to Jeremiah, "Cheer up, the worst is yet
to come."

III. Messages and events from the reign of Jehoahaz
(609 BC)
A. Grief after Megiddo (8:14 to 9:1)
B. Lament for Jehoahaz (22:10-12)
IV. Messages and events from the reign of Jehoiakim
(609-598 BC)
A. From before the battle of Carchemish (605 BC)
1. A warning to Jehoiakim (22:1-9,13-23)
2. Return to the old ways (6:16-21)
3. The Temple sermon (7:1 to 8:3; 26:1-24)
4. The potter and the clay (18:1-23)
5. The sermon from the broken bottle (19:1 to
20:18)

6. Messages from a linen waistcloth and shattered jars (13:1-17)
7. Attack upon idolatry (10:1-16)
B. From after the battle of Carchemish
1. Ultimate fate of Judah and the nations (25:1-38)
2. Jeremiah, Baruch, and the scroll of sermons (36:1-32; 45:1-5)
3. The lesson from the Rechabites (35:1-19)
4. Drought and pestilence (14:1 to 15:19)
5. Prayer from the persecuted prophet (15:10-21)
6. Jeremiah's personal life and the doom of Judah (16:1 to 17:8)
7. Appeal for personal deliverance (17:9-18)
8. Lament over God's wrath (9:2-26; 10:17-25)
9. Rebellion against the covenant (11:9-17)
10. Devastation by hostile neighbors (12:7-17)

Some of the more dramatic preaching of Jeremiah's life come from this period. Here we see him joining the great line of prophets in his acts of prophetic symbolism. Such acts made his messages all the more memorable and effective. This was a time of intense trial for Jeremiah. He was almost lynched following his great sermon against the false and foolish reliance upon the Temple. During this time he felt most alone, yet came to establish his relationship with Baruch who became his faithful friend.

V. Messages and events from the reign of Jehoiachin (598-597 BC)
A. Sermon against the king (22:24-30)
B. Lament over the approaching doom (13:18-27)
VI. Messages and events from the reign of Zedekiah (597-586 BC)
A. From his accession of the siege of Jerusalem (January, 587 BC)
1. The figs in the Temple (24:1-10)
2. A letter to the exiles (29:1-32)

      3. The necessity of submitting to Babylon (27:1 to 28:17)

      4. Messages against the lying prophets (23:9-40)

      5. A sermon of future hope (23:1-8)

  B. During the siege of Jerusalem (587-586 BC)

      1. Promise of Jerusalem's fall (21:1-14)

      2. A message of King Zedekiah (34:1-7)

      3. A sermon when the siege was temporarily lifted (37:1-10)

      4. Rebuke concerning treatment of Hebrew slaves (34:8-22)

      5. Jeremiah's arrest (37:11-21)

      6. Jeremiah's prison life (38:1-28)

      7. A promise to Ebed-melech (39:15-18)

      8. Sermons of hope, delivered from prison (32:1 to 33:26)

  C. After the fall of Jerusalem

      1. Zedekiah's fate (39:1-10)

      2. Jeremiah's freedom (39:11-14)

VII. Messages and events from the time of Gedaliah and afterwards (587-586 BC—. . .)

  A. The remnant in Judah and the assassination of Gedaliah (40:1 to 41:18)

  B. The future of Israel and the new covenant (30:1 to 31:40)

  C. The flight of the remnant (42:1 to 43:7)

  D. Messages against Egypt (43:8 to 44:30)

VIII. Messages concerning other peoples, generally undated

  A. Egypt (46:1-28)

  B. The Philistines (47:1-7)

  C. Moab (48:1-47)

  D. Ammon (49:1-6)

  E. Edom (49:7-22)

  F. Damascus (49:23-27)

  G. Kedar and Hazor (49:28-33)

  H. Elam (49:34-39)

  I. Babylon (50:1 to 51:64)

IX. Historical appendix (52:1-34)

In the latter days of Judah's history and beyond, Jeremiah had the opportunity to do what he had wanted to do all along—preach a message of hope. However, just as he had not been believed during Judah's good times when he proclaimed judgment, so he was not believed during its bad times as he proclaimed hope. He had the sad but bitter lot of being rejected from beginning to end. Further, just as he had been called upon dramatically to act out the truth of his messages of judgment by denying himself a wife and family, so he also had to demonstrate his faith in his messages of hope by investing in what appeared to be worthless land (32:1-44).

At the end of his ministry, Jeremiah was offered an opportunity by Nebuchadnezzar to go to Babylon and live out his last days in relative ease. Nebuchadnezzar had wrongly assumed that the prophet's proclamation of the necessity for Judah to submit to Babylon meant that Jeremiah supported the Babylonians. Jeremiah chose to remain behind in Judah, suffering the privations and hardships of the people he loved. Tragically, after the assassination of Gedaliah, the prophet was carried away from his beloved land by some of his own people, apparently dying in exile, a captive of those he had given his life to save.

25

Zephaniah

Like the pent-up force of a sweeping hurricane or the more sudden but equally destructive force of a tornado, the message of Zephaniah swept down upon the heads of the people of Judah and Jerusalem. His fury was unleashed upon the idolatrous practices of his people but primarily was addressed to the leaders of the people. Although expressing some concern with the injustices which abounded, he struck primarily at the infidelity which was at the root of immoral living.

Authorship, Date, and Unity

Insofar as the actual authorship of the book is concerned, once again we have no statement at all within the book itself. While there is no reason to believe Zephaniah could write, neither is there any reason to doubt it. If his genealogy is correct in 1:1, he was most likely of royal descent and, therefore, quite likely to have had more education than most people of his day.

The question of unity is quite difficult. Every verse in the last two chapters and many of the verses of the first has been denied to Zephaniah by one commentator or another. In fact, if every verse which has been denied to him were to be taken away, we would not have enough of his message left to consider at all. While there is no question but that the book as we now have it is what God intended us to have, it also appears that there is really not sufficient evidence to deny the basic content of the book to Zephaniah himself. Even if there are a few later editorial additions, the basic theme and the essential content must be assumed as coming from the tongue, if not the pen, of Zephaniah.

The title verse of the book assigns the ministry of Zephaniah to the reign of Josiah (1:1). This would place it in the period from circa 640 BC to 609 BC. His attack upon open idolatry and its related practices make it likely that he preached prior to the major Josianic reform, which is dated in 622 BC. Further, some sort of major crisis was apparently confronting the land. The only such crisis, which fits into the period from the beginning of Josiah's reign (640 BC) to the reform (622 BC), would be the Scythian invasion. (See Chapter 23, the historical background of the seventh-century prophets.) If this is the proper time, Zephaniah's ministry must have begun about 626 BC, the same time as Jeremiah's. There is no way of knowing who began first, but they could not have been far apart in initiating their preaching. Zephaniah could have broken the long silence of a prophetic word which had endured from the death of Isaiah.

Some interpreters have suggested that Zephaniah's ministry extended to the end of Josiah's reign. However, it appears more likely that his ministry was brief and was concluded by the time of Josiah's reform, if not before.

Zephaniah the Prophet

Of all the information about the prophets in the Old Testament, only Zephaniah has a full genealogy given, going back four generations: "The word of the Lord which came to Zephaniah the son of Cushi, son of Gedaliah, son of Amariah, son of Hezekiah" (1:1). Three things stand out in this geneology. First, Hezekiah was not a very common name in this period of Judah's history, so there would have been little reason for establishing Zephaniah's ancestry so far back if this were not the Hezekiah who was king in the days of Isaiah, in the latter part of the eighth century BC. That would make Zephaniah the great-great-grandson of King Hezekiah and a part of the royal family. It would explain his love for Jerusalem and his familiarity with the royal affairs.

Zephaniah's heritage might have enabled him to have had a better education than his contemporaries.

The second noticeable feature of the genealogy is that three of Zephaniah's ancestors and Zephaniah himself had names compounded with Yahweh. This would indicate the family loyalty to God, even (and especially) during the time of Manasseh's wicked reign. At a time when apostasy was the rule of the day, Zephaniah's family had maintained their faithful commitment.

The third feature of significance is the name of Zephaniah's father, Cushi. This is the normal word in the Old Testament for an Ethiopian. If it has that meaning here, though most scholars deny it, Zephaniah's father may have been a convert to Judaism who had married into this branch of the royal family. The fact that he was a convert is implied by the name given to Zephaniah, still a compound of Yahweh. It is also possible that Zephaniah's father was a Hebrew who had received his name from having served as an ambassador to Ethiopia, but this appears far less likely.

Zephaniah's name means "Yahweh hides" or "Hidden of Yahweh." Such a name was bestowed upon him during the evil reign of Manasseh, probably indicating the faith of his parents that he was to be hidden by God and brought forth to his people at a later time. Other than his name and genealogy, we know little else except what we can infer from his preaching. Some have suggested that he is to be identified with Zephaniah the priest in the time of Jeremiah (Jer. 52:24; 2 Kings 25:18). However, this is unlikely, as we have no other indication of such an identification.

Since King Josiah, a great-grandson of Hezekiah, was only eight years old when he began to reign about 640 BC, Zephaniah, the great-great-grandson of Hezekiah, must have been quite young when his ministry began. This may be confirmed by the fierceness of his prophecies, frequently a characteristic of youth. Because his messages were so fierce, he also likely died young!

When he began to preach, he poured forth the fury of such loyalty, when contrasted with the parallel development of apostasy, his messages may have been a major force behind the reform of Josiah.

The Content of the Book

I. Title verse (1:1)
II. The terrible punishment of God's people (1:2 to 2:3)
   A. Portrayal of utter destruction (1:2-6)
   B. Portrayal of sins and sinners (1:7-13)
   C. The nearness of the Day of Yahweh (1:14-18)
   D. An urgent invitation to escape (2:1-3)
III. Punishment upon foreign nations (2:4-15)
   A. Philistines (2:4-7)
   B. Moab and Ammon (2:8-11)
   C. Ethiopia (2:12)
   D. Assyria (2:13-15)
IV. God's ultimate salvation (3:1-20)
   A. A final woe upon Jerusalem (3:1-7)
   B. The conversion of the heathen (3:8-10)
   C. The sifting of judgment among God's people (3:11-13)
   D. God's final deliverance (3:14-20)

There is probably no more vivid view of the terrible searching judgment of God than that which is found in this book. Zephaniah's intimate familiarity with the precincts of Jerusalem and with the behavior of its inhabitants are set forth in detail. Further, he, as with most Old Testament prophets and most New Testament preachers, saw the Day of Yahweh as quite imminent; it was on the very threshold.

Even with such a scathing attack, the prophet also saw that judgment had a redemptive purpose, proclaiming:

> Seek the Lord, all you humble of the land,
>   who do his commands;
> seek righteousness, seek humility;
>   perhaps you may be hidden
>   on the day of the wrath of the Lord (2:3).

In the Temple worship of that day, anyone with a physical

deformity was not allowed to enter the precincts. They were outcasts. However, Zephaniah viewed the ultimate grace of God as including all outcasts.

> And I will save the lame
>   and gather the outcast,
> and I will change their shame into praise (3:19).

Thus, the mercy of God will ultimately triumph over the sinful rebellion of His people.

26
Nahum

A knowledge of the world of the ancient Near East, as well as the history of Judah, is necessary to understand the book and preaching of Nahum. Although that is true of many of the prophets, it is more important with Nahum than most of them.

Authorship, Unity, and Date

The date of the ministry of Nahum can be set within precise limits. He preached after the destruction of Thebes (the capital of Egypt) by the Assyrians in 663 BC (3:8) and before the fall of Nineveh in 612 BC, for the basic purpose of his message was to predict the fall of Assyria and its capital. However, placing his ministry within those bounds becomes a bit more difficult. Some have suggested Nahum's ministry be placed closer to the earlier date; others, closer to the latter. The reform of Josiah may have set the stage for the hope of deliverance for Judah from the Assyrian overlords. If that were not the time, the date is probably between that time and the fall of Assyria. The note of gloating over Assyria's downfall appears to be more than a prediction; it appears to be the declaration of a fact that should also have been visible to the people of Judah.

A number of scholars have denied the first chapter to Nahum, saying that it is an acrostic (alphabetic) psalm of late origin. However, they then go on to point out that only part of the alphabet is represented. Many interpreters have attempted to reconstruct the entire psalm as an acrostic, but interpreters do not agree on how it should be (or even if it can be) done. The poetry of 1:2 to 2:2 does not appear to be of the same exalted quality as the rest of the book. However, that in itself is not a sufficient reason for denying this part of the book to Nahum.

The book itself gives no indication of who wrote it. However, the book most likely was written and circulated shortly after it was composed by the prophet, for there would have been little meaning to his audience long after the fall of Assyria.

The book appears to have two title verses. The first is: "An oracle concerning Nineveh." The second is: "The book of the vision of Nahum of Elkosh" (1:1). This kind of introduction is not usual in the prophetic books, but there is no reason to doubt either. It may have been, if Nahum himself were the author, that the first title was his own, while the latter one was added by a later editor to identify the author.

Nahum the Man

As is true with several of the Minor Prophets, we know nothing about the prophet outside of the title and what little may be deduced from the book. We know nothing of Nahum's heritage, not even the location of Elkosh. Four locations have been suggested. It has been identified with a site in Galilee known as El Kouze. This identification was apparently first made by Jerome. It assumes that Nahum was probably an Israelite whose family had remained in the region following the destruction of that nation by Assyria in 722 BC. The second location suggested is Capernaum. This assumes that the actual name of that town was Kepher Nahum, "the village of Nahum." According to the supporters of this view, the name of Elkosh was changed in honor of Nahum after his ministry. This location would also presume that Nahum was an Israelite. The third suggestion has been that the village is to be identified with a modern village some twenty-four miles north of Nineveh. The modern village is known as Elkush or Alkosh. If this is correct, Nahum's family probably would have been among the Israelite captives carried off by the Assyrians.

Any of these three suggestions would give a clear basis for the deep hatred which the prophet showed toward Assyria, but the third one would do so overwhelmingly. The fourth suggestion would locate Elkosh in southern Judah, probably about twenty-five miles southwest of Jerusalem. This location would explain Nahum's concern for Judah and Jerusalem. Although no location is certain, it appears that one of the first three might be more likely, perhaps either Capernaum or near Nineveh itself.

Nahum was one of the greatest poets in the Old Testament. Even in English translation, the vividness of his description of chariots and horses, as well as of the tumult of battle, make readers see what he saw and feel what he felt.

Some interpreters are extremely critical of Nahum because of his harshness toward his enemies. The spirit of vindictiveness is utterly foreign to the God of love, yet it is a human attitude. That Nahum never directed his attack to the sin of his own people offered as reason for rejecting this book as a part of the Bible. However, such reasoning misses the entire point of the book. Nahum recognized that any kingdom, his own or another, which was built upon the principles characterized by the Assyrian Empire must ultimately collapse in a world ruled by a just and holy God. In the final overthrow of Nineveh, God's righteousness was given a demonstrable vindication.

The Content of the Book

I. The title of the book (1:1)
II. God's nature revealed (1:2-15)
    A. His attitude toward people (1:2-3a)
    B. His power in nature (1:3b-6)
    C. His justice and judgment (1:7-8)
    D. Wrath on Assyria and deliverance for Judah (1:9-15)
III. The destruction of Nineveh (2:1-13)
    A. The plunderer's arrival in Nineveh (2:1)
    B. The restoration of Judah (2:2)
    C. Description of the battle (2:3-9)
    D. The silent desolation (2:10-12)
    E. God's final word to Nineveh (2:13)

IV. Reasons for Assyria's fall (3:1-19)
   A. Nineveh, the bloody city (3:1-7)
   B. The fall of Thebes (3:8-10)
   C. The just fate of Assyria (3:11-19)

Nowhere in the world's literary masterpieces is there found as vivid and moving description of war as is found in the oracles of Nahum. The emotional appeal is strengthened when the vivid battle scene is contrasted with the silence after the battle.

> Desolate! Desolation and ruin!
>   Hearts faint and knees tremble,
> anguish is on all loins,
>   all faces grow pale! (2:10).

The end of a kingdom built on violence is sure and certain violence. Those who lift up the spear shall die by the spear. That is the justice of God. The Lord still reigns.

27

Habakkuk

The book of the prophet Habakkuk, although not of major significance from the standpoint of either length or great theological insights, is quite significant for any thorough student of the Old Testament. It should put to rest the old idea that the Hebrews were never given to philosophical inquiry. The first two chapters of Habakkuk are deeply involved with the philosophical issue of theodicy. The prophet was greatly concerned with how a just God can allow evil to exist in the world. The book is filled with wisdom materials, which may raise the issue of whether the Hebrew wisdom movement was the basis of this development of Hebrew philosophy. Though that question is outside the bounds of this discussion, we shall return to it in the introduction to Old Testament wisdom.

Habakkuk the Man

The name *Habakkuk* literally means "Embrace." Possibly loving parents gave it as an expression of their joy at enfolding the young child in their arms and hearts. It also clearly describes the prophet's relationship to his people, for he truly enfolded his nation into his heart. Nothing is told us concerning his home, his family, or his vocation.

Habakkuk's ministry was apparently quite different from that of other prophets. His message seems to have been less of an assault upon his people for their sins than a questioning of God because of the suffering of the righteous among his people. A number of wisdom forms are found in the book. In fact, the entire book may be said to be in the form of wisdom materials. If this is true, Habakkuk was probably trained as a "wise man" of Israel. He may have been a scribe by vocation, although that is not at all certain. In the sense of being a prophet, he falls into the category of a "seer" or a visionary. In both chapters 2 and 3 he records divine visions, things he was inspired to see and to understand.

The date of the ministry of Habakkuk has been assigned to periods as far apart as the 700s and the 300s BC. However, in general, most interpreters assign his ministry to the time of Jeremiah, near the end of the seventh century BC. Habakkuk referred to the imminent Babylonian (Chaldean) invasion of Judah (1:6), so he probably was ministering just prior to Nebuchadnezzar's first invasion circa 597 BC. The extremely vivid descriptions of Babylonian warfare make it likely that they had already performed such feats of arms that the people of Judah would have heard about them. This would have been after the great victory over Assyria at Haran in 612 BC and possibly even after their final crushing at Carchemish in 605 BC.

Habakkuk was a man of sensitive feelings and deep thought. The facts of life did not agree with the popular theology about God, so he sought an understanding of God that was also in line with his personal experience. He was a man of deep faith, for he took his doubts and questions to the only One who could help him—God Himself. Through his pilgrimage of doubt and faith, Habbakuk was given a new insight into the nature of God, of faith, and of the way of life for a person devoted to the service of God.

Authorship, Unity, and Date of the Book

The book strangely appears to have two title verses: "The oracle of God which Habakkuk the prophet saw" (1:1), and "A prayer of Habakkuk the prophet, according to Shigionoth" (3:1). Further, the fact that chapter 3 appears to be quite similar to the forms of many of the psalms, while being wholly unlike the earlier material of the book, has caused many interpreters to deny this final chapter to Habakkuk. While it is obvious that the final chapter has been correctly called a psalm, it is also clear that this very difference in form and intent would call for a difference in structure and style. It does appear to be the precise kind of song for which the solution to the problems of the first chapters would call.

It is significant that the Dead Sea Scroll commentary on Habakkuk deals only with chapters 1 and 2. There is no question but that the canon of the prophets was closed by this time, so we must at least raise the question as to why those commentators left out the final chapter. This may reflect a belief that it was by someone other than Habakkuk. However, the psalm does bring the book to a natural close. Though this final chapter may have been added later, there is insufficient evidence for drawing this conclusion with certainty.

The date of the writing of the book probably followed closely upon the ministry of Habakkuk. If he were a "wise man" of Judah, he certainly would have known how to write and could have easily produced the book himself. The first two chapters appear to have been an oral report of his personal encounters with God, and the final chapter appears to have been a literary production from the beginning.

The Content of the Book

I. The problem of the prophet (1:1 to 2:20)
  A. Title to the section (1:1)
  B. The first question: Why did God not respond to the injustices which the prophet saw among his people? (1:2-4)
  C. God's first answer: The wicked in Judah were about to be punished by the rising power of Babylon (1:5-11)
  D. The second question: Why was God using evil people as His instruments of justice? (1:12-17)
  E. The prophet's fearful waiting for God's answer (2:1)
  F. God's second answer: The righteous shall live in faithfulness (2:2-5)
  G. A series of woes against evil practices (2:6-19)

> H. A final call to silence before the judgment of
>   God (2:20)

The prophet had serious doubts about God's nature. The wicked were prospering, and God was apparently doing nothing about it. In response to Habakkuk's query, God responded that His patience did not mean that He did not care. Judgment was coming. Yet when the prophet realized that the evil Babylonians were the instrument of God's judgment, he was even more bothered. Continuing to question God, he became a bit fearful over his audacity. But God did not appear to be threatened by Habakkuk's doubts or questions.

At this point, God responded to Habakkuk with an important message and a command to record it so boldly that even those hurrying by could read it. The ultimate solution was simply this: "The righteous shall live by his faithfulness" (2:5, author's translation). The Hebrew has no word for *faith* in the New Testament sense of that word as trust or commitment. Rather Habakkuk was commanded to keep on being faithful to God even when he had doubts and unanswered questions. God was still sovereign and would eventually take care of things. Just how important this concept is can be seen in that it was quoted three times in the New Testament, each time with an enlarged meaning (Rom. 1:17; Gal. 3:11; Heb. 10:38).

Without all of his questions being solved, but with his ultimate direction assured, the prophet turned back to his mission. He pronounced a series of woes upon the evils he saw among those around him.

> II. The psalm of Habakkuk (3:1-19)
>   A. Title (3:1)
>   B. The prophet's awareness of God from others
>   (3:2-3)
>   C. Consideration of His mighty acts (3:5-15)
>   D. Fear at the coming judgment (3:16)
>   E. The quiet hope of faithfulness (3:17-19*a*)
>   F. Final musical notation (3:19*b*)

Having groped through the dark night of his own soul, the prophet had something to sing about:

> Though the fig tree do not blossom,
>> nor fruit be on the vines,
> the produce of the olive fail
>> and the fields yield no food,
> the flock be cut off from the fold
>> and there be no herd in the stalls,
> yet I will rejoice in the Lord,
>> I will joy in the God of my salvation (3:17-18).

Such was the end of the prophet's quest for certainty in an uncertain world. Even when he did not know all the reasons for what happened, he could still trust God. So can we.

28

Obadiah

Obadiah is the shortest book of the Old Testament, containing only twenty-one verses. As far as can be determined, there is no reference to the book or the prophet in the New Testament. The book has been described as "Obadiah's Indignant Oration" and a "Hymn of Hate." Both titles are somewhat unfair to this prophet of Judah and to his message of justice. However, little, if anything, concerning the love of God can be seen in this book.

Historical Background

In trying to determine a date for the book, we must begin by seeking the situation which called it forth. The title verse gives no information, for it simply states, "The vision of Obadiah." A major calamity had befallen Judah and Jerusalem; the Edomites, instead of coming to the aid of their brothers, or at least staying aloof from their tragedy, had joined in with gloating and finally looting and capturing fugitives and turning them over to the enemy (cf. vv. 10-14).

Four occasions might be considered as possibilities. The first was the invasion of Shisak of Egypt, shortly after the division of the kingdom. This is not likely, for the kinds of plunder described in Obadiah did not occur then. Further, the Edomites apparently remained subject to the Hebrew kingdom of Judah at this time. The second possible occasion might have been the invasion of Judah by Joash of Israel (2 Kings 14:8-16). That, however, is unlikely, for the enemy in Obadiah is described as "strangers," a term which would hardly be applied to the people of Israel.

The third suggestion focuses upon the attack of the Philistines and Arabians in the reign of Jehoram (2 Chron. 21:16-17). This is to be dated circa 845 BC. Some prefer this date, as it might allow for the identification of Obadiah the prophet with Obadiah the servant of King Ahab of Israel (cf. 1 Kings 18:3-4). However, the fact that this invasion is not mentioned in Kings makes it unlikely to be the serious crisis to which the Book of Obadiah refers. Further, since the name *Obadiah* means "Servant of Yahweh," a name frequently found in the Old Testament, there is no necessity for trying to identify Ahab's servant with the prophet. The expression "servant of Yahweh" is usually translated, but may be a name in some of the places where it appears. Further, it may not be a name here but only a description of an otherwise unnamed prophet.

The fourth suggestion is that the time described by Obadiah immediately followed the destruction of Jerusalem by Nebuchadnezzar in 586 BC. The bitter hostility the Hebrews felt toward the Edomites seems primarily to date from this time (cf. Lam. 4:21; Ezek. 25:12-14; 35:1-5). Although the third suggestion may be correct, the fourth one appears to be the more likely time for the setting of the message of Obadiah.

Authorship, Date, and Unity

As noted, we cannot actually be sure that Obadiah is a name. It has been suggested that the book was simply an anonymous prophecy to which the title, "The vision of the servant of Yahweh" was added. Though this is quite plausible, since most of the prophets are named; it is more likely that Obadiah was the name of the prophet behind the book. There is no indication as to who wrote the book, the prophet or a disciple.

The Book of Obadiah, only twenty-one verses long, has been subjected to such scrutiny that some scholars have identified a Proto- and a Deutero-Obadiah. Further, some scholars have identified three or four sources behind it. With such a short book and such limited evidence, any such analysis is extremely problematical, carrying such studies to the point of ultimate futility.

Striking parallels have been demonstrated between Jeremiah 49:7-22 and Obadiah, as well as between Obadiah and Joel. Commentators generally concede that Jeremiah took Obadiah and modified it to suit his purposes. The date of Joel is quite uncertain, but it is almost as probable that Joel also borrowed some of his material from Obadiah. If these two thoughts are correct, the Book of Obadiah was held in high esteem by his people and the prophets.

Since Jeremiah was quite an old man at the time of the destruction of Jerusalem and could not have lived too long thereafter, the date of the Book of Obadiah might be placed immediately after the fall of Jerusalem, if we accept the fourth date suggested. The freshness with which the destruction is viewed further enforces this conclusion. It should be noted that some interpreters do not date the writing of Obadiah until about the fourth century BC, but this seems to be quite unlikely.

The Content of the Book

I. Title verse (1)
II. Message to Edom (2-14)
   A. Punishment upon national pride (2-4)
   B. The nature of the coming judgment (5-10)
   C. The acts which made judgment necessary (11-14)
III. The coming Day of Yahweh (15-21)
   A. Judgment on the nations (15-16)
   B. The exaltation of God's people (17-20)
   C. Yahweh's supreme rule (21)

While the brevity of the book and its subject limits its application, several memorable teachings are in the book. The graphic assertion that self-exaltation can accomplish nothing before the power of God is set forth:

> Though you soar aloft like the eagle,
>   though your nest is set among the stars,
>   thence I will bring you down, says the Lord (v.4).

Further, Obadiah was quite sure of the absolute nature of divine justice, proclaiming:

> For the Day of the Lord is near upon all the nations.
> As you have done, it shall be done to you,
>   your deeds shall return on your own head (v.15).

But the prophet's ultimate hope did not rest in vengeance upon his people's enemies. To the contrary, his ultimate hope rested in the sovereignty of the living God.

> Saviors shall go up to Mount Zion
>   to rule Mount Esau;
>   *and the kingdom shall be the Lord's* (v.21, author's italics)

On that note his brief message came to an end. It was enough.

29

The Sixth-Century Prophets

History, unlike books, seldom is arranged in neat little pigeonholes or categories. For convenience's sake, interpreters divide one group of Hebrew prophets from another by calling them seventh- or sixth-century prophets. This is based on the nature of their ministries as much as on the actual dates of their lives. Jeremiah and probably Obadiah performed a part of their ministries in the sixth century, and Ezekiel's ministry clearly overlaps with these two men. Therefore, in setting the stage for the sixth-century prophets, some of the information will overlap with the background of those already identified as seventh-century prophets.

The Prophets of the Sixth Century

Four Hebrew prophets ministered during the sixth century. Ezekiel began his ministry in "the fifth year of the exile of King Jehoiachin," 593 BC (Ezek. 1:2). Haggai and Zechariah both began their services in "the second year of Darius," king of Persia, in 520 BC (Hag. 1:1; Zech. 1:1). The ministry of Daniel began in "the third year of Jehoiakim king of Judah," which was 606 BC (Dan. 1:1). His ministry continued at least until the reign of Darius, 521 BC (Dan. 5:31; 6:1-2). However, since the Book of Daniel is not among the canon of the Prophets but among the Writings in the MT, we shall not deal with that book until we get to that section of the canon in our studies.

The Historical Background

To fully understand the plight of the Hebrew people during the sixth century BC, we need to remind ourselves of the rebellion of King Jehoiakim against Nebuchadnezzar of Babylon in 601 BC, following the Babylonian defeat by Egypt. Judah enjoyed a few years of relative independence while Nebuchadnezzar rebuilt his army. In 598 BC, however, the armies of Babylon marched. Jehoiakim died, possibly by assassination, on December 7, 598 BC, and Jehoiachin became king.

In an attempt to spare his city and his people the devastation of war, the eighteen-year-old Jehoiachin surrendered to Nebuchadnezzar on March 16, 597 BC. At that time, he and his court, along with some of the leaders of Jerusalem, were carried as captives to Babylon; Zedekiah was placed on David's throne as Babylon's puppet. This was the first deportation. Ezekiel and Haggai may have been among that group of captives.

Zedekiah was a weak king, wanting to do what was best for his people, but too easily swayed by advisers of whom he was afraid. He, therefore, adopted a pro-Egyptian policy that eventually led him to rebel against Babylon in 588 BC. By January of 587 BC, Nebuchadnezzar's armies were in the land, devastating the countryside and besieging Jerusalem. Although defeat was briefly held off by the approach of relief from Egypt, the city finally fell to the Babylonians in 586 BC. A horrible destruction was wreaked upon the city. Zedekiah was forced to watch his sons executed, then was himself blinded and carried captive to Babylon, along with a significant number of others. This was the second deportation.

Gedaliah was appointed governor over Judah but was shortly thereafter assassinated. Fearing reprisals from Nebuchadnezzar over the murder of his governor, a large number of Hebrews fled to Egypt. The armies of Babylon were soon back in the land of Judah, carrying out additional punishments against the recalcitrant Hebrews and deporting another group of captives—the third deportation.

At this point, conditions stabilized for the Hebrews; actually, four separate groups of Hebrews can be identified during this period. First, the captives in Babylon were probably better off than any others. They were essentially allowed to do live as they pleased. They went about their own affairs, worshiped as they chose, and existed in separate settlements. Their lives were generally prosperous with very little interference. The only major restriction was that they were not allowed to return to Judah. Communication was fairly easy between them and their homeland.

In stark contrast to the Babylonian captives' situation was that of the people who had survived the wars and continued to live in Palestine. For them, civilization had almost ceased. The devastation of war had left their cities and villages in ruins, and their vineyards and olive orchards had been utterly destroyed. All of their energy and attention was spent on survival. Life was hard, hope was gone, and the rewards of their labors were meager. Further, because of their political and military weakness, they were the victims of countless assaults by raiders and plunderers from among their enemies.

The third identifiable group of Hebrews were those who had fled to Egypt. Jews had settled at Elephantine in upper Egypt, on an island in the Nile. This settlement may predate these refugees, or it may have been established by them. They erected a temple to Yahweh; but the old Canaanite influence was still among them, for they also worshiped a female consort to their God. Life was neither particularly hard nor extremely easy. They who had been delivered from Egypt as slaves had gone back as refugees. Over the years, some of the refugees apparently drifted back to Palestine, but the majority remained in the land of Egypt.

The fourth and final group of Hebrews is not actually an identifiable "group." During the years of war, numbers of Hebrews had fled their land, scattering throughout the ancient Near East. These Jews established settlements in cities throughout the Mediterranean world. Their settlements clearly endured, being strengthened by additions from time to time until they were a significant factor in the Roman Empire.

From the early days of the century until 539 BC, each of these various groups of Hebrews maintained its own independent existence. Those in Babylon actually prospered more than any of the others. Further, because many of the leaders were there, the Babylonian Jews had a more creative existence. The synagogue was founded in captivity in order to help maintain worship and identity. Much of the Hebrew literature appears to date from this period. In addition, the Jews made a real place for themselves in Babylon in both business and government.

The armies of Cyrus moved into Babylon in 539 BC, defeating the city and taking over its empire. As a part of his policies, Cyrus instituted a plan that allowed Babylon's former captives to return to their homelands and rebuild their sanctuaries and cities. The edict allowing the Jews to return was a part of this policy (2 Chron. 36:23; Ezra 1:2-4; 6:2-5). Part of the edict decreed that those who chose not to return were to aid the task of the returnees by sending offerings. This suggests that the Jews had been successful enough to want to remain and to be able to send offerings. Most of the Hebrews living in Babylon at that time had been born there. The dream of the return had been real, but when the actual opportunity came, a large number chose to remain behind.

Those who did return with exuberance faced extreme difficulties upon their arrival. The task of rebuilding was greater than they had imagined. Further, the people they found in Palestine were dispirited and resented those who returned. People in the neighboring areas, particularly in Samaria to the north, feared the zeal of the resurgent Jews and did everything possible to prevent their rebuilding. Finally, shortly after their return, the land was hit by several years of drought and poor harvests. Thus the immediate enthusiasm disappeared, and the task of rebuilding the Temple remained undone. This situation continued until 520 BC.

At that time Haggai and Zechariah came forth, calling for a renewed dedication to accomplishing the task for which the Hebrews had returned in the first place. The urging of the two prophets drew the people back to their task. The work of rebuilding was begun again, and the new Temple was finished in 516 BC (Ezra 6:15). This, coupled with the fact that Judah was no longer a kingdom but a province of the Persian Empire, directed the Hebrew's attention more toward religion than toward government. From that time, faith more than national allegiance held the Jews together. The Jewish civil authorities were subservient to the religious authorities. Although faith had been a vital part of their existence before, from this time on it was the central part. This is the background for understanding the ministries of Ezekiel, Haggai, and Zechariah.

30

Ezekiel

Of all of the books of the prophets, none appears quite as foreign to the contemporary audience as Ezekiel. The unusual visions, the strange behavior of the prophet, and the shifts between prophetic oracles and extremely legalistic cultic detail strike a modern reader as being almost beyond comprehension. For these reasons the book is frequently neglected or ignored by Old Testament students. Yet its impact upon the developing theology of the Old Testament, as well as its use in the New Testament, make its study not only important but vital.

Major Issues

Several major critical issues have been raised by scholars in this century in regard to the study of Ezekiel. Among these perhaps the first in importance is the date of the ministry of the prophet. Related to this is the nature of the prophet himself. Wide disagreement exists as to what kind of a person this prophet actually was. Also of significance is the question of where Ezekiel carried on his ministry. Finally, the question of the authorship and unity of the book has also created an important area of study. Only after we have considered these basic issues will we be in a position to consider the content of the book and the message of the prophet. However, before we can deal with these considerations, we need to face the historical question of the actual canonization of the book.

The Canonization of the Book of Ezekiel

The rabbis had a long debate over whether Ezekiel belonged in the Old Testament at all. The debate hinged upon three basic considerations. First, they had a problem with the fact that God had appeared to Ezekiel outside the land of Palestine. However, as more and more Jews were scattered around the Mediterranean world, this became a nonissue since such a position would have alienated or excommunicated a large body of loyal Hebrews. The second problem had to do with the extremely vivid visions of Ezekiel. This was basically foreign to the Jewish people. However, toward and into the New Testament era and the rise of apocalyptic literature in Zechariah, Daniel, and the numerous interbiblical apocalyptic works, this, too, became a nonissue. Such visions became an accepted part of Jewish Scriptures. The third issue focused upon the apparent disagreements between the cultic regulations found in Ezekiel and those found in the Levitical laws. However, according to the Talmud, after having burned three hundred jars of oil to light his lamp, Hananiah ben Hezekiah was able to reconcile most of the differences. Thus the rabbis concluded that the book should be a part of the Latter Prophets, although it was never to be read in synagogue services and no one was allowed to read it who was under thirty years of age, being too immature to face its message.

Such reservations regarding Ezekiel have not been expressed by the Christian community. The book is quoted more than sixty times in the New Testament, of which almost fifty occur in the Book of the Revelation. It has been regularly used in the churches, although not nearly as much as Isaiah and Jeremiah.

The Date of Ezekiel's Ministry

The date of Ezekiel's ministry has also become the source of a great deal of disagreement. He has been identified as being a preexilic prophet of Israel whose message was later edited and redated to the exilic period. Others have suggested that most of the Ezekiel material is quite late in the postexilic period and that redactors placed the oracles back into the exilic period in order to give them authenticity. However, the dating of Ezekiel's oracles is quite precise, giving the impression that the prophet may even have kept some form of journal from which this material was drawn. With three exceptions, the dated oracles move in chronological sequence through the book. The following table will help.

Dated Oracles in Ezekiel

Reference	Subject	Date
1:2	Inaugural vision	July, 593 BC
8:1	Temple vision	Sept. 592 BC
20:1	Confrontation of the elders	Aug. 591 BC
24:1	Announcement of Jerusalem's plight	Jan. 588 BC
26:1	Oracle against Tyre	?, 587 BC
29:1	Oracle against Egypt	Jan. 587 BC
29:17	Oracle about Egypt to Nebuchadnezzar	Apr. 571 BC
30:20	Oracle against Pharaoh	Apr. 587 BC
31:1	Oracle against Pharaoh	June 587 BC
32:1	Lamentation over Pharaoh	Mar. 585 BC
32:17	Lament over Egypt	Apr. 586 BC
33:21	Announcement of Jerusalem's fall	Jan. 585 BC
40:1	The vision of the restored Temple	Apr. 573 BC

The call of Ezekiel is dated quite precisely to July 593 BC, and his last recorded oracle is placed in April 571 BC. His ministry may have continued beyond that date, but we have no way of knowing. No valid reason has been offered to force us to question those dates. Both the historical and geographical references fit in quite well with this background.

The Nature of the Prophet

Unfortunately, the attention which has been given to the strange and unusual elements in the personality of the prophet Ezekiel have totally distracted many interpreters from the prophet's message. But such elements cannot be ignored. His actions have been described as going all the way from the bizarre to the grotesque. In attempts to explain him, he has been diagnosed as being neurotic, psychotic, schizophrenic, and cataleptic. He does appear at times to fit into the category of an ecstatic prophet. He is different from any of the other prophets of the Old Testament. But medical or psychological diagnoses from such a distance are difficult, if not impossible, to make. Ultimately, they appear to be basically unjustified. Who is to say what is normal in a person's relationship to God? It appears to be far better simply to admit that Ezekiel's experience is different from that of others in the Old Testament. But attempts to explain his "abnormalities" merely cloud the issue. Though different, he was clearly a prophet of God, a human spokesman of divine truth to his people and to subsequent generations.

Ezekiel was a Hebrew who had been carried as a captive by the armies of Nebuchadnezzar to Babylon. He lived in an exilic settlement near the Chebar canal. He was a priest, the son of Buzi. Ezekiel means "God strengthens," and it fell his task to strengthen the weakened hopes and faith of those who had been uprooted from their homeland by the consequences of war. He was married, and his wife died suddenly while he was in exile (24:15-18). He, like Jeremiah, was called upon to give a visible demonstration that he really believed what he had been preaching, being required to refrain from mourning over the death of his beloved companion.

His devotion to God was such that he was willing to make a fool of himself again and again in order to get his message across to his people. Further, he was deeply in love with his people, entering into their sufferings and sharing them fully. In many ways, he proclaimed essentially the same message to the people in exile which Jeremiah had been preaching to the people in Judah. The popular theology of his day claimed that the defeat of a people was equal to a defeat of their god. Ezekiel said that it was not so. The defeat of Judah had not been a defeat for God. Rooted in his preaching is a theology of exile, that God was working through Israel's suffering to accomplish His purposes.

Ezekiel may have been about thirty years old when he went into exile. The enigmatic verse in 1:1 may give this information. That was an important year for a priest, for it was the time when he began his service in the Temple. For Ezekiel, separated from the Temple, it may have become important as he discovered that he still had a ministry for his God.

Numerous debates have been held as to the actual location of Ezekiel's ministry. It has been located wholly in Babylon or partially in Jerusalem and in Babylon. Although no final conclusion is possible from the evidence we have, it appears most likely that his ministry was confined to Babylon with the Jerusalem passages being visionary. This becomes even more likely when we remember how much of his ministry was visionary.

Although Ezekiel made no reference to any contemporary prophet, he obviously dealt with many of the same issues which confronted Jeremiah. He also clearly set the stage for the later development of apocalyptic literature. His visions and vivid images were picked up, enlarged, and reapplied by the apocalypticists who followed him. His messages were shocking, but he lived in a shocking time. Perhaps that was the only way he could get the attention of the people who needed to hear him.

The Unity of the Book

The authorship of the book was questioned as far back as the time of the Talmud, when the rabbis said that it had been written by "the men of the Great Synagogue." However, until recent times no one seriously questioned the book's unity. As late as 1913 S. R. Driver could point out that no major question to its unity had been raised. That did not long endure. Since then, the attack has been carried so far that some deny all but about one-eighth of the book to the prophet. Attempts to reach any kind of scholarly consensus on what comes from Ezekiel and what does not have utterly failed.

Those passages most often questioned deal with individual responsibility (3:16-21; 14:12-23; 18:1-32; 33:7-20), those addressed "to the mountains of Israel" (6; 36), and the legal materials (40 to 48). However, there is no significant difference between these and other Ezekiel materials. Neither is there any reason to doubt all of these being actual concerns of the prophet-priest. Some evidence of a late editing may be demonstrable, but there appears to be little reason to doubt the book's unity. Since Ezekiel was a priest and the material is carefully dated the prophet himself was likely the original author.

The Content of the Book

The message of Ezekiel, for all of his eccentricities and strange symbols, is very much in the mainstream of Old Testament prophetism. His warnings and his demands are essentially the same as that of his predecessors. Further, although his vision of the future focused more upon Hebrew worship and its ritual than did that of his forerunners, his ultimate hope rested in the coming kingdom of God, just as theirs had.

    I. Introduction and setting (1:1-3)
   II. Ezekiel's call and commission (1:4 to 3:27)
      A. The vision of God (1:4-28)
      B. The Divine commission (2:1 to 3:1)
      C. The prophet's obedience (3:2-3)
      D. The task specified (3:4-11)
      E. Empowered by God's Spirit (3:12-14)
      F. Ezekiel's initial response (3:15)
      G. The Divine reaffirmation (3:16-27)

The statement of the setting leaves us with a major unanswered question: To what does "the thirtieth year" refer (1:1)? Many suggestions have been made, though none can be held with certainty. Since priests normally assumed their priestly office at that age (Num. 4:3) and since Ezekiel was a priest, this may be simply a reference to his age. However it is interpreted, no evidence justifies an emending of the text. Three things about the prophet as a prophet are clearly identified in these initial verses (1:1-3). First, he was among the exiles, enduring what they endured. A message has more authenticity to its hearers when its bearer is going through or has gone through what they experience. Second, Ezekiel was a visionary, receiving much of his revelation through visions, yet there was to be no doubt that his message was "the word of the Lord" (1:3). Ezekiel was the mouthpiece, but God was the source. Third, he was not limited to being a mouthpiece, God's hand was upon him (1:3). The power of God had been imparted to him and sustained him through his ministry.

We have a tendency to get so bogged down in the details of Ezekiel's initial vision of God as to miss its impact. Ezekiel and his fellow captives were in Babylon. According to the popular theology of the day, God was limited to Palestine and dwelt in the Temple upon the Temple mount. The exiles, thus, felt utterly isolated from the God of their fathers. The march from Jerusalem to Babylon had been a long journey to the northeast and then an even longer journey to the south down the Tigris-Euphrates Valley. When the prophet saw God coming to be with them, He was coming from the north (1:4), following the same path they had traveled. Ezekiel's first great discovery was that they were not alone, God was coming to them in exile. That sounds quite ordinary to us, but it was a shocking new revelation to most of the exiles.

In trying to interpret the prophet's vision, we need to note carefully that he was trying to describe the indescribable. Over and over again, he described something as looking "like" something else. This is always the problem of trying to put God's revelation into human language. Our words and our experiences are too limited to prepare us either accurately to describe or adequately to understand the full content of God's truth.

The title "son of man" is used approximately ninety times in this book as an address to Ezekiel. On one hand, it is probably to be understood as a form of address. On the other hand, it is probably not to be identified with the apocalyptic use in Daniel 7:13, nor is it to be equated with its use by Jesus as a term of self-designation. Here it apparently stresses Ezekiel's humanity when seen against the background of God as the source of his message.

As Ezekiel became fully aware both of the suffering of his people and the message God had for them, he was overwhelmed with the immensity and awesomeness of his task. He actually had nothing from himself to say to them. At the same time, he became even more fully aware that he did have a message from God for them. He had both the task and the responsibility to warn them of the impending consequences of their acts. Even as they endured one judgment, they faced an even greater judgment to come.

   III. Judgment in acts and oracles (4:1 to 7:27)
       A. Jerusalem's siege in symbolic acts (4:1-17)
       B. The destiny of Jerusalem's people following the siege (5:1-17)
       C. Destruction to the high places (6:1-7)
       D. Mercy to a remnant (6:8-10)
       E. Judgment upon all idolatry (6:11-14)
       F. Terror and grief at the coming judgment (7:1-27)

The symbolic acts other prophets occasionally performed became essentially a standard way of life for Ezekiel. At the very least, such a dramatic presentation of the prophet's message made it memorable. The prophets seemed to believe that the very "acting out" of their messages released God's power into a situation to see that the message of the symbolism came to pass. The Book of Jeremiah shows us that a number of people in Babylon were living in the hope that Judah would eventually be victorious over Babylon and that the captivity would come to a rapid end (Jer. 29:1-32). Jeremiah, from Jerusalem, sought to destroy that false hope. In these passages of Ezekiel, the prophet was trying to do the same thing from Babylon. He wanted his compatriots to be aware that Jerusalem was going to be besieged and defeated. Hope in a quick end to the captivity was a false hope.

    Ezekiel proclaimed to his people in Babylon that the ultimate judgment was directly caused by the idolatrous practices they had followed and their families and neighbors were still following. This was a warning to the exiles not to continue in such folly. Yet as he proclaimed such judgment, Ezekiel pointed out that the abundant mercy of God was going to spare a remnant of the people. Ezekiel was clearly not rejoicing at the divine judgment upon sin. Rather, he was grieving over it and terrified by it.

In a second set of visions, symbolic acts, and oracles, Ezekiel attacked in unmistakable terms the idolatry and false religion of his people. His very dramatic vision of the glory of the Lord departing both from the Temple and ultimately from Jerusalem should have forever put to rest the idea that God's blessings upon the Temple and His people were forever automatically assured. The beliefs of false religion sound good but ultimately lead to destruction. Ezekiel did have a genuine hope in God's redemptive blessings, but he was utterly devastating in his attack upon the false, empty hopes to which his people clung.

  C. The prophet's lament (19:1-14)
  D. The story of Israel's apostasy (20:1-44)
  E. God's ultimate judgment (20:45 to 24:27)
   1. Against the southland (20:45-49)
   2. Concerning the sword (21:1-32)
   3. Yahweh's indictment (22:1-31)
   4. Allegory of the two women (23:1-49)
   5. The judgment accomplished (24:1-27)

No prophet appears to have used as many different methods of communicating as Ezekiel. In this section of sermons, we see him as a master of allegory. As was true of many of the prophets, he is also seen as a master of wordplay, or puns. His use of the terms *Oholah* for Samaria and *Oholibah* for Jerusalem (23:4) is a magnificent example. *Oholah* means "she who has a tent," while *Oholibah* means "my tent is in her." This was an apparent reflection upon the fact that Samaria had a sanctuary at Bethel, but the Temple of God had been in Jerusalem.

The most graphic message the prophet communicated came at the death of his wife (24:15-24). His grief was demonstrated by silence rather than by outcry and tears. His message was that the exiles' devastation would be equally as great when Jerusalem finally fell.

To this point, Ezekiel's message was one of doom and judgment. However, he was also told that, when the news of the final fall of Jerusalem reached him, his mouth would be opened anew and that he would have a new message for his people. When the numbing grief of their homeland's destruction was going to be most overwhelming, God was going to have a new word for His people.

 VI. The foreign prophecies (25:1 to 32:32)
  A. Oracles against Amon, Moab, Edom, and Philistia (25:1-17)
  B. Judgment against Tyre (26:1 to 28:19)
  C. Oracle against Sidon and Israel's restoration (28:20-26)
  D. Judgment against Egypt (29:1 to 32:32)

Like the foreign prophecies of the other prophets, those of Ezekiel are of little interest to most biblical students. He delivered more oracles against both Tyre and Egypt than most other prophets did against any particular foreign nation. These foreign prophecies reflect Ezekiel's firm commitment to the fact that Yahweh was sovereign over all nations and that, as His prophet, he had an obligation to issue pronouncements against some of those peoples, even though they were outside the main limits of his basic ministry.

VII. Ezekiel's messages of hope (33:1 to 48:35)
    A. Oracles of restoration and hope (33:1 to 39:29)
        1. Issues of responsibility (33:1-33)
        2. Shepherds and the Shepherd (34:1-31)
        3. The defeat of Edom proclaimed (35:1-15)
        4. The restoration of Israel (36:1-38)
        5. The vision of the valley of dry bones (37:1-14)
        6. Oracle of the two sticks (37:15-28)
        7. God's utter sovereignty seen with Gog and Magog (38:1 to 39:29)
    B. The vision of the restoration of Temple and land (40:1 to 48:35)
        1. The new Temple (40:1 to 43:27)
        2. Laws and ordinances (44:1 to 46:24)
        3. Allegory of the sacred river (47:1-12)
        4. Tribal boundaries (47:13-23)
        5. Allocation of the lands (48:1-29)
        6. The new Jerusalem (48:30-35)

Ezekiel's view of the future included the restoration of the whole nation. Those who would seek to divide this into sacred and secular restorations have missed the point that to him there was no such division. All of life was sacred, lived in the presence of the Lord God of Israel. He obviously had a view of the Messiah in his hope of restoration, but his primary focus was not upon how God was going to accomplish his purposes but upon the fact that he was going to do it. Again his priestly concerns showed up in his vivid description of the renewed Temple and ritual. Like Jeremiah,

Ezekiel had few messages of hope for his people until the darkest days following the destruction of Jerusalem had settled upon them. At that time he was allowed to see the light of God's hope shine into the darkness of their despair.

31
Haggai

The prophets of the postexilic period are not generally as memorable as those who came during the period of the Hebrew kingdoms. In general, they were not concerned with great issues of ethics, morality, or theology. However, they did address the significant crises of their day. Such a man was Haggai and such was his ministry.

Haggai, the Man and His Ministry

The ministry of no person in the Old Testament is as precisely dated as that of Haggai. His entire ministry appears to have been limited to only five messages, all delivered in the last half of 520 BC. These messages are all dated to the second year of Darius, king of Persia, two being delivered on the first day of the sixth month, one on the twenty-first day of the seventh month, and two on the twenty-fourth day of the ninth month (1:1,13; 2:1,10,20). Using our modern system of dating, these appear to have been August 29, October 17, and December 18, 520 BC.

No biographical information, as such, is given about Haggai. On the basis of 2:3, some interpreters suggest that he had seen the Temple of Solomon before its destruction by Babylon in 586 BC. If this were correct, he would have been an old man in 520 BC, which may account for the brevity of his ministry. Another suggestion is that because of his interest in ritual and the Temple he may have been a priest. This latter suggestion appears less probable than the former.

Haggai's ministry was aimed at one thing—the rebuilding of the Temple. The Jews had returned from exile, after the decree of Cyrus, with great hopes and excitement. However, they were met by a poverty-stricken, frightened, dispirited group of citizens who had remained in Judah during the Exile. Some attempt may have been made to rebuild the Temple at that time; but by 520 BC, nothing of significance had been accomplished. Then Haggai, aided shortly thereafter by Zechariah, began to proclaim the necessity of getting on with the building. He encouraged the discouraged and prodded those in authority. When the rebuilt Temple was dedicated in 516 BC, it stood primarily as a monument to the ministry of this one man. His ministry is mentioned in Ezra 5:1 and 6:14, but nothing else is said of him in Ezra. His ministry was brief, to the point, and accomplished what it was supposed to do. No more could be asked of any prophet.

Authorship, Unity, and Date

The book appears to have been written at the same time Haggai was preaching, for there appears to be no awareness of the completion of the Temple reconstruction in 516 BC. However, the introductions to each of the five messages appear to reflect the hand of someone other than Haggai, probably a disciple who recorded and edited the materials. There have been no serious questions concerning the unity of the book,

The Content of the Book

I. The first sermon: the time to build (1:1-11)
   A. Title verse (1:1)
   B. Selfish concerns (1:2-4)
   C. Portrait of economic problems (1:5-6)
   D. The command to build (1:7-8)
   E. Real and potential judgment (1:9-11)
II. The second sermon: promise of God's presence (1:12-15)
   A. The decision to obey (1:12)
   B. Haggai's encouragement (1:13)
   C. The work begun (1:14-15)

Haggai's first sermon gives a vivid description of inflationary times and the lack of personal satisfaction from anything which was done. "He who earns wages earns wages to put them into a bag with holes" (1:6). "You have looked for much, and, lo, it came to little; and when you brought it home, I blew it away" (1:9). The people had been devoting all their attention to their own needs and none toward the Temple in which to worship and by which to glorify God. They were wrong.

There is some disagreement as to the date of the second sermon or even if it actually was a second sermon. If the first one were addressed to the governor and his council, they may have made the decision immediately to begin work. At that time, Haggai would have offered his sermon of encouragement. The work, then, began twenty-three days later, "on the twenty-fourth day of the month" (i.e., Sept. 21; 1:15).

  III. The third sermon: encouraging the discouraged (2:1-9)
    A. Title verse (2:1)
    B. Contrast between the old and the new (2:2-3)
    C. Promise of future glory (2:4-9)
  IV. The fourth sermon: the need for patience (2:10-19)
    A. Title verse (2:10)
    B. The contamination of evil (2:11-13)
    C. Waiting for God's blessing (2:14-19)
  V. Fifth sermon: promise to Zerubbabel (2:20-23)

After the work on the Temple had begun, it quickly became obvious to those who had seen the glory of Solomon's Temple that the new one was going to be poor by comparison. This crisis was met by the prophet's assurance that the real glory of the Temple would come from what God would do, not from their building. However, another crisis arose about two months later when the prosperity the prophet had promised for the people's faithfulness had not come to pass. By a question concerning the law, Haggai reminded the people that uncleanness was more contagious than holiness, thus it would take longer than they had expected for the blessings of God to begin to come to them. The fruit of holiness were going to be slow in coming, but he assured them that they would come.

Haggai's final word was addressed to the governor, Zerubbabel; calling him the signet was an assurance that God's seal was upon his work (cf. 2:23). Unfortunately, since this was also coupled with Haggai's description of the coming Day of the Lord, some people may have assumed that the governor was being designated as the Messiah. This may account for the fact that Zerubbabel disappeared from history at this point; for Persia apparently intervened, removing him from office. Darius was still in the early part of his reign, and any suspicion of such a threat would have been dealt with quickly and harshly. Although some commentators contend that Haggai himself considered Zerubbabel to be the Messiah, the book gives no indication that this was so. Zerubbabel's work in rebuilding was assured and the future kingdom of God was assured, but these were not necessarily the same thing.

32

Zechariah

Zechariah was the second of two prophets whose ministry began with the insistence that the time had come to rebuild the Temple following the return from exile, Haggai being the other. However, his nature, his ministry, his preaching, and his book are all quite different from Haggai and offer some significant problems.

Zechariah, the Man and His Ministry

Zechariah's name means "Yah (abbreviation of Yahweh) has remembered." By so naming their son, his parents may have been expressing joy at the deliverance of the Jews under Cyrus. If this were so, Zechariah would have been in his mid to late teens when he began his ministry as a younger contemporary of Haggai. However, the name can be "Yah is remembered." It is more likely that he was born a bit earlier, yet was still a young man at the time of the beginning of his ministry. In this case, his name expressed faith that the exiles still served Yahweh. He was youthful, visionary, and idealistic. He is also mentioned in Ezra 5:1 and 6:14 with Haggai. We know that Zechariah's ministry extended from the eighth month of the second year of Darius to the fourth day of the ninth month in the fourth year of Darius (1:1; 7:1). However, it is quite likely that it extended far longer than that. He was a descendant of Iddo, probably one of the priestly families (Neh. 12:16). There was a deep-flowing messianic theme to his preaching. He placed a major emphasis upon visions and is clearly a forerunner of the development of Old Testament apocalyptic.

417

Authorship, Unity, and Date of the Book

The first eight chapters of the book are clearly a unit, written by the same person, most likely a disciple of Zechariah, or possibly the prophet himself. However, scholars have long debated whether chapters 9 through 14 are really to be connected, or even whether they are from one, two, or more hands. Chapters 9 and 12 each have an independent title, being called simply "An Oracle." Further, their style, vocabulary, and setting are quite different. In 1 through 8, Jerusalem and her neighbors are at peace, while in chapters 9 through 14 there appears to be international turmoil and an impending siege of Jerusalem. Further, a time of conflict and great shedding of blood appears to have been immediately upon the horizon.

Dates have been suggested for chapters 9 through 14, varying from preexilic Jerusalem, just before its final defeat at the hands of Babylon all the way to circa 350 BC. If these words were from Zechariah himself, they come from late in his life, long after the setting of the first eight chapters. Further, if they were from him, there is no identifiable historical setting. Instead, they must be understood as a kind of apocalyptic drama. On the other hand, if they were not from Zechariah, they are probably two or more anonymous prophecies which have been attached to the book because of a slight similarity in apocalyptic style.

All of the Book of Zechariah was clearly known to the writers of the New Testament. Chapters 9 through 14 were used by the writers of the Gospels, while chapters 1 through 8 had a major impact upon the Book of the Revelation. Jesus obviously sought to fulfill the prediction of the coming King by His triumphal entry into Jerusalem. (cf. Zech 9:9; Matt. 21:5; John 12:14-15).

The Content of the Book

I. Visions and proclamation (1:1 to 8:23)
   A. Invitation to return to Yahweh (1:1-6)
   B. A series of visions (1:7 to 6:8)

1. The night vision of the man on a red horse (1:7-17)
2. Four horns and four smiths (1:18-21)
3. The man with the measuring line (2:1-13)
4. The vision of the Joshua on trial (3:1-10)
5. The vision of the golden lampstand (4:1-14)
6. The vision of the flying scroll (5:1-4)
7. The vision of the woman in the ephah (5:5-11)
8. The vision of the four chariots (6:1-8)

C. A series of messages (6:9 to 8:23)
   1. The messianic crowning of the priest (6:9-15)
   2. Proper worship and proper morality (7:1-14)
   3. Ten messages from Yahweh (8:1-23)
     a. His jealousy for Zion (8:1-2)
     b. His return to Zion (8:3)
     c. The gift of life (8:4-5)
     d. His marvels (8:6)
     e. His redemption (8:7-8)
     f. His encouragement to the builders (8:9-13)
     g. His new purpose (8:14-17)
     h. His worship (8:18-19)
     i. His future for Zion (8:20-23)

Zechariah's messianic emphasis took hold of the idea of the Messiah being the "shoot from the stump of Jesse, and a branch . . . out of his roots" as Isaiah had proclaimed (Isa. 11:1). Jeremiah had also used the concept. By the time of Zechariah, the "branch" appears to have become a technical term for the Messiah. Zechariah tied this concept in slightly with the idea of the Servant (cf. 3:8). He also tied the priesthood into the messianic hope with the image of the crowned (kingly) priest (6:9-14).

II. Coming world changes (9:1 to 11:17)
   A. An oracle against the nations (9:1-8)
   B. The coming King (9:9-10)

    C. The Lord's deliverance and provision (9:11 to
      10:12)
    D. The destruction of Lebanon (11:1-3)
    E. The Shepherd and the shepherds (11:4-17)
III. The great Day of the Lord (12:1 to 14:21)
    A. The tragedy of Jerusalem (12:1-5)
    B. Grief over the Pierced One (12:6-14)
    C. Ministry of the Messiah (13:1-9)
    D. Yahweh's holy kingdom (14:1-21)

Anyone familiar with the Gospels will easily be able to see
the impact these latter chapters had upon them. The point
of this entire section appears to be twofold. First, Yahweh
will bring His Messiah to Israel and the world in His own
way, through the avenue of suffering. Second, the work of
the Messiah will ultimately open the way to cleansing and
to the establishment of God's kingdom.

33

Other Prophetic Books
Jonah, Joel, and Malachi

The books of the prophets Jonah, Joel, and Malachi need to be considered independently of any other prophetic book, insofar as their historical background is concerned. The reason for this isolated treatment is that each of these books has unique problems of dating or interpretation which do not lend themselves to treatment in chronological relationship to other prophetic books.

Jonah

Probably no other book in the Old Testament has received such diverse treatment by interpreters in their essential approach as Jonah. Yet these interpreters have reached similar conclusions in regard to the basic message of the book. Many interpreters approach the Book of Jonah as a piece of literal history. Others approach the book either as a piece of fiction or as a modified form of historical novel, or more precisely, a historical short story. This latter group assumes not only that a basis of fact is behind the book but also that the author took literary license in order to communicate theological truth.

One basic issue confronts the interpreter deciding how to approach the book: inspiration. Some people believe God can only inspire writers to record history. These people have no place in their concept of inspiration for even the possibility that God might inspire other kinds of literature to communicate truth. Such a position imposes a limit upon God He may not have imposed upon himself. If, however, an interpreter believes God could have inspired any kind of literature He chose, the possibility that this book is something other than pure history can be raised and seriously considered. Commentators have spent so much time arguing about the book that they have missed its message. That has been a real boon to the powers of evil; for as long as God's people do not probe a book's message, they are not going to apply it.

If the book is literal history, we are faced with the dilemma that we have no historical record from Assyria of any wholesale repentance of the nation, even though we have information from every year of Assyrian history during the time when Jonah would have been ministering. There is also some difficulty with the idea of a foreign capital responding in such a way to a foreign prophet preaching in an unknown language.

On the other hand, if the book is another kind of literature, why would the writer make such a ridiculous figure out of a man who otherwise was a successful prophet? Scholars differ as to whether Jesus' references to Jonah (Matt. 12:38-41; 16:4; Luke 11:29) mandate a literal interpretation.

Without question, the story of Jonah has some basis in fact. However, it is also possible that the story was told with embellishments to expand it into an allegory or a parable concerning Israel and God's missionary purposes.

The Question of Dating

All we know of Jonah outside of this book is recorded in 2 Kings 14:25, which states that he was a very successful prophet in Israel during the reign of Jeroboam II. That background is important in understanding the message of the book. The date of Jonah's ministry must be put in the first half of the eighth century BC. But the book was written after the destruction of Nineveh in 612 BC, for it speaks of Nineveh in terms of how it used to be rather than how it presently was.

The message of the book appears to be aimed at setting forth a missionary imperative, especially toward hated enemies. Almost all commentators agree that the most likely historical occasion for its writing was around 400 BC, at a time when Israel was turned inward and had little or no concern for anyone other than itself. Written at such a time, Jonah himself would have represented the people of Israel, failing to be a blessing to those to whom God had sent them. They consequently faced the storms of God's judgment and were sent into exile (the fish). From that place they had turned to God and had been delivered. Then, as Jonah was given another chance, so were they. The point is, the people of Israel needed to recognize that God loved others beside them. Unfortunately, the Israelites of the postexilic era had once again turned their spiritual concerns (and all others, for that matter) inward. To such a time, the missionary message of Jonah would have come with stinging pointedness.

The Content of the Book

I. The futility of fleeing from God's will (1:1-17)
   A. Disobedience to God's call (1:1-3)
   B. The terrible storm (1:4-6)
   C. Jonah's confession (1:7-16)
   D. The great fish (1:17)
II. Deliverance (2:1-10)
   A. The prayer of Jonah (2:1-9)
   B. Jonah brought back (2:10)
III. Fruitful obedience (3:1-10)
   A. Jonah's message (3:1-4)
   B. Nineveh's repentance (3:5-9)
   C. God's mercy (3:10)
IV. The great lesson of God's love (4:1-11)
   A. Jonah's anger (4:1-5)
   B. God's lesson on pity (4:6-11)

Jonah did not want to go to the people of Nineveh because they were the hated oppressors of the Hebrews. Jonah's narrow nationalism dulled any concern he should have had for them. Second Kings indicates that he had been a very successful prophet. His awareness that God was merciful opened the possibility that his predictions concerning Nineveh might not come to pass and he couldn't face that possibility (cf. 4:2). This was precisely the kind of message Israel needed around 400 BC.

In this book, the foreigners appear to be far more sensitive to God and to good than Jonah. The seamen on the boat were more ethically sensitive than was Jonah. The Assyrians were quicker to hear God's word and to respond to it. This, too, was a lesson Israel needed. Far too frequently those who do not know God reflect more love and concern than do God's own people. The book has a striking message, stabbing the heart of the complacent and those who do not seek to share God's love with others.

Joel

Joel, of all the books in the Latter Prophets, is the hardest to assign to a specific period, either as to a date of ministry or to a date of writing. Of the prophet himself, almost nothing is known. His name, *Joel,* means "Yahweh is God"; it shows up in various forms throughout the Old Testament. It is the reverse of Elijah, "God is Yahweh." That has led some interpreters to identify the two or to suggest that they ministered at the same time. The name of his father, Pethuel, does not occur elsewhere in the Bible.

Joel showed an intense interest in the Temple and in its worship, which has led some commentators to suggest that he was a "cultic prophet," that is, a prophet officially associated with the Temple. He may also have had some connection with the Levitical priesthood itself.

The Date of Joel's Ministry

Establishing the date of Joel's ministry is the primary issue in the study of the man and his book. Three very different suggestions have been made. These are an early date, around the time of the reign of Joash in Judah, placing Joel near the last quarter of the ninth century BC; a late date, placing his ministry in the Persian period, probably around 400 BC; and a median date, placing his ministry during the last days of Judah, at the time of Jeremiah, sometime around 610 to 600 BC.

The majority of interpreters have supported the late date

based upon the following considerations. (1) No name for a reigning king is given in 1:1, as was normal for all preexilic prophets. (2) Temple ritual was emphasized more than ethics, unlike the preexilic prophets but very like the postexilic ministries of Haggai, Zechariah, and Malachi. (3) The Northern Kingdom of Israel is not mentioned, apparently having long been off the scene. (4) Israel, as a title, is used for Judah, something which no preexilic prophet did, lest it lead to confusion in understanding. (5) The leaders in the nation were the priests, a situation which was true primarily in the postexilic period. (6) The Exile had apparently already taken place (3:1-2, 17). (7) The reference to the Greeks (3:6) indicates that Israel had already had contact with them, something which did not occur until around 400 BC or later. (8) The symbolism makes it appear that this may be a step toward apocalyptic literature, a clear postexilic development (9) Numerous passages in Joel show affinity with Amos, Zephaniah, Isaiah (both sections), Ezekiel, and Malachi and make it clear that Joel's ministry followed all of them. (10) Neither Assyria nor Babylon are mentioned.

Those supporting the early date base their position upon these reasons. (1) The absence of the mention of a king and the prominence of the priests would fit perfectly in the early days of Joash, when the priest Jehoiada was regent in Judah. (2) With a message only for Judah, no reference to the Northern Kingdom was necessary. (3) Israel could certainly apply to Judah and, in Joel's context, would have offered no confusion. (4) The foreign enemies did not need to be mentioned, for anyone would have been aware who they were. (5) The mention of the Greeks did not have to refer to a nation but could have been a reference only to bands of slave traders, a situation which could have been possible at this time. (6) No reference to the Exile is so clear that it could not also have been applied to this era. (7) Clear ethical teachings are present, for example: "Rend your hearts and not your garments" (2:13).

Until recently, almost all discussion centered upon these two alternatives. However, in the period since World War

II, a number of commentators have asserted that the best date for the book is near the end of the seventh century BC. The reasons for this suggestion are as follows. (1) Most of the arguments for dates at the extremes are based on silence, the absence of evidence rather than its presence. Such arguments are always doubtful. (2) Many of the objections to the extreme views can be eliminated with a date between the two. The great similarity among Joel, Zephaniah, and Jeremiah make it likely that he ministered at the same time as they did.

Obviously, no consensus has been reached, but it does appear that the arguments for the late date are the strongest. Fortunately, the date of Joel's ministry does not affect the validity of his message. We can hear the voice of God speaking through it even though we cannot accurately reconstruct its background. In some ways, the very fact that it can be made to fit into three such divergent periods of Judah's history show just how universal is its application.

The Nature of the Locust Plague

The other major issue for interpreters of Joel focuses upon the locust plague (1:4; 2:25). Three different interpretations have been offered. (1) Many have suggested that this was simply a figure of speech, referring to attacking armies. However, no agreement has been reached as to which armies were intended. Further, the locusts are compared to real armies in chapter 2, something which makes no sense if they already stood for armies. (2) Others have suggested that the locusts were apocalyptic images of some kind of unearthly creatures that would devastate the earth in a great, future catastrophe. However, the symbolism of Joel seems far more like that of the typical prophetic message than the apocalyptic symbols of Daniel or of the Revelation. (3) The locust plague was literally that, a plague of devastating locusts that served as the inspiration for a vision of the ultimate Day of the Lord. No sufficient reason has been offered for rejecting the obvious interpretation that the prophet's land had been devastated by locusts and that he used that event as the basis for his message. A true prophet can always see the hand of God at work in the everyday world. The book was probably written shortly after the message was delivered in order for it to have the most meaning to its recipients.

The Content of the Book

    I. Title verse (1:1)
   II. The devastation of the land (1:2-20)
      A. The coming of the locusts (1:2-4)
      B. The universal effect (1:5-12)
      C. A call for a solemn assembly (1:13-14)
      D. A portent of the Day of the Lord (1:15-20)
  III. The coming Day of the Lord (2:1-17)
      A. The coming devastation (2:1-11)
      B. A call to repentance (2:12-14)
      C. Religious leaders to lead in a fast (2:15-17)
  IV. God's blessings upon their repentance (2:18 to 3:21)
      A. Physical blessings (2:18-27)
      B. Spiritual blessing upon God's people (2:28-32)
      C. The whole earth called to judgment (3:1-21)

Joel called his people to a time of genuine penitence as a means of averting the coming judgment, saying:

> . . . rend your hearts and not your garments.
> Return to the Lord, your God,
>   for he is gracious and merciful,
> slow to anger, and abounding in steadfast love (2:13).

Further, he foresaw the day when God would pour out his Spirit upon all flesh (2:28-29), a text which served as the basis for Peter's sermon at Pentecost (Acts 2:16). Joel's ultimate hope was in the promise of God, "I will restore. . . ." (2:25) and the ultimate assurance of its fulfillment, "When I restore . . ." (3:1).

Malachi

The prophetic canon of the Old Testament and apparently the ministry of Old Testament prophets themselves came to an end with Malachi. There is a question as to whether Malachi itself is a name or a title, and, therefore, whether we even know the name of this last prophet of the Old Testament times.

The Man Himself

Malachi literally means, "My messenger" and shows up in 3:1 where it clearly does not refer to the author. The translators of the LXX did not see the word as a proper name. Further, the Jewish authors of the Targum did not see it as a name, asserting that Ezra was the author.

Zechariah 9:1; 12:1, and Malachi 1:1 all begin with the same Hebrew word, *massa'*, "burden" or "oracle." Some interpreters have suggested that these last three oracles of the prophetic canon were all written by the same person and that the first two became associated with Zechariah by accident. But the Hebrew of the three is quite different, and it is unlikely that they were written by the same person. The possibility that they may be three anonymous oracles by different authors should not be ruled out.

However, the analogy of prophecy would suggest that Malachi is a proper name, for we do not have any other prophetic book whose central figure does not have a name. Recognizing that the issue is far from certain, we shall approach the book as though Malachi were the name of the prophet who spoke these words.

The man himself was obviously quite courageous, for he faced opposition from both priests and people undaunted. He addressed a time when worship was half-hearted and carelessly done. The whole nation approached God as if anything would do, as if He really was not very important or powerful. Malachi's style was very much that of the priests and the wisdom writers, and he may fit well into either or both categories.

His ministry has been associated with that of Ezra and Nehemiah. The Temple had been rebuilt and worship had been going on for a long time, long enough for the excitement to die down. Admittedly, the entire problem of the ministries of Ezra and Nehemiah is quite complex (see those chapters), but the message of Malachi appears to fit in well with a time ten or more years after Ezra's abolition of mixed marriages. The reference to the governor (1:8) would indicate a foreign person, not Nehemiah. Thus we must date the book after Ezra and either during the period of Nehemiah's return to Persia (ca. 430 BC) or after Nehemiah's second visit to Jerusalem (ca. 420 BC).

The Book

The book itself appears to be a unit, for the didactic (teaching) style shows up throughout. Further, the message appears to be quite uniform and consistent. There is little reason to doubt that it was written shortly after the ministry of Malachi himself. It could have been written by a disciple. If Malachi were a part of the wisdom movement, he could have written the book himself. Its careful organization may reflect the fact that it was written from the beginning and was not originally an oral presentation.

The Content of the Book

    I. Title verse (1:1)
    II. God's love for Israel (1:2-5)
       A. Doubted (1:2*a*)
       B. Demonstrated in history (1:2*b*-5)

The affirmation of Yahweh's love for Israel and hatred for Esau (Edom) has offered problems. However, the Hebrew words used here reflect God's gracious choice and His rejection. It was not that He had hated Esau as we think of hate. Rather, He had chosen to bless Israel and had not offered the same blessing at that time to Edom. His choices had been demonstrated in their respective histories.

    III. Israel's neglect in responding to God's love (1:6 to 4:3)
       A. Failure of the priests (1:6 to 2:9)
          1. Laxity in ritual and sacrifice (1:6-14)
          2. Carelessness in priestly service (2:1-9)
       B. Failure of the people (2:10 to 4:3)

1. Mixed marriage and easy divorce (2:10-16)
2. Cynicism (2:17)
3. The coming judgment (3:1-4)
4. Moral failure (3:5-6)
5. Failure in tithing (3:7-12)
6. Blatant skepticism (3:13-15)
7. Prospect of punishment or blessing (3:16 to 4:3)

IV. A call to remembrance (4:4)
V. The divine promise (4:5-6)

The Old Testament prophets drew to a close with a severe castigation upon the people for gross immorality, skeptical infidelity, and improper worship in approaching God. But this part of the canon also drew to a close with a distinct forward look, a hope for God's future acts of power and blessing. The priests were guilty of despising the God who loved them and had redeemed them and whom they served. The people had become doubtful that God was of any significance at all. Thus they were all warned, "The Lord whom you seek will suddenly come to his temple" (3:1). The Coming One was going to bring judgment to those who had turned away from Him. However, He promised that there was also "a book of remembrance" before God, with the names of those who were faithful in their service of God. Judgment and hope, promise and fulfillment, sinful people and confronting Lord, on those notes the Old Testament prophets faded away, having prepared the way for Him who was God's ultimate message to sinful humanity.

Part V
Introduction to the Study
of the Writings

34

Hebrew Poetry

This discussion of the nature and characteristics of Hebrew poetry could have been considered before the books of the prophets since much of the prophetic material is in poetry form. However, such placement might have reinforced the old idea that all authentic prophetic material is poetry. That is simply not so. Though prophetic material is not always poetic, poetry is the normal form for the psalms. Thus the study of Hebrew poetry is appropriate in this section on the Writings. The information on poetry given here is applicable to the use of that form in other parts of the Old Testament.

The Nature and Purpose of Poetry

Poetic literature in any language is used for a specific purpose. Poetry is used by an author either to communicate a truth more vividly or more memorably than can be done with prose or to communicate a truth that has a meaning too profound adequately to be communicated by straightforward prose. The words of Hamlet in Shakespeare's play of that name, "To be, or not to be: that is the question," have been recited over and over through the centuries. Yet if the author had placed in his hero's mouth the question, "Shall I commit suicide or not?" few people would have ever bothered to ponder, much less repeat the words. The poetry made Hamlet's plight vivid, memorable, and expressed emotions literal prose could never have shared.

If we are going to understand poetry properly, we need to read it over and over until we begin to *feel* what the poet *felt*. Poetry should elicit an emotional response. Until it does, we probably have not understood it properly. Reading and rereading poetry is the first and basic tool toward its understanding and appreciation.

The Characteristics of Hebrew Poetry

Before we consider two basic characteristics of Hebrew poetry, we need to consider a noncharacteristic. To most contemporary biblical students who have grown up in a Western culture, poetry has been normally characterized by rhyme. Words at the end of lines are expected to rhyme with words at the ends of other lines in some kind of repetitive pattern. However, although this is true of English poetry, it is not true of Hebrew poetry. *Hebrew poetry does not rhyme.* Thus, what to us is the most common characteristic of poetry does not even exist in Hebrew poetry.

Rhythm

The rhythm, meter, or beat of Hebrew poetry is one of its major characteristics. This has to do with the number of stressed or emphasized syllables in a line or verse. The usual term applied by technicians to a line of Hebrew poetry is a stich. One line of a two-line unit is called a distich and one of a three-line unit is called a tristich. While the stressed syllables are more easily identified in Hebrew than in an English translation, scholars still do not wholly agree in many instances as to how these stressed syllables should be identified. However, we do know enough about them to be able to identify three main patterns which occur in Hebrew poetry.

1. Each line has three beats. The 3:3 is the most frequently used pattern of beats in Hebrew poetry. Much of the Book of Job uses it and it is the most common pattern found in the Book of Psalms. Consider these examples.

The earth/is the Lord's/and the fulness thereof,
the world/and those who dwell/therein (Ps. 24:1).

Who forgives/all/your . . . diseases (Ps. 103:3).

2. Each part of a verse has two beats. Although not as

prevalent as the foregoing, the 2:2 is another very common rhythm. Being a very short beat, it resulted in a staccato type of movement. It was used for the expression of deep, heartfelt emotions such as exuberant joy, excitement, fear, or awe. Such are felt in the following.

> The nations/rage,//the kingdoms/totter;
>   he utters/his voice,//the earth/melts (Ps. 46:6).

> Blessed is he/whose transgression is forgiven,
>   whose sin/is covered (Ps. 32:1).

3. A third common rhythm is the 3:2. It is a slower, off-beat rhythm and is named *qinah* which means "lament." It is normally used to express grief or lament. Like music in a minor key to people of Western culture, to the Hebrew ears the very beat itself called forth a mood of utter and overwhelming grief. It is very prominent in the Book of Lamentations. Further, it was quite commonly used by the prophets in expressing their grief over Israel's sin or over the coming judgment. Illustrations of this meter can be seen in the following.

> O Lord my God,/in thee do I take refuge;
>   save me/from all my pursuers,/and deliver me (Ps. 7:1).

> Many bulls/encompass me,
>   strong bulls/of Bashan/surround me (Ps. 22:12).

Parallelism

The most obvious and major characteristic of Hebrew poetry is parallelism. While some scholars have identified multiple categories of parallelism in the Bible, these can basically be classified under three major headings.

1. Synonymous parallelism. Synonymous parallelism describes that technique of Hebrew poetry where the author says something and then repeats the same thought with similar words in the second line. Consider these examples.

> He who sits in the heavens laughs;
>   the Lord has them in derision.
> Then he will speak to them in his wrath,
>   and terrify them in his fury (Ps. 2:4-5).

> What is man that thou are mindful of him,
>> and the son of man that thou dost care for him? (Ps. 8:4).

> The heavens are telling the glory of God;
>> and the firmament proclaims his handiwork.
> Day to day pours forth speech,
>> and night to night declares knowledge (Ps. 19:1-2).

2. Antithetical parallelism. This is the direct opposite of synonymous parallelism. In this instance the second line takes the thought of the first line and expresses it in a reverse concept. This, too, is more easily seen by examining illustrations.

> For the Lord knows the way of the righteous,
>> but the way of the wicked will perish (Ps. 1:6).

> Many are the pangs of the wicked;
>> but steadfast love surrounds him who trusts in the Lord (Ps. 32:10).

3. Synthetic parallelism. As the title indicates, synthetic parallelism is not parallelism at all. At times, there is a parallelism of Hebrew structure only, not of thought. At other times, and far more commonly, the second line takes the thought of the first and carries it on beyond, almost in a stairlike progression. These illustrations will make this clearer.

> Blessed is the man
>> whole walks not in counsel of the wicked,
>> nor stands in the way of sinners,
>> nor sits in the seat of scoffers (Ps. 1:1).

> Surely goodness and mercy shall follow me
>> all the days of my life;
> and I shall dwell in the house of the Lord
>> for ever (Ps. 23:6).

> Thou didst with they arm redeem thy people,
>> the sons of Jacob and Joseph (Ps. 77:15).

Parallelism is an important characteristic of Hebrew poetry to recognize, for it aids in interpretation. The Hebrews used it as a technique of emphasis. It underscored the truths which they were expressing. However, while we do know something about both rhythm and parallelism, by our studies in the Ugaritic literature we have discovered that we do not know as much about such techniques as we once believed we did. These characteristics of Hebrew poetry are not well enough understood to be used as a tool for textual emendation. They are well enough known to be an aid to interpretation.

35

The Psalms

Of all the books of the Old Testament, the Book of Psalms has probably been more loved and appreciated by most people of all the ages. It has certainly been the most used by contemporary Christians as a source of timeless devotion. At the same time, some of its more brutal passages have presented problems for the contemporary interpreter, as they fall short of the Christian ideal of love and forgiveness toward one's enemies.

The Book of Psalms occurs first among those books which make up the section of the Hebrew canon known as the Writings. In the MT it bears the title of "Praises." In the LXX is identified by the title *Psalmoi,* whose best translation is "melodies" or "songs." The LXX title has come down to us through the Latin Vulgate. One ancient codex identified the book by the title of *Psalterion,* which refers to songs accompanied by stringed instruments. From this we have another frequently used title for this book—the Psalter.

The Nature of the Book

The Book of Psalms was the book of hymns, prayers, anthems, and liturgical readings the ancient Hebrews used in worship. For a long time it was thought that all of these various poems had been used in Israel from its earliest days, with most of them having been written by David. However, beginning with the latter part of the nineteenth century and continuing until the middle of the twentieth century, interpreters dated the psalms later and later until it almost appeared doubtful if any were preexilic compositions. It was

439

generally believed that many, if not most, of the psalms should be dated in the Maccabean era.

From the beginning of the form-critical work of Hermann Gunkel, however, there has been a revolt against this approach to psalm study. Throughout this century, more and more interpreters have pushed the dating of the psalms back into the era of the Hebrew kingdoms, concluding that the overwhelming majority of the psalms were preexilic and were used in the Temple of Solomon as the basic source of liturgical materials for Hebrew worship.

As noted in our study of the Book of Leviticus, Psalms and Leviticus should be studied together in order to get the best grasp of Hebrew worship. Leviticus presents the basic form of the sacrificial system which was used in ancient worship. The Psalms give the actual content of that worship, presenting the basic meaning, attitudes, and intent of worship.

The Book of Psalms is the longest book of the Old Testament. It contains 150 psalms. They should not be referred to as chapters. They are no more chapters than are the hymns in our hymnals. The book is also subdivided into five smaller books or collections. These are clearly separated from one another and identified as separate books. Each of these books ends with its own doxology. Psalm 1 is generally thought to serve as the introduction to the entire Psalter and Psalm 150 serves as the doxology for the whole collection. The doxologies obviously bring each collection to a natural and formal conclusion.

> *Book I:*
> Blessed be the Lord, the God of Israel,
> from everlasting to everlasting!
> Amen and Amen (41:13).

> *Book II:*
> Blessed be the Lord, the God of Israel,
> who alone does wondrous things.
> Blessed be his glorious name for ever;
> may his glory fill the whole earth!
> Amen and Amen!
> The prayers of David, the son of Jesse,
> are ended (72:18-20).

Book III:

Blessed be the Lord for ever!
Amen and Amen (89:52).

Book IV:

Blessed be the Lord, the God of Israel,
from everlasting to everlasting!
And let all the people say, "Amen!"
Praise the Lord! (106:48).

Book V:

This is glory for all his faithful ones.
Praise the Lord! (149:9*b*).

Of each of the five books, only the last one does not have a clear conclusion ending with an amen. Obviously, it was the only one which did not need such a clear conclusion. If Psalm 150 is the end of the last book, then the conclusion would be:

Let everything that breathes praise the Lord!
Praise the Lord! (v.6).

A great deal of discussion has ensued as to whether this separation of the Psalter into five books is natural or artificial. Those who have seen the division as artificial have suggested that dividing the book into five separate collections is simply an artificial attempt to parallel the five books of the Law with five books of song. This may be so, but we need to consider additional evidence before drawing a final conclusion. Consideration of the content of the five books, especially as regards their usage of the divine names produces some striking results. Consider the following table.

Occurrences Of Divine Names in Psalms

Book	Yahweh	Elohim
I (1 to 41)	273 (86.4%)	43 (13.6%)
II (42 to 72)	30 (15.5%)	164 (84.5%)
III (73 to 89)	44 (43.6%)	57 (56.4%)

IV (90 to 106)	103 (84.4%)	19 (15.6%)
V (107 to 150)	190 (87.6%)	27 (12.4%)

We immediately notice that in books I, IV, and V, *Yahweh* is used significantly more frequently than *Elohim* and that the reverse is true in regard to book II. Just as striking is the fact that in book III the usage is fairly evenly distributed between the two names, with *Elohim* slightly predominating. This extreme variation in the pattern of the usage of the names for God from book to book makes it highly unlikely that the division into separate books was either accidental or capricious. Rather, it appears far more likely that the books each had a separate existence and were later gathered into one large book. This idea is further reinforced by a comparison of Psalms 14 and 53. Those two psalms are alike except that each uses a different name for God. It appears that each collection included the psalm, using the divine name which was preferred in the worship center where each was used. This can be seen elsewhere, but this is the most striking in this instance.

Scholars have long conjectured, from a great deal of supportive evidence, that *Yahweh* was the name for God preferred in Jerusalem and in the southern part of the land while *Elohim* was the name preferred at Bethel and among the northern tribes. If this were so, book II was most likely the hymnbook of the northern tribes, with its use apparently centered in the shrine at Bethel. Books I, IV, and V appear to have been used in the Jerusalem Temple either before the division of the kingdom following Solomon's death, during the long time following the division before the fall of the Northern Kingdom in 722 BC, or in the very last years of the Southern Kingdom. The most likely time for the collection of book III would have been shortly after the fall of the Northern Kingdom, when the refugees from the north were being assimilated into the worship of the Southern Kingdom. While this specific reconstruction is obviously problematical, it is highly likely that the variation in the use of the divine names was the direct result of divine inspiration upon separate people in separate places at specific times in Hebrew history, as they sought to worship God.

The Titles of the Psalms

Most English translations of the Book of Psalms indicate titles for some of the psalms. Although scholars generally agree that these were added to the psalms long after they were written and, therefore, have limited historical value, they do clearly indicate strong ancient traditions concerning many aspects of the psalms. They are worthy of serious consideration in regard to what they do tell us about the psalms and their use in Israel's worship. The titles to the psalms can be collected and studied in four different categories.

Titles Descriptive of the Nature of the Psalm

Many titles appear to reflect the editor's opinion concerning the character of the psalm itself. There are several major titles of this type.

1. Psalm (*mizmor*): appears to indicate a piece of music to be sung with an instrumental accompaniment. This title occurs fifty-seven times.

2. Song (*shir*): seems to be a general term for a song, occurring about thirty times.

3. *Maskil:* usually only transliterated, as the meaning is uncertain. The Hebrew root relates to wisdom, and it has been variously interpreted as applying to a song which required a great deal of skill either to sing or to play or as applying to psalms whose content was generally assumed to make people wise. This title occurs thirteen times.

4. *Miktam:* another term only transliterated, at whose meaning we can only guess. It was probably a musical term, but its nature has been lost in antiquity. Some scholars have suggested that it is generally used of psalms with a special emphasis upon redemption or atonement. However, this is not easy to demonstrate conclusively. Other scholars have suggested that it refers to an especially pure or "golden" musical accompaniment. The term occurs six times.

5. Prayer (*tephillah*): a term with an obvious meaning which occurs five times.

6. Praise (*tehillah*): a term which occurs one time only (145), although it actually came to be used as a title for the entire Psalter. It is derived from the word *hallel*, meaning "to praise."

7. *Shiggaion:* a term which means "to wander" and has been interpreted as referring to a wild, ecstatic tune. It occurs one time only.

Titles Referring to the Musical Setting or Performance

Numerous titles appear to identify either the tune to which a psalm was to be sung or something significant about the musical setting or performance. Fifty-five different psalms begin with the notation: "to the chief musician" or "to the precentor." Titles such as *alamoth* and *sheminith* appear to refer to the musical pitch. Other titles clearly refer to particular kinds of instruments that were to be used in accompaniment. *Gittith* may refer either to an instrument or to a tune from the Philistine city of Gath. Many titles which appear to refer to the musical setting are totally obscure and are likely to remain so.

Titles Related to Authorship

Several of the psalms are associated with the names of individuals. Such titles have frequently been translated to indicate authorship. However, from the standpoint of Hebrew grammar and syntax, such is not necessarily the case. For example, the title to Psalm 3 begins by saying, "A Psalm of David." The Hebrew expression can be legitimately translated in several different ways. (1) It can be properly understood as "A Psalm by David." (2) It can just as legitimately be translated "A Psalm dedicated to David" or "about David." (3) It can further be translated "A Psalm in David's style" or "after the manner of David." The point is simply that the title by itself does not give any specific indication as to the actual authorship of the psalm.

Of the psalms associated with names of individuals, David occurs seventy-three times, Asaph occurs twelve times,

Solomon is used two times, and Heman, Ethan, and Moses occur one time each. In addition, the sons of Korah, probably referring to a Levitical choir, occurs eleven times in titles.

Psalms Related to Occasion

Several psalm titles also attempt to give the historical occasion which called forth the original writing of the psalm. For example, Psalm 3 states: "A Psalm of David, when he fled from Absalom his son." Further, Psalm 51 is entitled: "A Psalm of David, when Nathan the Prophet came to him, after he had gone in to Bathsheba." Since these titles were added long after the writing of the psalms themselves, they may be of questionable historical value. Further, since the title may not be ascribing authorship, these titles may be indicating a dedication to David with those specific historical backgrounds being the setting which the psalmist was writing about.

However, it should be obvious that too quick a rejection of the value of these titles is not wise either. Granting that the Hebrews were careful in preserving ancient traditions, whether oral or written, these titles may be setting forth the actual original setting of the psalm.

The Value of Psalm Titles

All of this brings us to the basic issue of precisely what the value of the psalms' titles is for the contemporary student. At the very least, they reflect what was believed about the psalms at the time of their final compilation and editing. At the most, they could be assumed to be historically valid in establishing the basis for the writing of the psalms. They clearly reflect the usage of the psalms in the history of Hebrew worship and music. But not all psalms had titles. No satisfactory reason has been found to explain why some psalms had titles while others did not. Those psalms which did not have titles were called "orphan psalms" by ancient rabbis.

One final item concerning the study of psalm titles should be noted. J. W. Thirtle, in a study of psalm titles based upon the Psalm of Habakkuk (Hab. 3), pointed out that this was the only psalm in the Old Testament which is set off by itself. That psalm opens with the words: "A prayer of Habakkuk the prophet, according to Shigionoth." It ends with the words: "To the choirmaster: with stringed instruments." This made Thirtle conclude that, in general, literary information was placed at the beginning of a psalm while exclusively musical comments were placed at the end. Though this conclusion has not been accepted by all interpreters, it does appear to offer a solution to some problems. Among these is the title to Psalm 88 which, as it stands, actually appears to be attributed both to the sons of Korah and to Heman. If the first part of this title were actually the conclusion to Psalm 87, the problem would no longer exist.

The Forms of the Psalms

As might be suspected from the very nature of poetry, Old Testament form critics have identified a number of clearly recognizable forms in the Psalter. In addition, numerous psalms also show evidence of being composites, made up of parts of two or more different forms. The major forms have been given the following classifications.

Hymns of Praise

These basically focus upon the adoration of God. They usually begin with an introductory call to worship where the intention to praise God is set forth. This is followed by a statement of reasons for praising God. The psalm is usually concluded with a repetition of the call to worship or a call to praise, which is often an expansion of the initial call to worship.

Psalms of Thanksgiving

These usually differ from the hymns of praise in that they are based upon the need to express gratitude to God for specific blessings granted. They normally begin with the offering of praise or with a statement setting forth the intent to praise God. Then comes a description of past difficulties or troubles which is accompanied by a description of how God sent relief from those troubles. The conclusion is a public declaration of gratitude to God for His acts of relief.

Psalms of Lament

A major dimension of Hebrew worship was lament, something which is left out of much modern worship, in spite of the fact that many people come to worship with a deep sense of hurt or agony. The laments are normally set in the *qinah* beat and are divided between individual laments and corporate or community laments. The community laments are usually less structured. Most laments begin with an opening plea for deliverance addressed to God. This is followed by some kind of description of life's troubles, along with a confession of trust in God. Then is set forth an appeal for deliverance with a promise or commitment to praise God when the deliverance came.

Royal Psalms

These psalms are not as tightly bound by structure as they are by content. They normally relate to some experience in the lives of Israel's kings. However, because of the kingly imagery found in them, they were readily acceptable to presenting Israel's messianic hope.

Liturgical Psalms

These psalms were obviously designed for public reading (or singing), usually in an antiphonal manner, and were apparently a regular part of Israel's public worship. In addition to antiphonal responses, they were also frequently structured around a series of questions and answers, with the priests and the congregation taking the two parts.

Psalms of Confidence

These psalms are quite similar to the confidence section of the psalms of lament. They are identifiable by their strong affirmation of personal confidence and trust in God. Most Christians find their favorite psalms in this category.

Wisdom Psalms

These psalms are usually identified by the short, pithy sayings similar to those found in the Book of Proverbs. They are further identified by the fact that their concerns are those normally shared by the wisdom movement and its literature. They are particularly concerned with the issues of retribution and reward, as well as with the constant problem of the prosperity of the wicked.

Mixed Types

Many of the psalms are of mixed types, not wholly fitting into one category or another. Specific parts of such psalms can be identified with one of the categories, but other parts fit other categories. Identifying individual forms can be of help in interpretation.

Technical Matters in Psalm Study

Several terms need to be defined to help the student read commentaries on the psalms with better understanding. *Selah* is a Hebrew word which occurs frequently within the psalms. It should normally not be read aloud because it was a notation to the singers and the musicians. It appears to have meant "pause." We are not sure whether it was an instruction to the singers to pause for a musical interlude or whether it instructed the musicians to pause, allowing the singers to proceed unaccompanied. It may have suggested that there be a long rest for both singers and musicians in order to allow the hearers an opportunity to ponder what had just been sung.

Stichos is a term applied to a line of Hebrew poetry with *stichoi* being the plural form. One part of a two-part line is usually called a *distich* and one part of a three-part line is called a *tristich*. What we normally would identify as a stanza or a verse is called a *strophe*.

Approaches to Psalm Study

Interpreters have made several different approaches to the study of the psalms. These have had varying degrees of success in helping to open the understanding to the message of this great literature.

One of the older and earlier approaches can be characterized as the "Davidic historization" approach. This assumes that all of the psalms were originally written by David, and the attempt is made to find an event in David's life which might have served as the background for each psalm. This appears to have been done, at least to some extent, by those who added the titles to the psalms. However, the approach is of dubious validity. First of all, if the seventy-three titles which connect individual psalms to David were attributing authorship (and that is doubtful, as we have seen), that still leaves numerous psalms attributed to other persons and a large number with no specific attribution. Second, we know so little of David's life, even if all seventy-three of the "Davidic" psalms were by him, we would always be on doubtful ground in identifying specific events as the bases for particular psalms.

Another quite ancient approach to psalm study, at least for Christians, has been to see in all the psalms (or at least, most of them) predictive references to the life of Jesus. This has been called the "Christological" approach. Without question, several of the psalms add significant detail to the messianic hope of the Old Testament. It is also without question that the Spirit of God led the early Christians to see numerous references to Christ in the psalms. However, at the very best, this is still quite limited insofar as the content of the entire Psalter is concerned. Such an approach is far too limited in its perspective to be an adequate tool for interpreting all of the psalms.

The third approach to the study of the psalms has been that of "historization in Israel's life." This approach seeks to recognize the fact that many of the psalms, if not all, sprang from historical faith experiences in the ongoing history of Israel. Such an approach seeks to identify a specific historical event or experience in Israel's life which gave rise to each psalm. It is no more satisfactory than taking a hymnal and trying to identify the specific historical event which called forth each hymn in it. Unless we have some knowledge of the actual writing of a hymn, we cannot make such a determination merely by reading the hymn itself. The very fruitlessness of such an approach can be seen by the fact that those who tried this approach have not been able to agree with one another on the historical background of each psalm. If the approach were valid, it would yield similar results when applied by different interpreters.

Each of these approaches may be of some value in determining the possible background of various psalms. They seem to be quite limited, however, in any attempt to understand the larger collection of psalms. Two other approaches appear to have been more fruitful.

The form-critical or worship-centered approach appears to offer a better understanding of the Psalter. This recognizes the fact that the psalms were used in Israel's worship. They were a part of the festivals, the great national celebrations as well as the times of private worship. This approach seeks not so much to determine what called the psalm forth in the first place as to identify how it was used by the people of Israel in its normal *Sitz-im-Leben*. Just as today people use hymns because of what they mean to the worshiper at that moment, not because of the event which called them forth, so it is assumed that these ancient hymns were used in a like manner. This approach seeks to focus upon what the worshipers were saying when they used a psalm. Such an approach appears to make the psalms far more meaningful and helps contemporary readers to more easily understand them. Further, such an approach recognizes the fact that the psalms are basically timeless; they speak to and from the hearts of worshipers of all ages and places.

Closely related to this is what I choose to call the "theological" or "faith-centered" approach. The Book of Psalms was the hymnbook of the ancient Hebrews. It was treasured by them because it expressed their faith in words which became more meaningful with every repetition. Thus as we come to grips with the basic faith which is expressed by the Psalter, we have come face to face with the basic faith of those ancient people. This was not merely God's revelation, it was Israel's faith proclamation. Some interpreters believe it is possible to study the whole of Israel's faith or theology from the psalms themselves. It is also this fact, that here we have the faith of the ancient people of God, that makes the psalms live in the hearts of today's people of God. Their very timeless proclamation make them easier to understand in all generations and in a variety of cultures.

The Content of the Psalms

Obviously any attempt to outline the Book of Psalms as a whole would be as fruitless as trying to outline a modern hymnal. Modern hymnals do sometimes collect hymns under specific general headings. The Book of Psalms does not even appear to do this. However, in order to try to get an introductory grasp of the content of the Psalter, I am going to identify some of the basic themes or subjects which are treated there. While I will not try to place every psalm under a particular heading, I will direct you to representative psalms in each category.

Psalms of Faith and Confidence

Three of the more significant psalms of this category are 23, 27, and 46. The twenty-third Psalm is probably the most familiar psalm. This great statement of utmost confidence in God has made its way into the world's treasury of great literature. There are few words which have become precious as,

> The Lord is my shepherd,
> I shall not want (v.1).

Further, one of the more graphic expressions of trust in God's love and care is found in the words,

> Surely goodness and mercy shall pursue me
> all the days of my life (v.6; author's
> translation).

Sharing equally as great a confidence, but less familiar, are the words of Psalm 27:

> The Lord is my light and my salvation;
>> whom shall I fear?
> The Lord is the stronghold of my life;
>> of whom shall I be afraid? (v.1).

The psalmists, however, were secure not only in the presence and power of God but also in His redemptive nature. The recurring refrain of Psalm 46 boldly states: "the God of Jacob is our refuge" (vv. 7,11). Jacob was the supreme Old Testament example of a confidence man and a smooth-talking scoundrel. Yet God had taken that man, transformed him, and turned him into the great patriarch of Israel. The psalmist found hope in the belief that the God who could use a man like Jacob could use him also.

Psalms of God and Nature

Perhaps the supreme example of the praise which the psalms expressed to God in regard to His majesty and beneficence as seen in the world of nature is Psalm 104. It sets forth God's greatness and His genuine care for all things of the earth. Further, the psalmist recognized that all of the world of nature is dependent upon God.

> These all look to thee,
>> to give them their food in due season (v. 27).

Because of God's care for nature, the people could also shout:

> I will sing to the Lord as long as I live;
> I will sing praise to my God while I have
> being (v.33).

Psalms of Praise to the Creator

Closely related to the psalms of God and nature are those which specifically focus upon Him as Creator. Two of the more familiar of these are Psalms 8 and 19. In Psalm 8 Israel praised God for His creation of mankind. The psalmist was overwhelmed by the awesomeness of the universe and the insignificance of man in comparison. At the same time, he acknowledged the even more overwhelming fact that God has honored mankind as the crown of His creation.

> When I look at thy heavens, the work of thy fingers,
>   the moon and the stars which thou hast established;
> what is man that thou are mindful of him,
>   and the son of man that thou dost care for him?
> Yet thou hast made him little less than God
>   and dost crown him with glory and honor.
> Thou hast given him dominion over the works of thy
>   hands;
>   and hast put all things under his feet (8:3-6).

Psalm 19, on the other hand, offers praise to God for an orderly universe, controlled by law. The psalmist found a basis for praise in the orderliness of natural creation. A basis for praise was also found in the law of God by which life is governed. This may be somewhat strange to us who see law as an infringement of freedom. To the ancient Hebrews, law made life livable and was one of God's good gifts; worthy of praise was God's law which brought the gift of life to Israel.

Psalms Praising God's Mighty Acts

God's acts of creation and sustenance in the world of nature can clearly be called might acts. However, I use this particular classification to refer to God's mighty acts in history. These show up regularly throughout the psalms, but the two psalms wholly devoted to His great acts in history are 78 and 105. At first glance, it might appear strange that anyone would wish to sing about history. However, Christians find great joy in singing about the crucifixion, the resurrection, and Jesus' birth, as well as other less significant events in His life. These are historical events through which God revealed Himself in mighty acts. To the people of Israel, events centered around the Exodus and the entry into Canaan, as well as other great events, were of no less significance. Through those acts God demonstrated His loving choice of them as His people. Thus these songs were not so much songs of history as they were songs of redemptive love at work. They sang of these

> so that they should set their hope in God,
>   and not forget the works of God,

but keep his commandments;
and that they should not be like their fathers,
    a stubborn and rebellious generation,
a generation whose heart was not steadfast,
whose spirit was not faithful to God (78:7-8).

Psalms of Exuberant Praise

Because of God's great acts, His sustaining grace and
mercy, His continual presence and comfort, the psalmists
also led Israel to burst forth in exuberant praise. Many
psalms can be found with this basic theme. Two of the more
familiar are 100 and 103. The constant undercurrent of the
entire Psalter can be summed up in the words:

Bless the Lord, O my soul;
    and all that is within me,
    bless his holy name!
Bless the Lord, O my soul,
    and forget not all his benefits,
who forgives all your iniquity,
    who heals all your diseases,
who redeems your life from the Pit,
    who crowns you with steadfast love and mercy,
who satisfies you with good as long as you live
    so that your youth is renewed like the eagle's (103:1-5).

The basic theme of these psalms was a call to praise God
with song, dance, service, and all of life.

Psalms of Anguish

As noted, lament was a major part of Israel's worship.
They recognized that frequently a sense of deep hurt either
led people to God or drove them there. These hurts sprang
from a variety of causes, as they still do. Psalm 22 sets forth
the utter agony of being alone, isolated from companions
and from God. Jesus found here a cry of dereliction which
He uttered from the cross. "My God, my God, why hast thou
forsaken me?" (v.1; Mark 15:34). Yet even that psalm of
agony ends with the assurance that God is still sovereign
and will ultimately be victorious, "For dominion belongs to
the Lord and he rules over the nations" (v.28).

The psalmists were also grieved when they were prevented from joining in corporate worship, crying out,

> As a hart longs for flowing streams,
>   so longs my soul for thee, O God.
> My soul thirsts for God, for the living God.
> When shall I come and behold the face of God? (42:1-2).

Perhaps the greatest agony of the human heart, however, was found in the crisis of guilt. The memorable fifty-first Psalm shares this grief across the years and the cultures.

> Have mercy on me, O God,
>   according to they steadfast love;
> according to thy abundant mercy
>   blot out my transgressions (v.1).

The ultimate need for cleansing is most vividly expressed.

> Create in me a clean heart, O God,
>   and put a new and right spirit within me.
> Restore to me the joy of thy salvation,
>   and uphold me with a willing spirit (vv. 10,12).

Among the psalms of lament, however, some are quite striking to those who seek to live by the Christian ethics of love and forgiveness. For example, the harshness of the psalmist's pleas for vengeance in Psalm 109 has become a stumbling block to many. These were written long before the time of Jesus. If Christians have a difficult time living by Jesus' teachings of love, how much more difficult was it for these ancients who had never known Him to forgive their enemies? Further, human nature frequently cries out for vengeance. The psalmists recognized that anger and hatred are a part of the hurts which humanity shares and that these hurts need to be taken to God.

Psalms of Practical Wisdom

The wisdom movement of the ancient Near East seems to have been designed to find out what went into "the good life." Israel developed such a movement, but with one major difference. That difference was God. To Israel, whatever went into the good life, it had to be lived in the presence of God. Israel's Wisdom movement permeated all of its national life. Numerous psalms focus upon the issues of practical wisdom as it related to the good life.

The very first psalm is one such, directing attention to the nature of a godly life.

> Blessed is the man
>> who walks not in the counsel of the wicked,
> nor stands in the way of sinners,
>> nor sits in the seat of scoffers;
> but his delight is in the law of the Lord,
> and on his law he meditates day and night (1:1-2).

Here is vividly portrayed the way into sin, as one progressed through the verbs: "walks" . . . "stands" . . . "sits." The way to avoid such a descent is plainly to be found by delighting in God's way, a life characterized by regular, habitual study of it.

These psalms just as vividly contrast the way of the fool, who says in his heart: "There is no God" (14:1). In contrast, we are shown the character of those who are able to enter into the presence of God. The life of the godly man is described in Psalm 15 by a series of brief characterizations which ultimately gave a firm foundation to life.

Such psalms also deal with the issues of good and evil, with a special emphasis upon the question of why the wicked seem to prosper. After grappling with such a question, the psalmist finally found an answer.

> But when I thought how to understand this,
>> it seemed to me a wearisome task,
> until I went into the sanctuary of God;
>> then I perceived their end (73:16-17).

The answers to ultimate issues of human wisdom were to be found in the presence of God. To the Hebrews, this was worth singing about.

Psalms of Kingship

The Hebrews also found something worth singing about in the divine care of their human king. These psalms show their glimpses of the ultimate revelation of great David's greater Son, the One who would ultimately be *the* King. For the psalmists, God was sovereign and, thus, His king would reign under His protection until He Himself would be revealed as the King of Kings. Some of these psalms rather obviously refer to the human king, such as Psalm 2. On the other hand, others just as clearly go beyond that dimension, such as Psalm 110. Here the hope was firmly established which later bore fruit in the Epistle to the Hebrews uniting the King with the Priest, after the order of Melchizedek.

Psalms of Crises and Great Moments

The final category of psalms gathers to itself those psalms which do not fit anywhere else. Here is Psalm 32, a psalm of great personal forgiveness. Out of the overwhelming joy of being forgiven, the psalmist sang forth:

> Blessed is he whose transgression is forgiven,
> whose sin is covered.
> Blessed is the man to whom the Lord imputes no iniquity,
> and in whose spirit there is no deceit (32:1-2).
> I acknowledged my sin to thee,
> and I did not hide my iniquity;
> I said, "I will confess my transgressions to the Lord";
> then thou didst forgive the guilt of my sin (v.5).

Further, the psalmists rejoiced at the great moments of national worship, when the Hebrews gathered from all over the land to worship and praise their God.

> I was glad when they said to me,
> "Let us go to the house of the Lord!"
> Our feet have been standing
> within your gates, O Jerusalem! (122:1-2).

At these times, the national identity was most strongly felt and the people's allegiance to the Temple was most visible. At the same time, they had no illusions about their relationship to God. He did not belong to them; they belonged to him and were and were His stewards of the land and the world. They were reminded quite bluntly by God of this fact.

> Every beast of the forest is mine,
>   the cattle on a thousand hills.
> I know all the birds of the air,
>   and all that moves in the field is mine.
> If I were hungry, I would not tell you;
>   for the world and all that is in it is mine (50:10-12).

The surrounding nations believed that their gods could not survive without their worship and their sacrifices. In Israel it was not to be so. God did not need them. It was they who needed Him! That is a lesson we still need to learn.

The Faith of the Psalms

As noted, the psalms set forth the basic faith of the Hebrew people. God and man are the two basic focal points to that faith. These were the two inescapable realities. A religion which loses sight of either has failed to meet human needs. Their ancient faith also had two basic emphases: human need and divine providence. They were overwhelmingly aware that the plight of humanity was quite desperate as they faced the problems of sin, guilt, and evil. They were equally certain that God was sovereign, His purposes were good, and He would ultimately be victorious. The consequences of the divine sovereignty brought to the hearts and the lips of the Hebrews both praise and thanksgiving. They praised God for what He was and thanked Him for what He had done.

Finally, the faith of the psalmists can be characterized as having four dimensions. They always looked back to the past, to God's great acts of creation and more especially to His great acts of redemption and deliverance. In the present dimension of their faith, they were aware that God was with them, even when they did not "feel" His presence. Where they were, He was. Because of what God had done and because of their present experience with Him, they could look forward to being in His presence in their future. This gave them hope. The fourth dimension to the faith of the psalmists was timelessness. Their faith transcended time and speaks to the hearts of all people everywhere. This makes the Book of Psalms a universal favorite among people. Wherever we are in our spiritual pilgrimage, we can find psalms which express our inmost thoughts, our greatest hopes, and our utmost certainties.

36

Issues in Old Testament Wisdom

Most biblical students are familiar with several divisions of ancient Israelite society—generally the priests and Levites, the prophets, and the kings. Very few beginning students are familiar with that group which has come to be known as the wise men or with their movement which is called the Wisdom movement. Yet this group seems to go back to the very earliest days of Israel. Moses associated with himself in leadership position, "wise, understanding, and experienced men" (Deut. 1:13; cf. v. 15). Joab used a "wise woman" in seeking to get David to accept Absalom back into the court (2 Sam. 14:2). David had wise men as advisers in his court (1 Chron. 27:32). Some interpreters justifiably suggest that these are only descriptive phrases and do not apply to a specific class of people in Israel. With Solomon, however, the situation is more clear. He is identified as a wise man who was a collector and author of proverbs, whose fame as a wise man went throughout his world (1 Kings 4:32-34).

By the time of Jeremiah, the category of "wise man" had become a technical term, referring to a specific class of people in the same way the priests and prophets were specific classes of people. At that time, the people asserted, "Come, let us make plots against Jeremiah, for the law shall not perish from the priest, nor counsel from the wise, nor the word from the prophet" (Jer. 18:18). Further, it appears that in some instances at least, scribes were equated with wise men (Jer. 8:8-9). Finally, the Book of Job gives a vivid description of what a wise man was expected to be in Israel (Job. 29:7-22).

461

Definitions

Two definitions need to be clearly understood. (1) A *wise man* or a *wise woman* in Israel (or in the ancient Near East, for that matter) was one who had seriously pondered what was necessary to have "the good life" and, based upon his or her experience as well as being founded upon the experience of the ages, arrived at conclusions. They were not necessarily religious or cultic officials but were people who influenced their people through thought and intellect. (2) The *Wisdom movement* was that group of wise people in any age and of all ages who passed on the gathered wisdom of others. They were in a real sense the philosophers of their people, teaching and sharing the distilled wisdom of the ages. They passed their wisdom on through writing as well as teaching.

Wisdom in the Ancient Near East

The Wisdom movement was not a phenomenon limited to Israel. It was present in every culture from which we have literature. We have such materials from Egypt dating early in the twenty-fifth century BC and from Mesopotamia only shortly thereafter. The Bible itself shows a significant awareness of the wisdom movements of the nations contemporaneous with Israel. Sisera's mother counseled with her wise women in Canaan during the time of the judges (Judg. 5:29). Both Jeremiah and Obadiah reflect knowledge of Edom as a center of ancient wisdom (Jer. 49:7; Obad. 8), a fact which is well-attested throughout the ancient Near East. Further, Babylon also had a major wisdom movement as is clearly reflected in the Book of Daniel (Dan. 2:2, 13; 5:7,8).

Basically, these wisdom movements present us with an abundance of materials for study. This should not be surprising, for many of the wise men were numbered among the people who were able to write. That ability alone made it more likely that their materials should be recorded and should survive. The materials which do survive lead us to conclude that the wisdom movement generally reflected two kinds of approaches to their subject: prudential and reflective. Prudential material is usually made up of short, pithy sayings based upon the common experience of mankind. These are normally identified as proverbs. The reflective materials are more often the carefully thought-out philosophies of the ancients, generally dealing with the issues of suffering, justice, death, and the good life.

The Wisdom Movement in Israel

The Wisdom movement in Israel was in many ways quite similar, if not identical, to that of the ancient Near East. Its concerns were the same and its methods were also similar. This is only to be expected, as the basic concerns and issues of life are the same for people regardless of nationality, culture, or era. Furthermore, even as the concerns are the same, so the forms in which the thoughts are recorded are similar, sometimes with identical words. The Hebrew Wisdom movement primarily recorded its ideas in proverbs or in more reflective poems or essays. The wise men also frequently communicated their truths in riddles (Judg. 14:14) or in fables (Judg. 9:7-21). Their primary concern was that a person be wise rather than a fool. Folly was a quality of life to be avoided at all costs.

The Hebrew Wisdom movement made a major impact upon the Old Testament. This can be clearly seen by the literature readily identifiable as Wisdom. First, entire books can be recognized as Wisdom materials: Job, Proverbs, and Ecclesiastes. Further, both the Song of Solomon and Lamentations show much evidence of being Wisdom material, if not entirely so. Second, many psalms show significant evidence of being the product of the Wisdom movement. Third, a great deal of the prophets' preaching appears to have been influenced by wisdom. Fourth, even the Former Prophets show the influence of Hebrew wisdom in numerous places.

Hebrew wisdom is similar to that of the ancient Near East. In fact, it would be surprising if there were no similarity. However, a major difference does exist between the Wisdom movement of Israel and that of the ancient Near East.

That difference can be focused in the fact that Hebrew Wisdom material is found in the canon of the Old Testament Scriptures. To the Hebrew wise person, the basic definition of the good life was different. In Israel, the good life was a life lived in relation with God. The recurring refrain, "The fear of the Lord is the beginning of wisdom" (Prov. 1:7; 9:10) is clear evidence of this. Numerous statements similar to this also occur, emphasizing the faith basis for the good life. It is possible that "the fear of the Lord" refers not so much to awe or reverence as to the actual authoritative Word of God. If this is so, then the basis for the good life is even more precisely defined as being a life based upon God's revelation. Further, we dare not forget that, even when the Wisdom Literature does not directly refer to God, it is still a part of the canon. That fact by itself makes us deal with this material from a faith perspective. First and foremost, Hebrew Wisdom material is religious, not secular. Every other facet of it hinges upon this fact.

Wisdom in the New Testament

The influence of Hebrew wisdom can also be significantly seen in the New Testament. It is first felt through literary references. Even more, it can also be seen in the teachings of Jesus. In a very real sense, the Sermon on the Mount (Matt. 5:1 to 7:27) is far more closely related to the Wisdom movement's teaching methods than to the prophets' preaching. Jesus' relationship to His disciples is also quite similar to that of a wise man to his followers. The Christian community has long recognized in Jesus the ultimate fulfillment of the Old Testament ideals of prophet, priest, and king. This is clearly correct. But we need also to see in Him the fulfillment of the ideal wise man of the Old Testament. He is the Sage above all sages.

37
Job

The Book of Job is unique both in the Bible and among the world's literature. It is unique in form, content, and literary quality. As far as literature is concerned, no book in the Bible has made as significant an impact upon the world. It has captured the imagination of many of the world's great writers, regardless of their own particular literary interests or accomplishments. Whether the interpreter be Martin Luther as a theologian, Alfred Lord Tennyson as a poet, or Fedor Dostoevski as a novelist, they have universally acclaimed the Book of Job a literary masterpiece. It has truly been called the literary mountain peak of the Old Testament.

The book reaches out across the centuries and across the barriers of race and culture to touch the hearts and minds of contemporary readers. It is not sufficient to say that the work is technically excellent from a literary standpoint. It also captures the imagination of those who read it. This is due to its exceptional dimensions. It has the dimension of height, uplifting its readers onto the sublime plateau that brings us near to the eternal stars and the God who made them. It has the dimension of breadth, a spacious universal nature that transcends the barriers of creed, color, rank, and race. Finally, it has the dimension of depth, probing deeply into the soul of humanity where surge the profoundest needs and anxieties of the heart.

The Structure of the Book

No other book of the Bible is so highly stylized as is Job. It begins with a prose prologue (1:1 to 2:13) where the scene shifts back and forth from heaven to earth. This is followed by a long poetic section where the main drama is presented. This involves two complete dialogues between Job and each of his three friends in turn (3:1 to 14:22; 15:1 to 21:34). A final dialogue is quite abbreviated, containing only a very short speech from one of Job's friends and no word from another (22:1 to 27:22). This dialogue is followed by Job's meditation upon the nature of true wisdom (28:1-28) and a soliloquy setting forth Job's final defense (29:1 to 31:40).

At this point, a younger bystander speaks up, addressing both Job and his friends (32:1 to 37:24). Finally, when human wisdom has said all it can think of, God intervenes with two speeches which are followed by a speech of submission by Job (38:1 to 42:6). The book is brought to its ultimate conclusion with a prose epilogue (42:7-17).

From beginning to end, the careful planning of the book and its clearly developed pattern of thought show evidence of the literary creativity of its human author. The evidence of its divine inspiration is also felt throughout. The very carefully worked out plot has been studied by writers of many ages as a basis for their approach to creative writing.

The language of the book appears to be a relatively late Hebrew, at least in its poetic passages. It also contains a number of Aramaic words. The vocabulary is quite varied, using many words found nowhere else in the Old Testament. The text itself offers numerous problems to both translator and interpreter. The LXX text is significantly shorter than the MT, containing about four hundred verses less.

The Nature of the Book

Even a very hurried reading of the book reveals that it is of a very diverse literary character. It is clearly Wisdom Literature, dealing with those issues which were of major interest to the Wisdom movement and doing so in forms that were characteristic of wisdom. As noted above, the book has two brief prose sections with a major poetic section sandwiched between. Within this larger division can be found narrative stories, drama, epic poetry, laments, instruction, debate, proverbs, and dialogue. However, identifying these parts does not bring us any closer to identifying the literary nature of the book as a whole.

It has been interpreted as being nothing more than literal history. It has also been interpreted as being purely the literary figment of some author's imagination, inspired by God to communicate His truth. In addition, other suggestions have been made which appear to lie somewhere between these two extremes. Seeking to identify the literary nature of the book has nothing directly to do with the matter of its divine inspiration. It is a part of the Old Testament canon and as such fits under its rubric of inspired Scripture. However, for one who believes that God can only inspire history, the entire question is moot: It must be history. On the other hand, for those who believe that God can inspire any kind of literature He pleases, the issue is of significance.

Those who do not believe that the book is literal history point to the following reasons as the basis for their conclusion. (1) The scenes in heaven are clearly outside the realm of history. (2) The use of the significant numbers of seven, three, and multiples of ten in describing Job's family and his possessions are not likely to have happened in precisely that arrangement. Statistics would normally be expected to have more variety. (3) Human conversation does not normally take place in the ordered, stately fashion as that depicted of Job and his three friends. (4) The conversation of people does not normally occur in exalted poetry. (5) The similarity between the story of Job and those found in other ancient Near Eastern literature makes it likely that the story is the development of a common theme found in the region.

Those who support Job's literal historicity point out that the heavenly scenes could have been revealed by God. Further, the fact that numbers do not normally occur in so limited a selection or that conversations do not normally occur this way are no indication that they couldn't or didn't. Finally, the fact of the existence of similar stories has no direct bearing upon whether or not these events actually occured.

The interpreters who see this work as essentially or exclusively a literary work and not a record of actual events point to the careful plan and highly structured nature of the book. They suggest that this is normally the evidence of the planning of an author. An author has the liberty of arranging events so that they can all happen just in the way that is wished in order to communicate the message needed. Opponents of this approach point out that being abnormal or unusual does not make something impossible. They also point out that the reference of Ezekiel to Job indicates that he actually lived and that the story is literal history (Ezek. 14:14,20). However, the supporters of this view note that Ezekiel's reference could have been to the literary character rather than to a historical figure. Further, they also suggest that even if Job actually lived, this does not necessarily mean that this narrative is historical.

I think the ultimate solution lies somewhere between these two extremes. No sufficient reasons exist to deny that Job lived, endured catastrophe and suffering, faced these problems with unsympathetic friends, and eventually came through them sustained by God. The book does appear to be a literary treatment of a basic story under the inspiration of God. This ancient story was apparently chosen as the vehicle by which and through which God could deal with some of the basic problems of humanity which were confronting the Hebrew Wisdom movement.

The book has been described as an epic poem, an ancient Hebrew drama, or simply a major literary work. Others have noted that to call it an epic poem ignores the fact that the prologue and epilogue both are in prose. The opponents of the drama classification note that the earliest confirmed use of Hebrew drama occurred in the second century BC. While that may be true, it would not be true if the Book of Job was a drama. Hebrew drama had to begin sometime. This may have been the first attempt at such a production. If it were a first attempt, it was clearly a masterpiece. Nothing which followed it in Hebrew literature ever lived up to this one.

For my purposes, I conclude that the book is based upon

a series of historical events whereby an ancient worthy, Job, suffered personal catastrophe. This story was used by the inspired author as the foundation for a magnificent drama whereby he communicated God's truths to His people and ultimately to us. I view the book as a drama based upon history, speaking to the common problems of humanity and the deepest concerns of people of all times and races.

Date and Unity of the Book

As usual, the issues of the date and unity of the Book of Job are as involved with one another as they are in most other books. Since no mention is made of the Hebrew people or of the nation of Israel, the setting of the book has been variously interpreted as being in the patriarchal times before Israel existed or in the exilic times after the kingdom had come to an end. The descriptions of Job, his family, and his possessions seem to fit well into the times of the patriarchs. Further, the fact that Job offered his own sacrifices clearly sounds more like the times before the existence of a formal sacrificial system and a highly organized priesthood.

However, establishing the date of the setting of the drama does not necessarily help us identify the date of its final writing. Most commentators date the final writing of the book in the time of Solomon or in the exilic period, although some would date it near the end of the period of the kingdom, probably in the late seventh century BC. The reasons for dating it in Solomon's time rest upon the rise of the Wisdom movement at that time and the book's basic universality. Both qualities appear to have been characteristic of Solomon's reign. Those who date it as exilic point to the fact that its concerns and its teachings fit in better with that time than any other in Hebrew history. The glimpses of immortality certainly made no impact upon Hebrew thinking if it were preexilic. This late date would also explain its lack of emphasis upon the nation of Israel. Further, the use of some Aramaic terms and much late Hebrew would seem to support this conclusion.

Those who date the book near the end of the kingdom appear to be merely seeking a compromise with the other two views without much evidence to support such a conclusion. Regardless of the date assigned, the arguments upon which such a conclusion is based are more stylistic and theological than concrete. Such arguments are almost always precarious. The date of its final editing, however, clearly does not preclude that some of the content may be quite early.

Related to the issues of date are the issues of unity. No major section of the book has escaped question by the students of the book. Due to the fact that the prologue and epilogue are in prose while the rest of the book is poetry, some commentators have suggested that these were not an original part of the book. Others have suggested that these were all that was originally there, with the poetic parts being added later. Yet others, dealing with the same issues, suggest that the prologue may have originally been there with the epilogue not having been original, since it appears to reverse the entire basis for the book. The arguments based upon its literary structure (prose-poetry-prose) just do not stand up to examination. This kind of symmetrical arrangement is found in the ancient law code of Hammurabi (poetry-prose-poetry). It is also found in a linguistic nature in the biblical Book of Daniel (Hebrew-Aramaic-Hebrew). Further, we must admit the restoration of Job's fortunes in the epilogue do not fit in well with the idea of trusting God no matter what happens as set forth in the Yahweh speeches. On the other hand, for God to be just, the restoration was necessary since Job's agony had come as the result of a test permitted by God.

The next major section questioned by commentators is the third cycle of speeches (22:1 to 27:22). The particular problem here is not a matter of unity but the issue of the very short speech of Bildad and the missing speech of Zophar. Some commentators have assumed that somehow the text got confused in the passage of time. They have sought to reconstruct these missing speeches from other materials in Job which they believe appear to be out of place. It seems far more likely that this modification was in itself a dramatic instrument for indicating that the arguments of the friends had been useless and that they had actually run out of anything more to say.

Job's speech on wisdom (28:1-28) has also been viewed by numerous interpreters as an insertion that was not a part of the original work. Admittedly, it adds nothing to the basic consideration of the drama. On the other hand, the entire drama to this point has demonstrated the futility and emptiness of human wisdom. It appears that the author was fearful that his audience might become so disenchanted with human wisdom that they might assume it was utterly worthless. This chapter on wisdom appears to be an affirmation that real wisdom has value but that it comes from God, not from man.

The Elihu speeches (32:1 to 37:24) have also frequently been denied to the original work. More people have attacked these than any other part of the book. Some see them as an intrusion into the developing drama. They are said to add nothing. Further, some interpreters suggest that no other part of the book makes any references to them. It is possible that they were added later and are an intrusion into the drama. On the other hand, others have noted that the speeches appear to sum up the main points that had been made before this and thus set the stage for the Yahweh speeches. Whether they were by the original author or were added by a later editor, they are obviously a part of the inspired text as we have received it.

The second Yahweh speech (40:15 to 41:34) has also been attacked as not really belonging to the story, merely repeating what had already been said in the first one. Such an attack ignores the traditional approach in the ancient Near East of repeating things for emphasis. The very basic nature of Hebrew poetry is built upon this fact. There is little basis for denying this section to the original author.

The Content

Interpreters have generally suggested that the Book of Job was written to answer the question: Why do the innocent suffer? If this were the purpose, it failed thoroughly. I find it difficult to believe that God would inspire any book to answer a question without answering it. Further, although Job is referred to in James as being patient or steadfast (5:11), it does not appear that the major theme of the book focuses upon these ideas. Rather, it appears that the book explores (without solving) the various aspects of suffering, especially as it relates to those who are righteous. Further, it has a major emphasis directed upon what happens to the faith of a person (or a nation) who has all the forms of religion without much depth when suffering comes. Its basic message appears to be that people will never wholly understand the problems of suffering. That being so, they are called upon to walk with God in trust for His presence and in His wisdom. He will sustain.

    I. Prologue (1:1 to 2:13)
       A. Job introduced (1:1-5)
       B. The first crisis (1:6-22)
          1.   The heavenly court (1:6-12)
          2.   Job loses property and family (1:13-19)
          3.   Job reacts to his tragedy (1:20-22)
       C. The second crisis (2:1-8)
          1.   The heavenly court (2:1-6)
          2.   Job loses his health (2:7)
          3.   Job reacts to his illness (2:8)
       D. The third crisis (2:9-10)
       E. The friends of Job come to comfort (2:11-13)

In setting the stage for the rest of the drama, the prologue describes Job as a man of deep piety, blameless and upright, one fearing God, and departing from evil (1:1,8). However, there is also a possible hint of superficiality in his faith, for he took upon himself the religious obligations of his children (v.5). This may indicate that he viewed the act of sacrifice as sufficient, without any real commitment on the part of the sinner. Be that as it may, it is clear that Job was seeking to live a life of piety in spite of his wealth.

Satan is also introduced. Here he is a part of the heavenly council, serving as a sort of divine inquisitor into the lives of humankind. His very name means "Adversary," and this is precisely what he is, the adversary of God's human creatures. Satan is portrayed as having access to the heavenly court and as being a part of the heavenly council.

When Job passed the first test of his faith, Satan proposed a second onslaught. Even here Job did not fall victim spiritually to the physical attack. The third attack came from his wife. It may have been an unintentional attack, but it was no less real. Her words, "Curse God, and die" (2:9), have generally been understood as evidence that she had lost her faith and was seeking to lead Job to turn against the God who would have allowed such injustices to happen. However, she may have been urging Job to end his misery by committing spiritual suicide through cursing God. This may have been her cry of agony, seeking to help her husband escape from his misery through death.

Job still did not overtly sin in his response to the suffering he was enduring. But the biblical writer appears to be hinting that his attitude was changing. When we are told that "Job did not sin with his lips" (2:10), we may be seeing a hint that something was changing in Job's heart.

At this point, Job's three friends are introduced. They were truly coming to sympathize with him. When they saw his suffering, they sat down and entered into it with him. Such a time was not a time for words but a time for silence. They were ministering to him through their presence.

II. The main drama: Job's integrity on trial (3:1 to 31:40)
   A. Job's death wish (3:1-26)
   B. The first dialogue: what is God like? (4:1 to 14:22)
      1. Eliphaz: Job needs to repent (4:1 to 5:27)
      2. Job's response: his fate is undeserved (6:1 to 7:21)
      3. Bildad: Job is a heretic (8:1-22)
      4. Job: God has used power wrongly (9:1 to 10:22)
      5. Zophar: Job is foolish (11:1-20)
      6. Job: a glimpse of hope which fades into despair (12:1 to 14:22)

Job's death wish leaped forth from his lips as a protest against all that had happened to him. He was saying that since life made no sense why should he live at all? The popular theology of Job's day, like that in ours, insisted that blessing came as the result of goodness and trouble as a consequence of sin. Job's experience was telling him that this was simply not necessarily so. One of the most beautiful descriptions of death in all the world's literature is found in 3:12-19.

As Job's three friends began to speak, we can identify with each of them. Eliphaz appears to be the oldest. He was more philosophical than the other two and was clearly more courteous and considerate than they. At the same time, he showed a total lack of understanding of Job's problem. His whole approach was based upon the idea that no innocent person would ever suffer. Thus he concluded from the obvious fact of Job's suffering that he had to be guilty of sin. He urged Job openly to confess his hidden sins, knowing that then God would relieve him. It appears throughout that Eliphaz was more concerned with the logic of his position that with helping Job. In response, Job lashed out at God's injustice (6:8-13) and at his friends' failure to comprehend his situation (vv.14-30).

Bildad responded that Job was speaking heresy. Anyone who dared to disagree with the popular and ancient theology had to be a heretic. Bildad has been characterized as the traditional theologian, so sure of his answers that he never questioned the possibility that he might be wrong. For him, the wisdom of the past was better than that of the present. Present experience would never change his understanding of past traditions. Job again lashed out at God, accusing Him of the misuse and abuse of His power.

At this point, Zophar spoke up, accusing Job of speaking as a fool. Zophar can be characterized as the ultra-orthodox copyist. He had nothing original to say, merely quoting what other had said to him. Unfortunately, like so many others, when he had nothing to say, he said it quite loudly.

Job lashed out at the arrogant pride of his three friends:

> No doubt you are the people,
>> and wisdom will die with you (12:2).

His anger was increased because he knew his own experience and it did not fit into their theology.

> I have understanding as well as you;
>> I am not inferior to you;
> Who does not know such things as these? (12:3).
> Lo, my eye has seen all this,
>> my ear has heard and understood it.
> What you know, I also know;
>> I am not inferior to you.
> But I would speak to the Almighty,
>> and I desire to argue my case with God (13:1-3).

At this point, Job began to have a glimpse of the fact that if life went on after death, there would be a time and a place for everything to be made right (14:7-17). Having glimpsed the truth, his hope faded away into despair.

> But the mountain falls and crumbles away,
>> and the rock is removed from its place;
> the waters wear away the stones;
>> the torrents wash away the soil of the earth;
>> so thou destroyest the hope of man (vv.18-19).

Their popular theology had no hope for a life after death, and Job was not yet ready to comprehend God's great revelation.

C. The second dialogue: what happens to the wicked? (15:1 to 21:34)
  1. Eliphaz: Job needs to repent (15:1-35)
  2. Job, worn out, waits to die (16:1 to 17:16)
  3. Bildad: Job cannot escape from the trap of his evil (18:1-21)
  4. Job's only hope is God (19:1-29)
  5. Zophar proclaims a great irrelevance (20:1-29)
  6. Job: no ultimate justice in this life (21:1-34)

  D. The third dialogue: what has Job done? (22:1 to
   27:23)
   1. Eliphaz: Job must make peace with God
    (22:1-30)
   2. Job: God is absent (23:1 to 24:25)
   3. Bildad's final, feeble attack (25:1-6)
   4. Job's summary of his arguments (26:1 to
    27:23)

In the second dialogue, the friends had little new to say. Job,
on the other hand, came ever closer to the truth that there
is more to life than what happens on earth. He obviously
was quite aware that he was grasping for some great new
revelation from God.

> Oh, that my words were written!
> Oh that they were inscribed in a book!
>
> ....
>
> For I know that my Redeemer lives,
> and at last he will stand upon the earth;
> and after my skin has been thus destroyed,
> then from my flesh I shall see God,
> whom I shall see on my side,
> and my eyes shall behold, and not another (19:23-27).

But although he momentarily seized upon this magnificent
truth, so great was Job's enslavement to his past beliefs that
he could not hold on to this great new truth, he plunged
back into the pit of despair (23:1-17).

  III. Job's mediation (28:1 to 31:40)
   A. On the nature of true wisdom (28:1-28)
   B. On his final defense (29:1 to 31:40)
    1. Remembrance of the happy past (29:1-25)
    2. The overwhelming grief of the present
     (30:1-31)
    3. His final plea of integrity (31:1-40)

In a magnificent mediation upon wisdom, Job realized that
neither from the past nor from the present comes genuine
wisdom. True wisdom comes only from God (28:28). That is
something that no wise man of any other nation would ever

have said. Hebrew wisdom ultimately found its source in
God. Job at this point still had no answer. But he knew that
his friends did not have the answer either.

   IV. The Elihu speeches (32:1 to 37:24)
   V. The Yahweh speeches (38:1 to 42:6)
   VI. The epilogue: restoration (42:7-17)

A young man who had apparently been standing by
throughout the dialogue spoke up. Job had silenced his
friends, but it was left to Elihu to silence Job. No one hears
God when they are speaking. Elihu at least made an effort
to deal with Job's arguments. He had been listening to what
Job had said. He did not assume that Job was a sinner
worthy of such suffering. But he clearly did assume that Job
had misunderstood God. The basic point he made was that
God would not debate with Job, but He would speak with
him. Foundational to this was that Job must first listen
clearly to what God had said in the past before he would be
ready to hear God in the future. Further, he pointed out
that from the midst of his suffering Job had only seen the
bad and had forgotten or overlooked the good. Basically,
however, Elihu's theology did not differ much from that of
the three friends. His dramatic purpose was to get Job to be
quiet so that he could hear God speak. He did point out that
God was not indifferent to Job's suffering.

   Following that, God spoke to Job from the gathering
storm. Job and his friends had all insisted that they knew
the truth. God neither dealt with the problem of evil nor
attempted to justify His ways to Job. He did force Job to
acknowledge how little he knew about anything. He forced
Job to face and admit his own ignorance. God did not accuse
Job of crimes, He simply exposed his attitude as foolish. God
challenged Job, that if he were going to stand in judgment
upon God he should act like God. Obviously, Job could not
do this. He was forced to admit that he had been speaking
from his own ignorance.

   In response to God's confrontation, Job finally acknowledged his own limitations, saying,

> I have uttered what I did not understand,
>> things too wonderful for me, which I did not know
>>> (42:3).

He also confessed that his past relationship with God had been based simply upon what he had heard about God. Job's new faith was based upon a personal experience with God.

> I had heard of thee by the hearing of the ear,
>> but now my eye sees thee;
> therefore I despise myself,
>> and repent in dust and ashes (vv.5-6).

A final warning was sounded in the book against those who become bound by the traditions of the past or the popular theology which has never come to grips with the real nature of God. The three friends were bluntly told, "You have not spoken of me what is right" (42:7).

In this magnificent book, we find a much larger and more profound understanding of God than we normally see in the Old Testament. Further, there is at least a clarification of the idea that all suffering had to be the result of sin. That just was not and is not so. In addition, the concept of man is one of the highest in the Old Testament. Man could ascend to the heights with God when he accepted the wisdom of God, the source of all wisdom. The book stands as a severe judgment upon traditional views that suffering was the result of sin. But it was not merely the idea of suffering which was on trial, it was the whole concept of traditional theology which was on trial. It failed. Traditional, popular theology did not measure up to the revelation of God or the experience of man. Finally, it was seen that suffering could lead a person into a richer and more profound relationship with God.

38
Proverbs

The title of the Book of Proverbs comes from the Hebrew word *mashal* which basically means "to be like." It would appear that it was originally applied to those short, pithy sayings which indicated similarity between various human experiences. However, by the time of the period of the Hebrew kingdoms it has clearly come to refer to any sort of short, wise saying. From this it grew to include any kind of wisdom material. The date by which this transition was complete is impossible to establish with our present knowledge. It has been suggested that it was not finished until the time of the Exile. On the other hand, the transition in the meaning of *mashal* may have occured even prior to the time of Solomon.

Unity and Date

In order to establish the date of the writing of the book, we must first address the issue of its unity. The book is clearly divided into the following sections.

I. An essay praising and identifying Wisdom (1:1 to 9:18)
II. A collection of short proverbs attributed to Solomon (10:1 to 22:16)
III. Two collections of teachings from the wise (22:17 to 24:34)
IV. Additional proverbs attributed to Solomon (25:1 to 29:27)
V. Proverbs attributed to Agur (30:1-33)
VI. Proverbs attributed to Lemuel (31:1-9)

VII. An acrostic poem on the nature of the ideal woman
(31:10-31)

Section II, the major collection of proverbs, is attributed to Solomon (10:1 to 22:16) and is made up of 375 proverbs. Most of these are in short, two-line statements with the exception of 19:7. The first part of this block appears to be essentially made up of contrasting couplets, written in the antithetic style of Hebrew poetry. These are primarily found in 10:1 to 15:33. Such an approach emphasized the truth being presented by restating it from the opposite standpoint.

> A false balance is an abomination to the Lord,
>   but a just weight is his delight (11:1).
> A wise son hears his father's instruction,
>   but a scoffer does not listen to rebuke (13:1).

The second half of this major section turned away from this type of parallelism, using synthetic and synonymous parallelism. Synonymous parallelism is where the second line repeats the thought of the first in different words. Synthetic parallelism is where the second line completes the thought of the first. Synonymous parallelism:

> An evildoer listens to wicked lips;
>   and a liar gives heed to a mischievous tongue (17:4).

Synthetic parallelism:

> A fool takes no pleasure in understanding,
>   but only in expressing his opinion (18:2).

Interpreters have not been able to identify any logical arrangement for the proverbs in this section. They essentially deal with practical observations about the nature of daily life. There is little which can be specifically identified as religious. However, we dare not ignore the fact that this material was included as a part of the Hebrew Bible, obviously reflecting their belief that the whole of life must be lived in the presence of and at the direction of God.

Most scholars generally agree that this unit is the oldest

man regularly collected writings based on their teacher's works and attributed them to him in an attempt to honor him. Numerous interpreters have suggested that many proverbs may have come from later wise men who attributed them to Solomon. On the other hand, knowing how ancient the entire near Eastern wisdom movement is and acknowledging the fact that Solomon from the earliest times was considered to be the epitome of a Hebrew wise man, there is little reason not to accept the tradition that this unit came essentially from Solomon and his court, where such matters were collected (1 Kings 4:29-34).

Section IV is an additional collection of proverbs attributed to Solomon (25:1 to 29:27). These, however, are said to have been edited or perhaps collected by "the men of Hezekiah king of Judah" (25:1). This statement is normally assumed to be accurate, thus dating this collection to the end of the eighth century BC. These proverbs are generally longer than those in the earlier section. This may indicate that they have been enlarged over the passing years. However, no significant doubt has been raised to their essential Solomonic origin. The issues with which these proverbs deal are basically the same as those in section II.

The proverbs in 22:17 to 24:34 are generally assumed to be a separate section. The title is expressed by the opening words:

> Incline your ear, and hear the words of the wise,
> and apply your mind to my knowledge (22:17).

That this is the title appears to be confirmed by a second title found near the end:

> These also are the sayings of the wise (24:23).

These proverbs are longer than those attributed to Solomon, usually being made up of two or more verses. Further, frequently proverbs related to similar subjects are gathered together in subsections.

Numerous commentators have pointed out the remarkable similarity that exists between 22:17 to 23:14 and the Egyptian Proverbs of Amen-em-ope. The Egyptian source is now usually dated around 1000 BC. Debate has long raged as to which collection influenced the other. The general consensus is that the Egyptian material was the original but that the Hebrew material has been molded by long usage to fit the nature of Israelite life as being essentially lived in the presence of God. If this conclusion is correct, it would not be the first time that God had inspired His writers to find truth among the things He had revealed to others. In any case, it has clearly become God's revelation to Israel and to her successors. No reason has been found requiring a date for this material later than the earlier times of the Hebrew kingdoms, and possibly even in the time of Solomon.

No one has yet identified Agur, his father Jakeh, or Lemuel, the producers of sections V and VI (30:1-33; 31:1-9). They are all identified as being a part of the tribe of Massa. This tribe is said to have been descended from Ishmael and probably settled in the northern part of Arabia, being nomads (Gen. 25:14). No satisfactory evidence has been found to help us arrive at a date for this material. The emphasis upon the qualities of a good king in 31:1-9 make it likely that these were written at a time when the Hebrew kings were being seen to have fallen short of the divine ideal. However, this could have happened as early as the latter days of Solomon's reign.

If the identification of Massa is correct, the inclusion of this material in the Hebrew Bible is just one more evidence of the universal character of wisdom. It is also another indication that the inspired writers had no qualms at including truths from other places through which God spoke to them.

The last section of the book is a highly structured poem on the nature of a virtuous woman (31:10-31). It was written as an acrostic poem, each line beginning with the next letter of the Hebrew alphabet. This kind of structure was apparently a late development in Hebrew poetry and literature. The poem serves as an admirable conclusion to a book which focused its attention upon the nature and qualities of life lived in the presence of God.

Wholly different from the rest of the book is the first section (1:1 to 9:18). This is a long essay on the nature of wisdom, set in the form of a teacher addressing his pupil. The pupil is called "son" by his master, indicating something of the intimacy which existed in such pupil-teacher relationships.

Because of the differing structure and nature of the material, for a long time it was assumed that this material had to be quite late in Hebrew history. However, most scholars now acknowledge that a significant relationship exists between this material and some ancient Ugaritic and Phoenician literature. Since that material is all demonstrably pre-Israelite, there is no longer any significant reason for not dating this into the reign of Solomon. Those who conclude that this is later than Solomon see 1:1-7 as being the title to the entire book and not to this section, as such. However there is no legitimate reason for denying this to Solomon and his wise men. Almost certainly, the original composition was reworded in later times, perhaps even by the men of Hezekiah.

The most significant feature of this section is the personification of wisdom (8:1-36). Wisdom is pictured as a woman, calling God's people to learn her ways. She is described as having been God's assistant in creation (v.30). While this is a far cry from the clear revelation of the other two Persons of the Trinity (Son, Holy Spirit) in the New Testament, yet it was clearly a step in the preparation for that ultimate revelation of the nature of God.

The Content of the Book

Other than the identification of the major sections, it is almost impossible to outline Proverbs. The basic concerns of the book are those which are involved in living the good life. The major emphasis directs attention to the ultimate contrasts between a wise person and a fool. Folly is to be avoided at all costs. Numerous terms are used in Proverbs to describe the various kinds of folly to be avoided. Among the major ones are those of the self-confident fool, the outrageous fool, the misguided fool, the unintelligent fool, the naive fool, the scorner, and the brutish man. The emphasis upon folly is intended to show the pupil the things to be avoided if one would lead the good life. Wisdom leads one away from all kinds of folly.

This approach is further strengthened by contrasting the things which either lead one into folly or are the result of folly with those things which are the product of wise choices. These contrasts can be found between laziness and industry, between drunkenness and sobriety, between evil and righteousness, between praise and humility, between extravagance and thrift.

Interpreters have frequently pointed out that the motives generally given for living the good life are less than those encouraged by the New Testament. The emphasis frequently appears to be placed upon being good because it pays off in prosperity. However, as long as the Hebrews did not have the fully developed New Testament understanding of life after death, it was logical that a just God had to make things right in this life. Only as the hope for a life after death began to be revealed were they able to lift their vision from this world to the next.

On the other hand, we must not let this distract us from the ongoing emphasis that

> The fear of the Lord is the beginning of knowledge;
> fools despise wisdom and instruction (1:7).

One's relationship to God was the basis for wisdom and righteousness. Further, numerous proverbs call people to an ethical standard which was not motivated by profit but simply by the desire to be good, as God expected. Finally, the New Testament writers quoted frequently from Proverbs, a clear indication that its level of revelation is not nearly as antiquated as some would have us believe.

39

The Megilloth
Ruth, The Song of Songs,
Ecclesiastes, Lamentations,
and Esther

Among the Writings is a collection of five books known as the Megilloth, a Hebrew title which simply means "Rolls" or "The Scrolls." The five short books which make up this collection were read at five major Jewish festivals or fasts. The books and the festivals with which they were associated are:

> Song of Songs—Passover
> Ruth—Pentecost
> Lamentations—Fast on the ninth of Ab
> Ecclesiastes—Tabernacles
> Esther—Purim

No one of these books bears any specific relationship to another except for the fact that they are a part of the Megilloth and are, therefore, a part of the Writings.

Ruth

The Literary Nature of Ruth

Almost all commentators from all areas of theological persuasion agree that this little book is one of the masterpieces of the world's literature. The story has heart appeal, focusing upon personal tragedy with ultimate victory, and is bound together by numerous themes of selfless and devoted love. Its basic purpose appears to be the proclamation of the overarching sovereign love of God, who works in human lives even when the people do not know Him and are unaware of His working.

The date of the writing of the book has been disputed,

being set in the period of the judges by some, by others in the period of the Hebrew monarchy, and by still others in the postexilic period following Ezra and Nehemiah. Although the historical setting is clearly in the period of the judges, the reasons for placing its writing later are significant. (1) In the Hebrew canon, Ruth is among the Writings, the last portion of the canon. (2) Customs which were commonly practiced in the time of the judges have to be explained, as if they have long been abandoned. (3) Several Aramaisms appear in the style of the author. (4) The nature of life as portrayed in Ruth is serene and peaceful, while life as actually reflected in Judges was anything but serene. (5) Its basic message best met the needs of the postexilic community, with Naomi representing the returning exiles, Boaz representing the people who had been left behind, and Ruth representing the foreigners who came along with the exiles. As these three had produced Obed and ultimately David, so the three groups could be used by a loving God to establish His new kingdom of peace.

On the other hand, the evidence is not all clear. (1) The book may have not been canonized until the Writings, due to its sanction of foreign marriages. (2) The style of Ruth is more similar to that of 1 and 2 Samuel than to that of any other part of the Bible. (3) The explanation of earlier practices could be a later scribal comment to explain something that had long been abandoned. (4) The serene environment could have been true in Bethlehem for some part of the period of the judges.

Evidence for the monarchical period does not seem to deal with these problems any better than the two extreme suggestions. It appears rather to be an attempt to simply reach a compromise, which really solves nothing.

The Content of the Book

I. The sojourn in Moab (1:1-5)

During a time of famine, the family of Elimelech and Naomi moved to Moab, where their two sons married foreign wives,

Ruth and Orpah. During their ten-year sojourn, the two sons and Elimelech died.

II. The return to Bethlehem (1:6-22)

When Naomi started to return home, she urged both daughters-in-law to remain behind. It took a second urging before Orpah did so, but Ruth's words of commitment stand among the greatest declarations of loving fidelity the world has known:

> Entreat me not to leave you or to return from following you; for where you go I will go, and where you lodge I will lodge; your people shall be my people, and your God my God; where you die I will die, and there I will be buried (1:16-17).

When they arrived back at Bethlehem, Naomi protested her bitterness and emptiness to her neighbors, not recognizing that Ruth was there to sustain her.

III. The struggle with poverty (2:1-23)

The days of Ruth and Naomi were beset by intense struggle, but Ruth worked hard as a gleaner to maintain life. In her gleaning, she was befriended by Boaz, whose eye her beauty and gentle faithfulness had attracted.

IV. Ruth's boldness and redemption (3:1 to 4:12)

In Israel, there was a practice called Levirate marriage (cf. Deut. 25:5-10). If a man died without a male heir, it was the responsibility of the nearest of kin to marry the deceased's widow and the first male child was considered to be the legal heir to the deceased. Thus a man "lived on" in Israel, and his inheritance was not lost to his family. The responsibility of the nearest of kin also included buying or redeeming the property of an impoverished or deceased person to keep it within the family. At Naomi's suggestion, Ruth boldly went to Boaz to lay her claim before him. It was an act of faith, for she could either have been abused or rejected. Neither happened. Boaz acknowledged responsibility but had to deal with a nearer kinsman first. Of great human interest is the fact that Boaz did not allow the other man to see Ruth.

Instead, after laying the matter of the property before him, Boaz added, almost as an afterthought, that marriage with a foreigner went along with the deal. At that the man turned his responsibility over to Boaz. Thus Boaz and Ruth were married.

V. The line of David (4:13-22)

The fruit of the marriage of Ruth and Boaz was a son, Obed. He turned out to be the grandfather of Israel's greatest king, David. He also turned out to be the ancestor of great David's greater Son, Jesus. Thus God demonstrated His sovereignty through human love. Further, a lesson, which ought to have been remembered but wasn't, was presented in that "foreign" blood was introduced into the line of David. That which others might consider foreign or pagan, God through His love used to accomplish His purposes of redemption.

The Song of Songs

The title, "The Song of Songs" is taken from the first verse of the book. It is also known as "Canticles," from the Vulgate, and has frequently been simply called "The Song of Solomon," also based upon the first verse. The book had great difficulty being accepted into the canon, primarily because of its erotic nature. However, this objection was finally overcome, due primarily to its connection with Solomon's name and to its allegorical interpretations by both Jewish and Christian interpreters.

The Unity, Date, and Nature of the Book

The issues of unity, date, and literary nature of the book are all tied together. The book has been interpreted as all coming directly from Solomon. If this were correct, it establishes both the unity and the date. However, a close reading of the book reveals that he is mentioned in only two passages, other than the title verse (1:5; 3:7-11). The setting is obviously the time of Solomon, but he seems to appear only incidentally as background, rather than as a central figure.

At the other extreme, some interpreters see this book simply as a collection of unrelated love songs, compiled late in the postexilic period. The reasons given for this are its use of some Persian and Greek loan words and its steady use of the relative pronoun, a definite characteristic of late Hebrew.

The absence of historical references make any accurate dating quite difficult, but we can search for a time when its theme might have been important. That appears best found in the time when the Hebrew people were having trouble with the prurient appeal of Baal worship. This could be a response to that time of the monarchy, setting forth the beautiful side of sexual love, but without its degrading tendencies toward apostasy. If its original compilation or writing is to be set in that time, its final editing almost certainly must be found in the postexilic era.

Rather than see the book as a simple collection of love songs, another possibility is to see it as essentially a forerunner of musical drama. It apparently is the story of the love between a Shulemite maiden and a shepherd boy. While waiting for him, she falls asleep and dreams that she is taken to be a part of the harem of Solomon. Her dismay at this is dispelled when her sweetheart arrives and wakens her from her dream.

Interpretations of the Book

The rabbis had trouble with the erotic nature of the book and sought to escape it by viewing the book as an allegory of the love between God and Israel. Christian writers have had the same problem, frequently trying to avoid it by allegorizing the book into a story of the love between Christ and His church. Unfortunately, such interpretations have been wholly unsatisfactory. Any inquisitive schoolboy or schoolgirl has seen what their parents have often refused to see, the book is a story of the beauty of human love. Sexual love is one of God's gifts to His people. Used within His intent, it is beautiful. We should rejoice that God inspired His writers to sing of its wonder.

The Content of the Book

I. Title verse (1:1)

The title verse may attribute authorship to the great king, but the Hebrew expression can also be translated as a dedication: "which is for Solomon"; or as a notation: "which is in the style of Solomon." Either of these two translations is far more likely than the traditional one.

II. Act 1: the maiden waits for her sweetheart (1:2 to 2:17)

While waiting for the shepherd, she sleeps and dreams of his love for her and thinks about herself as attractive to him. At one point, she starts up excitedly, thinking she hears him coming (2:8), but she is wrong, and waits further.

III. Act 2: she sleeps and dreams (3:1 to 4:15)

She dreams of searching for her sweetheart, then thinks she awakes as Solomon's entourage passes by and she is taken to be a part of the harem.

IV. Act 3: her sweetheart comes, and she awakes (4:16 to 8:14)

Her sweetheart arrives, and she awakes to discover that she had not been carried away from him. They rejoice in one another's presence and love.

Ecclesiastes

The Hebrew title of the book is *Koheleth,* taken from its opening verse. The Greek and Latin translation of this have given us *Ecclesiastes,* the translation of the Hebrew title. The word seems to mean "one who assembles a congregation," apparently for the purpose of preaching to it. Thus many modern translations simply call the book "The Preacher."

Nature of the Book

Ecclesiastes is another book which had great difficulty being accepted into the canon. The rabbis debated its authority due to its humanistic, cynical perspective and its apparent contradictions. Christian writers debated its place in the canon until well into the fourth century AD for the same reasons. But while the religious leaders debated, the people had accepted it; it spoke precisely to their predicament, which is nothing if it is not human, occasionally leading to skepticism and cynicism, and often filled with contradictions. Often lay people are more sensitive to the truth than religious leaders.

The book has been much abused by interpreters who have sought to make something out of it which it is not. Clyde Francisco recognized that it was an informal essay about the highest good. The very nature of an informal essay is that it holds up various ideas to the light of experience (and in this case, revelation), casting aside those things which do not survive the examination.

As such, then, an essay is not necessarily a logical treatise (though the more formal ones may be). More often, such an approach reflects the confusion that is experienced in any life. No one of us lives logically. Therefore, to try to excise those parts of the book which do not fit into the logical development is to miss the very nature of the book itself.

Authorship and Date

Although Solomon appears to be the central speaker of the book, from the time of Luther interpreters have doubted that he was the author. The reasons for this are as follows. (1) Solomon is not mentioned anywhere in the book, with only infrequent allusions to the king or the son of David. (2) The references to "all who were over Jerusalem before me" would indicate a later time than Solomon (1:16; cf. 2:9). (3) The Hebrew language style and vocabulary is quite late. (4) It reflects a highly developed Wisdom movement, not one in its infancy. (5) The serious questions which are raised about life and faith point to a postexilic time, when such questions were being raised.

In general, most interpreters from all theological positions now date the book in the postexilic period, sometime between 400 and 200 BC. The unknown author adopted

Solomon as his speaker for the literary effect, primarily since Solomon's life-style of despotic abundance, characterized by excesses of all kinds, was the kind of life he was seeking to examine.

Any serious thought will point out the truth that the speaker or central character of any literary work is not necessarily the author. Further, the author does not even bother to carry this figure beyond the early part of the book.

The Content of the Book

The book holds up to the light of examination the conventional wisdom of the day. Seeking to point out that, while the intelligent man can raise questions about what God is doing and what life is like, the wise man recognizes that the ways of God are ultimately beyond the understanding of man and that people cannot sit in judgment upon God.

    I. Setting and theme: all is emptiness (1:1-3)
   II. Theme as seen in life (1:4 to 2:26)
       A. In everyday life (1:4-11)
       B. In the pursuit of wisdom (1:12-18)
       C. In the pursuit of pleasure (2:1-11)
       D. In the ultimate end of life (2:12-17)
       E. In labor (2:18-23)
       F. Conclusion: life must be enjoyed daily as it comes from God (2:24-26)
  III. A second analysis of the themes (3:1 to 5:12)
       A. Everything has its time (3:1-15)
       B. Death comes to all (3:16-22)
       C. The prevalence of oppressions (4:1-3)
       D. Greed which drives the amassing of wealth (4:4-12)
       E. Popularity (4:13-16)
       F. Conclusions: worship God properly and do not expect too much from life (5:1-12)
   IV. Third analysis of the theme (5:13 to 8:9)
       A. Lost wealth (5:13-20)
       B. Unenjoyed wealth (6:1-9)
       C. Empty life (6:10-12)

D. Conclusion: avoid extremes (7:1 to 8:9)
V. Fourth analysis of the theme (8:10 to 12:8)
  A. Injustice in legal systems (8:10-15)
  B. The inscrutability of God (8:16-17)
  C. The common element of death (9:1-10)
  D. Life's uncertainties (9:11-12)
  E. Conclusion: live life as it comes (9:13 to 12:8)
VI. Final conclusion (12:9-14)

Anyone who has thought seriously about life as it is and people as we are, will find much in Ecclesiastes with which to identify. Experience is seldom idyllic and often quite inexplicable. At the same time, the really wise man does not ultimately lean upon his own wisdom. The man of faith comes to the point where he proclaims: "The end of the matter; all has been heard. Fear God, and keep His commandments; for this is the whole duty of man" (12:13).

One of the most beautiful allegorical descriptions of the coming of age is found in 12:1-8. Anyone who observes those growing old around him or who faces the prospect of the oncoming frailty of age can recognize the emotions which prompted this and can identify with its descriptions.

Lamentations

Lamentations is usually found third in the books of the Megilloth in the Hebrew Bible, although this is not always the case. Its primary use in Judaism was at the annual feast held on the ninth of Ab (mid- to late July) to mourn the destruction of Solomon's Temple.

Authorship and Date

The versions have attributed the book to Jeremiah, based upon a late Jewish tradition. However, the authorship is quite uncertain, with many reasons being offered for its having come from someone other than the great prophet of Judah's last days. It is hard to conceive of Jeremiah standing around grieving when his book indicates that he was still calling his people to repentance. His grief would have been real, but his main message was always a call to turn back to God. Further, the poetry of Lamentations is quite studied and carefully planned. Jeremiah's poetry reflects far more spontaneity. The book is made up of five laments over the fate of Jerusalem. The fact that the *'ayin* and *pe'* letters in the acrostic are in a different order in chapters 2, 3, and 4 than the normal order of the alphabet, and different from that found in chapter 1, has led some to suggest that at least chapter 1 was by a different author than the rest. Chapter 1 may have been done at Babylon's first invasion in 597 BC, that the next three chapters came immediately after the destruction of Jerusalem in 586 BC, and that the final chapter was written later during the Exile. The book was likely written in Judah, rather than in Babylon, for it is difficult to conceive of anyone in Babylon saying, "her prophets obtain no vision from the Lord" (2:9) during the time of the main period of Ezekiel's ministry in Babylon. Some have suggested that chapter 3 may be the last chapter written since it is so personal, but that is not a necessary conclusion.

The Nature of the Book

The book is a series of five funeral laments or dirges over the destruction of Jerusalem. The first four are alphabetic acrostics, with each verse beginning with a letter of the Hebrew alphabet in order. Chapter 3 is a triple acrostic, with three verses beginning with a letter before the author moved on to the next one. As noted, the letters *'ayin* and *pe'* are reversed in the middle three chapters. The final chapter, while not an acrostic, has the proper number of verses, twenty-two. All suggestions that it, too, was originally an acrostic which has become confused in transmission have failed to offer any conclusive evidence to support this.

The *qinah* measure of Hebrew poetry is the main one used in the book. This had the same effect on the ancient Hebrews that playing music in a minor key does on contemporary Western people. It produced a mood of extreme grief and sadness. The purpose of using the acrostic form was to say that the grief was so all encompassing that every letter of the alphabet could be used to describe it.

The Content of the Book

Outlining the Book of Lamentations is like trying to outline a hymn book when all the hymns deal with the same subject. The author held his grief up to view, examining it like a diamond. Yet, in the midst of his overwhelming grief, he was also sure of the goodness and mercy of God.

> This I call to mind,
>   and therefore I have hope:
> The steadfast love of the Lord never ceases,
>   his mercies never come to an end;
> they are new every morning;
>   great is thy faithfulness (3:21-23).

Further, his ultimate assurance was that God is still sovereign. Jerusalem had been destroyed. The people of Judah were in exile,

> But thou, O Lord, dost reign forever;
>   thy throne endures to all generations (5:19).

With that kind of faith and hope, grief can be endured.

Esther

Each of the five books of the Megilloth present their own distinct problems. However, those involving Esther appear to be more difficult to solve than any of the others. Although numerous minor problems have been raised over the book, three stand out as a major significance.

The Problem of the Absence of the Name of God

The most striking feature of the book is that neither the name *Yahweh* nor any word for God appears in the Hebrew text. Considering the fact that the book is in the Bible and is, thus, considered to be a part of the revelation of God, this is extremely startling. Other books in the Old Testament focus upon the relationship between people and God. Even those which appear to be most secular, such as The Song of Songs or Ecclesiastes, include references to God. This one almost appears as if it had been carefully censored so that the name did not appear. Because of the omission of the divine name, it was one of the last books officially included in the Old Testament canon. One suggestion is that the name was left out due to the fact that the book was written during the Maccabean era, a time when the gulf between God and humankind was viewed as so great that the author was afraid even to refer to Him. That appears unlikely since numerous other books written in that time contain God's name. However, the book is read at the Feast of Purim, one of the most boisterous festivals in Judaism. It has been suggested that the divine name was left out lest sacrilege occur by referring to it at such times. While not wholly satisfactory, this may be the best suggestion.

The Problem of the Jewish Revenge

In retaliation for the violent anti-Semitic purge which had been planned against the Jews, they were allowed to defend themselves and to strike back. They did so with exuberant violence. In fact Esther asked for an extra day to continue the violence (cf. 9:1-15). Anyone who has been a victim of human atrocities can at least understand the very human desire for vengeance. However, even the Old Testament declares that vengeance is God's prerogative alone (Deut. 32:35). The book has come to be treasured by Jews who have endured great persecution in any age. Christians realize that it is a long way from the New Testament ethic of Jesus.

The Problem of Historicity

One of the major issues raised about Esther is whether it actually happened. No such queen as Vashti or Esther is found anywhere in the Persian histories. Neither is there any record of such a slaughter as that recorded in the book. But this story is presented with no indication that it was anything other than history.

Scholars are almost universally agreed that the Ahasuerus of Esther is the Hebrew name of King Xerxes I of Persia, who reigned about 485 to 464 BC. Numerous details of the Persian court given in the book do fit well with what we know of royal life at that time. Further, a recent document lists a Persian official whose name was quite similar to Mordecai. It is possible that neither Vashti nor Esther was the official queen but were the chief wives of the harem. The absence of any records of such sweeping vengeance in Persia is more serious, but arguments from silence are always dangerous. It does appear that the book clearly has a historical core. Whatever the ultimate decision, again we must face the fact that the book is a part of the inspired Word of God and must be treated as such.

Authorship and Date of Writing

The authorship of the book is clearly anonymous. The book could not have been written before the reign of Xerxes I and, thus, must be no earlier than about 464 BC, although this is by no means certain. It does appear to have been written quite a long time after the events it purports to record. It may have been one of the last books of the Old Testament written. There is little doubt that it is a single literary work, done by one author.

The Content of the Book

The book is essentially a narrative, telling of anti-Semitism at its worst and pointing out the excesses to which unleashed vengeance can lead.

   I. Esther's rise to queenship (1:1 to 2:13)
     A. The king's banquet (1:1-12)
     B. Vashti deposed (1:13-22)
     C. The search for a new queen (2:1-4)
     D. Mordecai and Esther introduced (2:5-7)
     E. Esther brought to the harem (2:8-11)
     F. Esther made queen (2:12-18)
     G. Mordecai saves the king's life (2:19-23)
  II. Haman's intrigue against the Jews (3:1 to 5:14)
     A. Haman's advancement to premiership (3:1-2a)
     B. Haman's hatred kindled against Mordecai and the Jews (3:2b-6)
     C. The edict against the Jews (3:7-15)
     D. Esther committed to intercede (4:1-17)

    E. Esther's intercession begun (5:1-8)

    F. Haman's hatred intensified (5:9-14)

  III. Esther's success (6:1 to 8:17)

    A. The king remembers his debt to Mordecai (6:1-3)

    B. Haman's mortification (6:4-13)

    C. Esther's request of the king (6:14 to 7:4)

    D. Haman's execution (7:5-10)

    E. Mordecai's elevation to Haman's place (8:1-2)

    F. The edict to save the Jews (8:3-14)

    G. The Jewish rejoicing (8:15-17)

  IV. The Jewish victory (9:1 to 10:3)

    A. The slaughter of the Jews' enemies (9:1-10)

    B. The time of vengeance extended (9:11-16)

    C. A Jewish celebration of deliverance (9:17-32)

    D. Mordecai's place in the kingdom (10:1-3)

For all of its gruesomeness, the story of Esther has some beautiful points. Mordecai's awareness of the providence of God as he appealed to Esther for help is a monument of such teachings: "For if you keep silence at such a time as this, relief and deliverance will rise for the Jews from another quarter. . . . And who knows whether you have come to the kingdom for such a time as this?" (4:14).

On the other hand, Esther's courageous response to her uncle's appeal is just as striking. Facing the ultimate possibilities of her decision she replied: "I will go to the king, though it is against the law; and if I perish, I perish" (4:16). Without our knowledge, God can and does bring us to critical times, where we alone can make a difference in ultimate outcomes. At those times, we, as God's people, need to have the kind of dedication which will allow us to take the ultimate stand, regardless of the outcome.

40

Apocalyptic Literature: Daniel

Introduction

One of the least familiar, least understood, and most abused kinds of literature in the Bible is apocalyptic literature. This is true of both the Old and the New Testaments. The term *apocalyptic* comes from a Greek word *apokalupsis*, which means the "unveiling," "uncovering," or "revelation." It is the first word in the last book of the Bible, where it is normally translated as "the revelation." The strange thing about this title is that most interpreters approach it as being the exact opposite of its meaning. Instead of being understood as a kind of literature designed to reveal or unveil something, it has normally been understood as making things more difficult to understand.

The Characteristics of Apocalyptic Literature

Only two full-blown apocalypses exist in the Bible: Daniel in the Old Testament and Revelation in the New. However, in both Testaments sections of individual books have been identified as having apocalyptic characteristics or as being "little apocalypses."

Several other apocalypses were produced by both Jewish and Christian writers which did not find their way into the canon of the Scriptures. As we study both the biblical and the nonbiblical apocalypses, several distinctive characteristics set this kind of literature apart from others.

Eschatalogical. The main emphasis of apocalyptic literature is almost always on the "end time." Its focus is upon the catastrophic events which precede and introduce the

499

end of the ages. On the surface, its attention seems to be directed to those things involved in the last events of world history as the final victory of God over evil takes place and His ultimate kingdom is introduced.

Dualistic. Apocalyptic literature is profoundly dualistic, giving graphic and vivid descriptions of the power of evil, of Satan (or the devil), of his cohorts, and of the conflict between good and evil, between God and Satan, and between the angelic hosts and the evil followers of the devil. Such a conflict is almost always described as if the powers of evil were just barely overcome. However, the power of God is *always* victorious in the end.

Symbolic. The literature of the apocalypticists is always highly symbolic. The symbolism appears generally to have been drawn from the great images of Israel's history. Further, the images of earlier apocalypses are used by later writers with even more vivid detail. Animal symbolism is highly developed.

Number symbolism. Related to the general symbolism of apocalyptic literature is the highly developed number symbolism of this literature. Numbers appear to be used not so much to give specific detail as to communicate truth through symbols. The repeated use of *three, seven, ten, twelve,* and their multiples adds further support to this concept.

Visionary. A very obvious characteristic of apocalyptic literature is the major use of vision. The writer or speaker is always the receiver of great visions, either while sleeping or awake. The revelation or the message is almost always couched in terms of things which were seen. It is not always clear whether these visions were seen by the eye or the mind. It really makes no difference. The message being communicated was that the author had not arrived at his truth by thought but purely through some form of revelation.

Angelology and demonology. Angels and demons play a far greater part in apocalypses than in any other part of the Bible. This emphasis upon the invasion of human experience by supernatural beings attains its highest development in such material.

Pseudonymity. At least insofar as nonbiblical apocalypses are concerned, the author is always unknown. The work is ascribed to some great saint or hero of bygone days. Judged by ancient standards, this was not seen as an attempt to be deceptive. Rather, it was an attempt to honor the figure of the past by pointing out the message he or she would have communicated to the present. This universal characteristic of nonbiblical apocalypses must at least make the student raise the question as to whether the same characteristic is to be found in biblical apocalypses.

The Messiah. God's Messiah plays a much greater part in apocalyptic literature than is usually found in ancient materials, either biblical or secular. He is regularly seen as introducing God's heavenly or earthly kingdom by over-throwing all the forces of evil. The Messiah reigns over the coming kingdom of God, which produces a time of peace for God's saints after a time of great trial and conflict.

Overwhelming woes. Apolcalyptic literature almost always sees the end of time as being preceded by a series of awesome woes upon the whole earth, as well as being upon the people of God. In such times, survival itself can be a divine gift. Ultimately, however, the saints are delivered from the foretold woes and their awesome destruction.

Numerous other minor characteristics of apocalyptic literature have been identified. However, it appears that these major ones are those commonly found and clearly identified in such writings.

The Origin of Apocalyptic Literature

Two basic suggestions have been made by scholars as to the origin of apocalyptic literature in Israel. Because of its highly dualistic nature and its emphasis upon symbolism, a number of authorities have suggested that this literature arose in Israel after its exposure to the Persian Empire and its Zoroastrian worship. This would assume that all such writings would have had to be produced after the defeat of Babylon by the Persians. The proponents of this view generally suggest that it arose late in the Persian period, reaching its height in Israel after the defeat of Persia by Greece (333 BC).

Some aspects of Persian thought may have influenced the final days of the Old Testament and the rise of apocalyptic. However, we do not need to look outside of Israel for the origin of this material. It appears to be the natural out-growth of the Old Testament prophetic movement. As the hopes of the prophets began to be deferred farther and far-ther into the future and as external oppression began to be felt more and more in Israel's experience, the people needed a new message from God to sustain or rekindle their hope. At a time of heavy persecution, God raised up His writers to offer hope to His people. Such a message predicting the overthrow of Israel's oppressing enemies had to be written in a code so that it would not be confiscated by Israel's oppressors. Under divine inspiration, the code was found in the great symbols of Israel's past. Such symbols would have been readily understandable to the people of God but incom-prehensible to those oppressors who were not familiar with their heritage. Therefore the impetus for apocalyptic came not from outside Israel but from inside. It arose as God's response to the people's immediate crisis, giving them a message of hope and assurance. Their present experience often made them question the sovereignty of God. The en-during message of apocalyptic was that God was in charge of this world. He still is!

The apocalypticists insisted upon the enduring principles of righteousness and spirituality. They also revealed a genu-ine sense of urgency. God's servants had to be about God's work, for the time was short. They looked forward with genuine hope to the ultimate introduction of the kingdom of God. They also looked forward to a time when God would make all things right at the great final judgment. Theirs was a message which needed to be heard by a despairing and despondent people. In times of great human catastrophe, the message of apocalyptic needs to be sounded again.

Daniel

Probably no book of the Old Testament has been the subject of such wide disagreement and heated discussion as has the Book of Daniel. Very few, if any, issues in the study and interpretation of Daniel have been dealt with dispassionately. Without any illusions concerning the probability of gaining significant support for all conclusions, we must at least seek to survey the basic issues which have been raised and try to gain some degree of clarity in our approach to the study of this part of God's revelation.

Daniel as a Servant of God

The one major consistency in the book is the portrait of Daniel himself. We know nothing of Daniel's family. However, he was clearly either of the royal family or a part of the nobility of Jerusalem (1:3). His name, "God is my judge," expressed the faith of his parents, indicating that his own faith had its roots in that received from his parents. He is also described as having an outstanding physical appearance and equally outstanding mental gifts (v.4). His later life shows him also to be a person of deep spiritual commitments and genuine spiritual insight, as well as one with a rich life of devotion.

He was carried captive to Babylon in the "third year of the reign of Jehoiakim" (v.1). This would have been about 606-605 BC. As a promising youth, Daniel was selected to be trained for the service of Nebuchadnezzar. Refusing to indulge himself in the king's delicacies, he maintained his religious purity and developed into one of the outstanding young men of the king's service. He rose to a position of some prominence in Babylon and eventually became one of the three presidents over the administration of the empire of Persia (6:2). He continued to serve until the reign of Cyrus. His last dated vision is placed in the "third year of Cyrus," about April, 536 BC (10:1,4). He was one who continued his secular vocation, while at the same time fulfilling his divine commission. His life serves as an example of one who devoted all of his energy to the service of God.

Unity and Authorship of the Book

The only claim made within the book to anything being written is found in the statement that Daniel "wrote down the dream" which had been given in the first year of Belshazzar (7:1). Long-standing tradition has assigned the authorship of the book to Daniel, but there is no biblical necessity for accepting that tradition. While some of the material may have come from Daniel, we probably know no more about the identity of the final human author than we have been able to discover about numerous other Old Testament books. The divine authorship and inspiration is without dispute.

Two major problems have been raised in regard to the unity of Daniel. Even a superficial reading of the book shows that a major difference exists between the content of chapters 1 through 6 and chapters 7 through 12. The first six chapters relate to the experiences of Daniel and his friends with Babylon and its successor. Chapter 7, however, moves into what is clearly apocalyptic literature. The focus of this section is not upon events but upon visions. Numerous commentators have suggested that these two sections of the book came from different authors and were written at different times. To a person reading only from an English translation, this might seem like a valid conclusion. But the issue is clouded by further study.

In the original language, 1:1 to 2:4*a* are written in Hebrew, 2:4*b* to 7:28 are in Aramaic, and 8:1 to 12:13 are once again in Hebrew. Further, the Hebrew of both the first and the last sections appears to be essentially identical in style and vocabulary. From a linguistic standpoint, numerous interpreters have suggested that the use of two languages is a clear indication of a lack of unity. However, the content of the two sections makes it appear less likely. The narrative sections and the visionary sections occur in both Hebrew and Aramaic.

Some scholars have suggested that someone translated a Hebrew original into Aramaic but was not able to finish it. This makes little sense, for there is no adequate reason for substituting the Aramaic portion for the Hebrew original. In addition, the very fact that the borders between the various language sections do not coincide with the border between the two different kinds of literature obscures the entire question. No one who supports the basic unity of the book has yet been able to offer a satisfactory explanation for the language differences. On the other hand, no one who maintains a diversity of authorship has been able to explain the evidences of unity between the beginning and the ending of the book or within the Aramaic section as it bridges the line between chapters 6 and 7. The evidence of the Dead Sea Scrolls throws no additional light upon the subject. I think the probability rests on the side of the basic unity of the book. However, in saying this, I am forced to acknowledge my own ignorance of any reason for the change between the two languages. The problem would not be nearly as difficult if the change were only made one time. The fact that it is made twice complicates the issue.

The Date of the Writing of the Book

A major source of controversy regarding the Book of Daniel relates to the dates that have been suggested for the writing of the book. Basically two dates have been suggested. Some propose an early date, shortly after the final dated vision. This has normally been given as being about 530 BC. On the other extreme has been the proposal of a late date, during the time of the Maccabees, probably around 168 BC. This would have been during the time of the Syrian king, Antiochus Epiphanes.

Those who defend the late date have offered the following as evidence for this position.

(1) The language of Aramaic was the successor to Hebrew. The major Aramaic section demands a late date. Further, the Hebrew itself appears to be late. In addition, fifteen Persian words and three Greek words are in the text. As S. R. Driver said: "The *Persian* words presuppose a period after the Persian empire had been well established; the Greek words *demand,* the Hebrew *supports,* and the Arama-

ic *permits,* a date *after the conquest of Palestine by Alexander the Great"* (333 BC).

(2) The second half of the book directs its main attention to the period of Antiochus Epiphanes. Our knowledge of other biblical books suggests that the period to which major emphasis is given is the period to which we should assign its writing.

(3) The detailed predictions of chapter 11 show in minute detail a familiarity with the period of Antiochus. However, as soon as we pass beyond that period, the account becomes quite general and shows no such predictive detail. With apocalyptic being a new kind of literature, the only way such a book could have been allowed to circulate may have been to make it appear as if someone in the past were predicting the present. Where the details cease to be specific is where we should place the writing of the book.

(4) The other apocalyptic works with which we are familiar first begin to show up in the Maccabean era. It is hard to understand there having been such a long gap if Daniel came immediately after the Exile. If, however, Daniel is also from this period, then there is no unexplained gap in the production of apocalypses.

(5) The theology appears to be the latest in the Old Testament. The doctrine of a resurrection is clearer than anywhere else in the Old Testament. Further, the vision of the Messiah as son of man (7:13-14) made no impact upon anything else in the Old Testament but was clearly developed in the interbiblical period and influenced the New Testament. This is inexplicable if the book is early but quite understandable if it is late. Finally, the doctrine of angels is far more developed than anywhere else in the Old Testament. That it had no influence on any other Old Testament work is also inexplicable unless it came at the end of the Old Testament era.

(6) That Daniel is not among the Prophets but among the Writings in the Old Testament canon would indicate its lateness. If it had been written around 530 BC, there is no reason to explain why it was not included among the books of the second section of the canon.

Those who support this position point out that to the ancients there was no moral or ethical problem in attributing a contemporary work to some ancient saint. This was seen to be a way of honoring the saint. According to these scholars, that such a thing could have been done in inspired Scripture offers no problem, for it was a common practice which everyone would have understood. Our task is not to stand in judgment upon the human author but to understand the message of the divine Author.

Other interpreters cite numerous evidences to support the early date. Primarily these are aimed at refuting those given for the late date.

(1) The language is not necessarily late. Aramaic could have been in use by the end of the Exile and certainly was in use shortly thereafter. Further, the Hebrew is no later than much of that which is found in books that are clearly from late sixth and fifth centuries BC. If Daniel served in the government of Persia, he could easily have learned fifteen Persian words which would have been understandable to his general audience. If, on the other hand, the book had been from the age of Antiochus, more than three Greek words should have been in it.

(2) The details of the reign of Antiochus Epiphanes were a miracle of inspiration. This was such a time of importance for the Hebrew nation that God inspired Daniel to address it in detail for the encouragement of the people of that time. The fact that such was not normally the way God worked does not force us to conclude that He could not or did not act in such a way.

(3) The detailed knowledge the book shows both of the late Babylonian and of the early Persian eras requires that the author came from that period.

(4) The rise of apocalyptic literature in the Maccabean era was due to the fact that since Daniel spoke of and to their era, his book began to make its influence felt at such a time, giving an impetus to copyists.

(5) The theological argument for lateness is insignificant. Even though its theology is late, it is not materially later than that of Isaiah 40—66, Job, and Zechariah. Further,

even if it had no influence on following books, this is no
reason for saying it did not exist. It could have been ignored
because it was so advanced that its readers did not fully
comprehend God's revelation. For that matter, can we say
that we fully comprehend it now?

(6) Daniel may have been placed in the Writings due to its
late acceptance into the canon, not due to its late writing.
Its Aramaic section may have influenced that. Furthermore, it was so different from the other prophets that it was
not accepted immediately as Scripture.

Another explanation may deal with both sets of evidences
and opinions. The book may have gone through two edi-
tions. The detail from the Babylonian and Persian eras
strongly suggest that the book had its origin in the early
Persian period but that it was later revised and edited in the
Maccabean era to speak with a new freshness to those troubled times. There is no necessity to conclude that God could
have inspired only one author. We have abundant evidence
of the New Testament writers taking Old Testament Scriptures and reinterpreting them and reapplying them to their
own age. Why could this not have happened within the Old
Testament itself? This would appear to build upon the
strengths of both arguments while eliminating the objections to each.

The Content of the Book

I. Narratives of Daniel and his friends (1:1 to 6:28)
   A. Daniel's commitment to purity (1:1-21)
     1. The tragedy of captivity (1:1-2)
     2. Faithfulness in a time of adversity (1:3-14)
     3. The rewards of a pure life (1:15-21)
   B. God of gods and Lord of kings (2:1-49)
     1. Nebuchadnezzar's dream (2:1-16)
     2. Daniel's interpretation (2:17-45)
     3. The king's acclamation (2:46-47)
     4. The advancement of Daniel and his friends (2:48-49)
   C. Affirmation of the God of Israel (3:1-30)

1. The king's image and his decree (3:1-7)
2. Shadrach, Meshach, and Abednego accused (3:8-15)
3. A statement of utter faith (3:16-18)
4. The deliverance from the furnance (3:19-27)
5. No other god so able (3:28-30)

D. Honor to the King of heaven (4:1-37)
   1. The king's proclamation (4:1-3)
   2. The king's dream (4:4-18)
   3. Daniel's interpretation (4:19-27)
   4. The dream fulfilled (4:28-33)
   5. The proclamation concluded (4:34-37)

E. The handwriting on the wall (5:1-30)
   1. The idolatrous feast (5:1-4)
   2. The writing (5:5-9)
   3. Daniel's interpretation (5:10-28)
   4. Daniel's reward (5:29)
   5. Belshazzar's death (5:30)

F. Praise to the living God (5:31 to 6:28)
   1. The king and his kingdom (5:31 to 6:3)
   2. Jealously in action (6:4-5)
   3. Daniel's faithfulness (6:6-13)
   4. Faithfulness punished (6:14-18)
   5. Faithfulness rewarded (6:19-24)
   6. Darius's praise to the God of Daniel (6:25-28)

The basic emphasis of this block of material appears to be the assertion of the utter sovereignty of Yahweh, the God of Israel. This sovereignty is demonstrated both in the experience of the Hebrews in exile and in the experience of the pagan people of Babylon. Note that on three occasions a pagan king is portrayed as acknowledging the sovereignty of the God of Israel. After Daniel interpreted Nebuchadnezzar's first dream, the king proclaimed: "Truly your God is God of gods and Lord of kings, and a revealer of mysteries" (2:47). After the terrifying experience as an outcast, he also explained:

I blessed the Most High, and praised and honored him who
lives for ever;
for his dominion is an everlasting dominion,
  and his kingdom endures from generation to
    generation" (4:34).

Finally, after Darius had seen Daniel delivered from the
den of lions, he proclaimed concerning the God of Daniel:

> for he is the living God,
>   enduring for ever;
> his kingdom shall never be destroyed,
>   and his dominion shall be to the end.
> He delivers and rescues,
>   he works signs and wonders
>   in heaven and on earth,
> he who has saved Daniel
>   from the power of the lions (6:26-27).

Three historical issues have been identified within this
section as major problems. The first has to do with the siege
of Jerusalem by Nebuchadnezzar in the third year of
Jehoiakim (1:1). There is no direct reference to such an
occurence in either the biblical records or in the Babylonian
records. Thus many interpreters have assumed that this
was either a figment of the author's imagination or a mis-
placement of the siege which occurred during the reign of
Jehoiakim's son, Jehoiachin (2 Kings 24:10-14; 2 Chron.
36:1-10). However, we are told that Jehoiakim became subservient to Nebuchadnezzar after some sort of invasion
(2 Kings 24:1) and that he was carried captive to Babylon
briefly (2 Chron. 36:6-7). Further, the Babylonian records
also record the submission of "the Hatti country" (which
would have included Palestine) before Nebuchadnezzar in
the summer of 605 BC. Thus while no siege is actually described at that time, it is neither impossible nor improbable.
To the contrary, the description of Daniel 1:1 fits in well
with other recorded data.

The second historical problem that has disturbed interpreters has to do with the identification of Belshazzar as
king of Babylon (5:1). Historical records from Babylon that

have been available for years make abundantly clear that no man by that name was ever king of Babylon and that the last king was named Nabonidus. However, more recent discoveries show that Nabonidus did not wish to be king and fled to a hermitage in the desert, leaving his son to serve as regent in his stead. That son's name was Belshazzar. To Hebrews living in exile, while he was not the actual king, Belshazzar was certainly the de facto king, exercising all of the powers of kingship. Thus to call him "king" is not inaccurate. Further, this illuminates why Belshazzar offered to make anyone who could interpret the writing the "third ruler in the kingdom" (5:7,16,29). He was the second ruler; thus the highest reward he could offer was to make the interpreter third. Therefore this problem has also become a nonproblem.

The third major problem has been the statement that following the death of Belshazzar "Darius the Mede received the kingdom" (v.31). Scholars have frequently and clearly pointed out that Darius did not become king after the death of Belshazzar and that he was not the one who took the city. However, in the best biblical manuscripts, 5:31 is actually 6:1. The two chapters do not need to be interpreted as immediately following one other. Chapter 6 begins by telling what happened when Darius became king. However, we still have a problem by calling him Darius the Mede. Three Persian kings were named Darius; but all of them were Persian, not Medes. The Medes had ceased to exist as an independent nation around 550 BC. Their territory became a province of Persia. Throughout the Old Testament, however, the nation continued to be called "the Medes and the Persians." The designation of Darius as a Mede may have been neither a racial nor a national reference but an idiomatic expression applied to one who was a ruler of Persia.

One of the greatest affirmations of faith found in the Bible is in the story of Shadrach, Meshach, and Abednego. When threatened with the fiery furnace (a documented method of punishment used in Babylon), they responded, "Our God whom we serve is able to deliver us from the burning fiery furnace; and he will deliver us out of your hand, O king. But if not . . . we will not serve your gods or worship the golden image which you have set up" (3:17-18). Expressing utter confidence in God's power to deliver, they also stated their commitment to be faithful even if He did not act on their behalf. They were utterly faithful to His commands, leaving their fate in His hands. What an example they have set for us!

II. The visions of Daniel (7:1 to 12:13)
    A. The first vision, dated in the first year of Belshazzar (7:1-28)
        1. The nature of the vision: the four great beasts and the son of man (7:1-14)
        2. The interpretation of the vision: the everlasting kingdom of God and His saints (7:15-28)
    B. The second vision, dated in the third year of Belshazzar (8:1-27)
        1. The nature of the vision: the ram, the he-goat, and the horn (8:1-15)
        2. The interpretation of the vision: Antiochus Epiphanes's destruction (8:16-26)
        3. Daniel's failure to understand (8:27)
    C. The third vision dated in the first year of Darius (9:1-27)
        1. The nature of the vision: the words of Jeremiah (9:1-2)
        2. Daniel's prayer for understanding (9:3-19)
        3. Gabriel's interpretation (9:20-27)
    D. The fourth vision, dated in the third year of Cyrus (10:1 to 12:13)
        1. The nature of the vision: the angelic presence (10:1-9)
        2. The angelic message (10:10 to 11:1)
        3. The oppression of foreign kings (11:2-44)
        4. Victory over foreign oppressors and over death (11:45 to 12:4)
        5. An exhortation to patience (12:5-13)

The four major parts of the apocalyptic section are all dated quite precisely. This is not normal for the later apocalypses. Regardless of how one dates the writing of this section, the message is essentially the same. The utter sovereignty of God is proclaimed over all historical forces and ultimately over death itself. This was an encouragement to God's people of any time who were enduring major persecution. Furthermore, the final admonition to wait patiently for God to act in bringing in His kingdom was also intended to bring encouragement to those saints who were losing patience and hope in the face of hostility. The forces of evil will ultimately be defeated.

41

Priestly Levitical Histories
1 and 2 Chronicles and
Ezra-Nehemiah

Introduction

Although the conclusion is not unanimous, most scholars of all theological persuasions agree that a relationship exists between the books of 1 and 2 Chronicles, Ezra, and Nehemiah. First, the books of 1 and 2 Chronicles appear quite definitely to have originally been one book. The same is true for the two works of Ezra and Nehemiah. Between each of these two collections is also a very great similarity of style, interest, and theology. The similarity is so great that even if these two collections of material were written by different authors their interests were so similar that a general introduction to the entire corpus can be profitable.

The Authorship

The question of the authorship of these four books hinges on the issue of the theological outlook and the concerns of the books. The Books of Chronicles tell the story of the Hebrew people beginning with the genealogies of Adam, picking up the history with David, and continuing through the deliverance from captivity by the edict of Cyrus (1 Chron. 1:1; 2 Chron. 36:22-23). Obviously, this historical narrative overlaps with both the Pentateuch and the Deuteronomic Histories (Josh., Judg., 1 and 2 Sam., 1 and 2 Kings). The major emphasis, however, rests upon the period of the Hebrew Kingdom. It is at this point that we confront the first strange phenomenon of the work. During the period of the divided kingdom, *only the history of Judah is followed.* Israel is not mentioned except where it interacted with the Southern Kingdom. A primary concern of these books appear to be with the house of David only or with the events localized around the Temple. Another possibility is that the writing was done so far after the destruction of the Northern Kingdom that there was no real interest in it. The concern may have been a combination of one or more of these factors. This concern with Judah was the result of the inspiration of God working upon the hearts and minds of human authors.

As we read 1 and 2 Chronicles, we become quite aware that a major concern of the books focused upon the worship at the Temple of Jerusalem. In the study of the Deutero-nomic Histories, I noted that the authors were far more concerned with the meaning of events than with events as simply something which had happened. This is even more obvious in the study of Chronicles. The author was primari-ly a theologian and only incidentally a historian. He empha-sized the ark, the Temple, the matters of the Levitical priesthood, and things of similar nature. This concern is expressed in the record of David's moving the ark and estab-lishing the orders of the priests and Levites for the service of the sanctuary. The foundation of the house of David is seen to rest more upon proper worship at Jerusalem than upon the political power of the kingship.

However, the emphasis upon priestly concerns did not eliminate a genuine awareness of the nature of the ministry of the prophets. Their attention to the need for repentance and a turning to God is emphasized throughout. When the people of God were seen to have obeyed God and to have followed his prophets, they were blessed. However, either ignoring or disobeying the prophetic word was always seen to have brought disaster.

The same concerns can be seen in the Books of Ezra and Nehemiah. In fact, the concerns are so similar that the Talmud asserted that Ezra was the author of all four books. This view has found some support among modern interpret-ers. A closer reading of the works seems to demonstrate that the material of Ezra and Nehemiah is more pedantic while that of Chronicles was written with far more flair for the well-turned phrase. More than likely, the books had separate authors but a common final editor. The basic concerns are common throughout; the vocabulary and style is different.

The Date of Writing

The date of the writing of these books cannot be established until the issues of authorship are considered. If Ezra were the author, the writing was done during the latter part of his lifetime. If the books were compiled by an editor after the time of Ezra, we must move on beyond his lifetime. Some suggest that the Chronicles were completed before the time of Ezra. Therefore, their writing is occasionally dated just after the edict of Cyrus. However, 1 Chronicles 3:19-24 indicates that the final author was at least familiar with five generations after the time of Zerubbabel. Since Zerubbabel was living at the beginning of the Temple reconstruction (520 BC; Hag. 2:2), the final writing would almost have been as late as 400 BC and could have been significantly later than that.

The Issues of Historicity

Numerous commentators have raised major questions concerning the historical accuracy of the material found in Chronicles and Ezra-Nehemiah. Two kinds of issues have been raised, the first has to do with the use of numbers in the books and the second with the writer's recording of events.

In the use of numbers, commentators have noted significant problems over the records of financial concerns. The large amounts of treasure David is said to have amassed stagger the imagination (1 Chron. 22:14). The hundred thousand talents of gold and the million talents of silver would have amounted to billions of dollars. However, we are not certain what the weight of a talent was in David's time. Further, the chronicler may have been using numbers as symbols rather than as literal figures. Either way, our ignorance of the nature of the data makes it quite difficult for us to stand in judgment upon it.

Other problems have been identified in the chronicler's use of numbers in regard to the size of armies. For example, Jehoshaphat is said to have had over a million men in his army (2 Chron. 17), yet he is seen as being hopelessly outnumbered by the armies of surrounding peoples which never achieved such a number (2 Chron. 20:12,15). The Hebrew term for a thousand (*'eleph*) may also have referred to a fighting unit (see Chapter 10). This would alleviate the supposed problem here.

The second major issue commentators have raised concerns the historical accuracy of the chronicler with events he recorded for which we have no other mention, either in the Books of Kings or in extrabiblical sources. Earlier interpreters frequently were quite skeptical as to whether the events actually occurred. However, newly found records from ancient countries have cast more light upon the subject. These records demonstrate that some events the chronicler recorded happened as they are described. This brings into serious question the attacks upon passages which cannot yet be checked externally. From an investigative standpoint, confidence in the work of the chronicler has been renewed, restored, and reaffirmed.

The Nature of the Duplicate Account

Why do we have a second account of the history of the Hebrew people? The first answer may rest in a comparison with the four Gospels and the life of Jesus. Each Gospel adds new details of the events of His life. Yet each one also adds a new perspective to the *meaning* of His life. This appears to be true in regard to the history of the Hebrew people. The priestly Levitical histories give additional data to our understanding of that history. But they also give a new interpretation of those events. The work of the chronicler reinterpreted the message of God's dealing with His people, applying it to the needs of the Hebrew people in the fourth century BC. In a sense, the chronicler was doing much the same thing a modern preacher does, taking an ancient text and applying it to a contemporary situation.

The second answer to the basic question has to do with the

matter of divine inspiration. We have the second approach to Israel's history because we needed it to hear the full message of God concerning that history. The question is not whether we will study one approach or the other. Rather, it is a matter of hearing God speak through both approaches.

1 and 2 Chronicles

The Books of Chronicles are the last books in the Hebrew Bible. With them, the canon of the Old Testament reached its ultimate conclusion. Ezra and Nehemiah normally precede the Chronicles, although they obviously follow in terms of historical time sequence. No suggestion as to why Chronicles follows Ezra-Nehemiah has achieved a consensus among scholars. The best suggestion for this order may be that they were written in this order. However, this is by no means certain.

The Hebrew name for the books is "The Events of the Days." In the LXX, the books are called "The Things Passed Over," apparently referring to the things omitted from the Hebrew history of 1 and 2 Kings.

The Chronicles' narrative of Hebrew history begins with the reign of David, following the death of Saul and his sons (1 Chron. 10:1-7). The preceding chapters give the genealogies, beginning with Adam and concluding with the priests, Levites, and the Temple servants. The historical narrative continues until the edict of Cyrus, king of Persia, who allowed the Jews to return from their captivity.

The Sources of Chronicles

The chronicler was more precise in listing his sources than any other Old Testament writer. Among those identified are:
1. The Book of the Kings of Israel (1 Chron. 9:1)
2. The Book of the Kings of Judah and Israel (2 Chron. 16:11)
3. The Book of the Kings of Israel and Judah (2 Chron. 27:7)
4. The Chronicles of the Kings of Israel (2 Chron. 33:18)

5. The Commentary (Midrash) on the Book of Kings (2 Chron 24:27)
6. The Chronicles of Samuel the Seer (1 Chron 29:29)
7. The Chronicles of Nathan the Prophet (1 Chron. 29: 29)
8. The Chronicles of Gad the Seer (1 Chron. 29:29)
9. The History of Nathan the Prophet (2 Chron. 9:29)
10. The Prophecy of Ahijah the Shilonite (2 Chron. 9:29)
11. The Visions of Iddo the Seer (2 Chron. 9:29)
12. The Chronicles of Shemaiah the Prophet (2 Chron. 12:15)
13. The Chronicles of Jehu the Son of Hanani (2 Chron. 20:34)
14. The Vision of Isaiah the Prophet (2 Chron. 32:32)
15. The Chronicles of the Seers (Hozai) (2 Chron. 33:19)

In addition to these sources, the chronicler appears to have used the books of 1 and 2 Kings. He most likely used other sources as well, some of which may have been passed on to him in oral form.

The Nature of the Work of the Chronicler

Far more than a historian, the chronicler was a theologian. While writing history, he was primarily proclaiming his faith in God. LaSor, Hubbard, and Bush well note that this work is frequently identified or classified as "dogmatic historiography," history written from a theological viewpoint. The Chronicles are the proclamation of the awesome and absolute sovereignty of God and the fact that all nations and individuals are responsible to Him for their actions. This proclamation was made with a firm and refreshing affirmation of faith to a people in the Persian era whose hope had dimmed and whose sense of responsibility to God had weakened.

The chronicler's emphasis upon Temple worship and practices has often been interpreted as being on a lower plane than the great social and spiritual concerns of the prophets. Such an interpretation does an injustice to the overall emphasis found in these books. The emphasis on proper worship was not presented in place of morality but in addition to a proper ethical and spiritual relationship to God. It was not a case of either-or but of both-and. The chronicler demanded both practical righteousness and proper worship from his people. Neither was considered adequate without the other.

The Content of the Book

Since we have already surveyed the history the chronicler records in our study of 2 Samuel and 1 and 2 Kings, an additional survey is neither necessary nor profitable (see Chapters 15 and 16). The basic content of the book falls into four divisions.

  I. The genealogies from Adam to the Temple servants (1 Chron. 1:1 to 9:44)
 II. The reign of David (1 Chron. 10:1 to 29:30)
III. The reign of Solomon (2 Chron. 1:1 to 9:31)
 IV. The nation of Judah to the restoration (2 Chron. 10:1 to 36:23)

Ezra-Nehemiah

Little doubt exists that the Books of Ezra and Nehemiah were originally one book. They appear in one continuous story and are found in the LXX as one book, 1 Esdras. As noted, they probably were written by the same person (or persons) who put 1 and 2 Chronicles into their final form.

From a historical standpoint, the books give data about the Hebrew people and their place in the Persian Empire which no other biblical source provides. They also present some of the more fascinating problems in Hebrew history in the Old Testament.

In the Book of Ezra, 4:8 to 6:18 and 7:12-26 were written in Aramaic. The first section may have been copied from the records of the Persian Empire and the second is an actual copy of a letter from King Artaxerxes. Both would have been in Aramaic and were left just as they were copied.

The Men: Ezra and Nehemiah

The two central characters of the books afford a real study in contrasts. Ezra was an awesome, uncompromising figure who appears to have struck terror into the hearts of those around him. Nehemiah was friendly, generous, loyal, and quite human. Ezra was every inch a man of the law while Nehemiah was quite clearly a man of the spirit. Ezra seems to have felt little concern for the human needs of his people. Nehemiah, however, was deeply touched by the plight of his people. Ezra seems to have been unemotional, while Nehemiah was a person who felt deeply.

When the author of Ecclesiasticus listed the roll of Israel's heroes, Nehemiah had a place among them while Ezra was omitted entirely (49:11-13). In 2 Maccabees, a slightly later work, Ezra was not even mentioned; but Nehemiah was acclaimed with honor and praise (1:18-36). Ezra was a scribe and a son of the law. Nehemiah was a servant of a foreign king, apparently well versed in the art of politics. Ezra's prime concern was keeping his people faithful to the law. Nehemiah's appears to have been to protect his people from their enemies.

Yet, by early New Testament times Ezra had achieved the greater stature in the memories of the Hebrew people. He is considered to be the founder of the great synagogue, the founder of Judaism as a religion, and the one who restored the law to Israel. In some traditions, he is even acclaimed as the man who rewrote all of the Old Testament after its destruction. Nehemiah seems to have been a person whom people would love; Ezra seems to have been, at best, only a man whom people respected. Yet both had their parts to play in God's economy for Israel in the midst of the Persian era.

The Problem of Chronology

A major debate has raged over the years concerning the order in which these two men ministered in Jerusalem. In order to fully comprehend the nature of the problem, note the following data from the Persian Empire.

The edict of Cyrus	539 BC
The reign of Cambyses	530-522 BC
The reign of Darius I	522-486 BC
The reign of Ahasuerus (Xerxes)	486-464 BC
The reign of Artaxerxes I (Longimanus)	464-423 BC
The reign of Darius II	423-404 BC
The reign of Artaxerxes II (Mnemon)	404-359 BC
The reign of Artaxerxes III	359- BC

The ministries of Ezra and Nehemiah are both tied in with the reign of a Persian king by the name of Artaxerxes. Ezra is said to have come to Jerusalem in the "seventh year of Artaxerxes" (Ezra 7:7-8). Nehemiah is said to have come in "the twentieth year of King Artaxerxes" (Neh. 2:1). Nehemiah went back to Persia after his first mission was completed but later returned to Jerusalem in "the thirty-second year of Artaxerxes" (Neh. 13:6-7).

The issue would be simple if the references designated which Artaxerxes was intended. However, the situation reflected in the books, along with other historical data, make it fairly certain that Nehemiah is to be connected with Artaxerxes I. Thus, his two returns are to be dated in 444 BC and in 432 BC. Ezra was also generally assigned to this period, his return being dated in 457 BC. However, in more recent times he has been assigned to the reign of Artaxerxes II, making his return in 397 BC.

The issue is quite involved. Those who pursue it in detail should refer to some of the standard commentaries. However, a major argument has hinged upon the fact that the high priest in Nehemiah's time was Eliashib (Neh. 3:1). The high priest in Ezra's time was Johanan, "the son of Eliashib" (Ezra 10:6). According to Nehemiah 12:10-11, Johanan was actually the grandson of Eliashib. This offers no immediate problem, for the Hebrew term "son" can simply mean descendent. But if Ezra's high priest was the grandson of Nehemiah's high priest, then Ezra must have come in the reign of Artaxerxes II, in 397 BC.

This was where the argument stood until a recently discovered list of high priests shed additional light upon the subject. The list mentions a high priest before the Eliashib of Nehemiah whose name was Johanan. His father was actually named Eliashib, indicating that these were common family names. Thus, Ezra could have come before Nehemiah. Given the fact that there was a Johanan as high priest before the Elahshib of Nehemiah, we no longer have any historical evidence to make it necessary to place Ezra's return after Nehemiah's.

If these two ministries were in the time of Artaxerxes I, we are forced to acknowledge that the two men served at the same time but that Ezra was primarily concerned with religious matters while Nehemiah was primarily concerned with political and military concerns.

The Contents of the Books

I. The return of the exiles under Zerrubbabel (Ezra 1:1 to 6:22)
II. The return under Ezra (Ezra 7:10 to 10:44)
III. Nehemiah's return and the rebuilding of Jerusalem's defenses (Neh. 1:1 to 6:19)
IV. The people's renewal and rededication (Neh. 7:1 to 13:3)
V. Nehemiah's second return (Neh. 13:4-31)

The major emphasis of these two books rests upon the physical strengthening of the city of Jerusalem and its spiritual reform. These two are not to be seen as two separate concerns but two effects of the same basic concern. The main issue was that the people of Judah were the people of God and they were to behave like it. Such people had no basis either for discouragement or for infidelity. Some of the measures followed by Ezra were quite harsh by New Testament standards. At the same time, there is never any easy way to correct an extended period of disobedience to God.

Appendix:
Chronological Tables

2000 to 1700 BC	Patriarchal period, Abraham, Isaac, Jacob, and Joseph; wanderings in Canaan; descent into Egypt.
1700 BC	Hyksos (Semitic) Dynasty rules in Egypt; primacy of Joseph
1550 BC	Hyksos expelled from Egypt; Israel remains in Egypt
1450 BC	Israel remained in Egypt, but some early migrations back to Canaan may have begun
1300 BC	Sethos pharaoh, ca. 1306-1290
	Ramses pharaoh, ca. 1290-1228; the Exodus from Egypt ca. 1270

	EGYPT	CANAAN	MESPOTAMIA
1250 BC	Ramses Merneptah, ca. 1228-1121	Joshua, entrance into the land	Assyrian expansion
1200 BC	Ramses III, ca. 1185-1150	Sea People invade northern coastal plain Othniel and Ehud, ca. 1200	
1150 BC		Philistines invade coastal plain Deborah, ca. 1145	
1100 BC		Gideon, ca. 1140 Jephthah and Samson, ca. 1100 Eli	
1050 BC		Samuel, ca. 1050-1020	
1000 BC		Saul, ca. 1020-1000 David, ca. 1000-961	
950 BC		Solomon, ca. 961-931	

Appendix: Chronological Tables

	EGYPT	JUDAH	ISRAEL	SYRIA	ASSYRIA
	Shishak	Rehoboam, 931-913	Jeroboam I, 931-910		
		Abijam, 913-911	Nadab, 910-909		
900 BC		Asa, 911-870	Baasha, 909-886		
			Elah, 886-885		
			Omri, 885-874	Hadadezer	Shalmaneser III
		Jehoshaphat	Ahab, 874-853		(Battle of Karkar, 853)
			(Elijah)		
		Jehoram (853) 870-841	Ahaziah, 853-852		
			Jehoram, 854-841		
			(Elisha)		
		Ahaziah, 841	Jehu, 841-814	Hazael	
		Athaliah, 841-835			
		Joash, 835-796	Jehoahaz, 814-798	Ben-hadad	
800 BC		Amaziah, 796-767	Joash, 798-782		
		Azariah,	Jeroboam II,		
		(791) 767-740	(793) 782-753		
			(Amos, Hosea)		
			Zechariah, 753-752		
			Shalluum, 752		

	EGYPT	JUDAH	ISRAEL	SYRIA	ASSYRIA
750 BC		Jotham, (750) 740-732 (Isaiah)	Menahem, 752-742		Tiglath-pileser III
		Ahaz, (735) 732-716 (Micah)	Pekahiah, 742-740 Pekah, (752) 740-732	Rezin	
	So		Hoshea, 732-722 Fall of Samaria, 721	(Damascus falls 732)	Shalmaneser V Sargon II

	EGYPT	JUDAH	ASSYRIA	BABYLON
700 BC	Tirhakah	Hezekiah, 715-687 Manasseh, (696) 687-642	Sennacherib Esarhaddon Ashurbanipal	Nabopolassar
			(Fall of Nineveh to the Babylonians)	
650 BC		Amon, 642-640 Josiah, 640-609 (Jeremiah, Habakkuk) (Nahum)		
	Neco II	Jehoahaz, 609 Jehoiakim, 609-598 (Zephaniah)		
600 BC	Hophra	Jehoiachin, 598-597 Zedekiah, 597-586 (Fall of Jerusalem, 586)		Nehbuchadnezzar

	JUDAH	BABYLON	PERSIA
550 BC	Gedaliah, governor of Judah	Nabonidus	Cyrus
		Belshazzar, regent	Cambyses
	(Daniel)	Fall of Babylon to Persia, 539	Darius I
	Return to Judah, 539		
	Rebuilding of the Temple (520-515)		
	(Haggai, Zechariah)		
500 BC			Xerxes I (Esther)
			Artaxerxes
450 BC	Ezra, 458		
	Nehemiah, 444		
350 BC	Samaritan schism		

Greece takes over the Persian Empire under the leadership of Alexander the Great, 333 BC.

Selected Bibliography

CHAPTER 1

Allen, J. Clifton. "Introduction," "Genesis," rev. ed. *The Broadman Bible Commentary*. Nashville: Broadman Press, 1973. 1.

Bright, John. *The Authority of the Old Testament,* Nashville: Abingdon Press, 1967.

Cate, Robert L. *How to Interpret the Bible*. Nashville: Broadman Press, 1983.

_____. *Old Testament Roots for New Testament Faith*. Nashville: Broadman Press, 1981.

Mowinckel, Sigmund. *The Old Testament as Word of God*. Oxford: Basil Blackwell, 1960.

CHAPTER 2

Baly, Dennis. *The Geography of the Bible*. New York: Harper and Brothers, 1957.

Bright, John. *A History of Israel,* 3rd ed. Philadelphia: Westminster Press, 1981.

Cate, Robert L. *These Sought a Country: A History of Israel in Old Testament Times*. Nashville: Broadman Press, 1985.

Hermann, Siegfried. *A History of Israel*. Philadelphia: Fortress Press, 1975.

Wright, G.E. *Biblical Archaeology*. Philadelphia: Westminster Press, 1962.

_____. *The Westminster Historical Atlas of the Bible*. Philadelphia: Westminster Press, 1945.

529

CHAPTER 3

Cate, Robert L. *How to Interpret the Bible.* Nashville: Broadman Press, 1983.

CHAPTER 4

Bright, John. *Authority of the Old Testament.* Grand Rapids: Baker Book House, 1967

Cate, Robert L. *How to Interpret the Bible.* Nashville: Broadman Press, 1983.

———. *Old Testament Roots for New Testament Faith.* Nashville: Broadman Press, 1982.

Clements, R. E. *Old Testament Theology, a Fresh Approach.* Atlanta: John Knox Press, 1978.

Goldingay, John. *Approaches to Old Testament Interpretation.* Downers Grove: Inter-Varsity Press, 1981.

Hayes, John and Carl Holladay. *Biblical Exegesis, a Beginners Handbook.* Atlanta: John Knox Press, 1982.

Mowinckel, Sigmund. *The Old Testament as Word of God.* Oxford: Basil Blackwell, 1960.

Robinson, H. Wheeler. *Religious Ideas of the Old Testament.* London: Duckworth, 1913.

Rowley, H. H. *The Faith of Israel.* London: SCM Press, 1956.

CHAPTER 5

Amerding, Carl E. *The Old Testament and Criticism.* Grand Rapids: William B. Eerdmans Publishing Company, 1983.

Clements, Ronald E. *One Hundred Years of Old Testament Interpretation.* Philadelphia: Westminster Press, 1976.

Habel, Norman. *Literary Criticism of the Old Testament.* Philadelphia: Fortress Press, 1971.

Hahn, Herbert F. *The Old Testament in Modern Research.* Philadelphia: Fortress Press, 1970.

Interpreter's Dictionary of the Bible. 5 vols. Nashville: Abingdon Press, 1962.

Koch, Klaus. *The Growth of the Biblical Tradition.* New York: Charles Scribner's Sons, 1969.

Patte, Daniel. *What Is Structural Exegesis?* Philadelphia: Fortress Press, 1976.

Polzin, Robert. *Biblical Structuralism.* Philadelphia: Fortress Press, 1977.

Rast, Walter E. *Tradition History and the Old Testament.* Philadelphia: Fortress Press, 1972.

Robertson, David. *The Old Testament and the Literary Critic.* Philadelphia: Fortress Press, 1977.

Rowley, H. H., ed. *The Old Testament and Modern Study, a Generation of Discovery and Research.* Oxford: Clarendon Press, 1951.

Sanders, James A. *Canon and Community: A Guide to Canonical Criticism.* Philadelphia: Fortress Press, 1984.

Soulen, Richard. *Handbook of Biblical Criticism.* Atlanta: John Knox Press, 1976.

CHAPTER 6

Archer, Gleason L., Jr. *A Survey of Old Testament Introduction.* Chicago: Moody, 1974.

Francisco, Clyde T. *Introducing the Old Testament,* rev. ed. Nashville: Broadman Press, 1977.

Weiser, Arthur. *The Old Testament: Its Formation and Development.* New York: Macmillan, 1968.

West, James. *Introduction to the Old Testament.* New York: Macmillian, 1981.

Young, Edward J. *An Introduction to the Old Testament.* Grand Rapids: William B. Eerdmans Publishing Company, 1977.

CHAPTER 7

Cate, Robert L. *Old Testament Roots for New Testament Faith.* Nashville: Broadman Press, 1982.

―――――. *These Sought a Country: A History of Israel in Old Testament Times.* Nashville: Broadman Press, 1985.

Finegan, Jack. *Light from the Ancient Past.* Princeton: Princeton University Press, 1946.

Francisco, Clyde T. "Genesis," rev. ed. *The Broadman Bible Commentary.* Nashville: Broadman Press, 1973. 1.

Heidel, Alexander. *The Gilgamesh Epic and Old Testament Parallels.* Chicago: University of Chicago Press, 1946.

von Rad, Gerhard. *Genesis. Old Testament Library.* Philadelphia: The Westminster Press, 1971.

CHAPTER 8
Cassuto, U. *Commentary on the Book of Exodus.* Jerusalem: The Magnes Press, 1967.
Cate, Robert L. *Old Testament Roots for New Testament Faith.* Nashville: Broadman Press, 1982.
_____. *These Sought a Country: A History of Israel in Old Testament Times.* Broadman Press, 1985.
Childs, Brevard S. *Exodus.* Old Testament Library. Philadelphia: The Westminster Press, 1974.
Honeycutt, Roy W. "Exodus," rev. ed. *The Broadman Bible Comentary.* Nashville: Broadman Press, 1973. 1.

CHAPTER 9
Cate, Robert L. *Old Testament Roots for New Testament Faith.* Nashville: Broadman Press, 1982.
Rowley, H. H. *Worship in Ancient Israel.* London: SPCK, 1967.
Snaith, Norman. *Distinctive Ideas of the Old Testament.* New York: Schocken Books, 1964.

CHAPTER 10
Cate, Robert L. *These Sought a Country: A History of Israel in Old Testament Times.* Nashville: Broadman Press, 1985.
Noth, Martin. *Numbers. Old Testament Library.* Philadelphia: Westminster Press, 1968.
Owens, J. J. "Numbers," *The Broadman Bible Commentary.* Nashville: Broadman Press, 1970. 2.
Wenham, Gordon. "Numbers," *Tyndale Old Testament Commentaries.* Downers Grove: Inter-Varsity, 1981.

CHAPTER 11
Phillips, A. *Deuteronomy.* New York: Cambridge University Press, 1973.
Thompson, J. A. *Deuteronomy.* Downers Grove: Inter-Varsity, 1974.

von Rad, Gerhard. *Deuteronomy*. Philadelphia: Westminster Press, 1966.

Wright, G. E. "Deuteronomy," *The Interpreter's Bible*. New York: Abingdon, 1953. 2.

CHAPTER 12

Cate, Robert L. *Old Testament Roots for New Testament Faith*. Nashville: Broadman Press, 1982.

_____. *These Sought a Country: A History of Israel in Old Testament Times*. Nashville: Broadman Press, 1985.

Fretheim, Terence E. *Deuteronomic History*. Nashville: Abingdon Press, 1983.

Noth, Martin. *The Deuteronomic History*. Sheffield: Journal for the Society of Old Testament Study Supplement 15, 1981.

von Rad, Gerhard. *Old Testament Theology*. New York: Harper and Row, 1962.

Wolff, Hans Walter. "The Kerygma of the Deuteronomic Historian." *The Vitality of Old Testament Traditions*. Atlanta: John Knox Press, 1975.

CHAPTER 13

Bright, John. *A History of Israel,* 3rd ed. Philadelphia: Westminster Press, 1981.

Cate, Robert L. *These Sought a Country: A History of Israel in Old Testament Times*. Nashville: Broadman Press, 1985.

Wright, G. E. *The Westminster Historical Atlas of the Bible*. Philadelphia: Westminster Press, 1945.

CHAPTER 14

Dalglish, E. R. "Judges." *The Broadman Bible Commentary*. Nashville: Broadman Press, 1970. 2.

Martin, J. D. *The Book of Judges*. New York: Cambridge University Press, 1975.

CHAPTER 15

Cate, Robert L. *Old Testament Roots for New Testament Faith*. Nashville: Broadman Press, 1982.

————. *These Sought a Country: A History of Israel in Old Testament Times.* Nashville: Broadman Press, 1985.

La Sor, W. S., D. A. Hubbard and F. W. Busch. *Old Testament Survey.* Grand Rapids: William B. Eerdmans Publishing Company, 1982.

Weiser, Arthur. *The Old Testament: Its Formation and Development.* New York: Association Press, 1968.

CHAPTER 16

Bright, John. *A History of Israel,* 3rd. ed. Philadelphia: Westminster Press, 1981.

Cate, Robert L. *These Sought a Country: A History of Israel in Old Testament Times.* Nashville: Broadman Press, 1985.

Hermann, Siegfried. *The History of Israel in Old Testament Times.* Philadelphia: Fortress Press, 1975.

Thiele, Edwin R. *A Chronology of the Hebrew Kings.* Grand Rapids: Zondervan, 1977.

————. *The Mysterious Numbers of the Hebrew Kings.* Grand Rapids: Zondervan, 1983.

CHAPTER 17

Cate, Robert L. *Old Testament Roots for New Testament Faith.* Nashville: Broadman Press, 1982.

Heschel, Abraham. "Introduction." *The Prophets.* New York: Harper and Row, 1955. 1.

March, Eugene. "Prophecy." *Old Testament Form Criticism.* San Antonio: Trinity University Press, 1974.

CHAPTER 18

Bright, John. *A History of Israel,* 3rd. ed. Philadelphia: Westminster Press, 1981.

Cate, Robert L. *These Sought a Country: A History of Israel in Old Testament Times.* Nashville: Broadman Press, 1985.

Hermann, Siegfried. *The History of Israel in Old Testament Times.* Philadelphia: Fortress Press, 1975.

CHAPTER 19

Honeycutt, Roy L. *Amos and His Message.* Nashville: Broadman Press, 1963.

Mays, J. L. *Amos, Old Testament Library.* Philadelphia: Westminster Press, 1969.

Wolff, H. W. *Amos the Prophet: The Man and His Background.* Philadelphia: Fortress Press, 1973.

CHAPTER 20

Anderson, Francis I. and David Noel Freedman. "Hosea." *Anchor Bible.* New York: Doubleday, 1980.

Honeycutt, Roy L. "Hosea." *The Broadman Bible Commentary.* Nashville: Broadman Press, 1972. 7.

Snaith, Norman. *Mercy and Sacrifice: A Study of the Book of Hosea.* London: SCM Press, 1953.

CHAPTER 21

Francisco, Clyde T. "The Authorship and Unity of Isaiah 40-66." Louisville: The Southern Baptist Theological Seminary, 1944.

La Sor, W. S. *Old Testament Survey.* Grand Rapids: William B. Eerdmans Publishing Company, 1982.

North, C. R. *The Suffering Servant inn Deutero-Isaiah.* Oxford: Clarendon Press, 1948.

CHAPTER 22

Snaith, Norman. *Amos, Hosea and Micah.* London: Epworth Press, 1956.

Wolff, Hans Walter. *Micah the Prophet.* Philadelphia: Westminster Press, 1981.

CHAPTER 23

Bright, John. *A History of Israel,* 3rd ed. Philadelphia: Westminster Press, 1981.

Cate, Robert L. *These Sought a Country: A History of Israel in Old Testament Times.* Nashville: Broadman Press, 1985.

CHAPTER 24

Bright, John. *Jeremiah,* Anchor Bible Series. New York: Doubleday, 1965. 21.

Cate, Robert L. *Old Testament Roots for New Testament Faith.* Nashville: Broadman Press, 1982.

Holladay, William. *Jeremiah: Spokesman Out of Time.* New York: Pilgrim Press, 1974.

Wood, Fred. *Fire in My Bones.* Nashville: Broadman Press, 1959.

CHAPTER 25

Watts, John. *The Books of Joel, Obadiah, Nahum, Habakkuk, and Zephaniah.* Cambridge: Cambridge University Press, 1975.

CHAPTER 26

Dalglish, Edward. "Nahum." *The Broadman Bible Commentary.* Nashville: Broadman Press, 1972. 7.

CHAPTER 28

Thompson, J. A. "Obadiah." *The Interpreter's Dictionary of the Bible.* New York: Abingdon, 1962.

CHAPTER 29

Bright, John. *A History of Israel,* 3rd. ed. Philadelphia: Westminster Press, 1981.

Cate, Robert L. *These Sought a Country: A History of Israel in Old Testament Times.* Nashville: Broadman Press, 1985.

CHAPTER 30

Klein, Ralph. *Israel in Exile.* Philadelphia: Fortress Press, 1979.

Taylor, J. B. "Ezekiel," *Tyndale Old Testament Commentaries.* Downers Grove Inter-Varsity Press, 1969.

Zimmerli, W. *Ezekiel.* Philadelphia: Fortress Press, 1979. 1.

CHAPTER 31

"Haggai." *Tyndale Old Testament Commentaries.* Downers Grove: Inter-Varsity Press, 1972.

Mason, Rex. "Haggai." *Cambridge Bible Commentary for the New English Bible.* New York: Cambridge University Press, 1977.

CHAPTER 32

Mason, Rex. *The Books of Haggai, Zechariah, and Malachi.* New York: Cambridge University Press, 1977.

CHAPTER 33

Mason, Rex. *The Books of Haggai, Zechariah, and Malachi.* New York: Cambridge University Press, 1977.

Wolff, Hans Walter. *Joel and Amos.* Philadelphia: Fortress Press, 1977.

———. *Jonah: Church in Revolt.* St. Louis: Clayton Publishing House, 1978.

CHAPTER 35

Durham, John. "Psalms." *The Broadman Bible Commentary,* Nashville: Broadman Press, 1971. 4.

Rowley, H.H. *Worship in Ancient Israel.* London: SPCK, 1967.

Weiser, Arthur. *The Psalms.* Philadelphia: Westminster, 1962.

White, R. E. O. *A Christian Handbook to the Psalms.* Grand Rapids: William B. Eerdmans Publishing Company, 1984.

CHAPTER 36

Crenshaw, J. L. *Old Testament Wisdom: An Introduction.* Atlanta: John Knox Press, 1981.

La Sor, W. S. D. A. Hubbard, and F. W. Bush. *Old Testament Survey.* Grand Rapids: William B. Eedmans Publishing Company, 1982.

Scott, R. B. Y. *The Way of Wisdom in the Old Testament.* New York: Macmillan, 1971.

CHAPTER 37

Gordis, Robert. *The Book of God and Man.* Chicago: The University of Chicago Press, 1965.

Owens, Mary Frances. *Ezra, Nehemia, Esther, Job. Layman's Bible Book Commentary.* Nashville: Broadman Press, 1983.

CHAPTER 38

Fritsch, Charles T. "Proverbs." *The Interpreter's Bible.* Nashville: Abingdon, 1955.

Scott, R.B.Y. *Proverbs-Ecclesiastes. The Anchor Bible.* New York: Doubleday and Company, 1965. 18.

Tate, Marvin. "Proverbs." *The Broadman Bible Commentary.* Nashville: Broadman Press, 1971. 5.

CHAPTER 39

Cate, Robert L. *These Sought a Country: A History of Israel in Old Testament times.* Nashville: Broadman Press, 1985.

Francisco, Clyde T. *Introducing the Old Testament,* rev. ed. Nashville: Broadman Press, 1977.

Gollwitzer, H. *Song of Love: A Biblical Understanding of Sex.* Philadelphia: Fortress Press, 1979.

Knight, G. A. F. *Ruth and Jonah,* 2nd. ed. London: SCM Press, 1966.

La Sor, W. S., D. A. Hubbard, and F. W. Bush. *Old Testament Survey.* Grand Rapids: William B. Eerdmans Publishing Company, 1977.

Moore, C.A. *Esther, The Anchor Bible.* New York: Doubleday, 1971.

Patterson, John L. *The Song of Songs.* Cincinnati: Standard, 1932.

Pope, Martin H. "Song of Solomon." *The Anchor Bible.* New York: Doubleday and Company, 1977.

CHAPTER 40

Owens, John J. "Daniel." *The Broadman Bible Commentary.* Nashville: Broadman Press, 1971. 6.

Rowley, H. H. *Darius the Mede and the Four World Empires*

in the Book of Daniel. Cardiff: University of Wales Press, 1959.

Russell, D.R. *The Method and Message of Jewish Apocalyptic*. Philadelphia: Westminster Press, 1964.

Young, Edward J. *The Prophecy of Daniel*. Grand Rapids: William B. Eerdmans Publishing Company, 1949.

CHAPTER 41

Cate, Robert L. *These Sought a Country: A History of Israel in Old Testament Times*. Nashville: Broadman Press, 1985.

Coggins, R. J. *The First and Second Books of Chronicles, Cambridge Bible Commentary*. Cambridge: Cambridge University Press, 1976.

Francisco, Clyde T. "Chronicles." *The Broadman Bible Commentary*. Nashville: Broadman Press, 1970. 3.

La Sor, W. S., D. A. Hubbard, and F. W. Bush. *Old Testament Survey*. Grand Rapids: William B. Eerdmans Publishing Company, 1982.